Governing

Governing Italy

THE POLITICS OF BARGAINED PLURALISM

David Hine

CLARENDON PRESS · OXFORD

Oxford University Press, Walton Street, Oxford OX2 6DP
Oxford New York Toronto
Delhi Bombay Calcutta Madras Karachi
Kuala Lumpur Singapore Hong Kong Tokyo
Nairobi Dar es Salaam Cape Town
Melbourne Auckland Madrid
and associated companies in
Berlin Ibadan

Oxford is a trade mark of Oxford University Press

Published in the United States by
Oxford University Press Inc., New York

British Library Cataloguing in Publication Data
Data available

Library of Congress Cataloging in Publication Data
Hine, David.
Governing Italy: the politics of bargained pluralism / David Hine.
Includes bibliographical references and index.
1. Italy—Politics and government—1945–   I. Title.
JN5451.H56   1993   320.945—dc20   92-30854
ISBN 0-19-876172-4
ISBN 0-19-876171-6 (pbk.)

3 5 7 9 10 8 6 4 2

Printed in Great Britain
on acid-free paper by
Bookcraft (Bath) Ltd
Midsomer Norton, Avon

Contents

Abbreviations

CGIL	Confederazione generale italiana del lavoro (General Confederation of Labour)
CISL	Confederazione italiana sindacati lavoratori (Confederation of Workers' Unions)
DC	Democrazia cristiana (Christian Democracy)
DP	Democrazia proletaria (Proletarian Democracy)
MSI	Movimento sociale italiano (Social Movement)
PCI	Partito comunista italiano (Communist Party)
PDIUM	Partito democratico italiano di unità monarchica (Democratic Party of Monarchist Unity)
PDS	Partito democratico della sinistra (Democratic Party of the Left)
PdUP	Partito di unità proletaria per il comunismo (Proletarian Unity Party)
PLI	Partito liberale italiano (Liberal Party)
PMP	Partito monarchico popolare (People's Monarchist Party)
PNM	Partito nazionale monarchico (National Monarchist Party)
PPST	Partito popolare sud-tirolese (South Tyrol People's Party)
PR	Partito radicale (Radical Party)
PRI	Partito repubblicano italiano (Republican Party)
PSDI	Partito socialista democratico italiano (Social Democrat Party
PSI	Partito socialista italiano (Socialist Party)
PSIUP	Partito socialista italiano d'unità proletaria (Socialist Party of Proletarian Unity)
UIL	Unione italiana del lavoro (Union of Italian Labour)

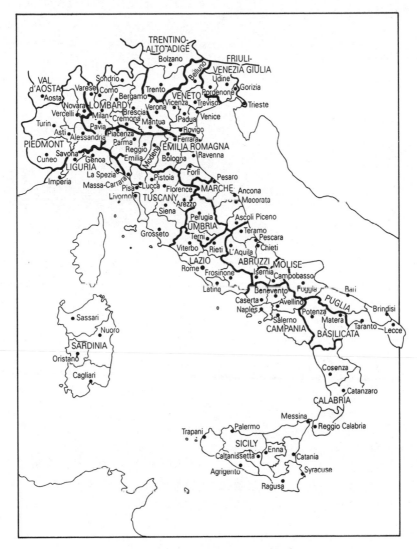

The Regions and Provinces of Italy

INTRODUCTION

The Debate on the Italian Political System

Bargained, multi-tiered, juridicized pluralism

For more than ten years, Italians have been engaged in continuous debate over the reform of their country's constitution. The debate has been conducted at several levels. At its simplest, it has been exploited by party leaders in the regular battles of attrition that punctuate coalition politics. The response from Parliament has been rather more elevated. The ambitious all-party parliamentary commission of inquiry—the Bozzi Commission—searched hard for a common diagnosis of the problems and common ground for reform, although its inconclusive report, published in 1985, was effectively an admission of failure.[1] Most sophisticated of all, though in practice no more influential than the Bozzi Commission, has been the steady commentary of jurists and academics. In recent years their scrutiny has made the Italian constitution one of Europe's most thoroughly analysed.

The Italian version of liberal-democratic parliamentary government has several distinctive features. It has generated a highly bargained pluralist democracy, with power dispersed across a wide range of arenas. Although in appearance the system is based on a strong version of party government, the ability of the parties to aggregate demands and respond to them by offering voters clear policy choices is limited. Moreover, the legal and constitutional system, and the structure and quality of the public administration, combine with the complexities of inter and intra-party relationships to complicate the implementation of policy once chosen by voters. Hence the title of this introductory section. The essence of Italian government cannot be captured in simple terms. It is a form of party government and in certain respects a very strong form, but that does not entail a simple or direct causal link between electoral demand and policy output that passes through a well-defined parliamentary majority built on programmatic parties. Interest groups have many different points of access to the system, and their interaction with fragmented parties and complex institutional procedures ensures that no single institution dominates. The system, in short, resembles the open pluralism of American political life as much as the generally more purposive style of European parliamentary government.

The features which limit clear-cut party government appear to be parts of an interconnected historical syndrome the origins and nature of which might be summed up as follows. After fascism and the disaster of World War II, Italian constitution-makers were anxious to build a more articulated democracy than the relatively unsophisticated parliamentary monarchy of the pre-fascist liberal state. Their main preoccupation was to prevent power again falling into the hands of an over-mighty leader. In partial contrast to their German colleagues, who faced a similar problem, they were more concerned to control and limit an executive which might become too strong, than to help it to survive in conditions of potential weakness. Thus both the constitution and electoral law were designed to disperse power rather than concentrate it. The constitution provided a series of checks and balances which, while stopping short of the separation of powers or outright federalism, nevertheless provided numerous ways in which Parliament, the executive, the constitutional and administrative courts, local government, interest groups, and (via the referendum) even the electorate could constrain and control each other. This was capped by a highly permissive version of proportional representation which ensured that the one potential source of power which might have held sway over the others, namely, a disciplined parliamentary majority supporting a purposive executive, could not materialize.[2]

Alongside these political features were administrative ones working in the same direction. The machinery of Italian government inherited from the liberal and fascist regimes was no less hostile to purposive government than were the divisions within and between parties. Until long after 1945, Italy's social and administrative infrastructure was well out of line with the standards of industrialized Europe, and in certain respects remains so. Reformed, rational, efficient bureaucracies could not, as in other European societies, be built upon long experience of an evolving administrative state. As post-war Italy became richer, it did start to generate the resources necessary to develop such a state; public intervention—aimed at both the productive economy and social redistribution—reached levels found elsewhere in Western Europe. But administrative development had to be a more hurried and improvised process, and the public service lacked the prestige and *mores* of the state traditions found further north. It was also more subject to party intervention and control. Moreover, the administration was never properly modernized. For a variety of reasons, explored later in this book, it reflected a nineteenth-century and highly legalistic outlook, and had difficulty adapting to the managerial, problem-solving ethos of the modern welfare state.

The system and its critics

The conventional critique

The consequences of this syndrome have been much discussed. They are said to have made the system a *static* one, in which policy change—whether substantive or, equally important, symbolic—is comparatively difficult to achieve. *Substantive* change is frequently prevented by the breadth of the coalition of interests needed to take decisions, and hence the likely existence of a veto group within it. This is not to say that the system is incapable of major policy initiatives, for important landmark examples stand out: currency reform in 1947; the development of the state-holdings sector in the 1950s; education reform, electricity nationalization, and various stages of the regionalization process in the 1960s; the gradual extension of welfare networks and the decision to take the lira into the EMS in the 1970s; reorganization of the process of southern regional aid and reform of the political executive in the 1980s; banking and local government reform in the early 1990s. However, such initiatives have generally taken an inordinately long time to materialize. Regionalism, for example, took twenty years. Moreover, when finally introduced, major reforms have been said to have taken the form of distinctly sub-optimum compromises, and their effective implementation frequently to have been prejudiced by the inefficiency or outright resistance of the public administration.

Equally *symbolic* change—alternation in government between competing groups of parties—has been impossible partly because of the static nature of the electoral system, which minimizes the translation of vote changes into seat changes in the legislature, but more importantly because of the shape of the party system. The dominant central position of the Christian Democrats has made their party an irreplaceable keystone of all coalitions. The allegedly less than perfect democratic credentials of the main opposition, the Communist Party, for many years made it ineligible as a coalition partner in the eyes of most minor parties, and even today its successor the PDS (Democratic Left Party) suffers from association with its communist progenitor.

The absence of alternation in government is unique in a major European country, and is widely regarded as a major defect in the legitimacy enjoyed by the Italian state. The symbolic change embodied in alternation provides democratic society with an important sense of political efficacy and involvement. However erroneous it may be, the belief on the part of voters that collectively they can affect political outcomes through their vote is probably a functional one for democracy. When that belief is denied to voters, the consequences are potentially corrosive of the legitimacy enjoyed by the system. This can happen if the party of their choice is consigned with unremitting regularity to the opposition, or if they feel they have no better alternative than to vote for a much-disliked governing party. To the party or parties in government, moreover, the absence of alternation gives an undesirable reassurance that, whatever they do, they will not be ousted from power. In the Christian Democrat Party, it has also clearly contributed to the division and factiousness of internal party life, a condition that would almost certainly be eased if the party felt greater need to demonstrate its unity and purpose.

The fact, finally, that bargained pluralism seems to have been *institutionalized* as the distinctive style of the political system is a source of special anxiety. It suggests that the system is now locked into a particular way of making decisions, making political reform very difficult, if not impossible. Those who participate in politics have grown accustomed to the system as it operates at present, have every interest in preserving it, and cannot predict their own fate in a reformed system. Moreover, the consequences of reform are too unpredictable, and too full of potential side costs, to make the risks worth running in any circumstances other than a dramatic crisis.

Defending bargained pluralism

Set out in this way the Italian 'syndrome' justifies the label. It is indeed a syndrome, not a model. But not all observers accept that the Italian political system has serious pathologies and is in drastic need of reform. One line of defence—focusing on the early post-war years—is concerned with the constraints on those who were seeking to rebuild a democratic system. It suggests that, in a country which hitherto had great difficulty establishing democracy, Italian politicians had little choice but to pursue a strategy of democratic consolidation that dispersed power and ensured that many important decisions were taken with the involvement of a wide range of social groups and political interests. Given the deep gulf between the political cultures of north and south, and the inheritance of class and religious antagonisms, this argument has some force. It is far from clear that in the early post-war decades there was a better route to the consolidation of democracy. Parties had to aggregate sharply contrasting interests, and coalition-building had to bridge major social divisions. Purposive government, backed up by a strong administrative state, may well not have been the best way of approaching this task. Instead, the open and inclusive system of multi-tiered bargained pluralism that was adopted may have allowed democracy to take root, where otherwise it would have failed.

The nature and role of the two main parties—the Christian Democrats and the Communists—illustrate this. The DC became an inclusive, inter-class party, consciously seeking to bridge the divide between north and south, landlord and agricultural tenant, employer and industrial worker. Although it defended Italy's status as a part of the Western capitalist system, it was far from simply a party of the middle class and business. From early on, entrepreneurial political leaders replaced traditional notables as the DC's representatives in the south, and this group quickly turned its attention to the task of stabilizing the non-Communist vote by the judicious use of public transfers to a wide range of southern interests, many from the least privileged strata in society. The Communist Party, for its part, quickly ceased to be an intransigent party of anti-capitalist revolution, if indeed it had ever been one. Depending on interpretation, the PCI was deterred, or seduced, from its allegedly revolutionary vocation, and began to participate in local government and behind-the-scenes parliamentary decision-taking. Its control over the most powerful part of the labour movement offered political leverage that soon gave it at least a minor stake in the existing social order. What might otherwise have been a head-on clash between two incompatible social alignments was therefore moderated by the ambiguous qualities each possessed. These qualities were to be fostered by other features of the political system—most notably the formal rules—which encouraged bargaining, compromise, and the sharing of power.

To be sure, not all early post-war Italian history reads as the unqualified pursuit of consensus. The most intense years of the Cold War, from 1947 to the mid-1950s, contain episodes that look very different. Most notable was the Christian Democrat attempt, in 1953, to break with the principles of proportionalism in the electoral system. The DC also studiously ignored several of the power-dispersing and liberal qualities of the constitution, and frequently took a tough line against communist control of the labour movement and areas of local government. Such strategies were never pursued with wholehearted conviction, however, and for each hard-liner in the DC, there was a liberal opponent. By the late 1950s, the latter were once again reasserting themselves.

Nevertheless, four decades on, the defence of the existing political order must be based on something other than its ability to consolidate the original democratic framework. A system in which power was highly dispersed may have been suitable for Italy immediately after fascism, and possibly even as late as the 1970s, but its continuing validity needs to be demonstrated. One way of doing so is to question the implicit assumption behind most criticism of the Italian political order directed at the lack of purposive government. At a very general level it can be argued that systems dominated by coherent majorities and strong executives over-simplify the process of public choice. Clear-cut and contrasting party programmes implemented by majority parties or cohesive coalitions give voters only a crude and distorted alternative. They are relatively insensitive to policy detail, and in societies in which voters have transitive preference schedules, they give highly misleading impressions about the distribution of policy preferences across the electorate. Majoritarian government, so such an argument would run, might be appropriate where there is a normal distribution of voters along a single policy continuum, but this is rarely the case, and probably does not apply to Italy.

However, between the relatively purposive governments of European states with cohesive, if not single-party, parliamentary majorities, and the bargained pluralism found in Italy, there is a wide gap. To defend the Italian system it would be necessary to deal not just in general principles but in specific features of Italian politics, and to show either that no more purposive system was necessary, or that it was not feasible without undesirable side costs. One long-standing scholar of Italian politics who appears to combine both approaches is Joseph LaPalombara, whose *Democracy: Italian Style*, appearing during a period of intense scrutiny and criticism of Italy's political order, raised much controversy for its apparent support of the political and institutional status quo.[3] He argued forcefully not only that the achievements of the political class were substantial, but also that political life, despite its apparent conflictuality and disorder, was informed by a greater level of agreement—among both élites and the mass public—than appeared to be the case. And he suggested that any attempt to reorder the complex system of institutions and tacit understandings on which the system was based could have negative consequences.[4]

How such arguments are to be assessed is unclear. As some of LaPalombara's critics have argued, it is, for example, uncertain what the underlying harmony of the system consists of, or how it is to be measured.[5] It is certainly inadequate simply to point to the many achievements of post-war Italian society—particularly in the field of material prosperity and social welfare—and conclude that if the political class has presided over such benefits, it must be a satisfactory political class.[6] The fact that the general qualities combined in liberal democracy and the market economy have delivered a prosperous society in post-war Italy says very little about whether a different *style* of liberal democracy (or indeed a different mix of private and public within the general framework of the market economy) would, either in the past or now, have produced more satisfactory outcomes.

Generalised judgements of whole political systems are in fact rarely very enlightening, and raise issues which go well beyond the competence of the political scientist. The study of political institutions must focus largely on processes, not outcomes. It can show how methods of political aggregation, and the formal rules and informal conventions of institutions, affect public choice and policy implementation. But the student of political science has no unit of measure comparable to monetary value in economics, and cannot therefore produce generalized balance sheets of public choice permitted by a given set of institutions and practices. To do so would demand a range of policy studies far beyond the scope of any single work, and a calculus for measuring preferences which even the most sophisticated exponents of public-choice analysis have not devised.

The focus of the book

This book is not therefore written to resolve the debate about Italy's system of government, nor to model its 'outputs', but to help clarify the terms of the debate, and to show what are the most distinctive and contentious features of the system, how they have arisen, and how they affect contemporary decision-making. It is divided into two parts: the first considers how political attitudes are shaped, and how demands are expressed through political parties; the second considers the constitutional and administrative structures through which parties and interest groups achieve their goals.

The emphasis in the first section is deliberately more on parties than on real interests. The main reason for this is that the convergence of European economies in the last four decades has created a range of interests and groups in Italy which is not fundamentally distinct from that in most other advanced European societies. There is a complex class structure, encompassing the same occupational status groups found in most mature economies; there are social divisions cutting across class and status groups, mitigating the effects of the latter, especially religion and territorial identity; and there are sectoral distinctions generating conflicts of interest between public sector and private sector, and between large-, medium-, and small-scale business, and so on. In all these respects Italy falls squarely into the European mould. What is distinct is more the way these interests are aggregated at the political level by the parties than the sorts of demands they bear in themselves.

The reason why this relationship is of interest is that Italy's political parties developed to some degree before the growth of the associational energy that generated a complex and articulated system of interest representation from the mid-1960s onwards. This is not to say that interest groups did not previously exist—they clearly did. Nor is it to argue that there was no linkage between particular parties and particular interests. But, as Alessandro Pizzorno noted many years ago, the development of the post-war party system took place initially at some remove from the real society in which the parties were competing for votes.[7] The result was that, in order to establish organizational roots and legitimacy, the parties consciously sought to colonize the interest-group universe. They did so fairly indiscriminately, so that, although their control was never very tight, and progressively weakened as time passed, the major parties each had links with a fairly undifferentiated range of groups. This had two effects. It fragmented the process of group representation, as a number of categorical associations (unions, small farmers, co-operatives) split along ideological lines. And it ensured that, even in an ideologically polarized political system, parties tended to represent very broad coalitions of interests. The fragmentation was further increased by what may be regarded as the single most distinctive feature of Italian society: the major disparity in economic development and living standards between the prosperous north and the backward south, and, within the former area, between the large-scale manufacturing conurbations of the northern industrial triangle and the more diversified economies of the central and north-east corridors.

Under these circumstances, political competition between parties involved the careful distribution of benefits to a composite and variegated set of clienteles; clear-cut lines of division between winners and losers were absent, and benefits and advantages tended to be disbursed to smaller and more defined groups than in most European states. Such disaggregation tended to make politicians especially vulnerable to sectional claims, generating a cumulation of distributive demands. Governments, meanwhile, were often unable to impose their own choices on the patterns of transfers and benefits. Without adjustment, reappraisal, and a clear set of objectives underlying these patterns, both the public sector, and public disbursements to the private sector, gradually became sources of significant distortion in the economy as a whole.

Party mediation of social interests, especially as it is affected by internal party structure, intra-party competition, and electoral law, is thus a distinctive feature of Italian political life. It generates an unusual combination of highly ideological and polarized public debate—the consequence of deeply rooted historical subcultures—and a highly pragmatic style of daily political brokerage. These issues are explored in the first four chapters. Chapter 1 examines the historical legacy for the modern party system of the three formative historical experiences that preceded the post-war republic. It underlines, in particular, the dual nature of the party system: in part the reflection of real social divisions, but in part the consequence of artificial political divisions unrelated to civil society. Chapter 2 analyses the social and economic foundations on which the parties built their support bases, and traces how the distributive struggle between competing social groups became gradually more complex as the balance of economic power between capital and labour changed, and the need to compensate other groups against the consequences of this change complicated the policy agenda. Chapters 3 and 4 then explore in more detail the structure of the contemporary party system. Chapter 3 examines the macro-politics of electoral competition between parties, the impact of the electoral system on political representation, and the nature of coalition-building. Chapter 4 descends to the micro-politics of party organization, policy-formation, intra-party competition, and political leadership, concluding with an assessment of how earlier theories of the nature of Italian party politics have been modified by a more detailed understanding of the internal operations of the parties.

The latter half of the book examines the formal institutions. Chapter 5 provides an overview of the constitutional order, Chapter 6 analyses Parliament and the representative process, Chapter 7 the political executive, Chapter 8 the administrative and legal framework, Chapter 9 subnational tiers of government, and Chapter 10 the increasingly important European Community dimension of Italian politics. These aspects of political life have traditionally received less attention in the literature on Italian politics, at least in English, than party politics and electoral behaviour. Partly this is because they have sometimes appeared to be of only secondary importance in a political system dominated by the informal brokerage of parties and coalition politics. Partly it is because the literature on them in Italian has traditionally been generated more by students of public and constitutional law than by students of political science—yielding a focus tuned more to procedural and legal detail than to the sociology of power.

The view that Italy's formal structures of government are poorly institutionalized, and therefore have little independent role in shaping political behaviour and policy outcomes, is however less tenable today than say twenty-five years ago. The republican constitution will soon be fifty years old. Other than the still rapidly evolving European Community tier of political life, its conventions and structures are now quite well established. Virtually all political actors have received their adult political socialization through republican institutions. Even the more recent innovations—regional government, the judicial activism of the constitutional court, and the abrogative referendum—are becoming familiar features of the landscape. The relationships established between the two chambers of Parliament, the political executive, the administration, subnational tiers of government, and the range of agencies which oversee these organs (court of accounts, council of state, the presidency of the republic, the constitutional court) are now firmly entrenched, and their rules and conventions have an important behavioural influence.

The final chapter considers what aspects of the constitution and of institutional, administrative, and electoral law might usefully be modified to improve the policy-making process. It is not a blueprint for reform, however, still less a comprehensive judgement on the quality of Italian democracy. There is almost certainly no reform, however incisive, which will cure the alleged ills of Italian political life at a stroke. A political system is not just the sum of the political parties and formal rules given to it by voters and constitution drafters; it is also the sum of the attitudes and values of its citizens and its political class, and these are not easily shifted by the stroke of a reforming pen. Occasionally, as in France with the advent of the Fifth republic, Germany with the Bonn republic, or Spain in its rapid and successful transition to democracy after the death of Franco, wholesale institutional reconstruction *can* help transform a political system. In Italy's well-entrenched liberal democracy, however, and in the absence of a de Gaulle, Adenauer, or Juan Carlos, such a transformation looks less likely. The attitudinal change necessary to underpin real reform—especially among members of the political élite—will probably come only slowly, thereby diluting considerably the impact of any formal institutional modification that Parliament and the electorate find themselves likely to agree upon for the foreseeable future.

1

The Weight of the Past

Italy's system of parliamentary democracy was established in the years immediately after World War II. Between 1943 and 1945 the peninsula was liberated from fascism and German occupation. In June 1946 the monarchy, which in formal terms had continued to operate during the fascist era, was abolished by popular referendum. On 1 January 1948 the republican constitution was promulgated. Italy thus embarked on the third regime in her eighty-seven-year history as a united state. The first—liberal Italy—was a rudimentary form of Parliamentary democracy, based on a restricted electorate. Its task in building the nation-state was formidable, and its record mixed. Unification was in many respects a lucky accident, engineered by a state, Piedmont, which imposed its own political system on the rest of the peninsula. It did so in a manner which could hardly be described as sensitive. The tensions generated in the struggle to democratize the political system eventually led to the collapse of the liberal regime and its replacement by fascism. From 1922 until the end of World War II normal political life and party development were suspended, and the country was subjected to a ramshackle and inefficient dictatorship. When democracy was restored, however, the political cleavages which had shaped the party system during the early period of state-building and democratization showed themselves to be remarkably durable. The division between secular liberals and the Church reappeared, as did that between the class-based parties of the left and the forces of the centre and right. What had changed was the balance between them, as became clear in the phase of political reconstruction between 1945 and 1948, which saw the drafting of the new constitutional framework and the struggle for the support of the newly franchised electorate.

The modern political system is thus the result of three fundamental historical experiences: political unification during the liberal era, fascism, and the brief but crucial period of resistance and reconstruction in the mid-1940s. The long-term impact of each is examined in this chapter.

Liberal Italy

Late unification as a nation-state

The history of the Italian state is far shorter than that of the Italian people. It begins only in 1861. Precisely why the peninsula should have been passed by in the first wave of European state-building cannot be investigated here.[1] The heart of the explanation lies in the economic and social disparity between the city-states of the so-called commune civilization of the centre-north, and feudalism in the south. Between the two lay the papacy: a territorial as well as spiritual power, and one with a vested interest in keeping the peninsula disunited. In examining modern Italy, however, the causes of the failure are less important than the consequences. From the sixteenth century Italy fell under the control of foreign powers and lost her central role in the European economy. Having been passed by in the first wave of state-building, she was condemned to wait until the nineteenth century for the second, which, when it came, sprang not from monarchical absolutism but from the generation of something approaching a middle-class national consciousness.

In the intervening centuries, the pace of social development was slow. In the centre-north, in fact, there was a regression, with a reversal of conventional class development as the cultural and commercial vitality of the communes gave way to a landed and privileged aristocracy. The chief result of this long delay was a society culturally quite unprepared for nationhood. The economic gap between north and south was formidable. The commitment of the great mass of peasants to the Italian nation was almost non-existent. The diversity of legal systems, of land tenure, and of dialect was enormous. An ingrained provincialism persisted for decades after the unification of 1861, as did the uncertainty of the ruling class about the political cohesion of the new state. The liberal constitution presided uneasily over a series of compromises—both economic and political—which seemed essential to hold the system together.

The effects of these compromises persist to this day. The most important was the widening of the gap between north and south. In the north, the *Risorgimento* signalled the emergence of an entrepreneurial middle class. A large part of the parliamentary class was drawn from its ranks, and public policy was aimed, not always successfully, at the development of a capitalist economy. In the south, the *Risorgimento* was in no real sense a class war between feudal privilege and the entrepreneurial middle class, because the latter hardly existed. Industry was at an embryonic stage; agriculture was poorly developed.

The peasants in this over-populated region produced only enough for subsistence, and the great estates were so badly managed that there was little capital accumulation. The old nobility had certainly fallen into decline, but the professional middle class, such as it was, tended to profit only to buy land and establish itself in the same parasitic relationship to the peasants as its predecessors.

The real social conflict in the south was that between the great mass of the population—the peasantry—and the old ruling class of notables and landlords, and in such a conflict the rulers of the new state were decidedly on the side of the latter. The Piedmontese had not descended on the south to liberate the peasantry, and had no intention of allowing a social revolution (dismantling the aristocratic estates) to follow the political revolution of unification. To do so would have threatened both the fragile unity of the new state and social stability throughout the peninsula. The privileges of the southern notables had to be preserved, for only in this way would they be induced to transfer their loyalty from Naples to Rome. Having obtained a united Italy, a single large national market, and a more rational administrative structure, the north was reluctant to put its gains at risk by objecting to this settlement.[2]

In the absence of reform in the south, the gap between the two halves of the country continued to grow. Industrial output doubled between 1880 and 1908, but development was largely confined to the north, particularly the Milan–Turin–Genoa triangle. This area enjoyed several advantages even before unification. In the liberal economic environment that prevailed after 1861, embryonic southern industries were exposed to fierce competition from more advanced rivals in the north and abroad, and frequently folded. Even when government policy took a more interventionist turn, it mainly benefited the north. In the 1890s, tariffs were raised to protect northern industries such as textiles, silk, steel, and heavy engineering. The contracts for military expenditure in Italy's first wave of assertive nationalism in the 1880s and 1890s also helped industry. Conversely, the chief side-effect of this nationalism, the tariff war with France, did great harm to southern agriculture, for the lucrative French wine market, to which southern vineyards were geared, was closed off at a stroke.[3]

Liberal Italy's adjustment to the political implications of unification had similarly far-reaching consequences. The immediate problem was to obtain legitimacy in the eyes of the two dominant social interests: the peasantry and the Catholic Church. To the majority of the peasants, unification's main result was that the oppression of Piedmontese tax-collectors was added to that of the local landlord. When anger and frustration spilled over into violence and banditry, the Piedmontese army replied in kind, and in the years after 1861 a virtual civil war was fought in the south. This problem was compounded by the attitude of the Church. It refused to recognize the new state, rejected the 1871 Law of Guarantees regularizing the position of the Vatican, and, most serious of all, it forbade Catholics to participate in Italian political life. At a local level, many priests were actively encouraging peasant agitation.[4]

Deprived of the support of both the peasants and the Church, and chosen by an electorate which accounted for no more than 2 per cent of the population, Italy's new liberal rulers were dangerously isolated from the real Italy. Faced with widespread social hostility and well aware of the deep-rooted cultural, legal, and administrative differences between various regions, the political class saw local autonomy as offering scope to the opponents of unification. It dispensed at an early stage not only with all thoughts of federalism, but with more limited schemes of local self-government. Italy was subjected to a rigid and centralized political system organized in the Napoleonic mould.[5] Administrative boundaries were based on a new unit, the province, similar in size and role to the French department. The key figure in this system was the prefect, a provincial governor dispatched from Rome, responsible only to the central government, and entrusted with the task of overseeing the administration and maintaining order. For many years the elective principle in local government was entirely absent, and even when, towards the end of the century, it was slowly introduced, central government, through its power of patronage, continued to exercise a controlling hand in most areas.

The new system was not entirely without benefits. It provided a minimally efficient and reasonably honest administration, and it brought uniform legal codes and a uniform educational system. But the price was heavy. Centralized control reinforced the sense for much of the peninsula that it was still occupied by a foreign power. In the long run there was an even greater disadvantage to centralization than its unpopularity. As Italian society became more complex and differentiated, the state acquired more functions, especially in the fields of social welfare and economic regulation. To a state as centralized as Italy, and with internal disparities as great as those between north and south, the problems of co-ordinating the growing number of ministries, of adapting policies to suit local conditions, and of ensuring at least minimal dispatch in decision-making came to assume ever more serious dimensions.

A second shortcoming of liberal Italy's political system, and one which similarly had lasting effects, lay in the nature of parliamentary politics. Nineteenth-century Italy failed to develop organized, disciplined, and clearly differentiated political parties capable of competing for the votes of a mass electorate. At the outset, the division between Cavour's 'historic right' of centralizers and monarchists and the Mazzinian left of radicals and democrats might have provided the basis for the development of a two-party system such as emerged at the same time in Britain. However, the Italian electorate was far too restricted to provide a stimulus to the creation of efficient disciplined party organizations. By the middle of the 1870s, the distinction between right and left had become very blurred, with the infiltration into the ranks of the left of large numbers of southerners who had no interest in reform of any kind. Divisions over policy were complex and cut across one another, rarely corresponding to a left–right division.[6] Prime ministers preferred to build parliamentary majorities not through party discipline but through *trasformismo*. This system led to the construction of a series of *ad hoc* alliances among the mass of unaligned parliamentary deputies. Forces on both right and left were 'transformed' into a large but unstable parliamentary majority. What resulted was barely definable as a *party* system in any meaningful sense until after World War II.

In such conditions corruption was rife. Deputies were bribed into supporting the government by the uninhibited use of patronage, both for themselves (honours, cabinet posts) and for their constituencies (railways, bridges, government contracts). It required delicate balancing of personal and local interests, and led to numerous changes of government as cabinets were reshuffled and new interests satisfied. Inevitably, it also led to a dramatic decline in the tone of parliamentary life. And when governments collapsed and re-emerged on matters having no relation to great issues of programme or principle, ordinary Italians could be forgiven for thinking that the political class was involved in little more than a thinly disguised conspiracy against the public.

By preventing the emergence of disciplined parties, *trasformismo* also undermined the possibility of alternation between parties in government and those in opposition. Indeed Italy has never really known the practice of alternation, since even with the advent after World War II of relatively cohesive parties the way in which government majorities were created continued to bear a resemblance to nineteenth-century practices. Broad coalitions spanning a considerable part of the political spectrum, and held together by the distribution of patronage, were still a feature of political life four decades after 1945. In such conditions party discipline was low and cross-party alliances frequent. The poor aggregative capacities of contemporary Italian parties, in fact, owe much to the habits and traditions passed down from the party system of the liberal era.

The failure of democracy

Liberal Italy's parliamentary practice provided an adequate if frequently unwholesome instrument for ruling a country with a restricted franchise, where the masses played no part in electoral politics. It could not cope with their emergence on the political stage, and herein lies the third and ultimately fatal flaw in the system: its inability to adapt to the new era of mass politics and self-assertive nationalism. From the end of the nineteenth century three new forces hostile to the liberal system began to develop. The first was the socialist movement. Working-class organizations began to appear among the industrial proletariat of Milan and Genoa, and the agricultural workers of the Po Valley, in the 1880s. In 1892 the Socialist Party was formed. It survived early persecution to develop an intellectual and white-collar, as well as working-class, following, and by 1913 was a major political force.[7]

In its turn, the socialist movement stimulated the rise of clericalism and nationalist reaction. The former reflected Catholic fears, that unless the Vatican's refusal to participate in Italian political life was tacitly reversed, socialism would establish an unchallengeable hold over the working class. The clerical movement was by no means united however. On the one side it contained progressive Christian Democrats, initially suppressed by Mussolini, but later to become the mainstream of the Catholic political world. On the other side there was a movement of clerical conservatism which, after the lifting of the papal *non-expedit*, ran parliamentary candidates of its own, but also provided support for any liberals and nationalists who would undertake to oppose anti-clerical measures in Parliament.[8] Nationalism was an even more diverse movement, and it too grew up partly inside the liberal block. It was backed by industrialists, landowners, and a variety of chauvinist conservatives seeking an assertive foreign policy and a firm line against the growing power of the labour movement. It had a natural base amongst those who wanted Italy to join the race for colonial acquisitions in Africa, and firm support from those—the arms industry and the steel lobby—with an interest in high military expenditure.[9]

The growth of these forces put new pressures on the ruling liberal block. Until the eve of World War I Giovanni Giolitti, the greatest of the practitioners of *trasformismo*, charted a skilful course through the troubled parliamentary waters they created. Refusing to panic in the face of working-class militancy, he attempted instead to compromise with the socialist movement by introducing a programme of minimum social reform, while restraining the extreme anti-clerical element in his own party, and accepting the need for a working compromise with the pervasive influence of the Church. In part against his own better judgement, he was also not above indulging in nationalist adventures where opinion demanded. In 1911 he embarked on a successful, if ultimately costly, military annexation of Libya.

In the end, however, his system collapsed around him. Socialism on one hand and nationalism on the other came under the leadership of more extreme forces, and the clerical movement headed towards the formation of its own party. What finally killed liberalism was the granting of virtually universal suffrage in 1912. Superficially, in the general election held the following year, the liberal block still enjoyed a majority of over a hundred, but the centrifugal pressures inside it were becoming unmanageable, and the difficulties it would face in the area of the mass electorate were clear.

Italy thus finally acquired the multi-party system which her fragmented society made almost inevitable under universal suffrage and proportional representation, and the difficulties of making the system work were ultimately to destroy the parliamentary framework. The onset of war postponed the confrontation with reality, but at its conclusion that confrontation could be put off no longer. From 1918 to 1922, successive liberal governments struggled to hold the centre against the challenge of socialism, political Catholicism, nationalism, and fascism. Eventually, exasperated, they invited Mussolini to abandon *squadrismo* for the premier's office, and within two years, through a combination of legality and violence, he had dismantled the parliamentary system and replaced it with the fascist state.[10]

Fascist Italy
Fascism and Italian political culture

The legacy of fascism is in many respects more elusive than that of the liberal state, despite its greater proximity to contemporary politics. None of the influences which it is tempting to attribute to the experience of 1922–45 is particularly tangible, for they largely involve attitudes and assumptions about politics, rather than concrete institutions or settled practices. One area in which the influence is relatively clear, however, is that of nationalism. During the liberal era, the nationalism of the *Risorgimento* was gradually replaced by a less healthy spirit of outwardly directed nationalism for which the absence of a strong military tradition, and the inability of the economy to support such a tradition, made Italy quite unsuited. Under Mussolini this spirit reached its apogee in the colonial adventures in East Africa. They brought little reward in economic terms, pushed the country towards the fatal embrace with Hitler's Germany, and led to a military record in World War II in Africa and the Balkans which was little short of disastrous.[11]

In the post-war era, as a result, the country has been happily free of aggressive nationalism, and this, and the absence of significant problems of decolonization, has not only limited the range of sentiments on which the parties on the far right can play, but has also enabled Italy's rulers to adopt a low profile in international affairs with policy built on the twin pillars of NATO and the European Community. These institutions of collective military and economic security had apparently served her so well that by the early 1970s there was virtually an all-party consensus (which even included the Communists) in their favour.[12]

In other respects, however, the impact of fascism on Italian political culture is less clear. It is impossible to say how far Mussolini provided an inoculation against a return to authoritarianism after 1945. It seems inherently plausible that the knowledge of what happened, in many cases the direct memory of it, has influenced the behaviour of politicians, and even ordinary voters. It appears to have exercised a restraining hand, and in the case of the left it bequeathed an almost obsessively cautious and conciliatory mentality. And it may well have made many voters think twice about deserting the parties of the centre at moments of particularly acute exasperation at the instability of coalition government. But there was no élite-led 'remaking' of Italian political culture in the way in which, it is sometimes argued, German political culture was 'remade' after World War II.[13] On the contrary, voters have continued to support allegedly extremist parties in quite large numbers throughout the post-war era. Moreover, if, at the brink, politicians have refrained from allowing the political system to come to a complete deadlock—as it did in 1922—they have allowed it to come perilously close on occasions, and the frequency with which governments come and go does not suggest a political class whose primary aim is a consensus in defence of democracy. This is not to deny that historical memory exists, that the common struggle against fascism is at times a powerful unifying myth, or that democracy is recognized as needing support precisely because on Italian soil it is a fragile plant. It is rather to underline the difficulty of weighing the effects of these factors, or of predicting when they will be invoked in concrete political action.

Moreover, fascism has left a direct legacy of authoritarianism, as well as an indirect legacy of democratic commitment. The Italian Social Movement, on the extreme right of the political spectrum, has been considerably larger than its counterpart in post-war Germany, and sees itself as the heir to Mussolini's politics. And closer to the heart of the political establishment there has been a more concealed strand of authoritarian reaction. This has arisen, at least in part, from the failure to purge the security services, the judiciary, and the bureaucracy of their fascist elements in 1945, and from the outlooks and administrative styles acquired by these institutions in the inter-war era. Various episodes testify to the presence of individuals prepared to conspire against democratic procedures, and there have been recurrent allegations that individuals in the security services have had connections with right-wing terrorist groups. Prominent among such allegations are three key incidents: the de Lorenzo plan to stifle left-wing opposition in the early 1960s; the P-2 masonic lodge scandal which came to light in 1981; and most recently the so-called 'Gladio' affair—the revelation of the long-standing state-sponsored underground militia network, trained originally as a stay-behind resistance movement in event of a Soviet invasion, but later, allegedly, linked with extreme right groups in the security services and elsewhere.[14]

Church and state

In at least one area, however, fascism left a very clear legacy. After six decades in which the Vatican formally refused to recognize the legitimacy of the Italian state, Mussolini finally managed a reconciliation. From early on, the Church had seen in fascism a more effective bulwark against the socialist movement than was to be had in its own offspring, the Catholic People's Party, much of which was dangerously sympathetic to the Socialists. In 1922 the Vatican abandoned the People's Party altogether, and henceforth gave much discreet support to Mussolini. In 1929, after considerable negotiation, it was announced that an agreement had been reached, formalized in a treaty and a 'Concordat' known as the Lateran Pacts, by which the Church finally recognized the legitimacy of the Italian state, and the Vatican City became a sovereign territory. In return, Catholicism became the official state religion, received a generous financial settlement, and obtained jurisdiction over marriage, and a wider influence over education. Catholic Action, the lay arm of the Church, was free to continue its work in youth education and other matters, as long as it abstained from political activity.[15] Although there was some friction over the interpretation of the agreement, it nevertheless stood the test of time, and indeed was incorporated into the post-war constitution.[16] Without question, the Concordat laid the basis for the survival of the Church's role in society in the 1930s and enabled it to emerge as one of Italy's most powerful social institutions in 1945: so powerful, indeed, that in the early years of the post-war republic it was able to act as a surrogate organizational network for the largest party.

The fascist economic inheritance

The second enduring legacy from the fascist era was a product of the regime's reaction to the depression of the 1930s. Italian industrial development was, and even today remains, highly dependent on the banking system, which had large direct investments in industry. In the 1930s, many banks were both merchant banks and deposit banks, and fell prey to the cardinal sin of borrowing short and lending long. With the equity collapse of the early 1930s, three—Banco di Roma, Credito italiano, and Banca commerciale—found themselves in difficulties that threatened the collapse of the financial system. They were rescued by the state, which thereby acquired large holdings in Italian industry, concentrating them in IRI (the Industrial Reconstruction Institute), which took over the holdings acquired from the banks.[17] By 1939 IRI had formal control of large parts of Italian industry, particularly in basic sectors such as steel, engineering, shipbuilding, aircraft production, and armaments.

Neither IRI nor any of the other institutions established with a similar purpose owed its origins to fascist ideology. They were the result of immediate economic necessity, and the relationship between government and the economy which they implied, and the problems they raised, were not in essence different from those which, in more recent times, the mixed economy has posed for governments of very different complexions. Equally clearly, neither the new role of the state in the economy nor the formal edifice of corporatism achieved co-ordinated state control. In the 1930s Italian society moved not towards totalitarianism but towards a shambling, inefficient, inordinately corrupt, and multi-centred state bureaucracy. By 1939 all attempts at effective co-ordination of the many centres of economic and administrative action had been abandoned; improvisation was the order of the day, and Italy drifted into war in a chronic state of unpreparedness.

Despite this, the economic legacy of fascism, in the shape of institutions such as IRI and the public-credit agency IMI, was of great consequence for post-war economic policy. These agencies were not abandoned as the detritus of an unwanted past, but were developed to become in turn one of the post-war economy's strengths, and more recently one of its serious problems. The great range of special regulatory agencies (established, in general, outside formal ministerial departments, and thus given considerable autonomy from central control) also survived, and left one of the most complex and labyrinthine administrative structures in the whole of Europe.

Resistance and Reconstruction

The years 1943–8 are the third, and most immediate, key to the contemporary political system. The way in which the war ended and politics was reconstructed had a more important and lasting impact than in most other European states. In France, for example, both the party system and the constitutional framework were considerably altered by later events. In Germany there was a substantial political vacuum before the Federal republic's constitution was drafted and the Bonn government was free of allied control. In Italy, in contrast, there was continuous political evolution from the fall of fascism in the summer of 1943 to the promulgation of the Republic and its first general election in 1948. By the end of this period the main lines of both party system and constitution were established, and Italy's place in the Western sphere of influence was assured.

The politics of the resistance

Political reconstruction began even before the war ended. At the armistice of September 1943 the Allies established their own military authority in the liberated southern section of the peninsula. However, for immediate tactical purposes the allies agreed to recognize the royal government, under Marshal Badoglio, which was thus accorded the status of 'co-belligerent': something more than a defeated enemy, if still less than an ally. The monarchy was not the only focus of political activity, however. As Italy's position in the war became progressively more hopeless, politicians of the pre-fascist era came together to form several party nuclei. Together these formed *Committees of National Liberation*—the political leadership of the resistance movement—with a co-ordinating centre in Rome.

The resistance was of profound psychological importance in liberating the peninsula. It gave the country a minimum of both self-respect and international respect, demonstrating that by no means all Italians were fascists. Certainly the 250,000 partisans who were active in it at one time or another were much more than a minor nuisance to the German occupying forces.[18] Not surprisingly, moreover, the relationship between the royal government, recognized by the allies, and the parties of the resistance movement was at first very difficult. The former had constitutional authority and symbolized political activity; the latter had the moral authority of anti-fascism, and symbolized the approaching era of democratic politics. Initially, the resistance parties refused to recognize the royal government at all, and only in April 1944, seven months after the armistice, did they join the government.

Surprisingly, it was the Communists—much the strongest of the resistance groups—who led this move. Their decision marked the determination of their leader, Palmiro Togliatti, to eschew armed insurrection when the Germans were finally defeated. This strategy was pursued until the spring of 1947, when the PCI was finally expelled from the governing coalition. There was no attempt to use the resistance brigades as a revolutionary army against the monarchy —however much the Communist rank and file might have been expecting this. At the end of the war the party kept its commitment to the allies and handed in its weapons.[19] The significance of the resistance movement was thus not just that it gave the Communist Party an important organizational and moral advantage over other parties. It also marked the beginning of the road to strategic moderation which distinguished the party from most other Western communist parties in the post-war era.

Admittedly, the PCI had little choice in 1945 but to work within the system. Italy was firmly rooted in the Western sphere of influence, and Togliatti knew that he would receive no direct military help from the USSR if he sought to impose communist rule by force. The resistance movement was therefore important in institutionalizing what was to become the core of the party's belief about itself and its strategy for winning power. Anti-fascist unity became a central organizing myth, justifying the party's later co-operation with parties of the centre and centre-right. It also enabled the Communists to argue, against sceptics in the 1960s and 1970s, that their subsequent ideological development was part of a consistent pattern of strategic thinking stretching back to the resistance. It was evident, they argued, in the PCI's 'polycentric' view of the international communist world in the 1950s, and in its support, after World War II, for a constitutional framework based on the dispersal of power, and a wide range of checks and balances.[20]

How much more there was to the PCI's strategic moderation than sheer necessity has been debated for many years. Sceptics of the PCI's commitment to democratic procedures naturally reject such claims as *ex post* rationalization. Left-wing critics attack the party strategy for its pessimism. The PCI leadership, so the latter claim, accepted the logic of the situation in which it found itself too readily. Out of such arguments grew not just a minor intellectual industry—interpreting Italy's resistance history—but also powerful and politically functional organizing myths for both left and right. What happened and why between 1943 and 1945 reverberated down the subsequent decades. The Communists used it to emphasize the historical continuity underlying their strategy—as indeed they had to if they were to reconcile their distinct communist ethos (Leninist origins, centralized organization, neutrality or even Soviet alignment on international issues) with an increasingly social-democratic path to power in a market economy and a liberal democracy. Yet by emphasizing this historical continuity they were constantly forced to defend and justify the past. Forty-five years after the war ended, what the partisan bands did or did not do as they helped liberate northern Italy was still haunting not only the Communist Party, but even the successor Partito democratico della sinistra (PDS) to which it finally gave way after the collapse of communism in Eastern Europe.

The new party system[21]

Six parties were present in the Committee of National Liberation. Two, the Democratic Labour Party and the Action Party, had not existed before fascism and were not to outlast the resistance. The others were reconstructions of parties present before the March on Rome in 1922. The Catholic People's Party reappeared as Christian Democracy (DC), and the old ruling liberal block as the Italian Liberal Party (PLI). On the left, the two parties which had split in 1921, the Socialists and Communists (respectively the PSI and PCI) reappeared to inherit the Marxist tradition. It was soon clear, however, that three parties would be more important than the others: the Christian Democrats, Socialists, and Communists. These were the only parties capable of reaching the new mass electorate which, with the enfranchisement of women, the increase in both turn-out and population, and virtually compulsory voting, was over four times greater than before fascism. To reach these voters, parties required large, efficient, organizational networks. Initially, none of the parties possessed such networks on a nation-wide basis, but in north and central Italy pre-fascist working-class traditions, combined with the recruits obtained from the resistance movement, gave the Communists, and to a lesser extent the Socialists, the rudiments of a mass organization. The Christian Democrats, for their part, if less well endowed with party activists, benefited from the nation-wide network of the Church and Catholic Action. These factors gave the three mass parties an important advantage over the others. This enabled them to build up additional flanking organizations—trade unions, peasants' and farmers' groups, co-operatives, women's organizations—providing a further, if less direct, means of contact with voters.

Nevertheless, in the presence of an extremely permissive system of proportional representation, it was always unlikely that the post-war party system would simplify to a straightforward division between Catholics and Marxists. First, the liberal political tradition, while greatly discredited by the collaboration of liberal politicians with Mussolini in 1922, was not entirely moribund. Secondly, many Italians had fared well under Mussolini and were fearful of the resistance parties. Others were loyal to the monarchy, abolished by 12 million votes to 10 million in a surprisingly close referendum in 1946. And on the left, the size and importance of the Communist Party proved a destructively divisive issue. Such factors guaranteed a complex pattern of minor parties surrounding the major ones.

The right

On the right, in addition to the Liberal Party, two other movements quickly arose. The monarchist lobby, sensing that the resistance optimism would not last long, demanded that the question of the retention of the monarchy should be put to a popular referendum. The conservative instincts of the southern peasantry were not quite strong enough to save the monarchy, but they created space for a small monarchist movement playing on these sympathies. Likewise, the many who had had an involvement, large or small, with the fascist regime, who had made quick profits from the War, or who had accepted fascism as a fact of life now wanted simply to start afresh without the moralistic purges threatened by resistance leaders. For such individuals, the curious *Uomo qualunque* (Common Man's Movement) succinctly captured the anti-party sentiments of the ubiquitous lower middle class of petty officials, shopkeepers, and peasant farmers. The movement was not to last, but only because the party which replaced it, the Italian Social Movement (MSI), encouraged by its success among former fascists, adopted an overtly neo-fascist stance in the 1948 general election, in clear but unpunished defiance of the constitutional bar on attempts to resurrect fascism.

The centre

The centre was dominated by the Christian Democrats. They won 35 per cent of the vote in the 1946 Constituent Assembly elections, against 15 per cent for the three parties of the right: Liberals, Monarchists, and Neo-fascists. Initially, the DC's leanings went in a progressive direction, and the tripartite coalitions of the early reconstruction era had a decidedly leftward orientation. Many Catholic activists had been involved in the resistance and had been influenced by its social radicalism. As the influence of the Church network on party organization increased, however, its conservative tendencies became gradually more marked. The economic problems posed by reconstruction also pushed the party in this direction, as many industrialists, rebelling against government controls, demanded greater entrepreneurial freedom and a more resolute stand against inflation. The clear evidence of the re-emergence of a social constituency on the right also strengthened the conservatives, the majority of whom were supporters of the monarchy. Thus when, in December 1945, the Christian Democratic leader Alcide De Gasperi captured the premiership, he almost immediately pushed the tripartite coalition in a conservative direction.

The left

In principle, the left was the strongest of the three main groups in the 1946 constituent assembly. It received 40 per cent of the vote—divided almost equally between Socialists and Communists—but its strength depended upon its remaining united. With the idealism of the resistance ebbing away rapidly, and the tensions of the Cold War impinging directly on domestic politics, unity on the left proved impossible to preserve for long after the 1946 elections. In a drama that was to undermine the position of the non-communist left, and leave the country with a weak and divided labour movement, the Socialist Party split into two under the increasing tensions of the Cold War. Giuseppe Saragat and 50 of the 115 Socialist members of the Constituent Assembly abandoned the party in protest against its continuing close links with the Communist Party, and founded the Italian Socialist Workers Party, later renamed the Social Democrat Party (PSDI).[22]

This split in the socialist ranks reflected a more fundamental division between pro- and anti-communist forces in the wider party system. The early months of 1947 were marked by the enunciation of the Truman Doctrine of the containment of communism, a major increase in East–West tension in Europe, and the announcement of Marshall Aid. These events had an immediate impact on the tripartite coalition of Communists, Socialists, and Christian Democrats. The promise of American assistance for a resolutely anti-communist Italian government encouraged the DC to expel the Socialists and Communists from the Council of Ministers and, albeit with some initial difficulty, form a new administration which immediately adopted sternly deflationary measures. Soon after, the Social Democrats and the small Republican Party joined the new government and the isolation of the Socialists and Communists was complete. Too late the latter realized that De Gasperi's gamble would succeed. Their attempt to organize demonstrations to bring the government down rebounded against them. With communist dictatorship in Eastern Europe an increasingly obvious fact of life, many Italians could have been forgiven for supposing that the Communists were on the verge of a similar coup in Italy.

It was therefore understandable that on 18 April 1948, in the first general election held under the new republican constitution, the Christian Democrats won a resounding victory. Their share of the vote increased from 35 per cent to over 48 per cent, while that of the Popular Front (a joint slate including both Communists and Socialists) received only 31 per cent. The 1948 election thus confirmed the relationships within the Italian party system which had been evolving since the liberation, but with one important new twist. The split in the socialist ranks meant that instead of three mass parties there were now, in effect, only two: the Christian Democrats and the Communists. The former—much the largest of all the parties—dominated the government; the latter, on the extreme left, dominated the opposition. The Socialist Party, in the wake of the secession of the Social Democrats, lost a large group of activists and approximately one-third of its voters; henceforth it was the largest of the minor parties, rather than one of the three mass parties. These minor parties now numbered six in all. Apart from the Socialists on the left there were two parties (the Social Democrats and Republicans) in a broadly left-of-centre position. On the moderate right were the Liberals, and on the far right the Monarchists and the Italian Social Movement.

Within the overall spectrum, the events of 1947–8 clarified the distinction between the so-called 'democratic' or 'pro-system' parties of the centre (Social Democrats, Republicans, Christian Democrats, and Liberals) and the 'anti-system' or 'extreme' parties of the left

(Communists and, at least until the late 1950s, Socialists) and of the right (Monarchists and Fascists). Henceforth, political life was dominated by the struggle to construct a stable coalition from this very heterogeneous centre group. When this eventually proved impossible, in the 1960s, the next best expedient, harking back to the pre-fascist practices of *trasformismo*, was to extend the group's boundaries by bringing parties of the left into the democratic fold.

The economics of reconstruction

The reconstruction years were no less vital in economic than in political terms. Between 1945 and 1950 decisions were taken which were critical to future economic development. The problems of reconstruction were formidable, with around 20 per cent of productive capacity lost. There were major shortages of supplies, most notably in energy and food, and the balance of payments was seriously in deficit. With exports and emigrants' receipts covering barely a third of the total import bill, normal sources of international finance were available neither to the state nor to private economic operators.

Despite these problems, the role of the political authorities in planning the allocation and production of resources was deliberately limited, and reconstruction took place under conditions of greater liberalism than in most European countries. The heterogeneous nature of the ruling coalition between 1945 and 1947 made effective economic policy-making extremely difficult. The left was anxious to promote a currency reform and a wealth tax, redistributing income away from wartime speculators. It also sought a forced loan to finance government expenditure, and strict control over foreign exchange. The moderates in the coalition took the opposite view. They were opposed to a currency reform on the grounds that the middle classes, whose savings would be adversely affected, had kept their faith in the currency during the war by investing in government bonds. If this faith were not returned there was a real risk of a new extremist movement arising on the far right.

In the absence of agreement between the parties of the coalition, economic policy after 1945 was dictated almost exclusively by the Treasury and the Bank of Italy, both of which, at the collapse of fascism, fell into the hands of the liberal economists who had been disapproving spectators of fascism's unsuccessful policies of state intervention, protection, and controls.[23] They rapidly set about implementing their own ideological vision, and this meant not only firmly resisting the plans of the left for currency reform and a wealth tax, but also systematically dismantling controls on foreign exchange and imports, reducing numerous other taxes, and holding government expenditure, and the government's printing presses, firmly in check.

Their strategy was pursued with great tenacity. Against a left which, with a few exceptions, was rather ignorant of economics, the liberal economists generally had the better of the argument. When they did not, the inaction which followed from the stalemate within the coalition tended to favour their strategy. The Keynesian revolution, beginning to influence economic policy in some other Western countries, found infertile terrain in Italy. The nature and promise of the mixed welfare economy was still little understood, and many on the left supposed that in the absence of a fully planned, socialized economy liberal principles were no worse than the limited intervention of a mixed economy. As on later occasions the Italian left subordinated economic objectives to political exigencies. The influence of the left in economic policy was not entirely absent. Legislation was introduced on inflation-indexing of wages, modest family allowances, minimum wage levels, rent controls, and the recognition, inside the workplace, of consultative workers' factory committees. But these measures proved not incompatible with the essentials of a *laissez-faire* order and were difficult to enforce.

Foreign aid and its conditions

Initially, however, economic liberalism was by no means an unqualified success, and by late 1946 its costs were becoming serious. Inflation, which had declined in late 1945 and early 1946, was again increasing rapidly. On the black market, the lira fell to a record low against the dollar, and with the initial American Aid programme scheduled to close there was concern about future international credits. The tensions inside the coalition reached breaking point. The moderates were determined to pursue a policy of devaluation and a tight credit squeeze, and the parties on the left were expelled from the coalition to facilitate this policy and win back waning American confidence. The new coalition immediately imposed a credit squeeze, raised the effective reserve ratio that banks were required to observe, and put strict limits on government expenditure. The measures were remarkably successful. Prices levelled off, the lira was stabilized, the authorities began building up foreign exchange against future speculation, and the first of the 1.5 billion dollars Italy was destined to receive under the Marshall Aid European recovery programme started to arrive.[24]

In laying the foundations for a more stable economy, in restoring confidence in the value of the lira, and in preparing the way for Italy's entry into the rapidly expanding international trade and payments system in the early 1950s, the measures were undoubtedly successful, although they have naturally been criticized by subsequent commentators for their severity and bluntness. Moreover, their consequences went beyond economics; the political changes which led to the split on the left and the exclusion of the Communists from government after 1947 were closely tied to the thrust of economic policy. The latter was aimed at undermining the power which the labour movement had established after the liberation. Dividing both the trade unions and the parties of the left was the prerequisite for the policies of low public consumption and high self-financed capital investment upon which the economic growth of the 1950s and 1960s was based. Priority had thus to be given to such explicitly political goals in the initial phase of development, and if this entailed holding aggregate demand to a level lower than that which was otherwise necessary, the long-term benefits were thought to outweigh the costs. By the end of 1948, Italy had safely embarked on the course of Centrist coalitions and economic liberalism which, in the radical political climate of the resistance, had looked impossible.

Conclusion

There are no clear standards by which to judge the question 'How heavily does the weight of the past hang on contemporary Italy?' Few, if any, West European states were reconstructed *tabula rasa* at any point in the twentieth century, and Italy certainly was not, even after 1945. Whether for Italy the emphasis should lie with continuity or discontinuity depends mainly on perspective. The Italian economy has undergone a profound transformation since 1945, reflecting a sharp break with previous economic models. The highly protected and regulated economy of the inter-war years gave way to an economic liberalism whose central plank was the insertion of the Italian economy into an open European and international trading system. Despite the persistence of a striking disparity in development, economic structure, and living standards between north and south, the overall economic and social transformation which has resulted from the adoption of this model has been profound, as will become clear in the following chapter.

In the political sphere too, it may be argued that there was a sharp break after 1945. Republican democracy stands in stark contrast—both with fascism and the old 'liberal' state—not just in having lasted, but in constituting a genuinely liberal, pluralist society, successfully integrating not just a small élite strata, but the great mass of the population. Comparisons with other Mediterranean societies underline this. Greece, Spain, and Portugal all shared many socio-political characteristics with Italy in 1945. They were relatively backward, agrarian societies, with hitherto protected economies, poor social infrastructures, weak and uncompetitive industries, and none was thought to provide fertile terrain for liberal democracy. Admittedly, in the north of Italy there was an industrial culture which considerably outranked anything found elsewhere in the Mediterranean, and which was the engine of a wider social modernization. It was Italian business interests which made it both feasible and necessary for Italy to insert itself into the emerging European economy, but even Italy at the outset was peripheral to that economy. Yet within a remarkably short time Italy had pulled itself away from its Mediterranean counterparts. It was the only one to adopt a genuinely liberal economic model, and the only one in which liberal democracy was successfully established. In Greece, democracy was under constant threat, and eventually succumbed to the military, to be re-established only in the mid-1970s. In Spain and Portugal too, the adoption of liberal democracy and an open economy had to wait until well into the 1970s.

Moving from the economic model of development, and overall regime choice, to the detailed features of the political system, the elements of continuity with the past become more important relative to those of change. The broad party choices that have endured since 1945 certainly derive from historically acquired partisan cleavages. The nature of relationships between voters and parties, and between the parties themselves, have marked elements of continuity with habits laid down in nineteenth-century political life. In particular there is a notable combination of two contrasting modes of political aggregation: on the one hand an exclusive and all-embracing sub-cultural vision of the social order (Marxist, integralist Catholic, neo-fascist), which offers its adherents an apparently unbargainable ideological programme; on the other, a personalized, unprogrammatic style of politics, based on the politician as patron or entrepreneur, and the voter as social client or individualistic consumer—a relationship determined by individually targeted, or at best highly localized, benefits and favours.

Clearly, these modes of aggregation are not exclusive, and, especially in the later post-war years, the parties have developed some capacity to pitch their electoral appeal to the middle level of bargainable programmes and issue agendas. Where they have not done so, new parties have emerged to challenge them. But that capacity has been profoundly affected by the inheritance of clientelism on the one side, and all-embracing ideology on the other.

Equally marked are the elements of continuity in administrative structures. The latter are less visible than party programmes and party–voter linkages, but no less important in determining the nature of a liberal democracy and the relationship between the citizen and the state—particularly where the state as social regulator develops an increasingly important role. The efficiency and fairness with which the state acquits its tasks of social redistribution (taxation, pensions, social assistance, health provision) and the productivity of other resources appropriated for social regulation and development (the judicial system, the military, education, environmental regulation, transport systems, etc.) have a major impact on the quality of liberal-democratic government. In this area, much more than in that of overall regime choice, or economic model of development, Italy is, as we shall see in later chapters, hampered by her past.

The reason is not difficult to discern. It is one thing to make a choice between competing political or economic philosophies; it is quite another to transform the attitudes, habits, skills, social standing, and other attributes of those who staff the machinery of state. Italy's transformation from agrarian society to modern industrial economy took place at a dramatic pace compared with older states like Britain or France, which had had far longer to build up efficient and prestigious administrative structures. Ironically, indeed, the problem in some ways grew worse after Italian unification. In the early phase, the country was governed by the Piedmontese state, itself modelled on the Napoleonic bureaucracy inherited early in the nineteenth century. That system had at least some of the virtues of efficiency, social prestige, and (relative) political impartiality of the system it emulated. Over the course of the twentieth century, however, the old Piedmontese virtues faded under the corrosive onslaught of fascist placemanship and corruption, and the gradual southernization of the (now Rome-based rather than Turin-based) central civil service. A further consequence of Italian economic dualism, in fact, was the failure of northern economic development to act as a motor for a parallel process of administrative modernization. The economic leadership of the country was located in the north, the administrative leadership in Rome. To have expected an administrative system as prestigious, efficient, and managerially self-confident as its French or British counterparts to develop under these conditions, and in a far shorter space of time, was, quite simply, unrealistic.

Both the political and the administrative legacies of the past thus hang heavily over modern Italian political life. In some respects the problems they generate have become more acute as time has proceeded. The poor aggregative capacities of political parties, and the apparent incapacity of the political system to deliver clear-cut alternation in power between competing groups of parties, reflects the contradictory pressures of ideological and subcultural polarization on the one hand, and petty clientelism on the other. The poor performançe of the public administration, and the divergent paths of factor productivity in the public and private sectors, reflect the inability of the state, burdened by the inheritance of the past, to keep pace with the development of the economy and civil society.

2

The Economic and Social Foundations of Contemporary Politics

In Italy as elsewhere, political life can only be understood in its economic and social context. Issues of social distribution form the most important part of the political agenda. In Italy's complex multi-party system they have a major impact on coalition-building. It is impossible to understand why Italian parties behave as they do without some understanding of the social context in which they operate, and the issue agendas they face. That is not to imply, however, that there are clear-cut relationships between social classes and particular parties. On the contrary, as the last chapter suggested, the differentiation between parties in this respect is comparatively low by European standards, with a great deal of overlap between parties in the groups and issues they promote, combined with a high degree of fragmentation in the articulation of the interests themselves. These features derive from the particular characteristics of Italy's post-war development:

- first, an intense process of industrialization telescoped into a far shorter period than in European countries further north;
- secondly, marked differences between regions, with not only a stark contrast between prosperous north and backward south, but also a major difference within the northern half of the country between the older industrial region of the north-west, and the so called 'third Italy' of the north-east and north-centre.

In the latter area small and medium-sized family firms have generated a growth process rather different from the large-scale manufacturing conurbations of the north-west.

This chapter describes the main phases of economic development through which Italy has passed since 1945 in developing these characteristics, and relates them to the gradually more complex relationships between government, capital, labour, and other interest groups which have developed at each stage.

The post-war era can be divided, very broadly, into three phases.[1] In the first—the 'economic miracle'—growth rates were prolifically high, and a major structural transformation occurred in the relative importance of agriculture and industry. This was the phase of so-called 'easy growth', when development gave rise to few serious tensions between the main objectives of economic policy: growth, price stability, external equilibrium. It ended in the recession of 1964–5. A second phase—a transitional one—covered the following decade. It began with a new growth spurt, based on a rather different mix of factors from the previous phase, and its main characteristic, from 1969 onwards, was the development of a growing industrial-relations conflict, accompanied by tensions between different economic constraints as governments acquired a wider range of policy objectives linked to social welfare, full employment, and regional development. The third phase runs from the mid-1970s to the present. It is marked by lower growth rates, greater cyclical variations in economic activity, and attempts, pursued in contrasting directions, and with variable success, to moderate the heightened distributive conflict over wages, profits, taxation, and subsidies.

TABLE 2.1 *Annual rate of increase of gross domestic product in Italy: 1951–1990*

1951	—	1961	8.2	1971	1.6	1981	1.0
1952	3.8	1962	6.2	1972	2.7	1982	0.3
1953	7.0	1963	5.6	1973	7.1	1983	1.1
1954	3.3	1964	2.8	1974	5.4	1984	3.0
1955	6.6	1965	3.3	1975	−2.7	1985	2.6
1956	4.3	1966	6.0	1976	6.6	1986	2.5
1957	5.1	1967	7.2	1977	3.4	1987	3.0
1958	4.9	1968	6.5	1978	3.7	1988	3.9
1959	6.6	1969	6.1	1979	6.0	1989	3.2
1960	6.0	1970	5.3	1980	4.2	1990	2.0
1951–60	5.3	1961–70	5.7	1971–80	3.8	1981–90	2.3

Sources: For 1952–60: K. J. Allen and A. A. Stevenson, *An Introduction to the Italian Economy* (London, 1974), 51; for 1961–89: Commission of the European Community, 'Annual Economic Report 1990–91', *European Economy*, 46 (Brussels, Dec. 1990); for 1990: *OECD Economic Surveys: Italy, 1990/91* (1991).

1950–1963: The Economic Miracle

In the two decades from 1951 to 1971, per capita income increased more than in the whole of united Italy's previous ninety-year history. The economic miracle spanned both decades, and came to an end only after the 'Hot Autumn' of 1969, but the really rapid phase of growth occurred between 1951 and 1963. The remarkable feature of this period was the sustained nature of economic growth. Until the recession of 1963–5, growth was within the range 3.3 to 7.0 per cent in every year except 1961, when it was no less than 8.2 per cent. No other European country managed such a smooth growth path. The rise in consumer prices only passed 3 per cent in two years between 1951 and 1962, and the rise in hourly wage rates was substantially below the growth rate of output. The increasing foreign-trade dependence of the economy brought no serious balance-of-payments difficulties. By 1957 Italy had overcome the chronic problems of the 1940s, and thereafter, in every year except 1963, it was able to record an overall balance-of-payments surplus. The balance on current account was not always so favourable, but when the invisible inflows from tourism and emigrants' receipts were added, they allowed Italy to build up substantial gold and foreign-exchange reserves.

Numerous indices of the later stages of industrial development appeared during this phase: high-technology engineering and automobile production, chemicals, and other 'advanced' products took an increasing share of the domestic market, and of exports, in comparison with such traditional goods as textiles. The economy continued to be characterized by the presence of many small firms (the average manufacturing unit in 1961 still employed fewer than ten workers) but a number of large, modern corporations, operating on an international scale (FIAT, Olivetti, Pirelli, ENI, Montecatini, Edison, Italsider), were also emerging.[2]

The origins of the miracle

The remarkable growth performance was the result of specific features of the period, several of which were not to continue after 1963.

The labour market

An important contributory element was the 'dualism' of the Italian economy, and the existence of a large reserve of unemployed or underemployed labour which could be utilized in the growth process. This dualism existed both *geographically* (a backward, largely agricultural south alongside the industrialized north) and *sectorally* (small-scale, low-technology, low-productivity firms alongside large modern enterprises). It meant that labour productivity could be raised by switching labour from the backward to the more advanced sectors of the economy.[3] Forty-four per cent of the labour force was still employed in agriculture in 1951. Moreover, unemployment stood at

9 per cent, and there were also major areas of underemployment, making the pool of labour available to industry substantial. Over the period from 1951 to 1963 a large proportion of excess labour was absorbed by industry (which increased its share of the labour force from 29 to 40 per cent) while the official unemployment rate fell to only 2.6 per cent.

This reserve of labour enabled investment and output to grow without any significant increase in wage costs. Firms were thus able to invest in new technologies, labour productivity increased rapidly as, in the absence of higher wage costs, did profits, completing a virtuous circle of growth through self-financed capital investment. Modest increases in wages and private consumption ensured that industrial expansion did not generate excess demand or draw in imports, or divert exports, to the domestic market. There were thus no real balance-of-payments constraints necessitating demand-deflationary measures to impede the growth process.

It was not only the slack labour market which kept labour costs low, however. The lack of differentiation of the labour market was also important. The low-level skills offered by most members of the labour force could be widely used. Political divisions within the trade-union movement constituted a further factor. The functional unity of Italian unions (i.e. the fact that they were *industrial* unions, each covering an entire industrial sector) was, in the 1950s and early 1960s, more than counterbalanced by a political disunity, dating from soon after World War II, by which three rival union confederations developed: one, the CGIL, largely communist-dominated; a second, the CISL, of mainly Catholic inspiration; and a third, the UIL, of predominantly social-democrat and republican origin. These divisions made effective union co-operation, whether nationally or locally, very rare; what little potential strength the unions possessed in the 1950s was frequently dissipated by inter-union rivalry.[4] Finally, Italian unions in the early post-war period were relatively inexperienced economic actors. Before 1922, the movement had been very weak. Under fascism it was suppressed entirely. In 1945 the habits of collective solidarity had to be learned anew, and unions had to establish not only moral authority in the workplace, but local and plant-level activists with bargaining skills and experience. This took time, and was especially difficult in the face of resolute employers determined to keep unions weak. It was also impeded by the ideological uncertainty of the Communist Party and the communist leaders of the CGIL, the main union confederation. Doubtful of the value of free collective bargaining, which they perceived as dividing workers rather than uniting them, they tended, in the 1950s, to see the union movement as an adjunct to the party and political action, rather than an independent movement looking after the immediate economic interests of its members.

These conditions gradually altered in the 1960s. The relationship between the level of unemployment and the power of organized labour changed. One of the two essential pillars of the Italian economic miracle—the existence of a continuous supply of cheap labour allowing high profits and high levels of reinvestment—was thus eventually undermined, but between 1951 and 1960 industrial wages only rose significantly faster than industrial productivity in one year.[5]

Exports

Particularly from the mid-1950s onwards, the Italian miracle was a prime example of export-driven growth. From Einaudi's liberalization of the 1940s, the basic thrust of public policy was the insertion of the Italian economy into the international market. In 1951 Italy entered the European Coal and Steel Community; in 1958 she became a founder member of the European Economic Community. Government policy encouraged sectors of industry catering for the high-income markets of Western Europe. Exports more than quadrupled in value between 1951 and 1963 and constituted much the most dynamic sector of aggregate demand, rising from 6 per cent to 13 per cent of demand over the twelve-year period: an annual growth of no less than 13 per cent.[6] In general, those sectors of industry with the larger share of production devoted to exports or with the most rapid growth rates of exports (vehicles and chemicals in particular) experienced the most rapid growth of productivity. It was in these sectors that the virtuous circle of export growth, leading to higher productivity through returns to scale and through new investment, was most in evidence.

Public investment

That growth in the peak years of the miracle from 1959 to 1963 was export-led is beyond dispute, but in the earlier years public investment was also important. Major investment programmes were undertaken in transport and communications, agriculture, and housing. In the early 1950s the rate of growth in these latter two areas was considerably higher than that in manufacturing industry. Industrial restructuring aimed to remove some of the potential bottlenecks in supply caused by lack of investment, and the monopoly power of certain large companies. The two most important developments were the modernization of the steel industry and the development of ENI (energy and petrochemicals).[7]

Both projects used public corporations inherited from fascism. Steel modernization was carried out through Italsider, part of the IRI group. By establishing several new large-scale integrated steel works, Italsider brought the previously low-productivity steel industry up to levels of competitiveness comparable to the rest of Europe. Italian engineering industries were thus assured of a continuous supply of low-cost steel, and exporting industries in sectors such as automobiles and domestic consumer goods were given important assistance.

ENI's development of methane gas deposits in the Po Valley created a network that extended throughout the industrialized north. It led to the rapid conversion of industry's energy source from coal to oil and gas, and to considerable balance-of-payments savings. ENI was also responsible for the development of modest petroleum deposits in Sicily. Astute manœuvres by its chief executive, Enrico Mattei, enabled it to challenge the hold of the main oil multinationals over Italian energy supplies. Its sideways expansion into petrochemicals, synthetic fibres, and fertilizers was also important. It broke the hold exercised by Montecatini over the price of many basic chemicals, and, especially in the late 1950s, the economy as a whole benefited from a substantial reduction in the price of chemicals and fertilizers.

It should be noted in passing, however, that the effects of the development of the public sector went beyond their propulsive economic consequences. The growth of the IRI and ENI laid the basis for a lasting cleavage in the Italian industrial structure between public and private, for the firms in the public sector were frequently in direct competition with those in the private sector. Unlike the major sectoral monopolies constituted by British nationalized industries, IRI and ENI were multi-sectoral holding companies, with interests in a wide range of activities, and without the same statutory limitations on their spheres of activity. The class of public-sector managers which emerged had similar attitudes towards profit maximization, market share, and new investment opportunities to their counterparts in the private sector, but they also enjoyed privileged access to political support and, in particular, public capital. As a result considerable conflict developed between the governments which sponsored their activities, and sectors of private industry. After the retirement of De Gasperi from the premiership in 1953, the growth of IRI and ENI greatly strained the previously close relationship between the Christian Democrat Party and *Confindustria*, the main employers' organization. In 1956 IRI broke away from *Confindustria* to found its own employers' association, *Intersind*, for companies operating under its aegis. Henceforth, particularly in the sphere of industrial relations, the latter adopted a very different strategy from *Confindustria* itself.

In later years, as the public sector fell under closer political control than in the 1950s and decisions over investment policy were increasingly dictated by short-term political considerations, the entrepreneurial dynamism displayed by public-sector managers deteriorated. This changed the performance of the public sector, but intensified conflict and rivalry between it and the private sector. The basis for this division, in many respects as significant as the other great division in Italian industry, that between large-scale and small-scale enterprises, was laid in the 1950s, and persisted right through to the end of the 1980s.

The costs of the miracle

North and south

The economic miracle was not achieved without costs, nor could it resolve the problem of the long-standing economic gap between north and south. The problem dates back to unification and even before. It grew worse during the industrial take-off at the turn of the century, and again as a result of World War II, which inflicted greatest damage on the southern half of the country. At the beginning of the 1950s, per capita income was only 68 per cent of that in the country as a whole.[8] This reflected several factors, including the larger proportion of the active population employed in low-productivity agriculture, the higher unemployment rate, and the considerably lower activity rate. Moreover, the disparity between areas *within* the south was itself substantial, with Basilicata and Calabria having per capita income levels barely one-third of the national average. In the Italy of the 1950s, with its rudimentary social services, such figures implied a huge reservoir of human misery, with high rates of illiteracy and infant mortality, and inadequate education. The slack labour market meant paternalistic and authoritarian labour relations, and together with the absence of organizing skills among the lower classes, or indeed the habit of collective action of almost any sort, it discouraged the formation of unions or class-based parties.

It would be wrong to suggest that the development of the years 1951–63 left these problems untouched. There was economic growth, and indeed the overall level of resources consumed in the south increased at a rate slightly above that in the economy as a whole. However, this was largely achieved through emigration and resource transfers. In terms of output, the gap, in relative terms, did not narrow at all. Gross product actually fell, as a proportion of national GDP, from 24.1 per cent in 1951 to 22.7 per cent in 1963, and throughout the period well over 80 per cent of *industrial* output continued to come from the north. In the labour market, the relative position of the south showed little improvement. In both north and south, unemployment was more than halved between 1951 and 1963, but the activity rate was still well below that in the north, and much of the pressure was relieved by the continuous net emigration, without which the unemployment figures would have been considerably worse.

Migration

Migration was the great social drama of early post-war Italy. The problems of over-population, land hunger, and rural poverty date back to the last century. Indeed the emigration rates for the period 1900–1920 were actually higher than those of the 1950s. Fascism, war, and depression combined to restrict the outflow to a trickle in the 1930s and 1940s, but with rapid rates of growth in northern Italy and the countries of the European Community in the 1950s, and the ending of restrictions on internal migration, the floodgates opened up once more. *Within* the south, there was a gradual emptying of the agricultural interiors, the great repositories of rural poverty, and a prodigious growth of the urban conurbations of the coastal plains: Naples, Palermo, Bari, Reggio Calabria, Catania. *From* the south, there was a huge outflow to Europe and northern Italy. In the decade 1951–60 a net figure of some 1.7 million southerners left the area. Between 1961 and 1970 the net departure was 2.3 million. From Italy as a whole, net emigration was 1.2 million between 1951 and 1960, and 1.1 million between 1961 and 1970. For the areas of out-migration, this implied rural depopulation; in provinces like Avellino or Campobasso, which suffered a contraction in population of more than 10 per cent over a decade, there was a dramatic decline in local commerce and services. Inevitably, it also led to a change in the structure of the population. Those who left in greatest numbers were employable adult males; those left behind were the old, the unemployable and illiterate, and wives and children.

Urbanization

Frequently, the human costs for those departing were as great as for those left behind. For migrants who settled in northern Italy, there was not only the hostility of the local population, but desperate inadequacy of education, social services, and housing. The latter was, and has remained, Italy's single most serious social problem. It gave rise to a veritable rape of the urban environment, with massive, politically uncontrolled speculative development around the edges of the major cities. It also became an acute political problem, for as the housing pressure grew, so did pressure to impose systems of fair-rent legislation. Inevitably, governments found themselves caught between two powerful demands. On one side was the property lobby, which included not just large-scale property companies but a host of lower middle-class landlords as well, all bitterly opposed both to rent control and to compulsory purchase of building land for publicly subsidized rented housing. On the other side there was an initially unorganized but gradually more vociferous tenants' lobby, which under Communist leadership was eventually to become a powerful exponent of rent control, albeit one whose very success probably contributed to the continuation of the housing-supply crisis in the 1970s and 1980s.

The interlinked problems of southern poverty, migration, and the urban crisis were only one manifestation of the shortcomings and the costs of Italy's rapid economic growth in the 1950s and 1960s. As we have seen, the state did intervene in economic life, but mainly in the sphere of fixed capital investment. Public consumption, and the provision of the social services of a modern welfare state, remained poorly developed. Radical critics of Italian economic policy in this period argued that this was the inevitable consequence of the model of export-led, free-market development on which the growth process was predicated. In their view development and under development were interconnected. The latter provided the labour supply on which growth in the advanced export-orientated sector could be based. Given the huge shifts in population, and the rapid urban growth, the extensive opportunities for speculative property development provided profits to be channelled back into industry. To divert resources towards infrastructure development in the south on a scale sufficient to enable the area to start to catch up would have threatened the export industries, and undermined the mechanism of export-led growth. To expand domestic consumption through major social welfare schemes would have threatened monetary stability and the balance of payments. From this complementarity between northern development and southern under development, the argument concluded, arose the paradox of a country which produced consumption goods for economies enjoying a far higher overall level of income than its own, while sustaining an area the fundamental needs of which (basic housing, education, agricultural infrastructure, urban transport, etc.) were still inadequately satisfied.[9]

It is doubtful that the choices being made, or their full consequences, were ever as clear to those in charge of Italian economic policy as this critique implies. It is equally uncertain whether there was any alternative model of development. Nevertheless, the basic incongruity of the combination of modernity and backwardness that Italy seemed to represent by the early 1960s was striking, and the policy problems it posed were to dominate political life over the following decade. The inadequacy of the state to cope with the consequences of economic growth and to remedy the poorly developed systems of welfare and social infrastructure, still less to close the gap between north and south, began to foster a more widespread consciousness of the costs, as well as the benefits, of economic growth. In its turn, this generated demands for extensive social reform, while within the labour movement it brought a gradual awareness of the movement's potential power in the labour market.

1963–1975: The Transition

Recession and recovery

The year 1963 represented a major turning point in post-war Italy. Politically, it marked the beginning of a new phase in coalition-building, described in the following chapter. Its essential feature was the emergence of the Centre-Left coalition: a recognition on the part of the ruling Christian Democrat Party that rapid economic growth had changed the political agenda and sharply increased the importance of social-welfare issues. To minimize the danger of the left eventually winning a majority on the strength of growing dissatisfaction with public services, inadequate infrastructure, poor housing, and so on, it was agreed, not without some dissent in the DC, that the Socialist Party should be prised away from its former alliance with the Communists and given a place in government. The new coalition which resulted—the Centre-Left—substituted the Socialist Party for the conservatively inclined Liberal Party as the DC's main junior partner. It was launched with extensive commitments to reform, raising expectations that the economic miracle would be followed by a new era of redistributive welfare reform.[10]

The year 1963 was however also a turning point in economic terms, and one that was inauspicious for such a shift in priorities. Henceforth, even the traditional objectives of price stability, external equilibrium, and growth proved increasingly difficult to reconcile. To these objectives others were now being added, including commitments to redistribution, both in income and in territorial terms, and to a higher level of employment. The result was increasingly tight constraints on policy-makers, and more limited margins for political manœuvre. The political expectations of the early 1960s were thus to prove difficult to fulfil and this, in turn, fostered a growing sense of social resentment and growing conflictuality in labour relations, eventually exploding at the end of the decade in the 'Hot Autumn' of labour unrest in 1969.

Recession

The recession of the mid-1960s cut the growth rate from 6.3 per cent in 1962 to 2.9 per cent in 1964: its lowest level since the beginning of the 1950s. The economy for the first time encountered a partial full employment ceiling, at least in northern Italy, boosting the hitherto weak and divided trade-union movement. Co-operation between the three main confederations improved, and wage demands in industries like engineering were pitched at a higher level. National wage agreements began to be supplemented by local negotiations over productivity allowances.

The result was a sharp acceleration of wages. From 1962 onwards they began to outstrip productivity growth; in 1963 unit labour costs increased by no less than 14.5 per cent, while productivity rose less than a third as much. The discrepancy led to a major redistribution of income. The share of labour in value-added in manufacturing rose from 58.6 per cent in 1960 to 70.1 per cent in 1964.[11] The consequences for investment, consumption, and the balance of payments were extensive. Investment in manufacturing suffered a 20 per cent fall in both 1964 and 1965. The rapid growth of incomes fed demand for consumer goods. To the cost-push of wage increases was added the demand-pull of an economy in which, for the first time, consumer durables and higher quality foodstuffs were falling within the reach of ordinary consumers. Such pressures were reflected on the current account of the balance of payments, as consumer imports were drawn in and exports diverted. On capital account, too, there was a marked deterioration, as Italian companies began to invest overseas. Once the balance of payments was in deficit, speculative pressures exacerbated the problem. A lower return on savings, an inflation rate which put a premium on present consumption, and a decline in profitability, all helped undermine the climate of business confidence of the boom years.

The entry of the Socialists into the governing coalition also affected confidence. It pushed the political centre of gravity to the left and promised measures which alarmed conservative opinion. The electricity supply industry was nationalized. Preliminary steps were taken to curb the speculative rise in land and property values resulting from urban growth. Plans were drawn up for a general system of compulsory public purchase of all development land at agricultural values. A 'withholding tax' on dividend income from shares was introduced to curb tax evasion. Plans were set in train for a system of economic planning which many feared would put strict controls on private-sector investment. In the event, controls on land development, dividend income, and private investment were all rendered ineffective, but in 1963 the defeat of the radical wing of the coalition was still over the horizon, and the confidence of investors, both large and small, was greatly shaken by the changed political climate.[12]

Recovery on a new basis

Labour militancy, inflation, the Socialist presence in the government, and the tight monetary policy deemed necessary to restore confidence combined to curb the impetuous economic development of the earlier post-war years. After 1965 Italian economic development changed. Output growth recovered to a respectable rate, but investment did not. The investment ratio in the period 1966–70 was one of the lowest in Western Europe.[13]

This deterioration in the quality of growth occurred despite cautiously expansionary policies by the authorities. Tight monetary policies were gradually relaxed, special sources of credit were made available for smaller firms, and a part of the burden of each firm's share of employee social-security contributions was temporarily transferred to the taxpayer. In conditions of slack demand and modest business expectations, however, the measures had little effect. Much of the liquidity created by the new monetary measures was absorbed by foreign investment, either by companies or individuals, or by Italian banks operating in the Eurodollar market: a clear indication of the decline in opportunities for profitable domestic investment since the 1950s and early 1960s. Despite intentions to the contrary, moreover, investment by public-sector firms, and other government-sponsored investment in the field of social infrastructure, both declined in the latter half of the 1960s.

The recovery that followed the recession of 1964–5 reflected this change. It was based on more fragile, short-term, and ultimately more destabilizing factors than the long boom of the economic miracle. In the absence of a major recovery of domestic investment, productivity growth had to be achieved by higher export volumes and more intensive use of capital stock. Exports did indeed rise, but this recovery was dependent on an international market environment which, by the end of the decade, was to become increasingly volatile. The second factor—the increasingly intensive use of existing capital equipment—

proved equally precarious. From 1964 to 1968, wage increases remained modest, compared to the marked increases in 1962 and 1963. The main triennial renewal of labour contracts passed off in 1966 with little difficulty. There was thus a slow recovery in the proportion of national income accruing to profits and dividends, after the radical redistribution in favour of wages and salaries in the first years of the decade. Italian trade unions were still relatively weak on the shop floor, preventing much resistance to the speeding up of production lines, more use of overtime, and greater reliance on piece-work. These measures were essential once the heady era of high investment and easy profits had passed. However, they exacted a heavy toll in deteriorating working conditions and were difficult to sustain, eventually generating the serious social tensions which erupted at the end of the decade.[14]

The Hot Autumn and the new climate of industrial relations

The basis of the recovery between 1966 and 1968—low public investment and intensified management pressure for labour produc-tivity—was the chief cause of the subsequent problems. Faced with a government which regularly postponed its promised social reform, and with employers who sought to increase output more by tightening workplace discipline than by investment in new plant and machinery, the labour movement finally rebelled. The result was an outburst of labour unrest—the so-called Hot Autumn—among the most intense, sustained, and bitter in any Western nation.

The causes of this change in industrial relations lie as much in politics as in economics. The overall level of unemployment fell only slightly between the 1966 wage round which engendered so little conflict, and the 1969 round which created so much, and there was still a substantial reserve of labour available through the continued exodus from agriculture. Nor did unionization increase significantly before the Hot Autumn itself. The two largest confederations, the CGIL and CISL, in 1969 organized approximately the same proportion of the work-force, around 32 per cent, as at the start of the decade. The dramatic increase which raised that figure to around 45 per cent by the end of the following decade appears to have been a *consequence* rather than a *cause* of the Hot Autumn.[15]

The origins of labour militancy in 1969 thus lie in political frustrations and social tensions as much as in labour-market condi-tions. The Centre-Left government, established in 1962–3 under a reforming banner, had raised expectations that education, transport, health services, housing, pensions, and other public services would be drastically improved. But faced with internal divisions within the coalition, and with the recession of 1964–5, it largely failed to fulfil those expectations. Moreover, with continued migration, directed by the late 1960s more to northern Italy than abroad, the industrial triangle was swelled by increasingly dissatisfied workers who, unlike their counterparts in Germany, France, and Switzerland, were full citizens of the country in which they worked. It was from this group, rather than the locally born, more disciplined working class, that the militancy of 1969 initially sprang.

The dimensions of the labour unrest itself have been extensively studied.[16] There was a massive increase in labour disputes, reaching an immediate peak in 1969, but remaining high until 1975. In 1969 an average of 23 hours were lost per employee through industrial conflict, compared with an average between 1959 and 1967 of fewer than 8 hours. Over the period 1968–75 as a whole, the average was 11.6 hours per employee. The 1969–70 round of wage-bargaining had acutely inflationary consequences. Hourly earnings in manufacturing industry rose by well over 20 per cent in 1970, compared to an average of only 6 per cent over the previous four years. As important as the immediate consequences were the wider changes in industrial relations that the Hot Autumn ushered in. Initially, the militancy was spontaneous and unorganized, and there is no doubt that union leaders were taken by surprise by its strength. Within a fairly short time, however, such tensions as existed between the established unions and the new activists were largely overcome, and the *ad hoc* systems of shop-floor leadership which emerged—in particular the so-called *delegati* (shop stewards)—were institutionalized as workplace representatives of the unions. This substantially increased the decentralization of union representation. By focusing union action on workplace issues it greatly contributed to overcoming the traditional political divisions between the three confederations. Although the plans laid down in 1970 for complete reunification of the three main confederations were never realized, the mutual trust and the co-ordination of strategy begun in the Hot Autumn were to last right through the following decade.[17]

The Hot Autumn thus fundamentally altered the climate of industrial relations in Italy, and unlike that in France in 1968, the change proved to be a lasting one. The shift in the balance of power in favour of labour was enshrined in a new legal framework, known as the *Statuto dei lavoratori* (Workers' Charter),[18] channelling shop-floor militancy in support of new issues appearing on the industrial-relations agenda: the control of the workplace environment, manning levels, reduction of the working week, and, most radically of all, a reduction of productivity incentives and of differentials between skill levels.

These issues had ramifications in the political sphere as well. The trade-union movement became a far more important participant in national political decision-making. For a period in the early 1970s the confederations even sought to use the new militancy to obtain explicitly *political* objectives in policy sectors that were connected to the work place only in so far as they contributed to the social wage (health, education, housing, pensions, etc.), but in fact it fairly quickly became clear that such ambitious corporatist-style bargaining was impractical.[19] Workers were unwilling or unable to gamble the returns from immediate shop-floor action on long-term political benefits, and governments could not deliver on their undertakings. However, once the union confederations settled on a range of industrial-relations issues that had more immediate consequences for their members—the indexation of wages against inflation, the control of public-sector prices, labour protection legislation, and redundancy pay—they discovered a level where they could exploit worker militancy very effectively to bring them into national bargaining networks with national employers' representatives, and with government.

The elements of an extensive tripartite bargaining structure thus began to emerge, although it would be wrong to consider it neo-corporatist, for it lacked the fundamental political strength guaranteed by a strong social-democratic party in power.[20] And it depended more directly than in northern Europe on a degree of latent conflictuality in industrial relations that was closer to the surface, and hence likely to erupt into outright industrial action. This conflictuality and the uncertainty of governments in their response to it gave the union confederations much leverage with employers and governments, and it was thus essential that shop-floor militancy should never be far beneath the surface of industrial relations. Moreover, the power given to union workplace representatives by the Statuto dei lavoratori, combined with residual political divisions between the confederations, denied the confederal leaderships the authority and hence the ability to deliver on bargains struck, enjoyed by leaders of more centralized unions in, for example, Germany or Sweden. In any case, it took time for an awareness of the consequences of the new climate of industrial relations to work through the trade-union movement. Only after the first oil shock, in 1973–4, did this awareness give the confederations the authority necessary to speak for the labour movement as a whole, and enable it to deliver on bargains struck.

Nevertheless, after the Hot Autumn Italy did move, slowly and hesitantly, in the direction of a system of national bargaining between major economic actors—albeit an inefficient one—and this reached its apogee in the years of so-called 'National Solidarity' in the latter half of the 1970s. The climate of industrial relations which evolved from the Hot Autumn thus had a lasting impact on the political agenda and the style of economic-policy decisions.

The consequences of the Hot Autumn

The conditions which followed the inflation of 1969–70 were substantially different from those of 1963. The reaction of the fiscal and monetary authorities was more restrained than earlier in the decade, but the recovery was still modest. Over the period 1970–3, Italian growth lay towards the bottom of the range for industrialized economies, and rates of gross fixed investment right at the bottom. The absence of stern deflationary measures combined with the new power—both legal and *de facto*—enjoyed by the labour force to prevent a repetition of the shake-out of labour, and of the rapid growth of labour productivity, which had occurred after 1963. As a result, in a regime of still fairly rigid exchange rates, the prospects for export-led recovery also diminished, and profit levels remained low for nearly three years following the Hot Autumn. Only in late 1973 was there a recovery, and when it came it was fuelled by domestic consumption, public expenditure, and by a particularly speculative form of investment, as much in stocks as in fixed capital. This led to a new round of wage settlements which reached levels not far short of those of 1969. The lira was allowed to float early in 1973, and the combination of wage increases and rising import prices drove inflation to the unprecedented level of almost 20 per cent, generating severe problems for the external trade balance throughout the rest of the decade.[21]

Economic policy during the period 1969–74 was equivocal. The breadth of the governing coalition guaranteed this. Even when the Socialist Party was briefly excluded in 1972–3, the Christian Democrat left retained an important voice, and for most of the period the Socialists were present in government and firmly opposed to any shift in economic policy intended to undermine union strength through drastic deflation or a change in industrial-relations law. Besides, the Workers' Charter legislation in 1970 worked in quite the opposite direction. As the brief and unsuccessful experiment in Centre-Right government in 1972–3 showed, there was no real alternative to the Centre-Left. If that coalition did not show reasonable sympathy to the demands of the labour movement, its support was likely to ebb away towards the Communists, and increase labour tensions.[22]

Equally important in preventing a resolute counter-attack on union power was the lack of united and effective pressure from the employers' lobby. The split in this lobby between public and private has already been described. Equally important was that between advanced, generally large-scale, enterprises on the one hand, and medium- and small-scale enterprises on the other. A part of the former group was willing to recognize that trade unions were now permanently rooted in their enterprises, and that accommodation and consensus, encouraged by a policy aimed at strengthening the discipline of union leaders over shop-floor workers, was preferable to outright confrontation. The short-run effects on corporate profitability of drastic deflation were seen as too high a price.[23]

A self-conscious and explicit policy of compromising with the confederal union leaderships to buy shop-floor peace nevertheless took time to develop, and only in the mid-1970s did the views of this section of the employers' lobby gain the ascendancy within *Confindustria*. Among smaller manufacturers, where short-run economies of scale were less important, the case for a conciliatory approach to union power was always regarded with scepticism. The split between large and small business, coupled with that between public and private, thus ensured that the labour movement faced not only a divided and uncertain government coalition, but an equally irresolute employers' front.

Labour relations and wage costs therefore became one of the core issues of economic and political life during the 1970s. The other was the problem of public expenditure, and this, too, was linked to decisions taken in the years 1969–74 stemming from the consequences of the Hot Autumn. Governments not only refrained from seeking to annul the changes in labour relations which were taking place; they adopted expenditure policies, and mechanisms of financing these policies, which greatly exacerbated their inflationary effects. Part of this expenditure was directly linked to demands made by the labour movement itself. It accounted for much of the rapid growth of expenditure on the deficits of pension funds and schemes of health insurance, and the growth of subsidies and transfers to industry, both public and private, to protect employment and pay for schemes of temporary redundancy.[24]

Moreover, there was an additional dimension to public expenditure development during this period that reflected the need to assist individuals and groups not protected by trade unions, whose position was threatened by inflation and who, in the early 1970s, seemed predisposed to turn to the politics of the extreme right in protest.

These traditional clienteles of Christian Democracy included small farmers, artisans, shopkeepers, and owners of other small family-run businesses. They too became the beneficiaries of transfers and other indirect support policies which swelled public expenditure in the new inflationary climate.[25] One of their main benefits was a fiscal system that institutionalized tax evasion on a massive scale. The so-called 'black economy' of unregulated and unrecorded goods and services, and second and third jobs, which has been estimated to add anything from 10 to 20 per cent to official Italian GDP figures, owes much of its existence to the widespread Italian enthusiasm for tax evasion.[26] Its implications for budgetary policy were dramatic, for while public expenditure rose during the 1970s, so did the level of deficit-spending, as tax revenue, particularly from the 'self-assessed' groups, failed to keep pace with extended budget commitments.[27] The result was not only, as elsewhere in Europe at this time, the rapid growth of public expenditure as a proportion of gross domestic product, but also the rapid growth of the budget *deficit*, which rose from just over 1 per cent of GDP in 1970 to over 10 per cent by the end of the decade.[28]

The years from 1969 to the mid-1970s are thus the crucial formative period for the issues which have dominated political and economic life in the last fifteen years. The response of the authorities to the combined effects of the Hot Autumn, the subsequent recession, and the first oil shock grafted the new strength of the trade-union movement on to the demands of traditional political clienteles. Such powerful pressures on government policy built highly inflationary consequences into the distributive battle over wages, taxes, transfers, and subsidies. The heterogeneous nature of these demands, and the inability of the coalition to take decisive remedial action, ensured that the social and economic tensions of the 1970s grew particularly acute. Decisive action to contain these pressures would have cost the governing coalition the support of many of the groups within the heterogeneous array of interests assembled under its banner. Faced by attacks from right and left, the most effective policy in the short term was to off-load the consequences on to inflation, and into the future, rather than make clear allocative choices in the present.

1975–1990: Stabilization, Adaptation, and the Cautious Return to the Market

The performance of the economy from the Hot Autumn to the mid-1970s was, by the standards of other European countries, rather poor. The performance over subsequent years has, again in comparative

European terms, been better. The average growth rate was admittedly lower than in the 1950s and 1960s, and the recession of 1981–3, when annual GDP growth averaged less than 1 per cent, deeper and longer than those of earlier years. From 1984 to 1990, however, Italy once again enjoyed significant growth, averaging 2.9 per cent per annum, and reaching 4.1 per cent in 1988. The growth rate in fact compares favourably with other European economies over this period; slightly above that in France and Germany, and slightly below that in the UK (before the UK's severe recession of 1990–1). Despite inflation, a high level of public indebtedness, and sustained distributive conflict, the Italian economy has shown signs of flexibility, vitality, and an ability to adapt to the changed circumstances in which the economy operates. The path by which Italy reached this condition, however, is by no means a linear one, and much of the flexibility and adaptability is the result more of autonomous social responses to economic challenges than of consciously planned public policy.

TABLE 2.2 *Rates of growth of gross domestic product in four European states: 1984–1990*

	1984	1985	1986	1987	1988	1989	1990
Germany	2.8	2.0	2.3	1.8	3.7	3.3	4.3
France	1.5	1.8	2.1	1.8	3.3	3.6	2.5
United Kingdom	2.1	3.7	3.5	4.7	4.1	2.2	1.5
Italy	3.0	2.6	2.5	3.0	3.9	3.2	2.0

Source: Commission of the European Community, 'Annual Economic Report *1990–91*', *European Economy*, 46 (Brussels, Dec. 1990). (Figure for 1990 from *OECD Economic Surveys: Italy, 1990/91* (Paris, 1991).)

'National Solidarity'

The economic recovery of 1973–4 coincided with the first oil shock. It was driven, more than in previous phases of growth, by domestic rather than export-led demand. For both these reasons it quickly generated inflationary pressures. However, the governing coalition was particularly weak, and anxious to do nothing to restrict the much-needed recovery in investment. Action to restrain inflationary pressure was therefore delayed, and when restrictions were finally imposed they were left on too briefly. In 1976, there was a further rapid upsurge in inflation, and in speculation against the lira, requiring the drastic step of a forty-day suspension in foreign-exchange dealings, a devaluation of the lira by 20 per cent, and a reimposition of restrictive measures, including an import-deposit scheme. The new recession that began in 1975 was thus of lasting duration; only in 1979, after further devaluations, and considerable restructuring of industry, did the economy recover. To achieve this recovery, a more fundamental adjustment in the relationship between government, employers, and the labour movement was seen as necessary, itself ushering in an important if temporary political change in the coalition.[29]

During the latter half of the 1970s, in fact, many of the implicit understandings on which politics and the labour market had been based were suspended. Fears were widely expressed that the entire market system was under threat, and that the values of liberal democracy were being eroded by terrorism and political extremism. Many on the left—especially in the Communist Party and the trade-union movement—were among the most apprehensive. For them the prospect of a collapse of business confidence and a massive recession was not seen as a vindication of socialism; rather, if such a collapse were to be accompanied, as the left feared, by a political backlash against terrorism, it was a likely harbinger of right-wing authoritarianism.[30] The business community, for its part, saw the critical factor as a more co-operative union attitude towards industrial restructuring and the recovery of Italian competitiveness, and if this meant sitting down on a regular basis with the confederal union leaderships to extract concessions from government to guarantee a minimum of industrial peace, this was regarded as a necessary price to pay.

This further *rapprochement* between business and unions began early in 1975, when a major agreement was signed between *Confindustria* and the main union confederations. It provided a guarantee of almost complete indexation of industrial wages against inflation, and a government-underwritten commitment to the payment of approximately 80 per cent of wages to workers temporarily made redundant in firms facing problems of structural adjustment—the so-called *cassa integrazione*.[31] In return for these concessions to the union confederations, employers sought a more stable industrial-relations environment, and some control (imposed by the confederations on industrial unions and shop-floor workers) over competitive and uncontrolled wage settlements well above the rate of inflation.

The role of government in these agreements was initially ambiguous, as was the degree to which they were supported by some sections of the business community. The indexation mechanism clearly institutionalized a new source of inflation into the economy, even if it pre-empted competitive leap-frogging in wage claims, and was looked on with some disfavour both by government and by small firms where unions were less well entrenched. Nevertheless, over the following two years a process of accommodation was gradually developed between capital, labour, and government, and it allowed some improvement in wage-bargaining, and labour flexibility. A further agreement, in 1977, induced the union confederations to continue their restraining influence over wage-bargaining, and to co-operate with plans for greater flexibility in the use of labour in areas such as shift work, overtime, and transfers between production lines. The unions also accepted minor adjustments to weaken the effect of wage-indexation, and a plan to transfer a part of the costs of employers' social-security contributions to indirect taxation. Slowly and painstakingly, and until the 1970s still largely on the basis of consent, the unions were induced to rethink some of the alleged advances won during the years following the Hot Autumn.

Naturally, agreements involving union concessions can only be understood against the political background, the chief feature of which was the incorporation of the Communist Party into the ruling coalition during the era of so-called 'National Solidarity'—a period running from the general election of 1976 to that of 1979. As will be seen in later chapters, such a coalition was dictated by political factors as much as economic ones. The Communists sought the mantle of respectability endowed by a role in government; the Socialists were anxious to protect themselves on their left flank.[32]

Structural adaptation

In its most pronounced form 'National Solidarity' was soon over. That it was short-lived was due, like the reasons for its existence, in part to political factors discussed in later chapters, and in part to economic ones. The latter included the increasing erosion of the power of labour, and the recovery of the international competitiveness of Italian industry at the end of the decade. The two were linked, reflecting the gradual adaptation of the economy to the consequences of the Hot Autumn, a process which made further overarching tripartite agreements like those concluded in 1975 and 1977 less necessary. Large firms started to devolve or subcontract much of their activity to smaller, more flexible enterprises, where unionization was lower and more flexible labour practices allowed. Frequently, this involved apparently archaic forms of work relationship, such as 'home' assembly work by women, or uninsured, untaxed 'second' jobs, in both of which cases employers could avoid the very high levels of social-security contribution applicable to permanent full-time labour.

The growth of small firms is one of the most striking features of the Italian economy in the 1970s and early 1980s, although its origins clearly lie in a process of social development that began much earlier in the post-war era. The 1981 census of industry showed that employment in manufacturing industry among large firms (500 employees or more) fell by 13.5 per cent over the period 1971–81, that in medium-sized firms (100–500 employees) was almost static, while that in small firms (employing fewer than 100) grew by 11.5 per cent. Equally striking were the regional concentration of this process and the regional clustering of particular industries. The development of small firms took place less in the industrial triangle (where traditions of unionization were strongly implanted, and unemployment was lowest) than in the so-called 'north-east corridor', an area stretching from the Veneto down the Adriatic coast through the Red Belt of Emilia-Romagna, Tuscany, and the Marches. Between 1971 and 1981, the share of total manufacturing output coming from this region rose from 20 to 23 per cent. Growth in the footwear and leather goods industries, and in precision equipment in the medical and high-technology fields, was particularly marked.

The basis of this development has been widely debated. It is argued that its concentration in areas which, until very recently, were characterized by small—often share-cropping—family farms, with large firms generally absent, reflects a process of structural adaptation permitted by small, semi-rural, socially cohesive communities. Such conditions have been seen as encouraging entrepreneurial qualities since the multiplicity of family-income sources (employment, self-employment, income from small farms, unpaid family labour for emerging small business) provides an underlying guarantee of business stability.[33] Much has also been made of the assistance given by 'quality of life' factors and by common features of the local social and political value systems of the 'social Christian' Veneto and the communist Red Belt. The Veneto, Emilia, Tuscany, and the Marches are regions that have suffered neither great out-migration to the older industrial areas, nor large-scale inward population movements from the south. Local government can therefore provide a comparatively advantageous 'social wage' in the form of efficient local social services. Moreover, both communist and Christian Democrat local political classes believe they can benefit from the development of small business, and actively cultivate a value system favourable to it.[34]

However, it was not just small firms for which the environment changed from the mid-1970s. For big business too, there were developments which substantially altered the industrial-relations climate. The gradual rise of unemployment slowly but inexorably eroded the ability of unions to rely on the discipline of their members. Absenteeism, the scourge of Italian manufacturing industry in the 1970s, declined steadily, while lay-offs and redundancy increased. Under such conditions, the employers' willingness to continue the agreements on wage-indexation and job security made between 1975 and 1977 also declined. The test came in 1980, when a major confrontation between unions and managements at FIAT over redundancies ended with a back-to-work rebellion by a large part of the work-force, and a serious defeat for the unions. Henceforth, employers' criticisms of wage-indexation became ever more insistent, and in stages the degree of protection it afforded workers' wages was reduced.[35]

A final reason why the era of National Solidarity collapsed was, of course, the difficulty the main confederations had in making it stick at company and workplace level. The period of so-called 'austerity', the imposition of which was probably pursued as rather too public a virtue by many of the Communist union and party leaders, was unpopular among many of the rank and file. Even if the balance of power was gradually turning against organized labour, there were sectors where the work-force felt itself sufficiently strong to be able to wrest greater concessions from management and resented the erosion of differentials that indexation created. This tension expressed itself in various ways: in support for so-called 'independent' unions, especially in the public sector; in declining electoral support for the Communists; and in conflict between militant shop-floor leaders and union officials. It did not apply everywhere. Frequently the militants overestimated their strength. But it undoubtedly added to the difficulties union leaders faced as the period of National Solidarity continued.[36]

The period 1974–84 thus witnessed a gradual adjustment to the dramatic political and economic changes in the first half of the 1970s. Until the end of that decade, the emphasis in this adjustment was largely on attempts at consensus and accommodation in the sphere of industrial relations—albeit imperfectly executed—rather than on attempts to reverse the changes themselves. Thereafter, the emphasis shifted. The adjustments in industrial structure, and the slackening of the labour market, led to a less accommodating set of relationships, and one less favourable than a decade ago to the labour movement, as can be seen, in Table 2.3, from the dramatic decline in days lost through strike action in manufacturing industry (although not, significantly, in public-sector services).

TABLE 2.3 *Labour disputes in Italy: 1965–1990 (millions of working hours lost per year)*

Year	Hours lost
1965	55.9
1966	115.8
1967	68.6
1968	73.9
1969	302.6
1970	146.2
1971	103.6
1972	136.5
1973	163.9
1974	136.3
1975	116.0
1976	71.2
1977	192.7
1978	71.2
1979	192.7
1980	115.2
1981	73.7
1982	129.9
1983	98.0
1984	60.9
1985	26.8
1986	39.5
1987	32.2
1988	23.2
1989	31.0
1990	36.3

Source: Istituto centrale di statistica, *Annuario statistico italiano* (various years).

The return to growth

In Italy, as in the European Community as a whole, the contrast between economic performance in the first and second halves of the 1980s is striking. As we have seen, the recession of 1981–4 gave way to an extended recovery which only ended in the winter of 1990–1. The factors driving the recovery were similar to those elsewhere in Europe: a weak labour market, resulting from the years of industrial restructuring; declining unionization and union power; the recovery of business confidence after the shocks of the 1970s; clear evidence that inflation was under considerably tighter control by the monetary authorities than in the previous decade; the execution of long-delayed investment plans; and the impact of economic recovery first in the USA, and then in the wider European economy.

During the long boom of the later 1980s, Italy embraced its affluence, and its attachment to the enterprise culture, with an exuberance that stood in remarkable contrast to the uncertainties of the 1970s. As in other industrial societies, private affluence, individualism, and conspicuous consumption once more seemed to become respectable values. Entrepreneurship was extolled as a fundamental social value by none other than the Socialist Party. At the level of public utterances, governments made much of Italy's prosperity for its own sake, rather than for the way it was used to pursue other social goals. A revaluation of the size of the black economy, together with some optimistic estimates of the real value of public services, enabled governments to revel in the so-called *sorpasso* (the point at which Italian per capita GDP overtook that in the UK), and an optimistic projection of short-term trends allowed them to look forward to a similar victory over France in the near future. For a while, early on in the boom, the notoriously unregulated Italian stock market shared this exuberance with an unprecedented bull run, built on the back of popular speculative enthusiasm for equities (although after the 1987 crash it settled into a more sober assessment of prospects).

There is no doubting the dynamism of the Italian economy during this period, nor its market-driven nature. However, the dilemmas of economic policy which built up over the years since the Hot Autumn had not melted away, and new ones were emerging. The degree of public regulation in the labour market, through wage-indexation, redundancy legislation, and social-security costs, remained controversial. Similarly, the alleged misallocation of resources arising from direct intervention in the manufacturing sector through state-holdings companies, and from indirect intervention through extensive systems of industrial subsidy and public procurement policy, continued to be a source of much criticism. And the chaotic and uneven redistributive mechanisms inherent in regional transfers, subsidization of low-productivity public-service employment, and fragmented welfare and pensions' networks were widely recognized as in urgent need of overhaul.

Meanwhile broader transnational developments in Europe were creating new pressures. In late 1978 Italy joined the European Exchange-Rate Mechanism. Until 1990, its participation involved 'wide-band membership', enabling the lira to float within parameters 6 per cent either side of a central rate, and until the later 1980s there were relatively frequent realignments within the system. Gradually, however, as Italian inflation edged towards the European Community average, revaluation receded as an option for the monetary authorities if they were to retain credibility domestically in the fight against inflation and externally in foreign exchange markets. In 1990 the lira moved to narrow-band membership (3 per cent parameters), and the last exchange controls were lifted.

Although undoubtedly a success in bringing the performance of the Italian economy in line with that of the core economies of France and Germany, these developments greatly increased the external pressure on domestic policy-makers. Labour-market policies or practices weakening the competitive position of Italian industry undermined overseas confidence in the lira, discouraged foreign direct investment, and encouraged Italian capital to migrate abroad. A high budget deficit—the result of incompatible competing claims on government—had similar effects. It forced up interest rates, penalizing domestic industry. And as the ERM moved in the direction of full monetary union it raised severe doubts over Italy's eligibility to join a system that would impose strict limits on the national budget deficits of all participating members.

Further problems were posed by the Community's Single Market Programme, which required member states to phase out many state aids to industry that came in the form of subsidies, access to special credit, and tax concessions. And working in the direction of regulation rather than deregulation, the Europeanization of Italian industry showed up two further areas of potential weakness: the absence of equity-market regulation and of anti-trust legislation. The narrow and unregulated Italian stock market made it difficult for Italy to extract the benefits of European financial-market liberalization, or to widen the base of equity ownership, while the absence of effective regulation of competition, mergers, and acquisitions permitted several large corporations to exploit positions of dominant market share to the detriment of competition and innovation.

In the latter half of the 1980s, therefore, Italy could celebrate its arrival as a major European economic power, yet remained aware—in a world of intensified international competition not just from within Europe, but also outside it—of the handicap represented by several structural bottlenecks to future development. These lay in the labour market, in industrial structure, and, most importantly of all, in the nature of the state. The capacity of the Italian state to absorb resources which it used inefficiently—in the health service, education, transport, and public administration—was an increasingly acute problem. The divergent paths of productivity growth between the public and private sectors were difficult to ignore, but difficult to correct.

A major reason for the persistence of this dilemma was that, politically, its implications did not translate into clear public debate or partisan division. Although there was a growing awareness, throughout the 1980s, of the irrational criteria on which Italian budgetary choices were based, and of the failings of the state, a clear distinction between a collectivist left and market-orientated right never emerged. The Communist Party itself suffered a long, slow decline, but its vote dispersed in a number of directions, and little of it appeared to drift towards parties that embraced a market-orientated philosophy unambiguously. In any case, since the left had never been in charge of the machinery of the state, it could claim, with as much justification as the right, that it stood for a reform of the public sector that would improve factor allocation. More importantly, the dominant party of the coalition, Christian Democracy, itself straddled the left–right divide, and in many respects was little less inclined to deregulation, privatization, and budget cuts than the parties of the left.

Society and Politics in Contemporary Italy

Social modernization

In the historical perspective of almost half a century, the most striking feature of contemporary Italian society is its transformation towards the European mean. Following the often frenetic changes of the early post-war decades, Italy had, by the end of the 1980s, acquired characteristics closely comparable to those of the older industrialized societies of Western Europe. In the 1940s, the Italian economy was still a semi-agricultural one, with a labour force distributed in a way similar to that of many of today's more advanced third-world economies. A little under half the labour force was employed in agriculture, with the remainder divided equally between industry and the tertiary sector. The industrial infrastructure was concentrated in the narrow confines of a triangle between Turin, Milan, and Genoa. Capital accumulation continued to pose serious problems. Whenever the economy approached the growth rates necessary to increase capital accumulation, it was prone to chronic balance-of-payments deficits. The prospects for rapid growth thus looked substantially poorer than elsewhere in Europe in the late 1940s. Yet by the end of the 1980s this difference from the older industrial economies had largely disappeared. Only 10 per cent of the labour force remained in agriculture, while 33 per cent were now in industry and 57 per cent in the tertiary sector.[37] Growth rates in the Italian economy in the intervening decades bore comparison with those of most other European economies, and even if per capita GDP was still below that in Germany, France, and (when measured by the standards of purchasing-power parities) even Britain, the gap had narrowed dramatically. The problems facing Italian policy-makers were in many respects similar to those faced by their colleagues in these other countries: how to achieve higher levels of productivity and technical innovation in an increasingly competitive international environment; how to maintain employment levels in an age of rising structural unemployment and lower rates of growth; how to cope with major distributive conflict between taxes, wages, profits, and welfare benefits; how to curb the long-term growth of public expenditure and its particularly rapid rise in times of recession.

This profound structural change has engendered wide-ranging social modernization. Dietary standards have changed markedly over the post-war period, with a major transformation in the type and quality of foodstuffs consumed. Health care, hygiene, and housing standards have also improved dramatically, especially in the south.[38] With rising living standards patterns of personal expenditure have changed considerably, and the proportion of income going to transport, hygiene, and leisure has increased markedly. The diffusion of popular culture through radio and television has brought to a country with traditionally ingrained provincial cultures and dialects a degree of homogeneity of values, language, and symbolism which, while still incomplete, represents a marked break from the early post-war era.[39] Education and social and geographical mobility have had profound impacts upon family life and attitudes, with a substantial increase in family breakdown, a retreat to the nuclear family model, and a decline in the size of the nuclear unit itself, from an average size of 4.0 in 1951 to 3.0 in 1981. As almost everywhere else in Europe, the most recent general census of population (1981) indicated near zero-population growth and an ageing population structure, presenting major implications for social-service provision and income distribution by early in the next century.[40] Perhaps most significant of all, the rise in the number of third-world migrants placed Italy, for the first time ever, in the category of countries with net inward migration. By the start of the 1990s, there were some 400,000 officially registered foreign residents from outside the European Community, and, including illegal immigrants, estimates of as many as 1 million in total. Their presence (despite the persistence of high official levels of unemployment) was a testimony to the combination of affluence and welfare networks which rendered menial and low-paid employment profoundly unattractive to ordinary Italian citizens.[41] In short a variety of indicators provide broad evidence of a major transformation in Italian social life, in a direction similar to that elsewhere in Europe.

The persistence of distinctiveness

Like all European societies, however, Italy retains distinctive features which reflect the path to modernization it has taken. These include a major regional imbalance between north and south, albeit somewhat different in nature from the past, and a complex class structure which, while assisting social adaptation to economic change, also generates major social inequalities and anomalies. Both features, in turn, have a profound impact on the political system, creating special interests to which the political class has to accommodate, and increasing the pressure on the state to intervene to mitigate distributional outcomes generated by the market.

The south

The most obvious unresolved problem remains that of regional imbalance. The south as a whole continues, despite three decades of special intervention policies, to lag far behind the centre-north by almost all indicators. The long phase of exceptionally low Italian growth, from 1975 onwards, affected the south more harshly than the north, and in some respects widened the gap between the two halves of the country. At the start of the 1990s, unemployment, at 20 per cent, was still over three times the level in the north. The proportion of the labour force employed in agriculture, at over 20 per cent, was more than double that in the north, and its productivity far lower. Equally worryingly, the main stimulant to a rising level of welfare in the south has been social transfers, often concealed as forms of employment support, and contained in a series of special items of legislation on youth employment, 'socially desirable services', disability pensions disbursed on an indiscriminate basis, agricultural redundancy benefits, and so on. A report in 1990 suggested, indeed, that this *benessere senza sviluppo* (prosperity without development) accounted for a major imbalance between disposable family income in the south and the resources effectively generated in the region. While the latter, on a per capita basis, was a mere 54.1 per cent of the north-centre level, the former, boosted by social transfers, amounted to 63.5 per cent.[42]

By the standards of the European Community, in fact, the south continues to rank alongside the regions of Spain, Greece, Portugal, and Ireland. According to an EC report on regional disparities, the seven most southerly regions (taking Sardinia as part of the south) all had levels of per capita gross domestic product below 85 per cent of the Community average. Ten regions of the centre-north, in contrast, had levels of per capita GDP above 115 per cent of the average, and ranked alongside the great majority of the regions of France, Germany, and the smaller northern states. No other European state has such an uneven distribution of GDP. Indeed, while over half of the 171 regions of the Community as a whole fell into the median group (GDP ranging from 85 to 115 per cent of the Community average) only three of Italy's twenty regions did so.[43]

Clearly, over the post-war period much progress *has* been achieved in absolute terms, if not in relation to the north. This was recognized in an official report in 1985, introducing a new mechanism of southern development aid. The report recognized that the lack of industrialization *per se* was no longer the main reason why the south was unable to develop a self-sustaining drive towards industrial development. Rather, poor technological infrastructure and systems of training, low levels of industrial productivity, and inadequate urban infrastructure were the major problems. The contrast between an industrialized north and a backward agricultural south had been replaced, at least to some degree, by a contrast in the efficiency with which resources— both labour and capital—were utilized. For any given activity, factor productivity was systematically lower in the south than the north.[44] The result of this diagnosis was new legislation on southern development (law no. 64, 1986) setting out a new philosophy of public intervention with a broader set of objectives than in the past, and with aid and investment incentives focused as much on the improvement of factor productivity and the modernization of technology as on the creation of new jobs in new industries.[45]

In the absence of a major overhaul of both public institutions and the attitudes and values of the southern political system, however, there are good grounds for scepticism about this new approach. The instruments of public intervention in the south remain poorly equipped to deal in a co-ordinated, efficient, and politically impartial way with regional development assistance. In certain respects, the situation has worsened over recent years; problems of social infrastructure—urban transportation, schools, and health services—have become acute. For business as for individuals the growth of organized crime has compounded the difficulties. It has infiltrated public life in several large urban centres—especially in Sicily, Calabria, and Campania —leaving the central state powerless to intervene effectively.

Moreover, the evident inefficiency and corruption of much public intervention in the south has begun, in recent years, to generate a backlash against transfers to the region. The most obvious recent manifestation has been the development in northern Italy of the so-called 'league' phenomenon: locally based parties protesting against the alleged southern domination of national politics and against the cost of inefficient income transfers from the 'productive' north to the 'parasitic' south.[46]

Even before the rise of the leagues, however, southern development policy was coming under strain from two other sources. The first was the poor financial performance of much of the south's large-scale public-sector enterprise, especially in areas such as steel and chemicals. Treasury pressure to limit the public cost of loss-making enterprises has increased greatly. The second has been the European Community, which has taken an increasingly close interest in Italian state aids to industry. The closure of the Bagnoli steel works, near Naples, has for long figured in the Community's plans for the restructuring of the European steel industry. More recently, and potentially even more controversially, the Community has started to take a close interest in state aids to FIAT that assist its southern investment programme.

The political implications of regional imbalance are, as we shall see in later chapters, quite profound. The style of southern political relationships has extended throughout the political system, affecting both state institutions and party organization. The criteria by which public resources are allocated is similarly affected by the outlooks of the southern political system, and this has jeopardized attempts in Italy over the last decade to emulate the efforts of other European states in establishing clearer and more efficient mechanisms of public choice. The state has, to a significant extent, been colonized by the south; an approach to the satisfaction of its political demands that has proved more effective than the creation of its own regional protest party. The development of an extensive system of clienteles built upon state-dependent beneficiaries of various sorts (public officials, welfare recipients, state-subsidized or protected business) has enabled the south to establish a firm grip on the Christian Democrat Party machine, and to exercise considerable influence in some of the smaller parties of government too. The strain placed upon the dominant governing party is formidable. The problem of internal coherence it faces is probably greater than that in any other major European party of the centre-right. Moreover, the south's influence does not, as we shall see, stop at the world of party politics. The bureaucracy, too, has become a preserve of the south, particularly at the higher levels, and this is widely considered to imbue it with the habits and outlooks of Italy's least modern, managerial, and innovative regional subculture.

The fragmentation of interest representation

The problems of the south clearly remain formidable, but they are by no means the only anomaly of the contemporary social structure. A more general feature, identifiable in many European societies, but in sharper relief in Italy than elsewhere, is differentiation between a modern, 'advanced' economy, sometimes seen as the 'centre', and various types of 'peripheral' or 'marginal' economy. Some sections of these latter types are clearly 'archaic' in that they survive, frequently through political protection, when normally they might be expected to have disappeared through economic rationalization. Other sections, however, are best considered not as 'archaic' survivals, but as *adaptations* of the modern economy, existing less because of subsidization or protection than because they are geared to particular product markets, and are built upon a very different system of labour relations from that of the 'modern' or 'central' economy.[47]

This conceptual distinction cuts across that between 'sectors' of the economy (agriculture, industry, services) as traditionally conceived, because each is itself to some degree internally divided between advanced, and peripheral and marginal, subsectors. Thus in the agricultural sector there are some 3 or 4 million people in either full- or part-time activity, of whom 1.5 million are probably in the efficient, relatively capital-intensive sector, the great majority as part of an employed labour force. The remainder are in small-scale farming units, employing no labour other than that from the family which runs the business. In this subsector viability depends in part upon various types of political subsidy (grants, loans, crop-damage compensation, artificial prices, pensions, and other social-security schemes) and in part upon a complementary income from part-time, frequently casual, employment in industry, often at low rates of pay and outside any 'regulation' by the social-security or tax authorities.[48]

The industrial sector is also divided in this way. As we have seen, the most unusual feature of Italian industry is that it is 'bottom heavy', with, by international standards, a very large number of small firms employing fewer than 100 workers. Thus alongside the 'central' or 'modern' capital-intensive economy, based on large industrial and financial groups, producing advanced products (automobiles, electronics, engineering, chemicals), and located largely in the industrial triangle, there exists a constellation of small-scale enterprises.[49] In part, these are linked vertically to the 'central' part of the economy, and represent the decentralization of production, noted earlier in the chapter, in response to labour-market changes from the late 1960s onwards. In part, however, they represent an independent sector which, through greater flexibility in the use of labour, compared to large-scale industry, can produce for the range of low- to intermediate-technology product markets (leather products, textiles and clothing, footwear) in which Italian exports have been notably successful in recent years.

Corresponding to this division in the industrial structure is an important division in the labour market. On the one hand there is a group of organized, highly paid workers, employed in large-scale enterprises, who through union action and protective legislation occupy a (relatively) privileged and secure position in the economy. Typically these are urban, adult males, in the northern industrial triangle (where adult male unemployment continues at rates far below that in other areas). On the other hand there is a 'peripheral' group employed in small firms, or artisan workshops, or as 'home-based' workers. Levels of unionization and state regulation are far lower, as are rates of pay. The majority are women, or young workers, and frequently the work itself is temporary and/or part-time. Among non-manual workers there are also distinctive characteristics in the labour market. The most significant is the small size of the *private* white-collar sector, and the relatively large size of its public counterpart, especially in the south. Here, too, the distinction between the 'central' and 'peripheral' work-forces is important, for the data for the private white-collar sector are generally considered to conceal an important *casual*, non-manual, labour force, especially amongst young graduates. Italy's very high level of graduate unemployment, and the apparent absence of an institutionalized channel by which graduates are fed directly into the labour force, is thought to cover over the existence of a 'peripheral' white-collar work-force, much of which, even before obtaining any formal qualification, is already employed in part-time or subcontracted work in sales, accountancy, design, programming, and research activities of various kinds.

A final distinctive feature of the labour force is the size of the 'old' (i.e. independent) non-manual group employed in commerce. As with their agricultural counterparts, a large proportion of those in this sector are there because *political protection* (either by default, as in the case of extensive, officially tolerated tax evasion, or by design, as in the case of extensive planning restrictions on large-scale, capital-intensive distribution chains) enables them to remain in business. As in agriculture, family incomes here too are supplemented by second jobs in the industrial sector.

The conceptual categories used in this description of the social structure of modern Italy are, of course, imprecise abstractions. The boundaries between 'central' and 'peripheral' sectors are quite indistinct, and any assessments of the numbers involved in them, or of the areas of the country in which particular sectors are prevalent, contains a good deal of arbitrariness. Such categories represent at most a distillation of the efforts of sociologists and economists to come to terms with important, but intangible, characteristics of contemporary Italian society. Yet despite their imprecision, they have a considerable utility. Neither the political subsidization of employment and the protection of economically threatened groups, nor the existence of peripheral or precarious, 'unregulated' employment, is unique to Italy. Most observers agree that in Italy they are extensive, however. They are widely seen as *functional*: both to an economy one of whose strengths lies in the flexibility and adaptability of its small firms, and to a political system in which *generalized* systems of social support—through generous unemployment benefits and other forms of assistance—have traditionally been poorly developed. In Italy the state intervenes, in aggregate terms, to approximately the same extent as elsewhere in Western Europe, as measured by the proportion of GDP accounted for by the public sector. What is distinctive is the less generalized, more particularistic, way in which it does so, the very diverse types of support and assistance it provides, and the way in which these activities are financed. This style has given rise to an epithet—*lo stato assistenziale* (the supportive state)—subtly different in meaning from its north European counterpart the *welfare state*.

The wide front on which the state intervenes has to be adjusted to the complex nature of Italian social structure. Clear lines of class conflict are difficult to define, as the range of state dependants and beneficiaries has gradually been extended. The result is a 'bargained' society in which distributive conflict is highly articulated, and the nature of both the party system and the formal political institutions, described in subsequent chapters, provides a multitude of channels through which groups and interests can make demands on public policy. Parties respond to this social fragmentation by casting their representative net very wide. Their attitude towards policy-making is, as a result, inclusive and incrementalist, rather than selective and programmatic. If there is a single reason why, in Italy, it is difficult for voters to make meaningful choices on the basis of party programmes, it is because, at least to some degree, all parties are making the same appeals to roughly the same extraordinarily wide range of social interests.

3

The Party System

Party Government and the Party System

Party-based democracy came to Italy relatively late. Organized, programmatic, political parties began to appear at the turn of the century, when the advent of universal suffrage generated the two mass parties—the Socialist Party and the Catholic People's Party—which laid the basis for competitive party politics. However, effective competition took time to establish. Although the two mass parties quickly expanded at the expense of the unstructured block of semi-independent liberal deputies from which Parliamentary majorities had hitherto been constructed, Mussolini destroyed the emerging party system before real party-based coalition government could evolve. It was thus only from 1945 that a structured system took root.

When it did so, however, it proved to be remarkably durable. The parties moved quickly to establish a strong party state. Links between party and society, initially tenuous after the suppression of independent civil association under Mussolini, were aided by the role parties played in reconstructing social organizations and interest groups. Assisted by the moral authority of the resistance movement, and by their near monopoly on organizational energy, the parties pursued an active policy of capture and colonization. This helped to lock substantial groups of voters into lasting partisan affiliation, and indeed, for the major parties, into subculturally distinct social communities.

Links between party and state were consolidated, at least for the governing parties, by a parallel colonization drive through the many public agencies inherited from fascism. Outside the career civil service of the central-government ministries, party appointment to managerial positions gradually became the norm. This control, shared out on a proportional basis between coalition allies, allowed the parties to exploit state agencies dealing with development, social security and welfare, housing, public enterprise, and local government. It did not always make them popular—indeed it generated a pejorative critique of Italy's *partitocrazia*—but it was important in solidifying the ties between parties, state, and, at least in some respects, civil society.

The influence of parties is felt in most areas of organized society. They dominate political recruitment, and party membership has become important for many types of public-sector administrative and managerial job, especially at senior level. They exercise wide influence over the interest universe. And in the absence of a prestigious, self-consciously evangelistic, bureaucratic class, they have assumed a central role in the policy-making process.

The strong form of party government Italy has experienced since 1945[1] has generated an enduring debate about the nature of the party system. Its terms have changed as the system has evolved. For many years, the focus was on the factors which caused and sustained such a fragmented, ideologically polarized, party system, and on the survivability of liberal democracy in the face of the challenges from political extremes on both left and right. Why did Italy have so many parties? Was there a process of long-term electoral polarization? How were coalitions constructed from such a system? How stable and effective could they be? Most importantly of all, could the system move from the stark polarization in which electoral choice appeared to involve all-or-nothing, unbargainable differences of ideological outlook, to a more moderate form of electoral competition in which parties offered voters differentiated programmes and thus meaningful choices about policies, sectoral options, and distributive outcomes within an agreed socio-economic and political framework?

Against apparently heavy odds, however, democracy survived, and was eventually consolidated. In recent years, it has been less and less possible to imagine Italian democracy being undermined by extremism. Yet what has been consolidated is often seen as unsatisfactory. The system is unable to generate clear-cut alternation in power between rival parties or coalitions. Earlier in post-war history this might have mattered less; indeed, it is possible the system might have been unable to cope with alternation. More recently, however, the lack of alternation has been seen as an encouragement to complacency and irresponsibility among the governing parties. The dominant party of the coalition—Christian Democracy—cannot be removed from office, even though it has sustained significant electoral losses in recent elections. The main opposition party—the PCI/PDS—has been unable to serve as the focus for an alternative, and indeed has suffered a dramatic electoral decline, even though satisfaction with the governing parties has also fallen. As a result, while there is now an agreed socio-economic and political context in which parties compete, the programmatic alternatives offered to voters within that context are not clear enough to have improved the process of electoral choice. In short, Italy's form of party government entails strong parties at the level of organization and control of the institutions of the state, but parties which, bereft of their ideological connotations, have been exposed as weak aggregators of policies and programmes.

Academic attention has therefore turned from the apocalyptic task of estimating the survivability of democratic party politics to the more mundane task of analysing the system's operational faults. In this vein, the main intellectual problems have focused on the parties as organizations, and on their failure to aggregate clear policy alternatives and transmit them to the institutions through which public policy is made. Moreover, new mechanisms of communication, new social movements, associational energy independent of the parties, and a growing demand for both enhanced participation and institutional reform have all begun to challenge the established order. Attention has thus turned to the question of whether significant electoral shifts or electoral reform may serve as catalysts for improvement. Is there a growing volatility in electoral attitudes? Is this volatility aiding or undermining the process of electoral choice? How could the party system be reformed and simplified?

This chapter and the next attempt to answer some of these questions. But they do not concentrate solely on the more recently posed intellectual problems. For the answers to the latter are not easily grasped outside the terms of earlier debate. To understand the extent of recent change in Italian politics, and the potential for further change, it is essential to understand the basic features of the party system as it has operated over the longer term. We begin with the fundamental historical determinants of the party system—religion, class, ideology, and territory—and show how these have combined with contingent political events to create the key features of the contemporary party system.

That system has traditionally been characterized by the presence of two major parties—Christian Democrats and Communists (now the PDS, or Party of the Democratic Left)—and a series of smaller satellites. The latter can themselves be divided into separate categories:

- parties of the democratic centre;
- parties of what can be described as the 'post–1968 fragmentation': a group containing parties on the left (some splits from established parties like the PSI and PCI), and protest parties of a more populist, although not on the whole authoritarian, type;
- parties of the authoritarian right.

In Fig. 3.1 these categories are set out for the various Parliaments elected between 1948 and 1992. Table 3.1 gives the basic electoral performance of these parties over the eleven general elections encompassed by these two dates.

TABLE 3.1 *Italian general elections: 1948–1992 (Chamber of Deputies)*

(*a*) Parliament I: 18 April 1948

	Vote (%)	Seats
Christian Democrats (DC)	48.5	305
Popular Front (PCI + PSI)	31.0	183
Socialist Unity (PSDI)	7.1	33
Italian Social Movement (MSI)	2.0	6
Monarchists (PDIUM)	2.8	14
Republicans (PRI)	2.5	9
National block (PLI)	3.8	19
S. Tyrol People's (PPST)	0.5	3
Peasants'	0.3	1
Sardinian	0.2	1
Parties not winning seats	1.3	
Total	100.0	574
Turn-out	92.2	

(*b*) Parliament II: 7 June 1953

	Vote (%)	Seats
Christian Democrats (DC)	40.1	263
Communists (PCI)	22.6	143
Socialists (PSI)	12.7	75
Social Democrats (PSDI)	4.5	19
Italian Social Movement (MSI)	5.8	29
Monarchists (PNM)	6.9	40
Republicans (PRI)	1.6	5
Liberals (PLI)	3.0	13
S. Tyrol People's (PPST)	0.5	3
Parties not winning seats	2.3	
Total	100.0	590
Turn-out	93.8	

(c) Parliament III: 25 May 1958

	Vote (%)	Seats
Christian Democrats (DC)	42.3	273
Communists (PCI)	22.7	140
Socialists (PSI)	14.2	84
Social Democrats (PSDI)	4.6	22
Italian Social Movement (MSI)	4.8	24
Monarchists (PNM)	2.2	11
Monarchists (PMP)	2.6	14
Republicans (PRI)	1.4	6
Liberals (PLI)	3.5	17
S. Tyrol People's (PPST)	0.5	3
Comunità	0.6	1
Val d'Aosta local list	0.1	1
Parties not winning seats	0.5	
Total	100.0	596
Turn-out	93.8	

(d) Parliament IV: 28 April 1963

	Vote (%)	Seats
Christian Democrats (DC)	38.3	260
Communists (PCI)	25.3	166
Socialists (PSI)	13.8	87
Social Democrats (PSDI)	6.1	33
Italian Social Movement (MSI)	5.1	27
Monarchists (PNM)	1.7	8
Republicans (PRI)	1.4	6
Liberals (PLI)	7.0	39
S. Tyrol People's (PPST)	0.4	3
Val d'Aosta local list	0.1	1
Parties not winning seats	0.8	
Total	100.0	630
Turn-out	92.9	

(e) Parliament V: 19 May 1968

	Vote (%)	Seats
Christian Democrats (DC)	39.1	266
Communists (PCI)	26.9	177
United Socialists (PSI + PSDI)	14.5	91
Italian Social Movement (MSI)	4.5	24
Monarchists (PDIUM)	1.3	6
Republicans (PRI)	2.0	9
Liberals (PLI)	5.8	31
Proletarian Unity (PSIUP)	4.4	23
S. Tyrol People's (PPST)	0.5	3
Parties not winning seats	1.0	
Total	100.0	630
Turn-out	92.8	

(f) Parliament VI: 7 May 1972

	Vote (%)	Seats
Christian Democrats (DC)	38.7	266
Communists (PCI)	27.1	179
Socialists (PSI)	9.6	61
Italian Social Movement (MSI)	8.7	56
Republicans (PRI)	2.9	15
Liberals (PLI)	3.9	20
Social Democrats (PSDI)	5.1	29
S. Tyrol People's (PPST)	0.5	3
Progressive group	0.1	1
Parties not winning seats	3.4	
Total	100.0	630
Turn-out	93.2	

(g) Parliament VII: 20 June 1976

	Vote (%)	Seats
Christian Democrats (DC)	38.7	263
Communists (PCI)	34.4	227
Socialists (PSI)	9.6	57
Italian Social Movement (MSI)	6.1	35
Republicans (PRI)	3.1	14
Liberals (PLI)	1.3	5
Social Democrats (PSDI)	3.4	15
Radicals	1.1	4
Proletarian Democracy (DP)	1.5	6
S. Tyrol People's (PPST)	0.5	3
Val d'Aosta left list	0.1	1
Parties not winning seats	0.2	
Total	100.0	630
Turn-out	93.4	

(h) Parliament VIII: 3 June 1979

	Vote (%)	Seats
Christian Democrats (DC)	38.3	262
Communists (PCI)	30.4	201
Socialists (PSI)	9.8	62
Italian Social Movement (MSI)	5.3	30
Republicans (PRI)	3.0	16
Liberals (PLI)	1.9	9
Social Democrats (PSDI)	3.8	20
Radicals	3.5	18
Proletarian Unity (PdUP)	1.4	6
S. Tyrol People's (PPST)	0.5	4
Trieste local list	0.2	1
Val d'Aosta local list	0.1	1
Parties not winning seats	1.8	
Total	100.0	630
Turn-out	90.6	

(*i*) Parliament IX: 26 June 1983

	Vote (%)	Seats
Christian Democrats (DC)	32.9	225
Communists (PCI)	29.9	198
Socialists (PSI)	11.4	73
Italian Social Movement (MSI)	6.8	42
Republicans (PRI)	5.1	29
Liberals (PLI)	2.9	16
Social Democrats (PSDI)	4.1	23
Radicals	2.2	11
Proletarian Democracy (DP)	1.5	7
S. Tyrol People's (PPST)	0.5	3
Sardinian	0.3	1
Val d'Aosta local list	0.1	1
Venetian League	0.3	1
Parties not winning seats	2.0	
Total	100.0	630
Turn-out	89.0	

(*j*) Parliament X: 14 June 1987

	Vote (%)	Seats
Christian Democrats (DC)	34.3	234
Communists (PCI)	26.6	177
Socialists (PSI)	14.3	94
Italian Social Movement (MSI)	5.9	35
Republicans (PRI)	3.7	21
Liberals (PLI)	2.1	11
Social Democrats (PSDI)	2.9	17
Lega lombarda	0.5	1
Green lists	2.5	13
Radicals	2.6	13
Proletarian Democracy (DP)	1.7	8
S. Tyrol People's (PPST)	0.5	3
Sardinian	0.4	2
Val d'Aosta local list	0.1	1
Parties not winning seats	1.9	
Total	100.0	630
Turn-out	88.9	

(*k*) Parliament XI: 5 April 1992

	Vote (%)	Seats
Christian Democrats (DC)	29.7	206
Democratic Left (PDS)	16.1	107
Socialists (PSI)	13.6	92
Italian Social Movement (MSI)	5.4	34
Republicans (PRI)	4.4	27
Liberals (PLI)	2.8	17
Social Democrats (PSDI)	2.7	16
Rifondazione comunista (ex-PCI)	5.6	35
Lega lombarda + Lega nord	8.7	55
Other leagues	1.2	1
La rete	1.9	12
Green lists	3.0	16
Panella	1.2	7
Pensioners' Federation	0.4	1
S. Tyrol People's (PPST)	0.5	3
Val d'Aosta local list	0.1	1
Parties not winning seats	2.7	
Total	100.0	630
Turn-out	87.2	

Sources: 1948–87: Istituto centrale di statistica, *Elezioni della Camera dei deputati e del Senato 14 giugno 1987* (Rome, 1989), 18–21; 1992: *Corriere della sera* (8 Apr. 1992), 1.

Determinants of the Party Spectrum
The continuity of historical cleavages

It is readily apparent from Fig. 3.1 that, in broad historical terms, until the 1992 general election the features of continuity were more marked than those of change. The two major parties of the 1940s—one renamed—were still the major parties at the start of the 1990s, even if their combined support had fallen quite markedly. Both parties have recently faced serious difficulties, but neither has quite lost its dominant position in its part of the spectrum. The smaller parties have increased in number over time; the fortunes of some have risen and those of others have fallen. The status of the Socialist Party has gone through particularly large changes. Some of the other minor parties, such as the Radicals, the Greens, and the local 'leagues', are relatively new entrants to party competition. In general, however, at least until

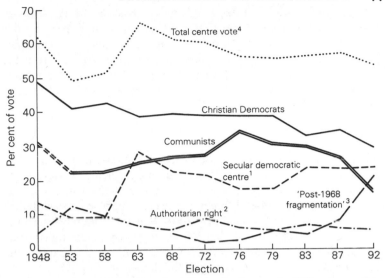

Notes: 1. The 'secular democratic centre' (the parties forming the DC's minor coalition allies) does not include the Italian Socialist Party until 1963.

2. The 'authoritarian right' includes the MSI and the parties running under a monarchist banner.

3. The 'post-1968 fragmentation' includes splits from the PSI and PCI, various new left parties, green parties, the Radical Party, and 'leagues' and other local movements.

4. From 1948 to 1958, and from 1979 onwards, the total centre vote is in general synonymous with the vote for the parties of the governing coalition. Between 1963 and 1972 it is between 4 and 7 percentage points larger since the PLI was not part of the ruling coalition. In the grand coalition (1976–9) the total centre vote was very much smaller than that for the parties of the governing coalition, since the latter included the PCI. At some other times one or more smaller parties (PRI, PLI, PSDI) withdrew from the coalition; in 1991, for example, the Republicans withdrew, reducing the size of the ruling coalition from 56% to 53% of the vote, and after the 1992 election to only 48%.

FIG. 3.1 The share of the total vote (Chamber of Deputies) received by the major parties/groups, 1948–1992

the 1992 election, the formula of 'two plus supporting six or more' continued to apply. To understand why, it is necessary to look at the durability of historical cleavages.

To describe any contemporary party spectrum is, at least in part, to describe the historical cleavages most salient at critical points in its emergence. As Lipset and Rokkan have persuasively argued,[2] the cleavages of the era of democratization, the party organizations, names, and identities to which they gave rise, and the loyalties of the electorate to those organizations, have proved remarkably durable almost everywhere. Thus, in Italy, although Mussolini suppressed party development for twenty years, the post-war system bore substantial similarity to that of the early years of the twentieth century.[3] Religion, class, ideology, and territorial conflict—the basic building blocks of most modern European party systems—all played a part in this pattern. Over time the meaning and intensity of such cleavages has changed, and if a party system were constructed from scratch in the 1990s, it would probably look very different. That it does not reflects the ability of established parties to adapt to new issues, and to keep alive those of past eras.

Religion

The ability to adapt is seen most clearly in the case of religion. The religious cleavage originally reflected the struggle between the Catholic Church and the temporal aspirations of the Vatican on one side, and the secular liberal ruling class which built the modern Italian state on the other. In nineteenth-century Italy this conflict was a form of cold war in which the Church refused to recognize the Italian state (formally it continued to hold out until the Concordat of 1928), and hence forbade Catholics to participate in political life.

However, a change was forced upon the Church from the 1890s by the emergence of socialism—a greater threat to the Church's moral and spiritual authority than even the secular state. Non-participation thus turned into active involvement, and a Catholic People's Party emerged to compete with the left for the allegiance of the newly enfranchised masses. Although the People's Party was clearly a party of religious defence, its relationship with the Catholic hierarchy was never easy, in part because its popular base, and the socially progressive outlook that this gave some of its leaders, brought it into conflict with traditional patterns of Catholic authority.

This ambiguity was nevertheless a source of strength for Christian Democracy, the post-fascist successor to the People's Party. Like some other European Christian democrat parties, the post-war leadership preached the values of class and international reconciliation, and further emphasized the socially progressive elements of its policy outlook.[4] Except in the areas corresponding to the old papal states, the DC was not identified with an unashamedly reactionary Catholic ruling class. It thus managed to avoid too close an identification with the Catholic hierarchy, constructing a broad inter-class coalition which placed it in a key position in the centre of the political spectrum.

In long-term historical perspective the Catholics thus displayed a remarkable adaptability. Outsiders in the nineteenth century, they became the establishment after 1945; unwilling to co-operate with secular parties in liberal Italy, they did so with alacrity in the republic. Religion has occasionally disrupted political life—especially when issues of divorce and abortion emerged in the 1970s—but every coalition has successfully spanned the religious/secular party divide. In this, Christian Democracy has been helped by the fact that anti-clericalism is largely confined to one region of the country, and there is virtually no Protestant sector to limit the scope of its appeal. Of little salience in day-to-day policy-making, its Catholic identity has thus been a largely positive influence for the DC. Even today it is a significant element holding together an otherwise disparate range of outlooks. However, as we shall see in the following chapter, it is by no means the only binding element, the common pursuit of power having increasingly displaced it. Moreover, as the secularization of Italian society has proceeded, the capacity of the DC's religious sociological roots to counteract the negative consequences of the party's long occupation of political power has gradually diminished, as the party's electoral set-backs in 1983 and 1992 have shown.

Class

The statistical correlation between party vote and social class has generally been low in comparison with countries in northern Europe. But class has had a major influence on the shaping of the Italian party system. Social conflict between employer and worker, and between landlord and peasant, has often been intense, especially in the first half of the century.

As we saw in Chapter 2 several factors have given rise to a complex class structure. One is the major variations in economic development between regions. Another is the persistence until fairly recently of a large peasantry, with a diversified pattern of land tenure. A third— more recent—is the importance of the small-business and artisan sector of the economy. In the early decades of the century, the industrial working class was thus smaller than in the more advanced parts of Europe, while the peasantry was larger, and, in certain areas, it was endowed with a profound sense of social grievance. The working class thus faced major difficulties in achieving its objectives, and was subject to serious internal divisions over the route to power.

From the 1890s onwards, Italy generated a class-based party of the left—the Italian Socialist Party—formed from an alliance of industrial and agricultural trade unions, peasants' co-operatives, and Marxist intellectuals. But while the PSI quickly established itself as the main party of the Italian left, and could fairly claim to be the chief political representative of the emerging unionized working class, and of a substantial part of the lower peasantry and agricultural day-labourers, it was always internally divided and threatened by competition from other radical groups.

After 1921, the secession of the pro-Soviet Communist Party split the Italian left into two, and later three, parties, all claiming to be the authentic representatives of the working class. Such claims were certainly not equally valid. After World War II, the party with the strongest working-class credentials was no longer the PSI but the Communist Party. The Socialists and Social Democrats gradually lost a clear-cut class connotation, responding to the competition from an organizationally stronger party on their left by hesitantly redefining themselves as socially composite parties of the centre. Class thus accounts for the genesis and evolution of a major part of the political spectrum, but does not, alone, explain the contemporary social base of the parties themselves.

Moreover, complexities in the class structure underlie the socially composite nature of the PCI/PDS vote. In much of north-central Italy, and parts of the Po Valley, the party traditionally represented share-croppers, and more recently artisans, small entrepreneurs, and many white-collar workers. This following was based partly on objective economic circumstances (conflict over agricultural contracts), partly on historical factors (deep-rooted republican and anarchist radicalism in what was once a conservative papal autocracy), and partly on outlooks inherited through family and community socialization (economic change replacing peasants with artisans and small businesses). As we shall see, the socially composite nature of the PCI had an important impact on its post-war ideology and strategy.

Ideology

Divisions based on class are often closely related to those based on ideology. But the two are not synonymous. Indeed, while in the formative decades of the modern party system attitudes to the social and political system divided the Marxist-inspired parties of the left from the so-called bourgeois parties (i.e. those committed to political pluralism), such issues have also divided the left itself. The party system has been marked as much as any in Europe by the great schism between Leninism and social democracy in 1921. What determined the relative strength of the Communists and Socialists thereafter was probably the product of fascism and the resistance movement, rather than the intrinsic appeal of either ideological outlook. But once a party with a close historical identification with a revolutionary rather than a parliamentary path to power established itself as the dominant party of the left, it undermined effective working relationships between centre-left and left for almost half a century.

On the right, too, ideology has left its imprint. Italy was the first struggling democracy in inter-war Europe to fall prey to authoritarian reaction. Even after 1945 there was a substantial group on the far right—the MSI and the Monarchists—unreconciled to the democratic framework. Most of its followers were poor, politically illiterate southerners whose vote was populist protest rather than clear ideological choice. But the MSI, the heir to the fascist legacy, has for four decades remained a major parliamentary problem, always winning enough votes to force the other parties of the centre and right to forge coalitions with at least a section of the left. Today, the MSI is no longer seen as a real threat to the system. It remains an essentially untouchable party for the purposes of coalition-building, but this is more a nuisance than a danger. Few suppose that there is any significant social or ideological constituency for reactionary authoritarianism on the right, other than amongst a small fringe of disgruntled activists who would nowadays win little support from business or even the security forces.

Similarly, as we shall see below, the sense in which the PCI remained an anti-system party became progressively less clear even before its change of name to the PDS. But the fact that it is only relatively recently—perhaps only in the 1980s—that Italy can be said to have reached a near consensus on the basic principles of its social and political system continues to determine both the shape of the party system and the relationships between its component parties.

Territory

The impact of territorial conflict on the Italian party system is also complex. The process of Italian unification was in many respects the conquest of the south by the northern liberal class, yet while the economic terms of unification for the south were harsh, they never led to the development of a significant, self-conscious party of territorial defence against control from the centre. This reflected the ability of the southern ruling class to infiltrate the established liberal ruling élite; it also reflected the paucity of organizational resources in this underdeveloped area. The 'southernization' of the Christian Democrat Party after World War II was further testimony to the willingness of the south to adapt to the centre rather than fight against it.

This is not to say that territorial politics plays no role in the party system, especially today. The south has never been able to generate its own party, but separatist and cultural minority groups in specific regions have. Thus Sardinia has spawned the Sardinian Action Party, while in the French-speaking Aosta valley in the far north-west there is the Union valdotaine, and in the German-speaking Tyrol, in the north-east, the Sudtiroler Volkspartei (SVP). None has possessed any strategic importance in parliamentary terms, but each has been significant enough to bring forth concessions from the centre, in the shape of special conditions of regional autonomy in their respective territories. Recently, in the wake of the revival of nationalist identity in

Central and Eastern Europe, these sentiments have again begun to stir—especially in the Tyrol.

Moreover, it is arguable that, at least until recently, Italy has contained not a single dominant national political culture, but rather several rival political subcultures, of which two—the Catholic subculture in the north-east of Italy, and the radical socialist subculture in the north-centre—were closely linked to the two dominant parties of the system. In fact, the basis of the subcultures was not exclusively territorial—if it were, the DC and PCI could not have been genuinely *national* parties, as they undoubtedly were. But both parties have had areas of particular regional strength. Furthermore, two other areas—not the preserve of a single dominant party—have also had distinctive territorial cultures. These are the north-west and the south and islands.

Distinct territorial identities reflect both history and contemporary economic conditions. The north-west industrial triangle is the most 'modern' part of the country. Containing the industrial conurbation of Milan, Turin, and Genoa, it is often described, in part misleadingly, as 'European' rather than 'Mediterranean' in outlook. The class structure approximates more closely than in other regions to that of advanced industrial societies elsewhere in Europe. The balance between left and right is more even than in the rest of Italy, and neither Christian Democracy nor the Communist Party is the unequivocally dominant party.

The north-east, in contrast, has been until recently the unchallenged bastion of Christian Democracy, although economic and social change has gradually pushed the real areas of DC strength away from the urban centres and out to the rural periphery.[5] Parties of the left have historically done badly here, in contrast to their performance in an adjacent area—the north-centre—which in certain socio-economic respects is rather similar. In the north-centre, anarchist and radical traditions of the nineteenth century, and acute tensions between landlord and peasant, have helped to create a Communist stronghold in the post-war era. Interestingly, the area known as the 'third Italy'—based on the dynamism of small and medium-sized enterprises—today straddles both north-east and north-centre, confirming that subcultural patterns rooted in history, rather than differences in economic structure, underlie the post-war Catholic/communist cleavage.[6]

The south and the islands, finally, are considerably poorer regions, where party organization is less solid, voter allegiances less stable, and political relationships are built around patronage networks and personalized political activity. In the south, contacts, small favours, jobs, and other individually aimed benefits are the small change of political life. The strongest party in the area, as in the north-east, is Christian Democracy, but its support is far more brittle than in the north-east, and at different times over the post-war era it has faced competition from parties in very different parts of the political spectrum. In the early 1950s, and again in the 1970s, it had to contend with the far right.[7] In the late 1940s and the mid-1970s it was strongly challenged by the Communist Party.[8] And particularly in the last decade the Socialist Party has used its access to government to mount a strong challenge as a rival source of patronage and political largess.

The basic fourfold division presented here is however a simplification of a very complex territorial pattern. All areas contain within them significant variations, and those variations have become greater over the years. Analysis of the territorial patterns of voting behaviour and political culture have identified enclaves inside large, politically homogeneous regions, and fringe areas that lie between such regions.[9] Thus in the south and islands, for example, cluster analysis has distinguished between: first, areas in which the predominant direction of political competition is between the DC and PCI; secondly, those in which it is between the DC and the political right (MSI and Monarchists); and thirdly, areas in which there is something approaching Christian Democrat dominance.[10] Explanations for these sub-regional variations then require complex analysis of the precise pattern of land tenure, the size and nature of urban centres, the role of the public sector in the local economy, etc.

A final territorial factor, which has emerged only in recent years, but which today is of critical importance to the party system, is the emergence in the north of a fundamental critique of 'Rome-based' misgovernment, and of the high and unproductive cost of transfer payments from the rich north to the poorer south. This is a reversal of the potential for territorial protest identified at the beginning of this section, under the long-term impact of—in the eyes of northerners—the 'southernization' of Rome. While once the capital was dominated by the northerners who engineered unification, during the twentieth century this connotation has gradually disappeared. As a result, it is not the south which feels itself to be the 'periphery', in relation to the administrative and political 'centre' in Rome, but rather the north.

Naturally, this sense of frustration is mixed in with a non-territorial grievance against the quality of Italian government in more general terms, and at the impossibility of alternation in power and of mechanisms by which the electorate can signal its frustration. The Lombard League, which in the 1992 election became Italy's second largest party throughout Piedmont, Lombardy, and the Veneto, had its counterparts in other parts of the country. They did not attract voters at the dramatic levels of 15–20 per cent achieved in the north, and in the south Sicily's *Rete* ('Network') certainly did not share the anti-southern sentiments of the leagues. Nevertheless, the fact that this protest was so dramatic in the north underlined the territorial dimension which was undoubtedly present.

Post-war determinants of relative party strength

Historical cleavages have dictated the overall shape of the post-war party system, generating parties of the organized working class, parties of the secular middle class, Catholic parties, and parties on both right and left which are perceived not to subscribe to the liberal-democratic framework.

Early post-war developments, described in Chapter 1, determined the relative strength between these broad groups. Christian Democracy inherited the leadership of the centre-right from the Liberals, and Communism took over the leadership of the left from the Socialists. The Christian Democrats, unlike the Liberals, were untainted by association with Mussolini in the early 1920s, and enjoyed the inestimable benefit of the vast network of the Church. They quickly came to be seen by the moderate and conservative electorate—and by Italy's Western allies—as the main political bulwark against the Communists. On the left, the Communists themselves benefited from their resistance record, and from the divisions within the Socialist Party.

By 1948, as a result, the party system had assumed the fundamental shape it maintained over the following four decades, and which is still identifiable even after the changes which occurred between 1989 and 1992. Until the late 1980s, changes to that shape were numerous, but were matters more of detail than of substance. They are considered below under six headings, but it should be remembered that even the proliferation of new parties over the last two decades still leaves the DC and PDS as the two largest parties, albeit with a combined share of the vote which in the 1992 election fell significantly below 50 per cent of the total.

Major party change

Declining Christian Democrat dominance

The position of the Christian Democrats was slowly weakened in the years after 1948, but without ever removing the party from its central role in all coalitions. In 1948, it had 48.5 per cent of the vote; by the early 1960s this had fallen to around 38 per cent, at which point it stabilized, before a further decline in the years from the mid-1970s to the early 1980s. In recent elections, the average support for the party has been standing at around 35 per cent, although in 1992 the party fell below 30 per cent for the first time ever. The long-term decline reflects both the crisis of secularization that has accompanied the advent of an advanced, consumer-orientated society, and the internal tensions of a party that attempts to represent both the modern market-orientated half of Italy, and the backward south.

The rise and fall of the Communist Party

The fortunes of the PCI/PDS, and with them the party's role in the political system, have gone through what by the early 1990s looked like a full cycle. For many years the PCI enjoyed an upward electoral trend, rising slowly from 20 per cent in the 1940s to reach a peak of 34.4 per cent in 1976. As it did so, the party established for itself a role of increasing influence first in local government and the trade-union movement, and then in Parliament, entering the parliamentary majority (though not the government) in the years 1976–9. Subsequently, the party has struggled to maintain its position. Declining public support for the welfare state and the power of organized labour—let alone for a more radical move towards a planned economy—affected the PCI even more than parties of the non-communist left. By 1987 the PCI's support was back at the levels of the mid-1960s: still the largest party of the left, but, for the first time, increasingly outmanœuvred by its smaller Socialist sister-party, which proved itself better able to adapt to the changing political and economic climate of the 1980s. The collapse of communism in Eastern Europe, and the crisis leading to the change of name to the PDS, and to the secession of the far-left group within the old PCI (discussed in Chapter 4), led to an even bigger fall in the general election of 1992, even if, by the standards of other West European communist and ex-communist parties, the fall was actually quite modest. By 1992 the PDS had a mere 16 per cent of the vote: still just ahead of the Socialists, but even with the additional 5.6 per cent for Rifondazione comunista, the left-wing secessionist group, still five points down on 1987, and thirteen points down on 1976.

Minor party change

The socialist movement

On the non-communist left, the problems of how to cope with the strength of the Communists and the Christian Democrats took the PSI and the PSDI through a series of unhappy breakups and reunions. As we have seen, the two parties split up in 1947 under the tensions generated by the Cold War. Nearly two decades later they were reunited, but the marriage lasted only three years (1966–9). Division took a heavy toll on the PSI over this period, not just through the 1947 secession, but again in the early 1960s, when the party's (pro-communist) left wing broke away to form a small separatist group, the inappropriately named Socialist Party of Proletarian Unity (PSIUP). The latter lasted only until 1972, when electoral failure led to a merger with the Communists. Its principal role was thus to act as a pipeline for draining off voters from the Socialist to the Communist Party.

Throughout the 1970s and 1980s the Socialist and Social Democratic Parties were rivals to be the main standard-bearer of social-democratic reformism. However, under Craxi the Socialist Party rediscovered its self-confidence and gradually pulled away from the struggling PSDI. By the 1987 election, it had clawed its way up to 14.3 per cent of the vote, to the PSDI's 3.0 per cent. Its position in the governing coalition, moreover, strengthened considerably as that of its larger but more divided Christian Democrat partner correspondingly weakened. Nevertheless, the PSI's electoral recovery has not been dramatic, and despite Craxi's flamboyant leadership, his strategy has remained vulnerable to the fate which befell the PSI under Nenni in the 1960s: that when the Christian Democrats and the government more generally became unpopular, the PSI too would suffer by association. As the long boom of the 1980s turned to recession in the early 1990s, just this happened, and, as in the 1960s, the PSI struggled to differentiate itself from the coalition of which it was part, paying the price for failure to do so with a small fall (from 14.3 to 13.6 per cent) in the 1992 election.

The far right

On the far right, the Monarchists, a largely southern party born out of the defeat of the monarchy in the referendum in 1946, found that their main *raison d'être* struck an ever-diminishing chord with voters. In 1972 they merged with the neo-fascist MSI in what was effectively a takeover by the latter. In the 1970s, the MSI itself enjoyed a brief period of popularity, though one largely confined to protest voters in the South. Locally, it has enjoyed remarkable but generally brief peaks of popularity, especially in parts of Calabria and Sicily, whenever a local grievance erupts at the expense of the Christian Democrats.

The new left

In a political system with as deeply rooted a Marxist subculture as that in Italy, and with as permissive an electoral system, it was inevitable that the left should throw up a range of *marxisant* groups some of which would gain representation in Parliament. Such movements began to emerge in the late 1960s, with the increase in dissent inside the Communist Party. In 1969, a group of radical intellectuals broke away from the party and formed the Manifesto Group, which subsequently elected a small number of its members to Parliament. At about the same time, the student movement and mounting labour unrest generated a political radicalism, particularly amongst younger voters, which created a small but important social constituency alongside and in some senses to the left of the Communists. As the PCI itself was incorporated into the ruling coalition, this constituency grew. It was occupied by a shifting group of parties, most of which did not get into Parliament, and one or two of which were probably the breeding ground for the terrorism of the late 1970s. The most notable party was PdUP (the Party of Proletarian Unity), formed in 1974 from the Manifesto Group, the remnants of the PSIUP, and the Proletarian Movement of Workers. It disbanded, largely through merger with the Communists, a decade later. A subsequent group, DP (Proletarian Democracy), formed in 1978, was still represented in the 1987 Parliament, with 1.7 per cent of the chamber vote. In 1992, however, it was overtaken by the new breakaway group from the Communist Party, Rifondazione comunista, which while in many respects owing its origins to the 'old' Marxist left not the 'new' one, nevertheless seemed destined to play a role not dissimilar to that of the PdUP and DP in previous legislatures.

Radicals, environmentalists, and leagues

The expansion of group activism and political participation in the 1970s did not just affect the Marxist left, however. Two of the more significant 'progressive' minor parties, the Radical Party and the Greens, were non-Marxist. An eclectic combination of environmental and civil rights causes, the Radical Party was distinguished less by a distinct ideology than by its flamboyant, participatory political style (dramatic public gestures and much use of obstructionist tactics in Parliament). It deliberately eschewed formal party organization and leadership, and succinctly captured the schizophrenic range of issues and philosophical cross-currents generated on the Italian left in the 1970s. Above all, it was a party of the 'post-materialist' generation, with a clear appeal to the affluent, participation-minded student and youth culture. In the later 1970s, the moderation and the heavy pedagogic style of the Communist Party pushed many such voters towards the Radicals.

In the mid-1980s, the Radicals began to lose momentum to the environmentalist movement, as the increase in environmental aware ness (particularly in the wake of the Chernobyl incident, and the 1987 referendums on nuclear power) began to take hold. In the 1987 general election the Green lists won 2.5 per cent of the vote, and in 1992, albeit divided between different tendencies, they won 3.0 per cent. Along with the Radicals, and other fringe left groups, they accounted for around 7 per cent of the vote and 34 representatives in the Chamber of Deputies in 1987. Such a presence constituted a significant change compared with the 1950s and 1960s, because of its effect not so much on parliamentary arithmetic as on the style of parliamentary and extra-parliamentary politics, and on perceptions of electoral competition. The group has never been large enough to change coalition arithmetic in a fundamental way, but it represents a dispersal of votes which puts all the established parties—Communists, Socialists, and Christian Democrats—at some discomfort, and has complicated political life considerably.

From 1987 onwards, however, the nature of non-Marxist and non-fascist protest against the governing parties took on new features. The 'new social movement' character of the Greens and Radicals was supplemented by sentiments which had much more to do with straightforward material concerns, as the northern leagues developed their critique of corruption and misgovernment by the Rome-based national political system, demanding radical measures of devolution to the regions in a new, fully federal, political system. At times this message, which had potentially racist overtones since it appeared to be directed at southerners, ran the risk of becoming an explicitly anti-immigrant protest vote similar to that for extreme right in Germany or France. At least until the 1992 election, however, this danger was contained.

Elections and Voting Behaviour

The electoral system

Italy's multi-party system is underpinned by highly permissive electoral laws. They provide a pure form of representation setting a very low threshold for entry to Parliament. For the lower house, the Chamber of Deputies, the country is divided into thirty-two constituencies, each containing a number of seats which varies from four in the smallest to over fifty in the largest. Voters choose their party (the *list* vote), and until the referendum of 1991 could also, if they wished, vote for up to three or four individual candidates on their party's list of candidates (the *preference* vote).[11]

In each constituency a *quota* is calculated, by dividing the total valid vote by the number of seats to be filled plus two. Each party's total list vote is divided by the quota to determine the number of seats it wins in any given constituency. Remainders across the thirty-two constituencies are aggregated in a national constituency, the effect of which is (partially) to compensate minor parties for their relatively large ratio of 'wasted' to 'seat-winning' votes, thereby making the number of votes a party wins across the whole country more proportional to the size of its parliamentary representation than would otherwise be the case.[12] To qualify for a share of the seats available from the national constituency, a party has only to obtain one local constituency seat, or 300,000 votes nation-wide.

Although, as Table 3.2 shows, there is a small premium offered to the larger parties, and a corresponding penalty to the smaller ones, the disparity between votes and seats is not great for any party. The consequence is a 'static' electoral system, giving no party a significant premium, and minimizing the effect of electoral change. Only once, in 1948, has the Christian Democrat Party won an absolute majority, and even then the majority was so small, and the party so divided, that the leadership deemed it prudent to invite other parties into the coalition.

TABLE 3.2 *The consequences of the electoral system for party representation (percentage share of valid vote and seats in Chamber of Deputies)*

	1979		1983		1987		1992	
	Vote	Seats	Vote	Seats	Vote	Seats	Vote	Seats
DC	38.3	41.6	32.9	35.7	34.3	37.1	29.7	32.7
PCI	30.4	31.9	29.9	31.4	26.6	28.1	16.1	16.9
PSI	9.8	9.8	11.4	11.6	14.3	14.9	13.6	14.6
MSI	5.3	4.8	6.8	6.0	5.9	5.6	5.4	5.4
PRI	3.0	2.5	5.1	4.6	3.7	3.3	4.4	4.3
PSDI	3.8	3.2	4.1	3.7	2.9	2.7	2.7	2.5
PLI	1.9	1.4	2.9	2.5	2.1	1.7	2.8	2.7
Other	7.5	5.0	6.9	3.8	10.2	3.8	24.7	20.8

The mechanics of the electoral system for the upper house of Parliament (the Senate) are different, but the end result is very similar to the system for the Chamber. Constituencies are of the single-member type, but unless a candidate wins 65 per cent of the vote (which almost never occurs) seats are allocated proportionately on a regional basis, by a variant of the d'Hondt formula. Despite this difference from the Chamber, and despite the difference in the minimum voting age (18 for the Chamber, 25 for the Senate), the party composition of the two houses has always been very similar, and differences which have existed have generally been of little political significance. The three tiers of local government (regions, provinces, and communes) each use a list system of proportional representation very similar in operation to that for the Chamber of Deputies. The one departure from this is in the smallest municipalities (those with a population below 5,000), where parties present joint lists, the largest party list being awarded an absolute majority of the seats on the council.

Electoral behaviour

The nature of electoral competition

In analysing Italian voting behaviour, it is important to distinguish between the macro-politics of overall party support and the micro-politics of individual voting decisions. Because the results of Italian elections rarely seem to affect the composition of governments, it is sometimes supposed that electoral behaviour is characterized by glacial stability. In fact the impression is probably no more the result of voter stability than of two other factors: first, an electoral system that minimizes the translation of vote changes into seat changes, and secondly the structure of the party system, which makes clear-cut change in the composition of coalitions very difficult. At least for the period from 1948 to 1977, net electoral volatility was about on the European average—higher in the early post-war years, lower later on.[13]

Moreover, aggregate levels of voter stability probably belie considerably higher levels of voter mobility between pairs of elections at the individual level. Measuring such movement is, however, notoriously difficult. Traditionally, survey data has been unreliable in Italy, because of low response rates and a suspicion, in a country with a wide party spectrum and an unwillingness to reveal party affiliation, that respondents do not always reply to survey questionnaires truthfully. In addition, when elections are quite frequent, and a large number of parties is crowded into the political spectrum, accurate recall data is likely to be impossible to obtain. For these reasons, in recent years

Italian political scientists have developed complex techniques for assessing volatility on the basis of aggregate data at the level of local polling stations.[14] They have concluded that at the individual level there are quite high levels of volatility—ebbs and flows which tend to cancel one another out at the aggregate level. Gross volatility may thus be considerably higher than net volatility.

However, exactly how 'open' this has made the electoral market place remains in some doubt—at least until the collapse of communist self-confidence in 1989–90. A substantial part of the volatility identified is more the result of electoral turnover, and variations in turn-out, than of straight switching by individual voters between pairs of elections. Turn-out has traditionally been high in Italy (around 90 per cent), partly because of the constitutionally backed view that voting is a 'civic duty' (failed observance of which is formally recorded). But in recent elections turn-out has been falling, most notably in the south, where differential turn-out can have a substantial impact on party performance.[15] In addition, evidence suggests that even those voters who appear consciously to choose their party at each election do so from a narrow range of alternatives. Flows of voters across defined limits still seemed quite limited, even in the elections of the 1980s. The same conclusion emerged from a major survey of voters in 1985, conducted by Mannheimer and Sani.[16] Only a small number of Communist and Christian Democrat voters appeared to be willing to vote for the other major party.

The most competitive part of the political spectrum, in fact, appears to be the centre, and the centre-left. There is substantial overlap between the potential electorates of the Socialist Party and the Christian Democrats, on one side, and between the Socialists and the Communists on the other.[17]

Electoral competition and subcultural blocks

This might suggest that the electorate is still divided into segmented blocks. Earlier in the chapter, we referred to the existence of strong subcultural groups in Italian politics, each closely, though not exclusively, linked to territorial concentrations of strength for par ticular parties. One of the primary unresolved debates in Italian political science is whether such subcultures still have the vitality that they had in the 1960s, when the Carlo Cattaneo Institute studied patterns of political participation in Italy, and concluded that subcultural segmentation was the major feature of Italian party politics.[18] The answer remains ambiguous. There seems little doubt that the strength of the subcultures has declined to some degree, and that fewer voters are subject to their organizational influence. On a strong interpretation of the concept, the proportion of the electorate thus encompassed could be as little as one-fifth or less.[19] Levels of religious behaviour have fallen on the Catholic side, while membership of trade unions has fallen on the socialist side.[20]

Projecting this dilution of the strength of subcultural networks into a decline in electoral support for the two major parties is, however, risky. In the first place, as such networks decline the parties may generate other bases of support. Secondly, it is necessary to distinguish between a restriction of the numbers of voters who are actually reached by the subcultures, and a general disintegration of the ability of the subcultural networks to channel voters within them towards particular parties. The former does not necessarily imply the latter.

This uncertainty is compounded by the different interpretations that the vicissitudes of recent elections have brought forth. Thus, after the Christian Democrat Party's major defeat in the regional elections of 1975, and the Communist Party's advance in 1976, some commentators supposed that only the Catholic network was in decline, and that the socialist network might even be advancing. Subsequent set-backs for the Communist Party, and the DC's renewed difficulties in the general election of 1983, suggested that *both* major subcultures were being eroded. In fact, however, the process was taking place much more slowly than was initially thought. A decade later, the Sani and Mannheimer survey still found a high correlation between exposure to subcultural influences and support for the two major parties.[21] This suggested that even if the subcultural influences encompassed fewer people, those who *were* reached were still, in consequence, inclined to vote Communist or Christian Democrat. This is also indicated by the apparent ability of the two major parties to survive periods of general electoral set-back most effectively in those areas where the subcultural networks remain strongest. In the 1992 general election, in the context of a substantial decline in support for the PCI from five years earlier in the country as a whole, the PDS vote held up notably well in the Red Belt heartland of Emilia-Romagna and Tuscany.

These complexities have stimulated various models to explain different types of motivation in the voting decision. One of the best known is Pasquino and Parisi's three-fold typology based on the concepts of *appartenenza*, *opinione*, and *scambio*.[22] The three categories correspond, respectively, to voters whose vote is an affirmation of tight cultural, group, or class identity; those who vote on the basis of a broad assessment of policies, leadership competence, fitness to govern, etc.; and those who vote on the basis of very narrow personal, local, or sectional interest—behaviour frequently referred to as clientelistic voting. Such a classification provides a framework for assessing which parties are dependent on which types of voter, and in what relative measure; how far the distribution of such voters in the electorate as a whole is changing; and how far each group is affected by other influences, such as the strength of party (as opposed to subcultural) identification, the performance of party leaders, etc.

Unfortunately, in a society where the number of parties is high, and the correlations, let alone causal linkages, between parties and specific social indicators are low, there are still rather few answers to these types of question. It seems clear that the strong subcultural bonds *have* weakened. It has been suggested that the clientelistic vote is more widely dispersed than in the past, though in reality this change probably came as early as the 1960s, with the entry into government of the Socialist Party. It is also widely assumed that the 'opinion vote' accounts for a larger proportion of the electorate than in the past, and hence that there is greater competitiveness in electoral politics than in the past. Parties *need* to adapt, since there are fewer 'captured' votes; but they are also *able* to adapt, since modern mechanisms of political communication enable them to reach wider audiences, and to penetrate the barriers which once insulated members of the subcultures from messages from other parties.

Changing electoral competition: winners and losers

It is a measure of the indeterminacy of most elections that, after nearly a decade and a half of 'electoral change', observers are still arguing about who are the winners and losers from a more open electoral market place. It would not be unreasonable to suppose that the changes described above should work to the benefit of the lay and moderate parties of the political centre. Italian society does indeed seem to have become more open, pragmatic, and secular in the last two decades, and these virtues, if such they be, are widely seen as demonstrating Italy's status as a mature, unequivocally European, market-based society, increasingly free of the Mediterranean under development which had once been the country's handicap. Whether such a self-image is strictly accurate is less important than the moral ascendancy it has managed to achieve, and the boost it might be expected to give to parties with few ties to the subcultural images and identities of the past.

The parties best placed to exploit this possibility ought to be the parties of the lay centre ('polo laico'), Socialists and Republicans especially, but also Liberals and Social Democrats. They should, in principle, be assisted by the fact that voters in the party space adjacent to their own (Christian Democrats and Communists) are, so the previously cited Mannheimer and Sani research suggests, willing to consider voting for the PSI and PRI, whereas they would not be willing to consider voting for alternatives further away on the spectrum. Such parties can thus expect to reap a 'secularization/modernization' premium.

As with many centre-located parties, however, their electorates will almost certainly prove more volatile than those with long-established traditions of voter identification based on subcultural or other social characteristics. If so, the proportion of their voters unwilling to consider voting for other parties will be lower. In short, the lay centre parties may be able to gain voters, but, in adverse conditions, they are more likely to lose them as well. And they face the ever-present risk that, as long as they remain in government with the dominant governing party, they will suffer from this association.

There is some evidence that these difficulties have indeed affected the PSI and PRI, and that it is more generally a difficulty for the so-called *polo laico*. Support for the PSI and PRI has increased in recent years, but inconsistently, and to some degree at the expense of other parties in the group, rather than of the two major parties in the system. Thus the PRI gained significantly in 1983 (following a period in which republican leader Spadolini held the prime minister's office), but slipped back in 1987 and in the European elections of 1989. It increased once more in 1992 after the PRI withdrew from the governing coalition, and attached itself to the anti-government sentiments sweeping through the electorate, especially the northern electorate, in the economic recession. The Socialists made what was by minor-party standards a major leap forward in 1987 (after the four years of Craxi's premiership), but the increase still took it only from 11.4 per cent to 14.4 per cent, and the party has undoubtedly lost some voters along the way to the Green lists, which contested their first general election in 1987, and subsequently to the Lombard League. The growth of the 'league' phenomenon, in fact, posed a threat to the electorates of both parties, although there was no evidence that they were suffering more than the Christian Democrats.

Thus, while the development of an electoral market place in the centre of the political spectrum is undoubtedly opening up electoral politics, the process is a slow and unsteady one. Voters in this part of the spectrum have certain features in common, but they are inclined to spread their votes in several directions. A part of the Socialist electorate is potentially available to vote for the PCI, and another part for the DC, while Republicans and Liberals tend towards alternatives among parties of the centre-right. This in the 1980s created a series of differentiated areas of competition. The PCI/PDS and the Socialist Party competed not only for each other's votes, but also for some of those which might go to the Greens or the Radicals. The Socialists themselves were competing in three segments of the market: on their left, with the PCI/PDS; towards the centre, both for voters inclined to vote for a lay centre party, and for voters willing to contemplate voting DC. The DC in turn overlapped not just with the centre and centre-left, but also with the right, where anti-communism, a degree of cynicism towards democratic politics, and a high level of clientelism are the key characteristics of the electorate. The minor lay parties themselves, including the newer ones like the Radicals and Greens, fight hard to differentiate themselves and rectify a cast of mind among many voters which tends to place them all in a single, rather uniform, political camp.

Under such circumstances, it is not surprising that Italian elections have failed to live up to the expectations raised by the appearance of greater competitiveness. Increasing voter mobility still washes around the edges of islands of stable attachments. The areas of competition have to date been inadequate to bring about real change. They also tend to be fragmented, and to concentrate on the narrow interface between pairs of parties or on issues which are not salient to a majority of the population. Like heated atoms, Italian voters therefore circulate with higher velocity and more energy, but in directions which seem to be mutually cancelling, or at least insufficiently clear to give any new impulse to the process of coalition-building. In so far as voters shift their votes, they do so by choosing new parties which cannot easily be used in assembling coalitions: Radicals, Greens, and most recently local parties such as the Lombard League.

Ironically, moreover, the most competitive area of the Italian electoral market continues to be the arc of parties which, for want of a narrower and more cohesive majority, are condemned to govern together. This not only limits the possibility that an alternative majority will emerge; it also undermines the stability of the existing majority. Paradoxically, twenty years ago, the instability of Italian coalitions was attributed, in a model of the party system known as *polarized pluralism* (examined in the following chapter), to centrifugal forces of electoral competition, and to fundamental antagonisms (religion, class conflict, attitudes to democracy) which separated the political parties. Today, it may be suggested that the problem is the increasing openness of the electoral market contained within the centre of the political spectrum, and the relative absence of electoral pay-offs for parties competing towards the left and right. It is to the problems of coalition-building thereby generated that we now turn.

Building Coalitions

In the absence of a workable parliamentary majority for any individual party, government in Italy is invariably based on *coalitions*. There are several ways in which parties can participate in coalitions. They may be present in the cabinet; they may form part of the parliamentary majority within which the government's programme is agreed, without actually holding any cabinet posts; or they may be willing to abstain in crucial confidence votes in Parliament, allowing the government to remain in office, despite voting against significant measures proposed by it. Thus, even though the Christian Democrat Party has been the backbone of every coalition, there are many permutations and styles of party coalition available. This section describes the principles on which they are built, and assesses the reasons for the extraordinarily high level of government turnover Italy has experienced since 1945.

In the forty-five years from the Liberation (April 1945) to the beginning of the 1990s, there were no fewer than fifty separate governments, presided over by nineteen different prime ministers. The average life of a government was thus just under eleven months. The longest-serving prime minister, De Gasperi (1945–53), headed eight governments. Aldo Moro (1963–8 and 1974–6) headed five. The record for the survival of a single government is held by Bettino Craxi, whose first government lasted three years, from August 1983 to July 1986.[23]

Eligibility

The major reason why coalition-building is difficult is the distinction between so-called democratic parties and those at the political extremes, whose commitment to democracy is alleged to be in doubt. This distinction arose at a very early stage in the post-war era, partly from the legacy of fascism, but mainly from the Cold War. While it has become gradually less important, especially in the 1980s, it has never quite disappeared. Even the transformation of the Communist Party into the PDS may not entirely dispel it, particularly since, as Chapter 4 demonstrates, there is substantial organizational continuity between the PCI and PDS, giving parties of the centre the opportunity to suggest that the Communist Party has simply changed its wrapping, but the contents remain the same. It was a distinction stressed above all by those who placed themselves squarely in the former camp, and who decided that they should not work with, or accept, the parliamentary support of parties whose commitment to the democratic system they considered suspect. The obvious candidates for exclusion were the Communist Party on the left, and the Neo-fascists and Monarchists on the right. However, in the early post-war years, the Socialist Party, anxious to preserve anti-fascist unity with the Communists, also found itself in this category, since its refusal to abandon its former alliance with the PCI made it unacceptable to the parties of the centre. In the 1950s and 1960s this attitude changed, and the Socialists came to be regarded as part of the democratic centre, becoming eligible for inclusion in the governing coalition, and indeed eventually becoming indispensable to its survival.

The branding of a party as 'anti-system' was in many respects an arbitrary matter, and the victims frequently protested their innocence. However, on the extreme right the links between former fascists and the MSI were extensive. In the case of the Communist Party various factors tended to undermine the party's democratic credentials: a history of close collaboration with Moscow, a commitment to a socialist economic model, and a party structure based for years on rigid adherence to the principles of democratic centralism. Moreover, comparative survey data regularly indicated that the ideological distance between left and right within the Italian electorate (as measured by self-placement on the left–right continuum) was wider than in most other European countries, suggesting that voters also conceived of politics in polarized categories.[24]

Once a party is successfully branded by its opponents as 'anti-democratic' it is very difficult to shake off the stigma, not so much among its own supporters or potential supporters in adjacent political space, but among the supporters of parties with whom a coalition might eventually be formed. The suspicion hanging over a party's democratic credentials thus becomes prejudicial to its chances of ever breaking through into the democratic part of the spectrum. This has created one of the major problems in Italian politics. A party like the Italian Communist Party—initially hostile to liberal democracy—can over time internalize the norms and values of such a system, and persuade large numbers of voters that it has done so, without ever quite becoming eligible for full coalition membership.[25]

The consequence of ruling out the parties at the ideological extremes as potential partners is that coalitions have to be constructed from a restricted democratic centre grouping which historically controlled around 60 per cent of the seats in Parliament, although this figure has fallen over time, and by 1992 was hovering only just above

50 per cent. Before 1960 the coalition involved only the Christian Democrats, Social Democrats, Republicans, and Liberals. From the beginning of the 1960s it included the Socialist Party as well, but within this expanded group the Christian Democrats continued to play the dominant role. Barring any major shift in the electoral support of the main parties, the DC could be replaced only if the Communists could woo away not just the Socialists, but some other parties of the centre too.

We should note finally, however, that the implicit assumption on which the discussion has so far been based—namely, that even if coalitions are unstable, they are at least self-sufficient while they are in office—is not entirely justified. The 'delimitation' or self-sufficiency of the majority has been a much-debated issue among the parties. Coalitions frequently come to depend, for their support on controversial issues, on parties which are not, in any of the three senses described above, participants in the coalition. Such dependence becomes necessary because the formal coalition has itself broken down on the given issue. One party or group within a party will rebel in a parliamentary division, either openly, or through the secret ballot or through absenteeism. In such cases, the parliamentary support or benevolent abstention of other parties, including those on the political extremes, may be necessary in order to get the proposals through parliament. But such support does not come without strings, and this gives all parties the possibility of at least some influence over the nature of coalition behaviour and parliamentary legislation whenever the formally defined coalition of parties is itself divided. This occurs quite frequently, and when combined with other aspects of parliamentary procedure it has given the Communist Party in particular a significant, if *concealed*, share in power which its normal role of public opposition belies.

Coalition-building conventions

Despite this last qualification the parties of the political centre are normally condemned to rule together. Given their diversity, and the frequency of government turnover, it is remarkable that in more than four decades they have succeeded in doing so with rather few complete breakdowns. Their success in sustaining coalitions is attributable mainly to the weight of past history: a broadly shared conviction that democracy must not be endangered by prolonged deadlock. This has given rise to certain conventions of coalition-building.

The first is that, if a government collapses, every effort will be made to construct a new one rather than resort to a general election. In a system in which coalitions are as brittle as those in Italy, a free fall into perpetual resort to elections would be a certain route to regime collapse. Irredeemable breakdown is therefore seen as a form of collective shame for the parties of the democratic arc, and a special stigma for any party which can be identified as particularly intransigent and hence culpable. To a large degree, this self-imposed discipline has worked. There has been no devaluation of the general election; between 1945 and 1992 Italy had only twelve general elections to the UK's thirteen, France's twelve, and West Germany's eleven. It is true that the parliaments elected between 1968 and 1983 did not run their full course, but all but the 1976–9 parliament ran for at least four of their allotted five years.

The second convention is that the President of the Republic (whose most important and politically influential task is to nominate a new prime minister, following consultations among party leaders) will always make extensive efforts to save a legislature and avoid premature elections. Although this occasionally involves controversial decisions, especially over the appointment of interim or caretaker prime ministers, it has, until recently, engendered remarkably little political controversy. This reflects not just the skill of most of the incumbents of the office, but also the acceptance by party politicians of the desirability that the president should play such a role. Some decisions *are* swallowed reluctantly, and do sometimes engender controversy.[26] But the need to embody the principle of stability and continuity in the figure of the presidency is rarely questioned.

The third principle—less explicitly and widely shared among the governing parties—is that if a coherent and self-sufficient coalition cannot be formed, the largest party, in practice Christian Democracy, holds office on a caretaker basis. Whether it does so in a disinterested and impartial way is sometimes disputed. Moreover, in recent years the Socialist Party has questioned the continuing validity of the principle.[27] Christian Democrat minority governments have nevertheless been an important mechanism by which the system has coped with periods of deadlock. Dissatisfied coalition partners have generally accepted their necessity, and have used them to maintain their distance from governments which they in practice have tolerated and held in office by selective abstention.

Coalition formulae

Despite the high turnover of governments, the scope for alternative formulae is extremely limited. As Table 3.3 shows, from 1947 to 1976 there were fundamentally only two formulae. The first, known as

'Centrism', included Christian Democrats, Social Democrats, Republicans, and Liberals. The second was the 'Centre-Left', in which the Socialists replaced the Liberals as the DC's main coalition partner, thus, at least in the 1960s, pushing the centre of gravity in the coalition from the centre, or even centre-right of the spectrum, towards the centre-left. In reality, the difference between the two was limited. It amounted to peripheral turnover rather than genuine alternation. In any case, in the 1970s the Liberal Party shrank almost to insignificance, and 'Centrist' coalitions no longer enjoyed a workable or even, after 1976, an arithmetic majority in Parliament. After 1979, in fact, the distinction between Centrism and the Centre-Left disappeared entirely, for both the Liberals *and* the Socialists were henceforth part of the ruling coalition: a formula known as the *Pentapartito*, or five-party alliance.

TABLE 3.3 *Coalition formulae in post-war Italy*

(*a*) *1945–1971*

Formula and its main party composition	Features
1945–7: Tripartism DC, PSI, PCI	Grand coalition of DC, PCI, PSI, and at various stages other smaller parties. Prime minister throughout: *De Gasperi*.
1947–53: Centrism PLI, DC, PRI, PSDI	Alliance of DC, PLI, PSDI, PRI. *Stable* phase of the alliance during the most tense phase of the Cold War. Parliamentary majority 362/574. Prime minister throughout: *De Gasperi*.
1953–60: Centrism DC, PLI, PSDI, PRI	Continued but less stable phase of the same alliance. Tensions between PSDI/DC-left and PLI/DC-right. Narrow parliamentary majority 300/590 (1953–8). Seven cabinets in 7 years; 5 different prime ministers.
1960–2: Transition PLI, DC, PRI, PSDI, PSI	Failure of attempt to extend coalition to extreme right (*Tambroni* experiment), followed by DC minority governments with no real parliamentary majority. PSI joins PLI (and PSDI, PRI) in 'benevolent abstention', under *Fanfani* premiership.

Formula and its main party composition	Features
1962–4: Centre-Left DC, PRI, PSDI, PSI	1. New alliance of DC, PRI, PSDI, PSI. Liberal Party excluded. 'Programmatic' phase, with PSI and DC-left in ascendancy.
1964–8: Centre-Left DC, PRI, PSDI, PSI	2. Stable phase of alliance, characterized by policy stalemate. Prime minister throughout: *Moro*. Two governments in four years. PSI accepts subordinate role to ensure coalition stability.
1968–71: Centre-Left DC, PRI, PSDI, PSI	3. New 'programmatic' phase. Tensions between PSI and DC-right over policy issues. First cautious opening to PCI in Parliament. Five governments and 3 prime ministers (*Leone, Rumor, Colombo*) in 4 years.

(b) 1972–1990

Formula and its main party composition	Features
1972–3: Centrism PLI, DC, PSDI, PRI	Return to government of Liberals in centrist alliance under Andreotti premiership. Narrow parliamentary majority 317/630. Prime minister: *Andreotti*.
1973–5: Centre-Left DC, PSDI, PRI, PSI	Resumption of Centre-Left, with increasingly benevolent Communist position in Parliament. Policy tension between PSI/DC. PSI eventually withdraws. Prime ministers: *Rumor, Moro*.
1976–9: National Solidarity DC, PCI, PSI	Two-stage extension of coalition to include PCI, first through benevolent abstention, then through inclusion in parliamentary majority. DC minority governments under *Andreotti*, but policy agreed with PCI, PSI, PSDI, PRI, PLI.

TABLE 3.3 (contd.)

Formula and its main party composition	Features
1979–92: *Pentapartito* PSI, DC, PLI, PSDI (PRI)	PCI returns to opposition. New coalition combining Centre-Left and Centrism in 5-party alliance of DC, PSI, PLI, PSDI, PRI. Initially very unstable, but increasingly cohesive. Succession of prime ministers including first non-Ch. Democrats: *Cossiga* (DC), *Forlani* (DC), *Spadolini* (PRI), *Fanfani* (DC), *Craxi* (PSI), *Goria* (DC); *De Mita* (DC), *Andreotti* (DC). Growing tensions in 1990–1, leading to Republican withdrawal in 1991 and major defeat for coalition in 1992 election.

third, far less exclusive, formula based on a 'grand coalition' covering most of the political spectrum. Such an arrangement is no less anomalous in Italy than elsewhere, and is only resorted to in extreme situations. Indeed, it is more incongruous than in Germany and Austria, where it has been based on an alliance of Christian Democrats and moderate Social Democrats, for in Italy it includes Communists as well. The formula was first used in the early post-war period, from 1945 to 1947. A modified version reappeared in the mid-1970s, in the shape of the 'National Solidarity' coalition, with the Communist Party joining the parliamentary majority, and even voting for the government in votes of confidence, though not holding seats in the Council of Ministers.[28]

'National Solidarity' owed its existence to two main factors. The first was the need to obtain Communist support for an incomes policy during the economic crisis of the mid-1970s. The price of this support was an acknowledgement of the PCI's credentials as an eligible partner within the coalition, an acknowledgement which the Communist leadership believed would confirm and justify the major changes in party doctrine and ethos which had occurred at an accelerating pace since the late 1960s. The Christian Democrats were unwilling to give the Communists the ultimate accolade of full cabinet status, but, albeit with some reluctance, were prepared to accept them as partners in the parliamentary majority.

The second, and more important, reason for the National Solidarity governments was the breakdown of the Centre-Left formula, and the impossibility of restoring Centrism. The Centre-Left became gradually less effective in the late 1960s and early 1970s. The Christian Democrats even tried briefly to restore Centrism in 1972–3, but opposition in their own ranks made this impossible, and later the formula became arithmetically unsustainable. From the late 1960s, the Socialists, exasperated by their failure to extract policy concessions from their coalition allies, began to think in terms of a left-wing alliance with the Communist Party: the *alternativa di sinistra*. Although this too was at the time arithmetically impossible, a first step towards it was to force the other parties to accept the Communists as an equal partner in the coalition.

The changing context of coalition-building in the 1980s

In the 1950s and 1960s coalition formulae, if not individual governments, were relatively stable. The country experienced a longish period of Centrist rule, ending in 1960, and, after a brief transition, an almost equally long period of Centre-Left rule from 1962 to 1971. Admittedly, within each of these two phases there were variations in the *stability* of the formula. The Centrist governments formed after 1953 were relatively divided, as were the Centre-Left governments formed after 1968. Nevertheless, the contrast with the 1970s, when the search for a stable formula became increasingly frenetic, is striking. Three times in succession Parliament had to be dissolved prematurely because of political deadlock, and three different coalition formulae —Centrism (1972–3), the Centre-Left (1973–5), and National Solidarity (1976–9)—were tried in quick succession.

The years since the early 1980s seem in some respects to represent a restoration of the relative stability of coalition formulae which Italy enjoyed in the 1950s and 1960s but the restoration is by no means complete. Two factors have changed. First, and most importantly, the electoral decline of the Christian Democrat Party has undermined its hegemonic rôle within the coalition. In the 1950s and 1960s, it dominated its coalition partners. It always held the premiership, and it expropriated the lion's share of the important ministerial posts, and most of the patronage available to central government. In the 1980s, to buy the loyalty of their allies, the Christian Democrats had to offer them considerably greater concessions. Thus the premiership passed firstly to the PRI and later to the PSI. Between June 1981 and April 1987 the DC only occupied the office for a nine-month caretaker interval. And although the so-called *polo laico* or 'lay' group of centre parties (PSI, PRI, PSDI, PLI) has not proved as cohesive as had been hoped at the beginning of the decade, it has negotiated a substantially increased share of ministerial posts. Since 1980 the lay parties have had as many Council of Ministers seats as the DC (together with the premiership), despite having little more than half the parliamentary strength of the Christian Democrats.

The second factor which differed in the 1980s was the new role of the PCI. Although, after 1979, the PCI returned to opposition, and suffered a long, slow, electoral decline, it did not return to ideological isolation. Its steady progress towards a position very similar to that of mainstream European social democracy continued. Its exclusion from government has therefore become an increasingly contingent matter, as other parties have sometimes been willing to acknowledge. At local level, moreover, the Communists have succeeded in establishing alliances with a wide range of parties, including Socialists and Christian Democrats. In Parliament, the party has been able to build implicit alliances with disgruntled elements of the coalition—most often those on the left of the Christian Democrat Party. And despite its frequent public arguments with Craxi's Socialists, there is always the hint that, with only slightly different parliamentary arithmetic, the Socialists might be willing to construct a left-alternative coalition—a hint which greatly strengthens the PSI in dealing with the DC.

Both these factors contributed to a more open style of coalition relationships, even before the electoral earthquake of 1992 threw established coalition relationships into question. The coalition formula remained largely unchanged from 1980 to 1992, but this concealed a more bargained set of inter-party relationships within Parliament, and within the government a more even balance between Christian Democracy and its partners. What occurred in the 1992 election seemed likely to further this tendency, if not actually to take the country back towards the open and inclusive coalitions of the 1970s. The urgent need for institutional reform, signalled by the electorate in both elections and referendums, once more made it necessary to contemplate coalition arrangements with the PCI/PDS. As party leaders searched for coalition solutions in the more difficult post-electoral environment, the case for renewed co-operation with the PCI/PDS to push through an overhaul at least of the electoral system increased substantially despite the slump in the PCI/PDS vote.

Italian coalitions and coalition theory

From the above discussion it should be evident that, while there are certain conventions governing coalition-building, these approximate more to self-imposed moral injunctions than formal rules. In fact, Italian coalition-building does not, as several writers have observed,[29] fit easily into any formal theory of coalition behaviour. Minimum winning coalitions are rare. In the case of the Chamber of Deputies elected in 1987, it would, in principle, have been possible to construct a coalition based on the DC and PSI alone, enjoying a majority of 26 (328 seats out of 630), instead of the 377-seat five-party coalition which was actually the norm. A left-orientated coalition of PCI, PSI, PSDI, Radicals, Proletarian Democrats, and Greens would have had a majority of 14, but was even less likely than a DC/PSI alliance.

Such coalitions are impractical for a number of reasons. Indiscipline in parliamentary majorities is frequent, so narrow majorities are dangerous. In any case, since majorities always straddle the centre, each faction within the Christian Democrat Party, and each minor party, has a different perception of where the centre of gravity in the coalition should lie, and hence of which party it wants in the coalition. Parties and factions also calculate that it may be better to have their immediate electoral rivals inside the coalition, where they assume some co-responsibility for government, than in opposition. The extreme example of this was the Historic Compromise, a coalition including well over four-fifths of the Parliamentary spectrum. It was the product of numerous factors, but the key element was the Socialist Party's determination to co-opt the Communist Party into the majority, both to increase the influence of the left as a whole, and to associate the PCI with the responsibilities of power, and hence stem the flow of votes from PSI to PCI.

Understanding the construction of Italian coalitions is thus a complex process. History, ideology, intra-party conflicts, and institutional rules all play a role. Broad ideological choice explains the nature of the centre-located coalition by which Italy is normally governed, and complex considerations of internal coalition balance explain why it is not of the minimum-winning variety. The picture becomes even more complex when explaining the distribution of power *inside* particular coalitions. First, cabinet posts vary considerably—both between themselves and over time—in perceived importance. The post of prime minister, and to a lesser extent deputy prime minister, are of high visibility and prestige, as are the Ministries of Foreign Affairs, the Treasury, Finance, Interior, and Defence. Other ministries are of value for their patronage potential: Health, Education, Posts and Telecommunications, Agriculture, and Public Works fall into this category—just before an election, they can be of great value to a minister or his faction.

Clearly politicians have some broad sense of relative value when distributing cabinet posts between the parties of the coalition,[30] but exactly how a given distribution is calculated depends upon mutually perceived strength at any particular moment. Clearly, during the 1980s the Christian Democrat Party felt itself to be somewhat more vulnerable to the demands of its coalition partners than in the 1950s and 1960s. It yielded not only the prime minister's office (see Chapter 7, below) but also a larger share of Council of Ministers seats. As Table 3.4 shows, in the 1963–8 Parliament the DC normally held over 60 per cent of posts in the Council of Ministers, while DC deputies constituted 67 per cent of the Centre-Left's 386-seat Chamber of Deputies majority group. In the 1980s, in contrast, its share of ministerial posts fell to 54 per cent and later 48 per cent, while its share of the Chamber of Deputies majority fell to only 62 per cent. The Socialist Party, meanwhile, saw its ministerial presence rise considerably more than proportionately to its increased parliamentary support; it obtained ten seats (out of thirty-two) in the 1989 Andreotti cabinet (including deputy prime minister, Foreign and Finance ministers) against only six (out of thirty) in 1983, and six (out of twenty-six) in 1963.

TABLE 3.4 *The shares of the DC and its lay coalition partners in the Chamber of Deputies majority and the Italian Council of Ministers*

	1963	1983	1989
DC			
Deputies	260 (67%)	225 (61%)	234 (62%)
Council of Ministers posts[a]	16 (62%)	16 (54%)	16 (48%)
Lay parties[b]			
Deputies	126 (33%)	141 (39%)	143 (38%)
Council of Ministers posts	10 (38%)	14 (46%)	17 (52%)

[a] For 1963 the first Moro government (formed Dec. 1963); for 1983 the first Craxi government (formed Aug 1983); for 1989 the sixth Andreotti government (formed Aug. 1989).

[b] In 1963 PSI, PRI, and PSDI; in 1983 and 1989 PSI, PRI, PSDI, and PLI. Note that in 1991 the Republican Party withdrew from the coalition; Prime Minister Andreotti took charge of the two formerly PRI-held ministries, thereby changing the balance back to a small DC majority in the Council of Ministers.

It can be concluded, therefore, that although there is a broadly proportionalist mentality in the distribution of seats in Italian governments, there are no precise rules. Parties bargain with each other and with the incoming prime minister, and occasionally engage in a game of controlled brinkmanship. Once the general decision to form a coalition has been taken between party leaders, no one will want the decision to be reversed, but those who feel themselves to be in the strongest political and electoral position (i.e. *in extremis* those who are least afraid of incurring electoral disapproval if there should be deadlock and a fresh election) are likely to be able to hold out longest for an improved share of ministerial posts.

4

Party Organization

Parties are important elements of the institutional landscape of liberal democracy. They aggregate interests into coherent programmes; they simplify choices for voters; they socialize voters, activists, and politicians into the political system; and they provide the personnel who compete for office. How effectively they carry out these functions is closely linked to how they are organized. Indeed, to understand how policy is made in most complex party systems it is necessary to examine not only the relations between parties but also the internal operation of individual parties. That, in turn depends on two main factors: the formal rules governing party life, and the behaviour of the individuals who inhabit the party as leaders, activists, and members.

In the case of political parties, the balance between these two dimensions is somewhat different from that in institutions which are more clearly defined by the (externally set) constitutional and legal order, such as legislatures, executives, the administration, or local government. Parties tend to get little attention in constitutional texts, and are little regulated by law, except in connection with election expenses and party finance when public subsidies are involved. Behavioural norms and internal rules—always less binding than external ones—are therefore the most important elements in the power structure of political parties.

These observations certainly apply in the Italian case. The constitution's few references to political parties provide no real constraint. Art. 49 simply legitimizes parties as a mechanism through which there is competition for public office, while arts. 72 and 82 refer to the role of parliamentary *groups*—clearly intended to be, in almost all cases, *party* groups. Legislation introduced in 1974 in the wake of a major financial scandal, and amended in the early 1980s, allowed for the public financing of political parties.[1] However, even though by 1985 each citizen was contributing some 1,500 lire (just over $1) to the upkeep of Italian parties, this legislation has not been thought to have contributed greatly to the transparency of sources of party finance or the probity in office of party representatives.[2]

To understand Italian parties, therefore, it is necessary to look at the internally set rules and behavioural conventions governing party life, rather than legislation laid down in the public domain. This also means dropping the assumption, widely held when studying the structure and operation of the party system as a whole, that Italian parties are unitary actors. They clearly are not. Parties which have long been institutionalized in a pluralist society, as in contemporary Italy, and which have developed complex relationships with interest groups on the one side, and the machinery of the state on the other, are far more than agents for mobilizing particular programmes. They are arenas in which competing demands vie for position, and avenues through which those who seek political office can realize their career aspirations.

The consequences for party cohesion and purposiveness vary considerably from party to party. In some, leaders are insulated from party pressures once in public office. In others the party as an organization and a decision-making unit plays a more important role, and leaders in Parliament or government are less likely to have a free hand. If, for example, there are different party leaderships corresponding to different institutional arenas—the party as an organization, the party in Parliament, the party in government, the party at subnational levels—then policy-making is likely to involve frequent interaction between these leadership groups. Parties may then be divided between factional groups which compete for power in each institutional arena. Factional competition may generate conventions and expectations about discipline and authority which make strong leadership difficult. Such a division of labour may reflect wider structural features of the political system; federalism, for example, has obvious consequences for the cohesion of parties. It may also reflect conscious choices made by political parties about the distribution of intra-party authority. Given these permutations, different parties in the same political system, and even employing broadly the same formal party structures, may, as in Italy, have different patterns of internal authority.[3]

The Italian Christian Democrat Party, and to a lesser extent its coalition partners, have deep internal divisions. Exactly what they are divided about is a complicated matter, explored later in this chapter. The key point here is that divisions between different institutional arenas, and between different factional groups, ensure that authority to make policy is rarely delegated to a cohesive leadership group in government. Rather, policy-making is a continuous process of reference back and forth between party organization, parliamentary group, government, and individual faction leaders.

Not all parties are of this type, however. Some are obviously too small to have complex articulated divisions. Moreover, the Communist Party was traditionally built on a highly centralized structure of authority, concentrated in the hands of those who control the party bureaucracy. Even before the transformation into the PDS, this had begun to change rapidly, but its persistence over several decades reflected a clear preference by the party for unity and discipline over freedom of discussion and the institutionalization of internal dissent. As we shall see below, this difference between the PCI and the parties of government has been reflected not just in different patterns of authority but also in different attitudes to party membership, activism, and grass-roots organization.

The contrast between the Christian Democrats on the one hand and the Communists on the other has been accentuated by the lack of alternation in power. The PCI could maintain its cohesion for so long partly because, at national level, it did not have to face the dilemmas posed by a proper role in government. The strains that this role places on the relationship between the Parliamentary leadership on one side, and party officials, workers, and activists on the other, only began to emerge in the PCI in the late 1970s, during the National Solidarity coalition, and then only in attenuated form.

The Christian Democrat Party, in contrast, has faced the same tensions faced by dominant parties in other systems—the Japanese LDP, for example, or the Indian Congress. Both nationally and locally, it has become the channel through which those who seek power for its own sake can obtain office and further their careers. And as a party whose *raison d'être* is management of the status quo rather than transformative ideological purpose, it has a relatively weak mechanism for filtering those attracted to it, and a relatively loose ideology to hold itself together. It is thus dominated by professional politicians: entrepreneurs, attracted to politics as much by considerations of career as programme or ideology. This may be true of more political parties everywhere than political scientists sometimes admit, but in few European countries is it as clear as in Italy.

This chapter explores the implications of these issues. It begins by considering the formal structure of power in various parties, and the organizational resources each enjoys. It then examines the informal structure, especially the causes of factionalism, and its consequences for the representative process and the programmes parties assemble. Finally, the chapter analyses the implications of the Italian style of party organization for models of the party system which have emerged in debates on that system over the last two decades.

Formal Party Organization

A common model

Italian parties are built on what looks at first sight like a common structure. Classic Duvergian distinctions[4] between cadre, branch, cell, and militia structures have become largely irrelevant over the years, as all parties, including those originally conceived to conspire against liberal-democratic institutions, have instead adapted to them. Thus, although the location of *effective* power varies, especially between the Communist Party and the main parties of the governing coalition, the formal organizational model parallels the tiers of Italian government: municipal, provincial, regional, and national. The grass-roots unit of party organization is the *sezione* (section), which in small communities corresponds to the *comune*, or municipal tier of government, and in larger towns and cities to wards and quarters. Above the section is the provincial party organization, which has traditionally been the most important tier below the national level, since it generally controls, either directly or through a special committee, the party's representatives in the provincial capital, and plays a major role in designating candidates in elections. It is in the provincial capital that the most important posts of power are available—city mayors, and the *assessori* (executives elected from and responsible to the city council) who are in charge of major departments of city administration.[5] In recent years the regional tier has become more important, as has the region as a unit of government, and it is now generally regarded as the filter through which delegates are selected to a party's national congress, but the provincial city organization remains the key subnational party unit.

At the national level, party organization is built around the congress, a gathering generally held every two or three years. The congress is a major trauma in party life, and not something to which parties can subject themselves annually, as in British political life. It is a fierce set-piece competition for control of the levers of party power. It normally elects a ruling council or assembly which meets regularly between congresses. It also elects, either directly or indirectly, an executive to run the party organization, headed by the national party secretary—in effect the party leader. From the congress major changes may emerge in the influence of individuals or groups which have a subsequent bearing on relations with other parties. If the party in question is in government, the congress may even affect the survival of the coalition itself.

The important point is that most Italian parties are built on a *direct* structure of party power, in which even those in elected representative office have to pay close attention to the balance of power inside the organizational structure. At least in formal terms, power emanates—with the qualifications added below—from the rank-and-file membership. It is from *party* bodies—whether nationally or locally—that electoral resources are managed, that official party statements emanate, that candidates are designated for elections, that ministers, mayors, *assessori*, etc. are selected when the party is in government, and, last but by no means least, that party nominees to public agencies, hospital boards, management teams, etc. are designated. Control of, or a major share in, the party organization is therefore a key political resource.

Naturally, because of the prestige, power, and remuneration involved in public office-holding, there is substantial overlap between top party leaders, the parliamentary class, and, for parties of government, ministerial office. No party (not even the PCI/PDS) is a classic apparatus party led from the party bureaucracy, dispatching mandated recallable delegates to Parliament and government. On day-to-day matters, the leaders of a party's parliamentary group, or the representatives of a party in national or local government, take decisions. On bigger questions, however, especially those connected with coalition strategy, the ultimate arena in which conflicts over power and policy are settled is that *inside* the party decision-making machinery. Members of the government, or of the legislature, may have a strong influence there, but governments will not last long, nor will groups of back-bench members of Parliament enhance their re-election prospects, if they try systematically to go against the party. Politicians thus have to maintain a close eye on their party base, and can never afford to neglect local political leaders and the need for a strong following among rank-and-file members.

The fact that power emanates from the rank and file does not, however, imply that there is a high level of participation and activism. On the whole there is not. Most studies of Italian parties—with the partial exception of those of the PCI—suggest active rank-and-file participation is fairly low, other than at election times and just before party congresses. Most members of most parties probably sustain little interest in questions of party policy, whether locally or nationally. The closest they generally come to expressing views on policy questions is to support the broad outlook of a particular group in pre-congressional debates. Because of the way congress debate is organized, this is a fairly remote and low-level form of involvement in the policy process. Pre-congressional debates focus on general statements of party strategy ('motions' or 'theses') which are either platitudinous or deal with questions of coalition strategy, rather than policy detail. Policy itself is determined by those elected to local and national party office, in consultation with outside party consultants.

Even in the PCI, activism was relatively constrained, with perhaps only one member in five or fewer attending local party meetings with any regularity. The PCI/PDS has admittedly come closer than the other parties to the participatory ideal of the mass-party model. In recent years, with the growth of less inhibited internal debate, and the end of democratic centralism, rank-and-file participation has, despite the party's declining membership, become more meaningful. However, most activity at the grass roots is still related to the party festivals and membership drives—activity which has little immediate bearing on intra-party policy-making.[6]

However, it would be wrong not to acknowledge the significance of the comparative solidity of post-war Italian party organization, and the positive contribution it has made to the consolidation of Italian democracy. Almost 4 million Italians have been in the habit of joining political parties (about one in every ten voters), and between them the parties still muster over 25,000 local party sections. Parties are therefore a major social institution linking society to the state. In so far as strongly entrenched parties with close organic links with society are important in locking voters and interest groups into stable patterns of political affiliation, it may fairly be claimed that Italian parties since 1945 have overcome many of the failings of the earlier party system. For an important element in the failure of mass democracy after World War I was the organizational weakness of the main parties, and the lack of solid ties between parties and society. Today, of course, this consolidation role is less necessary, but in the 1950s and 1960s it was vital in helping Italian democracy through difficult periods.[7]

Admittedly, in so far as the strongest and best-organized Italian party has always been the PCI, it might be argued that the organizational strength of communism was a part of the *problem* of democratic consolidation, rather than a part of the solution to it. The PCI itself, however, always denied that it was an anti-system party, and in the 1970s and 1980s, even before the transformation into the PDS, that claim grew harder to deny, particularly in view of the party's moderate and conciliatory stance through the profound economic crises of the 1970s. The party's firm grip on the left—both through its control of the main trade-union confederation CGIL, and through its wider party presence—was an important restraining influence, restricting the scope for destabilizing radical movements, and giving government and business a reliable interlocutor with which compromises could be made.

TABLE 4.1 *Party membership in Italy's main parties, 1950–1990*

	DC	PSI	PCI/PDS
1950	855,291	700,000	2,112,593
1955	1,189,348	770,000	2,090,006
1960	1,470,923	489,337	1,792,974
1965	1,613,314	437,458	1,615,296
1970	1,738,996	506,533	1,507,047
1975	1,732,501	539,339	1,730,453
1976	1,365,187	509,388	1,814,262
1977	1,201,707	482,916	1,814,154
1978	1,355,423	479,769	1,790,450
1979	1,383,650	472,544	1,761,297
1980	1,320,000	502,211	1,751,323
1981	1,385,141	508,898	1,714,052
1982	1,361,066	541,526	1,637,751
1983	1,375,687	554,389	1,635,264
1984	1,382,278	573,590	1,619,940
1985	1,444,568	516,265	1,595,281
1986	1,395,784	589,697	1,551,576
1987	1,812,201	616,071	1,508,140
1988	1,887,615	640,760	1,462,281
1989	1,875,324	663,212	1,421,230
1990	1,959,735	669,003	1,264,790

Sources: 1950–85: David Hine, 'Italy: Parties and Party Government under Pressure', in Alan Ware (ed.), *Political Parties: Electoral Change and Structural Response* (Oxford, 1987), 81. 1985–90: for the DC, data supplied by Signora D'Agostino, Ufficio tesseramento, DC, Rome; for the PCI/PDS, P. Ignazi, *Dal PCI al PDS* (Bologna, 1992), 101; for the PSI, data supplied by Dr Moraldi, Ufficio tesseramento, PSI, Rome.

Variations on the organizational pattern

The Communist Party

The PCI had, and to a large extent the PDS still has, a formidable organizational presence. It has been extensively studied over many years, and it is possible here only to summarize the dimensions of the edifice. Until 1989 the party never had fewer than 1.5 million members. It has a strong presence in the trade-union movement, especially in the largest of the three main union confederations. It has a major stake in the co-operative movement, and in various other commercial enterprises. It mounts an ambitious programme of summer festivals which are a cross between popular cultural gatherings and political propaganda. It runs a daily newspaper, *L'unità*, and other periodicals. And it takes very seriously its role of political education and stimulant to social and economic policy research, running regular party schools, research institutes, conferences, and so on. Throughout the 1980s, the PCI's organizational effort remained impressive. There was no dramatic collapse of morale, membership, and electoral support to parallel what occurred in France and Spain during the same period.[8]

Nevertheless, in recent years the party has faced major organizational problems. At the root of its difficulties lies the increasing unsuitability, in modern conditions, of the 'mass-party' model conceived by Palmiro Togliatti in the mid-1940s. Imported from Gramscian notions of hegemony through a 'war of position', the model suggested that a working-class party could build up such a powerful organizational presence in society that eventually its cultural, ideological, administrative, and labour-market strength would enable power to pass naturally (and non-violently) into the hands of the (communist-led) working class. Both ideologically and organizationally such a model now seems redundant. Ideologically, as we shall see below, few in the party are any longer clear what a classless society would look like, but most are certain that neither Leninist nor Gramscian notions of how to reach it lead to anything but shabby authoritarianism. Organizationally, such a party appears increasingly out of character with the pluralist and individualist society Italy had become by the 1980s.

In reality, the PCI was always out of character with a substantial part of post-war Italian society. On the positive side, it stressed honest and effective government in its local strongholds, and displayed an organizational efficiency and a cohesion lacking in most other parties. On the negative side, its ideas on economic management and government intervention seemed at odds with the dynamism of the private sector and more generally with the individualist ethos of Italian society. For three decades, the party's political and administrative virtues were sufficient—in the eyes of over a quarter of the electorate—to overcome what (at least on a short-term reading of the administrative capacities of the Italian state) must be considered the incongruous view that organized planning from the centre could be superior to the individualist ethos. By the 1980s, however, this illusion was becoming harder to sustain. Italy's working class was becoming more prosperous and internally diversified. Workplace ties and solidarity were being undermined. The traditionally solid agricultural day-labourers and share-croppers were disappearing. Their replacement by new members from the white-collar urban middle strata brought into the party recruits with a more tenuous commitment to repetitive organizational party tasks like selling party newspapers and making pasta for party rallies, and far less need of the networks of social support (working men's clubs, sporting and cultural associations, co-operatives, etc.) traditionally provided by the party. In a more affluent and consumer-orientated society, these things were increasingly available to the rank and file through the private market. Similarly, the increasing range and pluralism of the media—a multitude of television and radio stations, and a flourishing and diversified popular press—weakened the importance of old-fashioned face-to-face political communications through party meetings, workplace trade-union contacts, etc.[9]

These changes in the social context in which the party operated were paralleled by changes in the political context as it adapted to the liberal-democratic framework. By doing so, it increased its legitimacy, and thereby probably made marginal voters more willing to vote for it, but equally it surrendered much of its missionary evangelism, and gave committed party activists less of a reason for the sacrifices they had traditionally made to keep the party organization in peak condition. Its sense of clear and unequivocal moral purpose, and of the linear inevitability of its mission to reshape society—the communist *diversità*—was far harder to sustain once the party implicitly acknowledged that it was a competitor in a liberal-democratic game along with all the others.

It became even harder to sustain after what were widely regarded as the mistakes in political strategy of the 1970s. The period of 'National Solidarity', as we have seen, proved not to be an intermediate phase preceding communist entry into government in an unbroken upward trajectory of electoral support. Not only was the party relegated to opposition throughout the 1980s, but it showed, for the first time ever, that electorally it could go backwards as well as forwards. Indeed, all elections since 1979 have been a dogged rearguard action to minimize electoral losses, as the party's vote has drifted back first to the levels of the early 1960s, and in 1992 to a lower level than at any point since 1945. By the early 1990s there even seemed some prospect, indeed, that the PDS could be overtaken, electorally, by the PSI, returning the party to the position of subordination on the left that it last faced in 1946. Togliatti's 'mass party', capable of transforming voters into sympathizers, sympathizers into members, and members into activists on a mass scale, thereby protecting the party from the vicissitudes of electoral fortune, had shown itself to be incapable of operating under modern conditions.[10]

There are, therefore, many dimensions to the organizational difficulties which the Communist Party has faced in recent years. The end result—even before the change of name to the PDS—was to lower drastically the boundary wall between the party and the rest of Italian society. 'Being a communist' meant much less than in the past, and this damaged the sense of discipline, commitment, and organizational uniqueness on which the party traditionally depended. Membership declined both quantitatively (from a peak of 1.8 million in the mid-1970s to only 1.4 million in 1990), and probably also qualitatively. As participation and activism declines, numbers are kept up by recruiting whole families, and the membership ages through the low appeal of its youth sections.

Until the end of the 1980s, these problems were worrying, but the party faced genteel decline—managed in a fairly orderly fashion—rather than dramatic rout. However, the revolution in Eastern Europe in 1989 looked set to change this, threatening to leave the PCI attached to names and symbols (if not to the ideological essence) of positions now ostentatiously abandoned by the political systems in the East. To prevent events from overtaking the PCI leadership's cautious efforts to push the party towards an essentially social-democratic position, Achille Occhetto, who became party secretary in 1988, gambled on a complete relaunch of the party, under a new name and programme, as a more broadly based party of 'progressives and leftists'. What such a change might consist of we shall see below, but at the start of the 1990s the real aim was damage limitation rather than expansionist new departure.

Christian Democracy

Although the formal architecture of Christian Democrat organization looks very similar to that of the PCI, in practice intra-party life is quite different, first because the social bases on which the party was built are far more diverse than those of the PCI, and secondly because factionalism has created a different relationship between leadership and base, and a different meaning to membership.

In the early post-war era the DC was built as much around the social networks of the Church as around a solid base of grass-roots party sections. The lay arm of the Church, Catholic Action, was a key asset, giving the party a broad inter-class base. So were the Catholic trade-union confederation (CISL) and the Association of Christian Workers (ACLI). Over time, however, the first and last of these organizations declined very markedly, while the CISL took its distance from the party. The unfavourable ratio of members to voters, compared to the PCI, and the undesirability of depending on the Church, persuaded the party leadership to build up the party organization—a policy that bore some fruit in the 1950s, especially under the energetic secretaryship of Amintore Fanfani (party secretary 1954–9). By 1959 membership had reached 1.6 million, remaining at around this level for the next decade. In the 1970s it rose further still, reaching a peak of almost 1.9 million by 1973, giving the DC, at least on paper, more members than the PCI.[11]

In practice, however, the *quality* of Christian Democrat membership has always been lower than in the PCI. Research suggests that the level of participation and activism among Christian Democrat members is consistently below that of the PCI membership.[12] Grass-roots organizations in the DC are less well equipped than those in the PCI, in terms of offices, printing capacity, meeting rooms, etc.; they raise fewer of their own funds (and receive correspondingly more from party candidates and central party sources); they spend a greater proportion of their funds on election campaigning (and have less to spare for other local party work); and they hold fewer meetings and other activities.[13] This shows up most clearly in the annual budgets published by the central organizations of the two parties, which indicate that the PCI is able to raise more than twice as much, in membership dues and fund-raising campaigns, as is the DC.[14]

Much of the explanation for this lies in the geographical distribution of the membership. The highest concentration is found in the south of the country, not an area marked by high levels of associational energy or a sophisticated electorate,[15] nor indeed the area in which historically the DC has won its largest share of the popular vote. It is clear that in the south the motivation to join the DC is often connected less with broad political beliefs, or a desire to further the wider aims of the party, than with particular and highly personal considerations—jobs, favours, promotion, benefits—that stem from the local political world. This clientelist basis is also a reflection of grass-roots struggles for control of the party machinery. The more members a group can recruit, the better it is placed. Frequently, accusations of inflated membership figures emerge, especially in the run-up to party congresses, and from time to time local party branches have to be closed down or placed under the control of centrally imposed commissioners. But false members are probably less of a distortion of the true state of DC organization than members recruited by family, friends, and employers who are entirely passive—there simply to swell a faction's vote power.

A further example of this—again demonstrating the lack of congruence between DC membership figures and the predominant local mores—is found in the surprisingly high level of *female* party members in the DC, especially in the south. In 1986, 40 per cent of the DC members in the south and in Sicily and Sardinia were women, compared to an average (itself high compared with other Italian parties) of about 33 per cent in the centre and north. Given the considerably more advanced state of the feminist cause in the north, this is clearly counter-intuitive, and seems best explained by the tendency for males to enrol members of their family for reasons connected with the strengthening of internal party power groups.[16]

As a mechanism for involving its members in the life of the party, and maintaining a high level of commitment and activism, the Christian Democrat Party organization is thus clearly less effective than that of the PCI/PDS. Above all, this stems from the different functions the two organizations perform, reflecting the different positions of the two parties in the political system. The Christian Democrat Party has been permanently in power. It therefore faces complex questions about the designation of representatives to public office at all levels from the Council of Ministers downwards. Because of the extensive patronage networks linking parties to the public sector, the party is also an arena in which pressures and demands from a great variety of sources are focused. Inevitably, as a permanent party of government, it attracts to it all those individuals and groups who have some special sectoral or personal demand which they perceive to be better satisfied by going straight to whomsoever is in power, than by seeing their demand integrated into a broader programme of the party that—on wider political grounds—they might otherwise have preferred. Correspondingly, any party which has been in government so long—whatever its record—is tarnished in many eyes with policy failure, and is perhaps less likely to attract to its ranks those with a sense of reforming purpose and evangelical policy idealism.

The DC organization thus has to cope with these particularist roles alongside the more general task of propaganda, electoral work, programmatic commitment and rank-and-file activism. And it has to do so with a mix of policy activists in which the balance is tipped towards power-seekers rather than policy idealists. For the Communist Party, in contrast, it is possible to concentrate far more of its energies into the party organization's activist role, not least because it faces few distractions posed by the dilemmas of power and government.

Periodically, the Christian Democrat Party passes through a phase of collective soul-searching in which it reassesses organizational questions and tries to allocate a higher priority to the task of organizational efficiency. Under Fanfani's leadership in the 1950s, this clearly bore some fruit. More recently, the party has passed through two phases during which it has tried to reform and improve grass-roots party life by rooting out some of the worst excesses of inflated membership, and by attempting to concentrate the attention of party officials and workers less on internal power struggles, and more on efforts to improve the external image and standing of the party in the wider electorate. The first of these phases coincided with the Zaccagnini secretaryship from 1975 to 1980; the second with the early years of the De Mita secretaryship from 1982 to 1989. In both cases, the efforts followed periods in which the party had been severely damaged by scandal emanating from internal power struggles. As we shall see later in this chapter, however, neither attempt was particularly successful in changing the nature of internal party life.

The Socialist Party

The organization of the PSI is an instructive hybrid. In scope, it stands somewhere between the mass organizations of the PCI and DC and the modest machinery of the minor parties. In style, it is a combination of the activism of the PCI and the power-broking of the DC. From fairly early in the post-war period it was clear that the PSI would be unable to match the PCI's formidable party machinery. Once the main trade-union confederation had fallen into the hands of the Communists, the heartland of the labour movement was lost. Party membership by 1950 stood at only one-third that in the Communist Party, and the ratio between the two has rarely moved far from that figure over the following four decades. The Socialist Party lacked the network of flanking organizations (workplace cells, union branches, co-operatives, farmers' organizations, Church organizations) that assisted the PCI and DC. It could muster a branch in most Italian towns and cities, but its branches were smaller and poorer than those of the PCI, and considerably less active.[17]

As in the case of the Christian Democrat Party, moreover, the largest proportion of party members has come to be concentrated in the south. This was not the case in the early post-war years, and stands in sharp contrast to the geographical distribution of Communist membership. In the 1950s, only 25 per cent of PSI members were in the south and islands, the great majority being concentrated in the industrial triangle, where the party still had some claim to be a classical social-democratic party based on the blue-collar working class. By the 1970s, 50 per cent of the party's members came from the southern half of the country, with regions like Sicily and the poor and backward

Calabria having far more members than industrialized Piedmont. The class composition of the membership also shifted, with a substantial rise in the proportion coming from middle- and lower-middle-class backgrounds, and from public-sector activities such as the bureaucracy, municipal services, hospitals, broadcasting, etc.[18]

The reason for this change was simple. The longer the PSI stayed in government, the more it attracted to itself the same groups and individuals attracted to the Christian Democrat Party, and the more difficult it became—as long as the PSI was so evidently in a subordinate position to the DC—to retain those ideologically committed party activists who would maintain the effectiveness of party organization on the ground. The PSI thus faced the same dilemma as the DC, and with the same consequences.

As in the DC, such changes brought forth regular denouncements of the alleged degeneration and decline of grass-roots commitment.[19] However, to some degree at least the Socialists have, under the leadership of Bettino Craxi, gone beyond this neurosis. Their more recent model of party organization no longer lays such emphasis as in the past upon an extensive network of party branches, an army of professional officials, a high level of membership, and active rank-and-file participation. Instead, the ideal has become the *federal* party assembling under the PSI banner a wide range of interests, clubs, and groups. The latter are, in effect, swallowed whole without much effort to transform the individuals they contain directly into active party members. Traditional class-party images and structures—the hammer-and-sickle emblem, the *compagno* (comrade) ethos, the central committee, the union link—have all been set aside. Today the party attempts to communicate with its electorate not through this traditional mechanism, but through the media and advertising, and indirectly through non-party interest groups and associations which it attempts to line up on its side. Reforms to the party structure have incorporated this at the highest level. The long-standing central committee—the body, elected by the national congress, which was entrusted with major party decisions—has been abandoned in favour of a *national assembly*, nearly one-third of whose roughly 400 members are drawn from education, science and technology, business organizations, the professions, cultural circles, and so on.[20]

Such a change is, however, less interesting because it gives power to this or that social group in the party's decision-making structures than because it projects a message about the party to the voters—especially the lay middle-class voters it has been seeking to attract. The PSI has, in practice, proved itself even less capable of living up to the ideal of the federal party of the 1980s than to that of the class-based branch party of committed activists of the earlier post-war decades. The reality on the ground is a party of professional politicians and elected officials. Like most of the other minor parties of government, the PSI raises just enough resources, in virtue of its government role, to keep a minimal electoral organization in being. The party has a larger network than other minor parties, but it cannot come close to the social presence even of the DC, let alone that of the Communist Party. This has not prevented the balance of electoral advantage moving in the Socialist Party's direction, as it has appeared to do in the last decade. But where this occurs, it demonstrates the long-term erosion of advantages enjoyed by parties with strong organization, as the linkage between parties and society comes to depend on factors other than a mass army of party activists.

The Informal Power Structure

While the formal structure of Italian parties tends to follow a common pattern mirroring the representative institutions of the state, the *informal* power structure varies considerably, and raises complex issues of party democracy and internal party cohesion. In the PCI/PDS, a key concern for many years has been how to relax the grip of democratic centralism, and thereby enhance the party's democratic credentials, without slipping into the state of open factional warfare that has periodically dogged the DC and PSI. In these latter parties factionalism has been an endemic problem with a profound effect on the cohesion of coalitions and the ability of governments to push their programmes through into legislative form.

In the early post-war years both the Communists and Socialists employed a system of democratic centralism which made both parties vulnerable to accusations that, since they did not seem to practise genuine democracy inside their own organizations, they could not be trusted to respect the principles of a democratic society. In the Communist Party, while there were discernibly different philosophical outlooks present in the party leadership, rank-and-file members had few formal opportunities to express preferences between them, and the party maintained at least the façade of monolithic unity until relatively recently. In contrast, by the end of the 1950s, the Socialist Party had abandoned democratic centralism, and thereafter tolerated a fairly open system of competing power groups. In this sense, albeit with qualifications, the PSI could claim for many years to have been a more democratic party than the PCI. But it was also a far less united one, and the factionalism it displayed was widely seen as one of its major difficulties, projecting to the electorate the image of a divided, uncertain, and somewhat corrupt party, consuming in internal power struggles resources which might have been better deployed in competition with other parties.

The DC has suffered even more than the PSI from factionalism. Indeed, it is probably one of Europe's most divided parties. Its internal conflicts absorb prodigious amounts of time and energy, and make party management an extraordinarily difficult art. In many respects, the DC is better understood not as a single party but as a federation of factions, each of which, in government, has its own demands and interests to promote. Moreover, whereas in recent years the PSI has been able to overcome some of the worst effects of factionalism, the DC has not been able to do so, despite periodic attempts to boost the authority of its leaders and impose greater control from the centre.

Leadership and base in the PCI/PDS

The democratic centralism of the PCI's internal organization enabled the leadership to keep a firm grip on the party for many years after 1945. Those in charge drew their power from membership of the strong professional bureaucratic apparatus. The Communist parliamentary group overlapped with the apparatus, but was decidedly subordinate to it, as was the phalanx of officials at provincial level whose careers depended on not falling out with the leadership. The apparatus thus had ample resources to recruit and co-opt from below, to set the party agenda, to control debate, and to select candidates for elections.

Nevertheless, democratic centralism rarely had to be enforced by coercion. Bureaucratic manipulation alone did not maintain the commitment and activism of one and a half million members of the party. Shared values and an acceptance of the need for party discipline—particularly where party unity allowed the PCI to contrast itself favourably with the factionalized parties of the centre—was normally enough. When tensions arose, the bearers of new ideas or demands were frequently co-opted into the apparatus rather than suppressed. In a pluralist society democratic centralism could not be sustained indefinitely against the wishes of the rank and file without atrophication of party life. As memories of the anti-fascist resistance and of the labour conflicts of the 1950s faded into the past, the leadership increasingly accepted the need to test out its ideas among the rank and file, and to preface any major new initiatives with a careful, if sometimes manipulated, grass-roots debate.

Even if it had wanted to, then, the PCI could not insulate itself from the influences of social change and especially from the effects of the new social movements (feminism, gay rights, environmentalism, etc.) which emerged in the 1970s. Much of the party's post-1968 generation was affected by these movements, and twenty years on this group is now rising towards positions of influence at the top of the party hierarchy.[21] There has thus been a long-term shift in power relations and in the style of intra-party debate. It has been a gradual evolution, making clear turning points difficult to identify. Party leaders have had to listen increasingly carefully to sentiments expressed at the grass roots, and where necessary to adjust their strategy, sometimes quite substantially. Once debate ceased to be conducted in coded euphemisms, and spread out from the closed worlds of the central committee and the executive into the non-party media, the centralization of power and the cohesion of the party were certain to decline, even if the formal façade of democratic centralism remained.

This had become strikingly clear by the end of the 1970s. The period the party spent in a parliamentary coalition with the Christian Democrats and its allies during the era of National Solidarity put a profound strain on the relationship between leadership and rank and file. The PCI's withdrawal from the coalition in 1979 was to a large degree a response to the dissatisfaction of party workers and trade-union activists with what was perceived as the party's subordination to the DC, and to the costs for trade-unionists and Communist voters of the government's counter-inflation policies.[22] Even more unequivocally, the serious electoral set-back suffered by the party in the 1987 election stimulated an open and acrimonious debate in the central committee culminating—unprecedentedly—in a contested vote to install Achille Occhetto as deputy secretary.[23] By the mid-1980s, in fact, well before the collapse of communism in Eastern Europe, the PCI had shed the essentials of democratic centralism. Members could say what they thought publicly; party leaders engaged in open, occasionally heated, argument; decision-making procedures and elections gave real opportunities for debate and opposition.

The impact of 1989

In many respects, the PCI was better prepared to face the consequences of the dramatic collapse of East European communism in 1989 than any other Western communist party. It had long dissociated itself from centrally planned economic systems and authoritarian one-party rule. Its programme was essentially social-democratic and

European. Despite a *rapprochement* with Gorbachev after 1985 that had gone some way to repair the breakdown of relations between Moscow and the PCI in the early 1980s, the party was relatively free from the legacy of the Cold War.[24] It could claim, with some justice, that the popular rejection of communism in the East was consistent with its own criticisms of those systems over many years.

Organizationally, moreover, the party leadership did not need to make dramatic and unconvincing gestures to demonstrate its sympathy with the liberal spirit of the times. The long-standing *de facto* abandonment of democratic centralism was at least a partial defence against the party's past. Nevertheless, Occhetto—by now party secretary—recognized that to carry on as before, claiming that the systematic rejection of collectivism by the communist block called for no acknowledgement by parties of the left in the West, was impossible. Making a virtue of necessity, Occhetto called for a relaunch of the party under a new programme, a new name, and a new symbol.

The debate which ensued took the PCI through two acrimonious congresses (March 1990 and February 1991) and culminated, at the latter, in the transformation of the PCI into the Partito democratico della sinistra, and the secession of a small group of leftists (led by Armando Cossutta, previously closely identified with a pro-Moscow position) to form a new, unapologetically communist, party—*Rifondazione Comunista*—whose electoral prospects, though limited (perhaps 2 or 3 per cent), were not, given Italy's pure form of proportional representation, entirely forlorn. It confirmed not just the end of democratic centralism, but the emergence of a party with divisions approaching in depth and intensity those in the parties of the centre.

In this debate the leadership was fundamentally divided, with a Fronte dei no, headed by a group of older party leaders including Natta and Ingrao, campaigning against the Occhetto plan, and a group of reformers on the right, headed by Giorgio Napolitano, urging the party secretary to accept even more unequivocally an explicitly social-democratic ideology. The vote in favour of this relaunch was eventually approved by a two-thirds majority at the Twentieth (and last) Congress. The significance of the vote lay not just in its outcome (the PDS remains, after all, the direct heir to the PCI) but also in the fact that the party rank and file itself decided the outcome directly.

The debate brought out into the open, and partly rearranged, strands of thinking and power groups discernible for many years. The centre of the party was and still is occupied largely by the national and provincial apparatus officials. In the 1970s and early 1980s, this group supported the party secretary, Enrico Berlinguer, in his cautious evolution towards 'Eurocommunism'. It was the group that benefited most from the party's increasing integration into the political mainstream and its growing power in regional and local government, and even in Parliament. It favoured an evolution towards social-democratic ideology (though this epithet was always roundly rejected by those involved) but was fearful of too radical a shift, which might split the party and jeopardize its (at that time) apparently steady progress towards government. As long as the party remained a fairly centralized one, with a large number of professionals dependent, in career terms, on promotion from the party bureaucracy to elected office in Parliament and regional and city government, this group was likely to deliver sustained support to the leadership group and the national party secretary. It remains the dominant group in the new PDS.

On the left and right of the central apparatus were groups motivated less by perceptions of the need for organizational stability and continuity, and more by overtly ideological impulses. To the left there were two main positions, very different from one another as well as from the centre. The most distinct, but also much the smallest, was Cossutta's pro-Soviet group. Much more substantive was the party's radical conscience—the so-called Ingrao group—an identifiable element in PCI thinking since the mid-1960s.[25] Although clearly on the left, it was decidedly not pro-Soviet. Its distinctiveness came rather from its assertion of the need for a decisive break with the market framework (in contrast to the equivocal gradualism of the centrist group) and its stress on the role of the working class in the transition to a socialist economy (in contrast to the inter-class alliances emphasized by those further right). These two groups formed the basis for the Fronte dei no in the debate over the party's future, but they were joined by several older party figures—in particular Tortorella and former secretary Alessandro Natta who had previously been part of the apparatus leadership.[26]

On the right, the so-called 'social democrats' had long favoured a far more explicit recognition of the party's Western orientation. They had already been prepared some years before to recognize openly what the central leadership only finally felt it dare acknowledge in 1990—that the party had almost everything in common with Western social democracy, and the mixed capitalist economy, and shared almost nothing with the Eastern bloc.

Until 1990, the apparatus leadership group tended to hold the balance between the Ingrao group and the social democrats. In the debate on the party's relaunch it seemed at first to throw its weight behind the latter, but the need to restrict the size of the looming secession on the left, especially in the charged atmosphere of the Gulf War—the background to the Twentieth Congress—confirmed that the apparatus leadership continued to hold the centre against factions on both right and left. This muted what would otherwise have been a clear-cut two-way split between supporters and opponents of the relaunch of the party.

However, it had a further effect in underlining the continuity between the PCI and the PDS. Occhetto's aim in 1989 had been to restructure the left by bringing in groups and interests from all across the left of the political spectrum, including radicals, environmentalists, women's groups, and so on. The aim was similar to Craxi's goal of a federal party some years before: itself, as we have seen, largely unsuccessful.[27] Few such groups expressed an interest, however. The domination of the Twentieth Congress by the struggle between the factions of the old PCI, and the evident continuity involved in the apparatus leadership's balancing role between left and right, all but obliterated the *federative* aspects of the launch of the PDS. The continuity with the PCI was clear from the near identity of leadership, parliamentary group, grass-roots structure, and membership between the two parties.

This state of affairs did not bode well for the new party. It had finally made the symbolic break with its communist past that reformists had so long demanded, but the organizational continuity with the past still haunted it. Moreover, the one organizational feature which *had* changed was the emergence of open factionalism. The new party was deeply divided, covered a wide ideological spectrum, and openly acknowledged this. It was rapidly developing an internal power-sharing mentality that would institutionalize factionalism. Traditionally leaders of all its tendencies had been allocated seats inside the party executive, the parliamentary group, and local government, in such a way as to prevent the minority groups from isolation. But this had been done behind closed doors. By the early 1990s, the battle was out in the open, with the rank-and-file membership as arbiters. While the careers of so many in the new party depended upon the effectiveness of unity and cohesion, it remained to be demonstrated that the PDS was completely *un*manageable (and in this respect the departure of those who had joined Rifondazione Comunista seemed likely to prove a blessing in disguise). Nevertheless, holding the party together under the far more adverse conditions of a 'post-communist' European order looked likely to be extraordinarily difficult. The *diversità* of the former

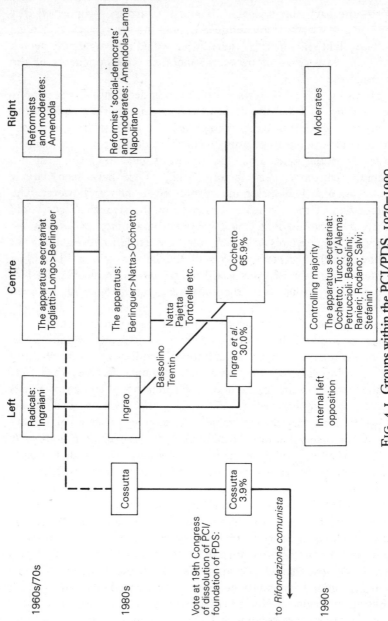

FIG. 4.1 Groups within the PCI/PDS, 1970–1990

PCI—its unity and discipline, and the commitment of its followers—had, it seemed, been permanently diluted.

Factionalism in the DC and PSI

The ubiquity of deeply entrenched divisions in Italian parties,
especially (but not exclusively) in the two main parties of government,
is striking. Broad political *tendencies* are not uncommon in many
European countries. Nor are *issue groups*, supporting particular
demands in one area of policy. The latter are specially common where
parties make a conscious effort to find semi-institutionalized places for
particular interests (farmers, unions, artisans, etc.) inside their
organization. In Italy, however, besides identifiable tendencies and
issue groups, there are also very clear-cut *factions*: well-organized
groups, present at various levels in the party, with a high level of self-
conscious cohesion running across a wide range of issues.[28]

Policy, ideology, and coalition strategy

The origins of this phenomenon are complex. In part, they lie in the
width of the policy spectrum and the number of parties. Facing
competition on both left and right, it is inevitable that, within some
parties of the centre-located coalition, there are wings which prefer
alliances not with other parties of the centre, but with those to their left
or right. After the Socialist Party joined the Centre-Left coalition in
the early 1960s, it contained within it a minority which preferred the
prospect of a left-wing alliance with the Communists to a Centre-Left
coalition with the DC. In the 1970s, such a preference briefly became
the officially declared objective of the entire party, and was partly
responsible for the Communist Party's entry into the parliamentary
majority.[29]

   The Christian Democrats, too, have faced internal divisions related
to alliance strategy. For many years there has been no alternative to a
coalition with the Socialist Party, but there has been a real argument
about the concessions which the DC needs to make to keep its
Socialist partner in the coalition. Ironically, those who are most
resistant to the PSI are inclined to look for assistance from the PCI/
PDS—for example in covert alliances in Parliament—as a way of
signalling to the PSI that if it becomes too demanding some things may
get resolved over its head. In short, it is not always to the Socialists that
those on the left of the DC look. In the DC's case, however, the party
is not divided just by alliance strategy, but also by the width of the
political spectrum the DC occupies. It has always claimed a centrist
vocation, and has an ideological self-image substantially different from
north European conservatism, or even from German Christian

Democracy. But 'centrism' is easier to define negatively than positively, and is less immune from internal divisions in bad times than good. In recent years, when political agendas everywhere in Europe have been focused on measures of market liberalization and on controls on public expenditure, the DC has faced a difficult dilemma over its attitude to the role of the state in economic activity, and to the size of the welfare system—questions to which we return later in the chapter.

Structural incentives of factionalism—the preference vote, and internal party rules

The existence of divisions over ideology, policy, or alliance strategy, important though they are, is nevertheless insufficient to explain the persistence and deeply rooted nature of factionalism in Italian parties. For a full explanation, we need also to consider some structural features of the wider political system: in particular, the nature of the electoral system; the way in which resources are mobilized to fight elections; and the rules govering the internal distribution of power in Italian parties.

The Italian electoral system is notable for two main features: its extreme proportionalism, discussed in Chapter 3, and the so-called *preference vote*. The latter determines which particular candidates on a party's list are actually elected, once that party's share of seats in a constituency has been determined by the list vote. Candidates with the highest number of individual preference votes, up to the number of seats due to the party, are declared elected. The effect is to make elections at the same time both inter-party contests and intra-party primaries. Frequently the latter are more bitterly fought than the former. The system is a major incentive to factionalism, since it puts a premium on exclusive alliances between groups of candidates within a party list. Candidates assemble as many personal followers as they can, urging them to concentrate their preference votes on themselves and their allies—the urging being more or less discreet depending on how disapproving of such a practice the party currently is.[30]

Until the referendum of 1991, voters had three, or in large constituencies four, preference votes to cast. They did not have to use them all. In the country as a whole, voters have tended to use only about 30 per cent of the preference votes available to them. Some have not used a preference vote at all; many have cast only a single list vote, often to support the well-known figure (*capolista*) at the top of their party's list of candidates. Moreover, there have been substantial variations in the use of the preference vote between regions and between parties. Voters in the south have been twice as prone to use the system as those in the north. Similarly parties of government and those with powerfully organized factions have had much higher levels of preference-voting than those in opposition. The explanation is not hard to find. The most ready source of preference voters is party members (along with their families and friends). Control of the party machine makes a faction the gatekeeper of party membership, and gives access to a solid core of preference votes for election and re-election. Where political relationships are of a clientelistic, individualistic type, it will be easier to recruit members who will play such a role. Hence the relatively high membership levels which both the Christian Democrat and Socialist Parties have developed in the south of the country. Control of the membership brings control of the party machine, control of the preference vote, and hence election to public office.

It should be noted that the referendum of 1991 changed the rules of preference voting.[31] Henceforth, voters would be able to cast only a single preference. The aim was to limit the extent of this internal electoral battle, and remove the incentive for *alliances*. Lesser-known candidates could no longer benefit from being part of an unofficial internal 'slate'. Eventually, such a mechanism may assist in dissolving the rigidity of factional alliances, but the habits of mind induced by many years of patron–client networking will take some time to erode.

A second sensitive point at which the preference vote has had its effect is on the struggle for public resources: jobs in the public sector, grants, licensing and regulatory authority, etc. Control of such resources is vital in mobilizing preference votes because party members have to be rewarded for their services, whether those services involve merely voting or campaigning more directly. Some of these resources will be distributed to individuals through the local-government networks of a particular faction. Others are mobilized through nationally constructed policies designed to appeal to well-organized interest groups capable of delivering disciplined blocks of preference votes. Pensioners, farmers, teachers, shopkeepers, and public employees provide obvious examples of groups in such a position.

It is thus clear that the assembling of large reservoirs of preference votes through the formation of intra-party cartels controlling party membership and the spoils of government has had the effect, over many years, of changing the nature and *raison d'être* of factionalism in the governing parties. Factions reflecting clear-cut outlooks on public policy or long-term party strategy have become progressively harder to distinguish from those which are alliances of convenience between political entrepreneurs seeking election and career advancement.

The incentives to factionalism have been enhanced in the Christian Democrat and Socialist Parties by a further factor: proportional representation in the distribution of power between factions inside the party organization. The Socialist Party has used internal PR since the early 1960s. The Christian Democrats adopted it formally in 1964, at the Ninth Congress, but had already been moving in this direction in practice for some years.[32] Its use is facilitated by the nature of debate in party congresses. As we have seen, these are set-piece battles between organized groups in the party. Each group presents a general statement of party strategy, and the support it wins amongst rank-and-file members in pre-congressional debate determines the size of its delegation at the national congress. Seats in the assemblies that run the party between congresses, and normally also places in the executives, are then distributed in proportion to the grass-roots support of each faction. Over the years, the precise rules have been varied. In the Christian Democrat Party there have been minimum thresholds for representation, and in 1973 proportionalism in the national congress was formally abandoned, but proportional voting on factional lists of delegates at the subnational levels of party organization was maintained, largely nullifying the impact on factionalism at the top of the party.[33]

In any case, whatever the formal rules, Italian parties prefer not to have disgruntled, isolated minorities in their ranks which undermine their credibility and purposiveness. If they are isolated in the party organization, such groups will conspire with other parties behind the scenes in Parliament and local government to cause trouble for their leaders. A share in the control of the party machinery is thus generally available to minorities at least in internally representative party assemblies and executives. It is normally also available in the spoils of public office (ministerial posts etc.) at the party's disposal. In this latter area, of course, the rules are rarely drawn with precision, and for many patronage posts (for example, senior managerial posts in public agencies, hospitals, banks, etc.) the rules cannot—for obvious reasons of public propriety—be written down at all. In these areas, arguments over the allocation of the spoils of office can be intense, and can hold up government decision-taking for long periods.

Factionalism and party reform

The intensity of factional divisions that these structural incentives have generated is shown in Figs. 4.2 and 4.3, which trace the divisions as they have developed in the Christian Democrat and Socialist Parties over the last three decades. They show that at its peak, in the early 1970s, the DC contained at least eight clear-cut, organized groups, and the PSI five.

The impact of the self-evident *disaggregation* of organizations one of whose primary purposes in the political system is the process of

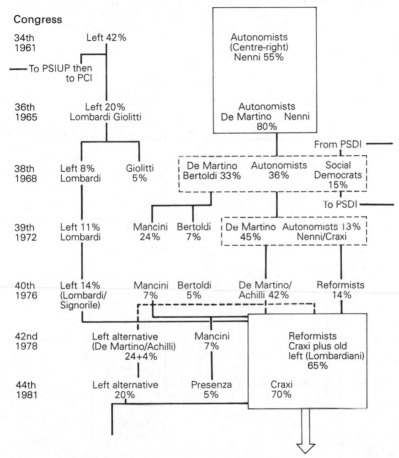

Note: At the three subsequent congresses (1984, 1987, 1989) the party was divided, albeit less rigidly, into the Craxi majority—over 70% of the party—and the left opposition minority. Within the majority group, however, there were a number of informal distinctions which did not crystallize to the point of the presentation of distinct motions and associated lists of candidates for office at the congress.

Sources: for 1961–72: David Hine, 'The Italian Socialist Party and the Centre-Left Coalition' (D.Phil. thesis, University of Oxford, 1978), 118; for 1976–81: W. Merkl, *Prima e dopo Craxi: le transformazioni del PSI* (Padua, 1987), 139.

FIG. 4.2 Factions and groups in the Italian Socialist Party since the 1960s

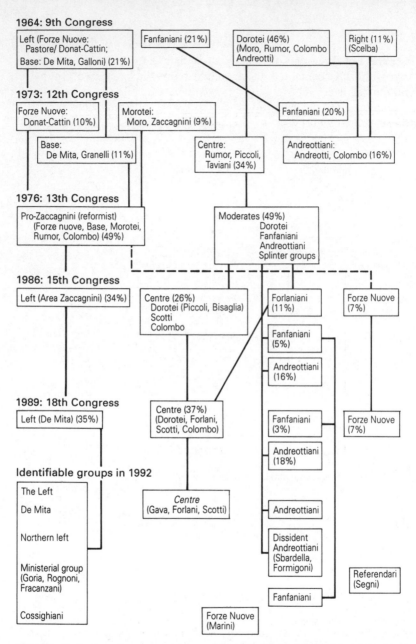

1964: 9th Congress

Left (Forze Nuove: Pastore/ Donat-Cattin; Base: De Mita, Galloni) (21%)	Fanfaniani (21%)	Dorotei (46%) (Moro, Rumor, Colombo Andreotti)	Right (11%) (Scelba)

1973: 12th Congress

Forze Nuove: Donat-Cattin (10%)	Morotei: Moro, Zaccagnini (9%)	Fanfaniani (20%)
Base: De Mita, Granelli (11%)	Centre: Rumor, Piccoli, Taviani (34%)	Andreottiani: Andreotti, Colombo (16%)

1976: 13th Congress

Pro-Zaccagnini (reformist) (Forze nuove, Base, Morotei, Rumor, Colombo) (49%)	Moderates (49%) Dorotei Fanfaniani Andreottiani Splinter groups

1986: 15th Congress

Left (Area Zaccagnini) (34%)	Centre (26%) Dorotei (Piccoli, Bisaglia) Scotti Colombo	Forlaniani (11%)	Forze Nuove (7%)
		Fanfaniani (5%)	
		Andreottiani (16%)	

1989: 18th Congress

Left (De Mita) (35%)	Centre (37%) (Dorotei, Forlani, Scotti, Colombo)	Fanfaniani (3%)	Forze Nuove (7%)
		Andreottiani (18%)	

Identifiable groups in 1992

The Left De Mita Northern left Ministerial group (Goria, Rognoni, Fracanzani) Cossighiani	*Centre* (Gava, Forlani, Scotti)	Andreottiani
		Dissident Andreottiani (Sbardella, Formigoni)
		Referendari (Segni)
	Forze Nuove (Marini)	Fanfaniani

Note: Figures in parentheses represent approximate share of congress delegates at the relevant congress.

Sources: 1964–89: Robert Leonardi and Douglas A. Wertman, *Italian Christian Democracy: The Politics of Dominance* (London, 1989), 114–115; 1992: *Corriere della Sera* (17 Apr. 1992), 7.

FIG. 4.3 Factions and Groups in the Christian Democrat Party since the 1960s

aggregation, is profound. The factions of Italian parties do not represent mere policy positions, or broad outlooks. They are highly organized, with a visible leadership, and a sense of identity and cohesion. They have an organizational framework running from national level right down to the local party sections. Most factions will be strongest in the home base of their main leaders, but those which restrict themselves to limited territories are unlikely to be very successful. Factions generally have a press agency, a national headquarters, their own financial resources, and are sometimes linked to a particular newspaper or magazine—especially if they start life as bearers of a distinct approach to policy or party strategy. Major groups, particularly in the DC, are likely to convene conferences and policy working groups. They are discussed openly in the press, and are recognized in the regular practice, if not also the formal rules, of the party congress, the party parliamentary group, and other party arenas. Factions thus have to be considered as part of the Italian institutional landscape in their own right.

The consequences of factionalism are extensive. Their existence gives sectional groups and local interests precise and open channels of access to political decision-making centres. Factions act as promoters of special interests, expecting in exchange financial or organizational support, preference votes, and party members. Such channels are far more easily accessible than in political systems where parties are more cohesive, political benefits are distributed at a more aggregated and generalized level, and discussion of policy is (relatively) closed off once government programmes have been agreed. Over an extended period, the internal fragmentation of Italian parties has laid down a style of party politics in which power is dispersed, and decisions which seemed to have been agreed are frequently contested and renegotiated. Party discipline thus gives way to a high degree of sensitivity to local or sectional pressures. In such circumstances, the capacity of the DC and PSI to aggregate interests, and to make clear choices between priorities, is severely limited.

Even in cases when parties are unitary actors, multi-party coalitions are hampered by the linkage between one issue area or decision and another. Policy is made through painstaking searches for compromise packages, with assent from any particular party frequently dependent on complex pay-offs. When two of the four or five parties of the coalition are themselves federations of factions, the intricacies of such arrangements are far greater. As we shall see in later chapters, many government decisions that might in other states be left to the relevant departmental minister's discretion through delegated legislation (if not indeed devolved to administrative action by civil servants) are, in Italy, highly politicized. They have to be negotiated between party leaders, approved formally by the Council of Ministers, and often require detailed parliamentary legislation because faction leaders do not trust ministers to use the power delegated to them in an acceptable manner. A related area in this connection involves public-sector managerial appointments, in which parties and factions take extremely close interest because of the administrative power that control of big-spending agencies can give.

The degenerative consequences of factionalism for representative democracy, as well as for individual parties, have been a major concern over the last two decades, not only among independent observers but also inside the two main parties. Both the Socialist Party and the Christian Democrat Party have made periodic efforts to reform themselves, and under Craxi's leadership the Socialist Party at least has made some headway in doing so, although more at national level than locally. The DC, however, has been largely unsuccessful in getting to grips with the problem. When political scandals linked to factional conflict erupt with particular force, or when the party's electorate shows signs of growing restive at the party's disunity, efforts are made which have a temporary effect, but the basic divisions have tended to emerge again quite rapidly.

Craxi and the reform of the PSI

The Socialist Party's efforts at party reform, like those of the Christian Democrat Party, stem from periods of serious electoral set-back. In the PSI's case, the most traumatic set-back experienced in recent years was the election of 1976. In that year, given the general shift to the left, the party expected to gain significantly. Instead, almost the entire shift to the left accrued to the Communist Party. The result was a profound sense of crisis. The party had for some years been divided into factions, and with the exception of the left-wing, the divisions between these bore little relation to real ideological or policy argument. At the Thirty-Ninth Socialist Congress in 1972, the party was split into five factions. Nominally, there was greater unity at the Fortieth in 1976, but only because the congress was held just before a general election. The absurdity of this state of affairs, in a party with less than 10 per cent of the popular vote, was evident, and it created the conditions under which, over the following five years, the rank and file and the parliamentary party proved willing, with an almost palpable sense of relief, to throw their support behind a single authoritative leader, in the shape of Bettino Craxi.

Initially, Craxi's task in uniting the party was far from easy. He was elected as a compromise between various groups, and seemed beholden to his sponsors from rival factions. However, his strategy of reasserting the PSI's identity, and distinguishing it both from the PCI and DC, proved an unexpected success, and helped him assert control over rivals in his own party. He argued forcefully that the PSI's role of broker between the Communists and Christian Democrats had been an expensive mistake encouraging the two to co-operate over the PSI's head. He preferred to replace the National Solidarity coalition—in which the PSI had no influence—with one which excluded the Communists, making the PSI arithmetically indispensable. His instinct proved correct. The Communists' return to opposition no longer threatened a haemorrhage of votes from the PSI to the PCI. In the changed social and electoral environment of the 1980s, it was the Communist Party which lost votes, and the PSI which started—albeit slowly—to gain.

The new PSI strategy had the great good fortune to coincide with the beginning of a long phase of strategic weakness for the Christian Democrats, during which they lost votes and became increasingly reliant on PSI support. In these circumstances Craxi's leadership proved a notable success. By stressing his own alleged purposiveness (*decisionismo*), exemplified first by his capacity to get a grip on the PSI's own warring factions, and later by his role as prime minister of post-war Italy's longest-serving government, Craxi also struck a response in voters apparently anxious for stronger and more cohesive government. Between 1979 and 1987, the PSI vote rose from 9.8 to 14.3 per cent—not a fundamental realignment, but enough to persuade the PSI of its debt to Craxi. For the first time since the 1950s the party had a leader capable of imposing his will on it, and of speaking for it in negotiations with other parties without having first to negotiate internally with a range of warring groups. Deputies and local leaders moved over to the Craxi camp, abandoning their previous group loyalties. With them they brought party members and preference votes. By the early 1980s Craxi controlled three-quarters of the party and, unlike his three immediate predecessors as party secretary, had established such a high personal leadership profile that he was clearly perceived across the party as a major electoral asset. Those who did not join the Craxi group found increasing difficulty in speaking out against the leadership. Gradually the opposition declined, some becoming deputies of the so-called 'independent left', some joining the Communist Party, others languishing in resentful isolation on the PSI left.

The revolution wrought by Craxi, on a party previously riven with divisions, reflected an adaptation to a more modern style of political leadership and of political communication with the party rank and file and its electorate than the Socialist Party had previously enjoyed. It was heavily dependent on Craxi's occupation of the prime minister's office (examined in Chapter 7) and his own media appeal. It was punctuated by combative gestures towards other parties and interest groups, and by a constant search for the political headlines. Craxi's contribution to the much-discussed syndrome of 'politics as *spettacolo*' has been considerable; some have even described his leadership as the rediscovery of 'charismatic' authority.[34] As a means of winning control of the party, the strategy depended on electoral success and a perception by his potential rivals in the party that as its prime electoral asset his leadership was unassailable.

There is no doubting Craxi's achievement in retaining control of the PSI for over fifteen years, suppressing the previously endemic factionalization, winning the prime minister's office, holding on to it for so long, and increasing his party's share of the vote. There are nevertheless real limits to that achievement. The party's electoral recovery was steady rather than spectacular, and in 1992 went into reverse. One of the main reasons for this reversal was the legitimate doubts that remained about Craxi's ability to overcome the substance of factionalism, rather than its surface appearance. These doubts spring from the substantial personal rivalries that clearly persist among his own lieutenants, and the battles for patronage and preference votes that continue, albeit under the overarching umbrella of a single 'Craxi faction'. These features show up in the periodic involvement of Socialists in cases of political corruption at local level. The most spectacular blew up in the Socialist Party's northern stronghold of Milan, in the winter of 1991/2, with dramatic repercussions on the city administration and on the PSI's vote in the area. In certain respects, indeed, the PSI is now projecting two contrasting faces to the world. One is the purposive and prime-ministerial leadership of the modern, media-orientated party; the other is the old party machine, based on local notables and political clientelism and rooted firmly in southern politics. The party's difficulty in reaching electoral take-off undoubtedly reflects this limit to the Craxi revolution. The internal reforms of the PSI represent only half a revolution. The structural incentives to factionalism and clientele politics rooted in the wider political system have prevented that revolution working right through the party, and constitute a significant limitation on Craxi's wider political strategy.

The (recurrent) failure of reform in the Christian Democrat Party

Efforts to eradicate factionalism in the Christian Democrat Party have also been closely associated with periods of electoral difficulty. When the party performed particularly badly, as in the 1975 regional elections, and even more in the 1983 general election, there followed a period of collective soul-searching, and loud protestations of the urgent imperative of party reform. The revelations of extensive political corruption that preceded these elections clearly demonstrated the electorate's concern at the corrosive party infighting bred by factional competition. The DC's response to each episode was to elect a new allegedly reform-minded party secretary (Zaccagnini in 1975 and De Mita in 1982) who would clean up party life, rediscover the Catholic idealism of the party's original mission, and restore confidence in the party.

Zaccagnini's efforts bore some fruit. His main success was to eradicate some of the malpractices in party recruitment that inflated membership rolls, and to reform the party rules by extending incompatibilities between the holding of party office and public office. Membership fell by half a million, from 1.8 to 1.3 million over the middle years of the decade, and never again reached the inflated heights of the early 1970s. However, Zaccagnini's efforts were overshadowed by the governments of National Solidarity of the later 1970s. With Councils of Ministers composed exclusively of Christian Democrats, his profile as DC leader tended to be overshadowed by Andreotti and others. In 1979 he was replaced by Flaminio Piccoli of the anti-Communist Preambolo alliance of the centre-right, in a move clearly intended to draw a line under both the party's efforts at internal reform and its alliance with the Communist Party.

Within two years, however, scandals—most notably those arising out of the P-2 masonic lodge affair—had once again brought the party low, this time costing the DC its hold on the prime minister's office. To keep the support of its coalition partners, it was forced to yield Palazzo Chigi to the Republican leader Giovanni Spadolini, and with the exception of a few short months in the winter of 1982/3 it was not to regain it until 1987. Following the P-2 affair, Ciriaco De Mita was elected secretary at the 1982 Congress, restoring to the leadership a figure from the party's left, and one committed to resume the work of reform begun by Zaccagnini.

In one important respect, Ciriaco De Mita had an advantage over Zaccagnini. With the prime minister's office in the hands first of Spadolini and then of Bettino Craxi, De Mita could adopt a far higher profile as leader than his predecessors, since there was no rival source of DC leadership in Palazzo Chigi. Craxi's domination of the PSI, together with the emergence of a more competitive electoral environment, underlined the importance for the DC of grooming a strong and effective political communicator who could counter the image of a fractious and divided party for so long projected by Christian Democracy. From the beginning, therefore, De Mita's efforts at reform were linked to his efforts to assert his own personal leadership, and to do so not only through control of the party organization, but also through his accession to the post of prime minister.

As we shall see in Chapter 7, however, the attempt to concentrate in the hands of a single individual both main leadership posts—party secretary and prime minister—was unacceptable to the party. As prime minister De Mita was a clear failure. He had to undertake to relinquish the post of secretary in order to win his party's nomination for the office. By the time he secured the nomination, his hold on the party was already slipping, and he survived in office only a year. But even before becoming prime minister, in the spring of 1988, his efforts to reform the party organization had run into insurmountable difficulties. The coalition of groups which elected him was from the beginning hesitant about thoroughgoing reform, and doubly so after the 1983 election which suggested that in the south efforts to purge the party of its worst clientelistic habits could actually cost it votes, rather than gain them.[35] By the mid-1980s, in fact, party reform was quietly being dropped. The party slipped back into its state of barely controlled endemic warfare. The alignments shifted somewhat, and with Craxi's hold on public opinion proving effective, DC leaders were forced to conceal their worst excesses. As a party reformer, however, De Mita proved no more successful in the long run than had Zaccagnini a decade earlier.

Party Organization, Electoral Competition, and Models of the Party System

The characteristics of party organization considered in this chapter, combined with the evident change in the nature of electoral competition analysed in Chapter 3, clearly limit the utility of traditional models of the Italian party system based purely on the direction of competition along an ideologically polarized left–right spectrum. The Italian party system was for many years singled out as one of the most enduring examples of a fragmented, ideologically polarized, party system: a type that has disappeared from most societies in which it was once present. The model contrasts, moreover, with the fragmented party systems of the smaller states of northern Europe. In these societies, as Sartori pointed out in the distinctive analytical framework which has come to be associated with his name, 'moderate' pluralism was characterized by a more limited ideological distance across the spectrum, and/or by a form of political segmentation held together by élite co-operation across party boundaries.[36]

In Italy, in contrast, the continuity with an ideologically polarized past, unmitigated by the cohesion and élite co-operation which comes from small-state status, seemed not to have been broken. Admittedly, the most cataclysmic element of the polarized-pluralist model—the prediction that the system would eventually collapse into authoritarianism—was never realized. Nevertheless, coalition-building was rendered difficult by the continued presence of parties which were either unacceptable for inclusion in government (such as the MSI) or whose status on this score remained in some doubt (the PCI, and perhaps more recently the Greens, the Radicals, and local leagues).

This ideological/subcultural model had its two most articulate spokesmen in Giovanni Sartori and Giorgio Galli.[37] They differed in their predictive conclusions. Sartori focused on the impact of centre-located coalitions on electoral drives, and hence on the possibility of polarization and system collapse. Galli emphasized the static qualities of the system: deeply entrenched subcultural blocks preventing any real electoral change because the party expressed by one of these blocks was permanently ineligible for government. What both commentators shared was the view that ideological distance permanently damaged the democratic framework.

Today, it no longer seems intuitively plausible to claim that the system is as polarized as in earlier post-war decades. However, it is still not easy—given the intellectual grip of such ideas—to explain why. A clue is offered by Paolo Farneti, who argued that in modern political conditions the direction of the basic polarizing electoral drive in the system had been reversed. Farneti's interpretative model, based on the concept of 'centripetal' (as opposed to Sartori's 'centrifugal') pluralism, started from the assertion that at some point in the post-war era (Farneti dates it from the mid-1960s) the system ceased to operate according to the logic attributed to it by Sartori.[38] It still contained several of Sartori's other properties, but not the crucial one: the centrifugal drive. Even if such a drive still existed among voters (which was itself doubtful) it did not exist among party leaders, who regularly found ways of constructing compromises to prevent the system collapsing into political deadlock. The most dramatic illustration of this was the era of National Solidarity in the 1970s. Far from exploiting the breakdown of the centre-based coalitions as a mechanism for undermining the system as a whole, the Communist Party acted in a moderate and responsible manner, shoring up an emergency government, and supporting it through a series of difficult political decisions.

Sadly, Farneti died before he could work out his ideas more fully by explaining in detail why party leaders should engage in coalescent and accommodating behaviour. A part of the explanation no doubt lies in directions explored in previous chapters. One is the deep-rooted pessimism of the main 'extremist' political party, the PCI, after its experiences of the early 1920s. Its conclusion—that intransigence contributed to the rise of fascism—has, as we have seen, marked the PCI's post-war political strategy with an almost obsessive caution.

A further factor, diffuse and intangible but critical as contextual background explanation, lies in social and economic change. In most democratic European societies after 1945 political discontinuities, and social and economic modernization, gradually succeeded in eradicating or confining to the fringes the scope for extreme parties. In contrast, peculiarities rooted in history conspired to leave Italy with what might be described as an unreformed and polarized party system. However, simply because Italy preserved the structure, labels, and organizations of an unreformed system did not imply that it was immune from the pressures of social and economic modernization. These pressures included rising levels of consumer affluence, the security of the welfare state, the changing class structure (especially the growth of the middle class), support for the liberal-democratic values and market-based political economy required by participation in the process of European economic integration, and growing scepticism of the utility of alternative non-market models of social organization, as they had developed in Eastern Europe. All these factors could influence both voters and party leaders even without a basic change in the structure of the party system itself. Such considerations are critical to an understanding of how contemporary Italian political leaders behave. The immediate focus of political debate may frequently be political failure rather than economic success, but this does not necessarily imply the absence of a basic consensus on liberal-democratic values and the market economy, or that such a consensus has no effect on the behaviour of the political class.

However, even these broad accounts of depolarization do not exhaust the range of explanations, because the nature of parties and party systems cannot be fully understood without taking account of life inside the party organization. From without, allegedly extremist parties may look as if they are, or recently were, the bearers of programmes and demands for the radical reordering of social relations or political institutions. However, such parties are also frameworks through which individuals acquire office, realize career aspirations, and perform roles in office which are similar to those performed by politicians in depolarized political systems. The fact that they do so through organizations and under banners which once symbolized radical political programmes may be of only secondary significance.

This is not to argue that parties which have undergone a process of depolarization towards a broad policy consensus retain no characteristics which affect their ability to perform effectively under such a consensus. Their performance can be affected by activist minorities which fail or refuse to recognize that depolarization has occurred, and continue to press for radical policy positions, confusing the message portrayed to the outside world. And other parties may find it convenient and electorally beneficial to ignore the process of depolarization and continue to brand the reformed, now moderate, party as an extremist organization. However, these qualifications do not undermine the importance of looking closely not just at names, labels, and concepts of organizational continuity with the past, but also at the role performed by the party in the contemporary political system.

It is here that a close analysis of party organization is instructive. Such an analysis, for Italy, suggests that political parties, or at least the three most important ones, have been converging to a common type, and that Duvergian distinctions between cell, militia, and mass parties are of little relevance. The PCI/PDS can no longer be regarded as a monolithic, conspiratorial organization led by a dedicated and cohesive revolutionary élite. On the contrary, it is open and inclusive, and its commitment to internal democracy cannot automatically be seen as significantly different from that of the parties of the political centre. Increasingly, it resembles other parties as an agency through which politicians realize career aspirations. Like politicians from other large parties, they too are dealing in votes and dependent on public money, and they have a strong stake in the existing order. When that order is threatened, they too will defend it, as the Communist Party demonstrated unequivocally in the 1970s.

If this analysis is correct, it suggests that the Italian party system today has rather little in common with polarized pluralism. It was always the strength of the Communist Party which gave the model its plausibility. On the far right, the MSI, though a nuisance, posed little threat, and its existence owed much to the electoral system. Indeed, given the resurgence of the far right in recent years in some allegedly 'depolarized' European party systems, it is surprising that the MSI has been unable to muster more than the 5 per cent it has been winning over the last decade. If, on the left, the PCI has disappeared both as a monolithic and self-conscious bearer of radical demands, and now indeed as an emotive 'communist' symbol, the case against the ideological/subcultural interpretation of the party system strengthens further.

The weakness of that case is essentially that it focuses too much on only one dimension of the existence of political parties—their ideology—and takes too little account of equally important dimensions like party organization, political mediation, and electoral representation. Whereas polarized pluralism suggested that the main problem of the Italian party system was the radical ideological incompatibility of Italian parties, an analysis focusing on these other dimensions might conclude quite the opposite: namely, that the main problem is the extraordinary similarity between the three major parties. Italy could be said to have three large parties of the centre, between them gathering nearly 80 per cent of the popular vote, but lacking real differentiation of programmes, and unable to articulate clear policy alternatives between which voters can choose. It would be wrong to press this argument too far, but both as organizations, and as broad catch-all coalitions of a wide range of social interests, the DC, PCI/PDS, and PSI share much in common, and certainly more than traditional models of the party system have acknowledged.

5

The Constitutional Order: An Introduction

Constitutions are best studied in their political context, not in isolation, and that is the approach adopted in this book. The detailed analysis of the key institutions—parliament, the political executive, the administration, and subnational government—is found in Chapters 6 to 9. Nevertheless, for the purposes of exposition, it is desirable to begin with a brief overview, looking not just at the main institutional features and how they interact (the 'letter' of the constitution) but also at its 'spirit'. This provides an opportunity to consider some of the institutions—especially the presidency of the republic, the constitutional court, and the judicial system—which serve as the guardians of the constitution and the rule of law, and which are not considered in greater detail in later chapters.

Social Rights and Citizenship

The constitution is divided into two parts: the preamble and the first part deal respectively with what are described as 'basic principles' and the nature of citizenship; the second part deals with institutional arrangements. The preamble and part one overlap: the 'basic principles' of the preamble are elucidated in the section on citizenship, which deals in turn with civil, ethical and social, economic, and political rights and duties. In this section there is a clear commitment to liberal political principles, as these have developed in Western societies since the late eighteenth century. Fundamental political and legal freedoms and equalities are asserted unequivocally: freedom to form parties and unions, to hold meetings, to express opinions, to enjoy privacy and due process of law, to travel, and so on.

However, the constitution's traditional liberal principles are directed mainly towards civil rights and institutional relationships. In the area of social and economic rights there are more substantive commitments of a twentieth-century type, some of which—particularly in the area of property—run counter to traditional liberal values. The early sections of the constitution are in fact quite heavily influenced by the principles of collectivism and social solidarity which dominated the political outlook of two of the three largest parties of the resistance (the PCI and PSI), and which indeed were by no means absent from Christian Democrat outlooks too. Thus, for example, art. 3 of the constitution is heavily imbued with the collectivist critique of the inadequacy of liberal political equality, and has been taken by Marxist jurists to imply an activist and socially egalitarian state.[1]

All citizens are invested with equal social dignity and are equal before the law, without distinction as to sex, race, language, religion, political opinions and personal or social conditions.

It is the duty of the republic to remove all economic and social obstacles which, by actually limiting the freedom and equality of citizens, prevent the full development of the human being and the actual participation of all citizens in the political, economic, and social structures of the country.

Certainly, a reading of the first two sections of the Italian constitution might suggest that many provisions are closer to a set of goals or long-term policy objectives—at best a programme for action—rather than a set of immediately redeemable rights. Unlike classical eighteenth-century liberal constitutions, the Italian constitution contains no inviolable 'right to property'. Instead there is a series of interventionist prescriptions. Thus art. 31 stipulates that the republic 'aids the family by means of economic and other provisions'. Art. 32 asserts optimistically that 'the republic safeguards health as a basic right of the individual and as an interest of the community, and grants free medical assistance to the indigent'. Art. 41 begins, 'Freedom of private economic enterprise is guaranteed', but continues, 'It cannot, however, be in conflict with social utility or with safety, freedom and human dignity.' Art. 42 asserts the apparently self-evident truth that 'Property is either public or private. Economic goods belong to the State, to public bodies, or to private persons.' Art. 44 promises that the law shall impose 'obligations on and limitations to private land ownership' in order to 'secure rational utilization of the land and to establish equitable and rational social relations'. Art. 46 'recognizes the right of workers to participate in the management of undertakings, in the manner and within the limits prescribed by law'.

However, the way in which these social goals were to be achieved was left to the discretion of future legislators. This was inevitable. The Constituent Assembly involved at most only a partial assertion of collectivist principles over traditional liberal values (and one which was rapidly fading as the Constituent Assembly was completing its work). The only form of compromise which was possible was one which alluded to various types of social and economic right, but which devolved to subsequent legislation (and hence, in effect, to the electorate) the task of fleshing out the content. The substance of many of the rights asserted is thus left studiously vague, and this applies not just to socio-economic issues but to others too. Thus, for example, art. 5 asserts that the republic 'which is one and indivisible, recognizes and promotes local autonomies'. Art. 9 commits the republic to promoting 'the development of culture and scientific and technical research' and to safeguarding 'natural beauty and the historical and artistic wealth of the Nation'. Art. 13, which asserts the inviolability of personal liberty, leaves it to the law to determine the maximum period of detention before sentence. In each case, subsequent legislation has to determine how far such action can be promoted without jeopardizing other policy objectives.

Italy is not unique in including within its constitution references to social rights in such a form that they are compatible with very different types of legislative backing and distributional outcome. The problem of defining the content and level of detail of a bill of rights is a long-standing one. Drafting a constitution by definition requires a broad measure of political consent among the parties writing it, and this makes precise commitments difficult to agree upon. Constitutions cannot enter into detail in such areas without becoming rigid and inflexible in the face of changing electoral and hence governmental opinion. The Italian constitution is nevertheless unusual in the extensive range of subjects to which it makes reference—extending to co-operatives, the artisan sector, the financial sector (including reference even to home ownership), the education system, the family, health, and so on.

The constitution has, as a result, often been criticized for its studied imprecision, and for the potential gap that is created between the formal rights of equality and social protection endowed by the constitution, and the objective capacity, or political willingness, of the state to give them substance at any particular moment.[2] Constitutional purists of the traditional liberal persuasion have also objected that, even where the substantive policy goals of a constitution are, in some general sense, shared widely, there is likely to be genuine room for disagreement about the appropriate pace at which they should be pursued, and about the relative balance between different goals where they appear to be in conflict. Resolution of these uncertainties (unlike those stemming from immediately redeemable rights) cannot, they argue, be achieved in a meaningful way by the jurisprudence of a constitutional court. It can only be achieved through electoral or parliamentary choice.

Whether a constitution *should* contain references to prescriptive policy goals is not a matter that can be resolved here. What should be noted, however, is that in long-term perspective the radical and potentially collectivist social values of the Italian constitution have found an echo in the broad thrust of social and economic intervention over the post-war era. Moreover, the constitution has been said to be part of the justification for the type of *sectional* intervention which, as we shall see in the following chapter, characterizes much Italian social legislation. The fact that the constitution makes specific reference to the need to provide assistance to a wide list of *enumerated* categories—illegitimate children (art. 30); large families (art. 31); able but indigent students (art. 34); employed workers (art. 36); female workers (art. 37); the disabled (art. 38); small farmers (art. 44); artisans (art. 45)—has even been identified by some commentators as the inspiration and justification for policies that pursue substantive equality through finely targeted legislation.[3]

Naturally, as time passes, and the original list of groups deserving of special treatment becomes dated, the constitution provides a progressively less useful guide to which groups deserve finely targeted benefits. As this happens, legislators may become just as likely, if they remain attached to the principle of targeted benefits, to take as their operating criteria not situations of objective need but rather the nature of the electoral pay-off to themselves. Certainly, Italy's steadily rising level of public intervention in the area of social welfare, culminating in mass systems of social insurance, a national health service, an active labour-market policy, and so on, has not been driven solely by the 1948 constitution. Most West European societies have seen similar developments irrespective of whether their constitution contains general prescriptions in this direction or not. Nevertheless, the Italian constitution has been an important justificatory source for parties and even governments, and much landmark legislation (for example, the 1969 *Statuto dei lavoratori*, or Workers' Charter) has been presented as the fulfilment of the aims of the constitution. Similarly, in its ever-expanding role as arbiter and interpreter of legislation, the constitutional court has had frequent occasion to refer to the substantive rights conferred by the first section of the constitution—even if it has often been sceptical about the extent to which they can be said to constrain legislators in particular directions.

Institutional Relationships

The second section of the constitution sets out the institutional geography: Parliament (arts. 55–82), the president of the republic (arts. 83–91), the government (arts. 92–100), the judiciary (arts.

101–13), the system of subnational representative government (arts. 114–33), and what are described as 'constitutional guarantees'—in effect the provision for interpreting and modifying the constitution itself (arts. 134–9). It is infused with checks and balances which are intended as a guarantee against the abuse of power by any one branch. The system is clearly intended to operate through legalism, mutual vetoes, and institutional bargaining umpired by a series of non-partisan institutional guarantors. As we have already observed, the constitution disperses power across a range of institutions, and contains few provisions which can be used to strengthen the power of the executive.

Legislature and executive

Thus there is no special protection for the government against the erosion of its Parliamentary majority as found in some other West European democracies. Whether devices like those found in say Germany or France[4] would make any difference to the problem of inter- and intra-party fragmentation, as it is found in Italy, is debatable, and is taken up in the concluding chapter. For the purposes of eliciting the spirit in which the constitution was intended, however, what is important is that no such provisions—effective or otherwise—were even included. Thus government legislation in its passage through Parliament enjoys no constitutionally backed special treatment, and there are no restrictions on private members' legislation, or on amendments to government legislation.[5] Nor is it intended that Parliament shall pass over to the government extensive generalized powers to introduce delegated legislation, as does, for example, art. 38 of the Fifth French republic's constitution. Arts. 76 and 77 of the Italian constitution provide for forms of delegated legislation, but they are couched in the negative—the emphasis being placed heavily on the limits of such actions, most notably in connection with *time* limits.

Admittedly, art. 77 has become an issue of great contention in the Italian constitutional order, as governments have increasingly made use of it over the last twenty years. It allows the government to issue emergency executive decrees having the force of law. They must be converted into ordinary law by Parliament within sixty days or they lapse.[6] As originally conceived by the Constituent Assembly, they were to be reserved for genuine 'emergencies', but in recent legislatures their number has grown to well over one every week. In effect governments are using the device to force on to the parliamentary agenda consideration of a wide range of decrees concerning issues as diverse as taxation, social welfare, energy policy, and broadcasting law.

In certain respects governments are succeeding, as the sustained and anguished protest from Parliament over the last decade has suggested. In reality, however, these protests are more about the damage done to rational parliamentary timetabling by the constant need to review emergency decrees than they are about the power they give to the government. Parliament has in fact been able to fight back quite effectively, not only by frequently declining to convert decrees into ordinary legislation, but by bargaining with the government over the content both of the decrees themselves and of other items of current legislation.[7]

The decree-law controversy thus underscores the extent to which Parliament has internalized constitutional values granting it exceptional—almost coequal—power with government on the content and detail of government legislation. Significantly, moreover, it is in this area that Parliament has made its mark, rather than in that of wider and more generalized parliamentary scrutiny of the thrust of government policy, and of the actions of the administrative system. As we shall see, in recent years Parliament has begun to develop its scrutinizing functions, but, in comparison with its negotiating power over legislative detail, there remains much ground to be made up. Equally significantly, the constitution itself is virtually silent on these other roles. It devotes a whole section to the drafting of legislation, but it simply leaves to the two chambers of Parliament authority to determine their own internal procedures (including by implication their committee structure and procedure), and adds, almost as an afterthought following twelve detailed articles on legislative drafting procedures, that the chambers can, if they wish, 'order inquiries into matters of public interest', in which case they establish internal committees with powers similar to those of judicial authorities. These issues are explored further in the following two chapters.

The legislature and other constitutional agencies

If, through the constitution, the legislature enjoys significant powers of leverage over the executive at national level, it is not supposed to do so—at least as far as the constitution itself is concerned—in its relationship with other constitutionally established sources of power. The constitution disperses power to, and entrenches the position of, subnational units of government, the ordinary and the administrative judiciary, the constitutional court, and the electorate (through the latter's right to repeal legislation via a referendum procedure). Each of these agencies was seen as having an important role in limiting the power of a cohesive parliamentary majority, and for each it was seen as vital to establish basic principles of autonomy.

The judiciary

For the legal system this entailed the establishment of a special agency interposed between the judiciary and the political world, in the shape of the *High Council of the Judiciary*. Art. 104 affirms that 'The judiciary is an *autonomous institution independent of any other power*', contrasting it by implication with a judicial system under the control of a national ministry of justice. The president of the High Council is the president of the republic. The Council itself consists of thirty members, two-thirds elected from within the various branches of the judiciary (eight from the court of cassation, four from the courts of appeal, and eight from the lower courts), and one-third elected by Parliament from the academic-law community and from practising lawyers. It oversees recruitment, promotion, assignment to particular benches, and disciplinary proceedings in the entire judicial corps. The judiciary, though part of the public payroll, is thus a self-governing body insulated—at least in principle—from the government or the parliamentary majority.

However, this essential political independence—emphasized by a Constituent Assembly that was taking as its reference point the experience of the fascist era—cannot entirely protect the judiciary from political controversy. There are various ways in which judges as individuals, and the judicial system as a whole, can become involved in politics. First, the dispensing of justice often involves the investigation of political corruption and fraud, especially, but not exclusively, at local level. Since judicial investigations take place in the full glare of the media, even the decision to investigate cases of alleged corruption, let alone to prosecute, can have wide-ranging political consequences. Secondly, the pursuit of organized crime—especially in Sicily, Calabria, and Campania—is controversial both because it is alleged to have political ramifications, and because organized crime in the south is so widespread and socially corrosive a phenomenon that the *technical* arguments about its suppression (e.g. the level of special assistance in terms of judicial and police resources, and personal protection, that judges should be given) become politicized. All these matters raise sensitive issues of expediency, and can leave members of the judiciary feeling abandoned or exposed by politicians if they feel they are being denied the resources necessary to do their job effectively and in reasonable personal safety. Moreover, in a society where the judicial corps divides along political lines, and where the political sympathies of examining magistrates investigating particularly sensitive cases may be known, it is hard for individuals to escape accusations of bringing political considerations into the exercise of office.[8]

There is also the more general question of efficiency in the use of public resources, and the sheer labour productivity of the overall judicial machinery. The political autonomy of the judicial system naturally means that although taxpayers' money is being dispensed, ministers cannot be held directly accountable to Parliament for the way that money is used, in the same way as for ordinary ministerial departments. This is especially serious in a country where the wheels of justice do appear to grind exceedingly slow, and where the backlog of cases in both the civil and penal court system is, by any European standards, exceedingly high. This issue is taken up again in Chapter 8. Politicians must bear the ultimately responsibility for the state of law and order in a society, and will be held accountable by the electorate. Yet criticism of the judiciary, of which there has been a great deal in recent years for its alleged inefficiency, can, when articulated by politicians, very quickly begin to look like the exertion of some form of political intimidation.

'Auxiliary' agencies

Beyond the ordinary judiciary there are also special judicial corps, which are less insulated from the political world, and indeed are first listed in the constitution under the heading 'Government', in a subsection entitled 'Auxiliary bodies'. These are the council of state and the court of accounts. The council, composed of some 400 councillors, part nominated by the government and part recruited by competitive examination, performs a dual function. It advises the government on legal and administrative matters, but it is also the highest court of appeal on matters of administrative law, dealing both with the protection of the individual *vis-à-vis* the administration, and—a sub-branch of this—with the employment conditions of public employees. The role of the court of accounts is somewhat different. It does not advise the government. Rather it exercises various con- trols—most *ex ante*, some *ex post*—over the legality of public expenditure, and in these duties it reports to Parliament, rather than the government. Its 500-plus magistrates, like the councillors of the council of state, are appointed in part by competitive examination, and in part by government nomination.

The impact of both these agencies on the legalism that pervades the governmental system is considered in more detail in Chapter 8. Here, we are concerned with their constitutional status, and in this connection what is of prime concern is the issue of political independence. As in the case of the ordinary judiciary, the formal separation of the two does not always correspond to the practice. In the case of the council of state and the court of accounts, while members of both bodies are protected from government in the sense that they cannot be retired, suspended, or transferred by politicians, the protection is less explicit in the constitution, and left to ordinary law. Moreover, the protection is weakened by the power of the government to nominate some members of both bodies—albeit generally from within the politically neutral public administration.[9] It is further weakened, in the case of the council of state, by the latter's dual role as government adviser and judicial body, and, even more seriously, by the common practice by which councillors, who constitute something of an élite administrative corps, membership of which is prestigious and sought after, are seconded into the personal *cabinets* of ministers as advisers.[10]

Both the post-war council of state and the court of accounts continue institutional and administrative traditions reaching well back into Italian history—indeed to the period before unification. A third body listed under the 'auxiliary' agency section of the constitution is an innovation of the republican period. This is the Consiglio nazionale dell'economia e del lavoro (national council of the economy and labour), whose 111 members are drawn from a wide range of economic and social interests. It is a consultative forum, bringing together both sides of the capital/labour divide, and providing advice to government, Parliament, and regional governments, particularly over labour-market questions, forthcoming legislation on economic and social-policy issues, and macro-economic management generally. It is thought of as performing a useful, but essentially background and low-key, role, and cannot be regarded as a major forum in the economic-policy field.

Regional and local government

The Italian constitution provides a minimum threshold for local autonomy, in the sense that the three tiers of subnational authority which it establishes—regions, provinces, and municipalities—cannot be abolished by the central authorities, nor their (constitutionally endowed) powers altered, except by constitutional change. As we shall see, this, combined with the sociological importance of local identity in Italian political life, ensures that subnational political institutions play a significant role in the political system. As all studies of centre–local relationships demonstrate, however (even those of fully fledged federal systems), the real extent to which political power is decentralized

depends on a range of factors—most notably financial arrangements—which are rarely set out in detail in a constitution. Italy is no
exception to this, as we shall see in detailed examination of Italian
regional and local government in Chapter 9. Even what the
constitution says about the formal legislative and administrative powers
of regional authorities is restrictive or partially misleading. It is
restrictive in that legislative power is to be exercised 'within the
fundamental principles established by the laws of the State . . .
provided that such legislation is not in contrast with the national
interest' (art. 117). There follow (arts. 125–7) three detailed
statements of the procedures by which the state ensures that these
conditions are observed. And it is misleading in that the list of policy
sectors set out in art. 117 as those in which the regions enjoy
administrative autonomy does not correspond to those which, in
practice, have proved some of the most important.

There is no doubt that Italian regional devolution has been for many
a disappointment, both for the unconscionably long time it took to
establish, and for the limits on regional autonomy when it was
established. However, the constitutionalization of the centre–local
relationship has been an important part of the bargained interaction
which has developed between local and national politicians, in which
outcomes are determined not just by informal political linkages but
also by the jurisprudence of the constitutional court, picking its way
carefully through the meaning of arts. 125–7.

The referendum

The final constitutional check listed here consists of the opportunity
available to the electorate to repeal both constitutional and ordinary
parliamentary legislation. Constitutional laws can, within three months
of their publication, be submitted to such a referendum on request of
one-fifth of either chamber of Parliament, 500,000 voters, or five
regional councils, but, to date, no such referendum has been held.
Most ordinary legislation (other than financial laws, pardons, and
treaty ratification) can be submitted to a similar referendum at the
request of 500,000 voters or five regional councils. To obtain repeal of
a part, or all, of a piece of legislation, a majority of the electorate must
vote (three referendums failed in 1990 for this reason, even though the
great majority of those who did vote supported repeal) and a majority
of those voting must vote in favour. The legislation detailing the exact
procedure for the holding of referendums was not introduced until
1974.[11] To date there have been eighteen such referendums, plus an
extraordinary one, permitted by Constitutional Law no. 2, 3 April

1989. The latter was defined as one of guidance ('di indirizzo'). Its purpose was to win plebiscitary support for a declaration that the European Parliament should be given authority to draft a text for a 'European Union' treaty for the European Community.[12] Whether it will prove a precursor of a new type of positive referendum, allowing voters, or indeed parties, to promote legislation which cannot get a hearing or a majority in Parliament, remains to be seen.[13] In addition, there have been around twenty other requests for the holding of a referendum which, having obtained the required 500,000 signatures, were either ruled as inadmissible subjects for a referendum by the constitutional court, or were overtaken by parliamentary action to repeal or amend the legislation in question.

TABLE 5.1 *Italian referendums 1974–1991*

Issue	Year	Result (%)[a]		Turn-out (%)
Divorce	1974	Yes	40.7	88.1
		No	59.3	
Reale Law (public order)	1978	Yes	23.5	81.2
		No	76.5	
Public financing of parties	1978	Yes	43.6	81.2
		No	56.4	
Cossiga Law (public order)	1981	Yes	14.9	79.4
		No	85.1	
Life imprisonment	1981	Yes	22.6	79.4
		No	77.4	
Right to carry arms	1981	Yes	14.1	79.4
		No	85.9	
Abortion reform (permissive)	1981	Yes	11.6	79.4
		No	88.4	
Abortion reform (Catholic)	1981	Yes	32.0	79.4
		No	68.0	
Wage-indexation	1985	Yes	45.7	77.9
		No	54.3	
Civil responsibility of magistrates	1987	Yes	80.2	65.1
		No	19.8	
Parliamentary immunity/ Commissione inquirente	1987	Yes	85.1	65.1
		No	19.4	
Siting of nuclear power stations	1987	Yes	80.6	65.1
		No	19.4	

Issue	Year	Result (%)[a]		Turn-out (%)
Subsidies to local govts. permitting nuclear power	1987	Yes No	79.7 20.3	65.1
Italian participation in nuclear programmes abroad	1987	Yes No	71.8 28.2	65.1
Field-sports legislation	1990	Yes No	92.2 7.8	43.3
Funding legislation for field-sports	1990	Yes No	92.3 7.7	43.3
Use of pesticides	1990	Yes No	93.5 6.5	43.5
Preference-voting in elections	1991	Yes No	95.6 4.4	62.5

[a] As explained in the text, the Italian referendum is *abrogative*; thus 'yes' indicates the level of support for the removal of a law, or part of it, from the statute book, and 'no' support for the status quo.

The eighteen negative or abrogative referendums held to date are set out in Table 5.1. The range of issues is very broad, as has been the range of promoters, who have ranged from the civil rights groups associated with the Radical Party to conservative Catholic interests. The device has certainly settled some high-profile issues the parties have been unable to handle themselves. It has also often driven a wedge between parties and their supporters, and, because of the inherent awkwardness of policy-making through the repeal of legislation, it has been a blunt instrument for eliciting exactly what voters want. Nevertheless, it has allowed the electorate to enter the policy process directly in areas where otherwise compromise, delay, or obfuscation would have been the natural result of a divided or deadlocked Parliament.[14]

Implementing and Changing the Constitution

Implementation

The constitutional arrangements described in the previous two sections did not come into being overnight on 1 January 1948. Constitutions grow into place in all societies, and Italy is no exception. Conventions associated with the institutional relationships, with the attitudes and expectations of political leaders and electorates towards such relationships, and with the jurisprudence of the constitutional court in interpreting the constitution have all taken several decades to develop. Moreover, in the Italian case changing political circumstances have profoundly affected the pace at which key parts of the constitution have been put in place. The liberal power-dispersing system of checks and balances on which the constitution is based was not set up immediately, because, at the height of the Cold War, and with a potentially fragile parliamentary majority, the dominant centrist coalition feared that if the system were implemented rapidly it would weaken the coalition's ability to govern. The result was twofold. First, much of the enabling legislation necessary to make a reality of the checks and balances in the constitution was delayed—in some cases over extraordinarily long periods. Second, the parties of the left, the Socialists and Communists—who might at the time have been expected to have favoured a centralized and *dirigiste* conception of state power—became enduring supporters of the checks and balances of the constitutional text, if for no other reason because they found themselves excluded from the governing coalition after 1947, and saw in a dispersed and decentralized power structure a way of influencing policy through Parliament, regional and local government, and through legal and constitutional constraints.[15]

Thus several key features of the constitution were delayed. The constitutional court only came into being in 1956, and thereafter inevitably took some years to make inroads into the overhang of fascist legislation on the statute book, much of which was incompatible with the civil and social rights in the republican constitution. The ordinary judiciary itself continued to harbour among its ranks the habits and outlooks of a past era. As for the referendum device, and the system of regional government, both were delayed even longer. Initially, only four of the five 'special' regions on the periphery were established; the fifteen ordinary regions had to wait until 1970. The referendum, too, was only put in place in 1970. And in more intangible ways, in Parliament, as we shall see in the following chapter, the power-sharing mentality only really began to affect the relationship between legislature and executive in the late 1960s, to be enshrined in the reform of the parliamentary regulations in the early 1970s.

Changing the constitution

While the constitution has therefore taken different shapes at different times, it is nevertheless a rigid one, unlike its pre-fascist predecessor. It cannot be changed by ordinary legislation, and where the constitutional court deems this to have occurred, the law itself is automatically revoked. Constitutional changes, of which there have been very few, require a special legislative procedure, and must be passed by each chamber of Parliament twice, in identical form, at an interval of three months, and on the second occasion must pass each chamber by an absolute majority of the whole house (i.e. not just a majority of those present and voting). Unless they are passed by a two-thirds majority at the second occasion, they can also be subjected to a referendum, on demand of one-fifth of the membership of either house, 500,000 electors, or five regional councils. Such restrictions are a powerful limitation on constitutional revision. The formal changes which have to date been introduced have been limited to relatively minor matters: the intervals between elections to the Senate; the number of members of the Chamber of Deputies; the number of justices of the constitutional court; the number of regional governments.

In effect, if the constitution is to be changed in a fundamental way—for example by establishing an executive presidency along the lines of that found in Fifth republic France, which would require the direct election of the president of the republic—then it has to be done either by broad inter-party agreement, or in a politically controversial way (i.e. by a bare majority). If done by the latter route it will inevitably devolve the final decision to the electorate, for a referendum becomes almost inevitable. To date, neither approach has been attempted. There has been much discussion of major institutional surgery, in an attempt to achieve broad inter-party agreement, but insufficient common ground has been found. Nor has a minimum coalition been cohesive enough and confident enough of mass support for its changes even to test seriously the parliamentary waters, let alone those of the wider electorate.

Institutional reform does not, however, have to be achieved through revision of the constitutional text itself. Many elements of the political order are governed by ordinary law, or indeed by no law at all. Of these, much the most important is the electoral system, which can in principle be changed by normal legislation. As we shall see in the concluding chapter, there are various ways in which electoral reform might be thought capable of changing the party system, and, through it, also the relationship between legislature and executive, which latter is widely seen as the unsatisfactory element of the existing constitution. At one point early on in the post-war period, electoral law was indeed changed, in such a way that any group of parties winning over 50 per cent of the vote would be accorded two-thirds of the parliamentary seats—a substantial premium which could have given the Christian Democrats an absolute majority over all other parties. In 1953, the DC and its three allies (PSDI, PLI, and PRI) failed by the narrowest of margins—0.15 per cent of the vote—to cross the necessary threshold to obtain the premium. By the next election circumstances had changed in the coalition. Those who had been unhappy about the procedure in which they had acquiesced regained the upper hand in the coalition, and the electoral system returned to the pure proportionalism of the *status quo ante*.[16] What the 1953 episode seemed to demonstrate, in fact, was that to bring about major institutional change through ordinary law was little less difficult and politically destructive of stable short-term coalition relationships than to do so through constitutional revision. The 1948 constitution had created a balance, and for the next three decades that balance could not be adjusted without consequences too unpredictable to be judged as worth the risk. Only in the 1980s did reform come back on to the political agenda in a serious way, and even at the start of the 1990s, after ten years of the debate, Italy still had not found enough common ground to begin the process of change. What that change might consist of, if and when it eventually comes, will be explored in the concluding chapter.

Constitutional Guarantors

The President of the Republic

The president of the republic is the first line of defence when it comes to protecting the constitution. He exercises this role in various ways. He enjoys modest (i.e. generally suspensive rather than absolute) powers of inspection, control, counter-signature, and nomination, in both the legislative and the executive field. Because he is not directly elected, and, as the constitution states, 'represents the unity of the nation', none of these powers approaches in political weight the power of, say, the US president to veto legislation, or of the French president to dissolve the National Assembly. It is a convention of the constitution that as far as possible Italy's president should be 'above' party politics, even if before election presidents have been practising politicians. As we have already seen in Chapter 3, it is not always easy or possible for the president of the republic to remain above party politics, especially when fulfilling his duty to nominate an incoming prime minister during a particularly difficult coalition crisis.

The president is elected for a seven-year term by an electoral college of the members of the two chambers of Parliament, strengthened by three representatives from each region (other than the Val d'Aosta, which has only one). Despite its non-partisan role, the presidency is much sought after by political parties. Of course, as in the case of nominees to other agencies carrying non-partisan, constitutional-guardianship roles, nomination tends to change the nominee in ways that the sponsoring party could not foresee. This was certainly the case with President Cossiga (elected in 1985), whose last years in office were spent in sometimes bitter feuding with his own Christian Democrat Party. Nevertheless, parties regard the presidency as a visible symbol of their standing, and will not relinquish lightly the opportunity to fill it. Presidential elections can thus be hard-fought battles, especially if no agreement has been reached between the parties before the balloting begins.

Such agreement is not always easy to achieve. First, it requires internal agreement on a single candidate by the Christian Democrat Party, which naturally contains several groups each championing a particular candidate. Secondly, it normally requires agreement between the DC and its coalition partners, most notably, in the last two decades, the Socialist Party. In addition, during the 1970s, it seemed to require the agreement of the Communist Party, given the PCI's influence over the coalition-building process. Even the first of these conditions can be hard to achieve. In 1971, the DC was bitterly divided over its candidate, with the result that the election of Giovanni Leone took no fewer than twenty-three ballots.[17] His election was the most divisive in the republic's history, being opposed not only by the Communist Party, but also by the Socialists. It broke an unwritten rule that the main parties will seek as broad as possible a consensus in election to what is constitutionally a highly sensitive office. In the two subsequent elections (Pertini in 1978 and Cossiga in 1985) the presidential election was set in the context of better (although by no means perfect) unspoken understandings about the distribution of party nominations to key 'institutional' appointments, including not only the presidency of the republic, but also those of the Senate, the Chamber of Deputies, and the Council of Ministers.[18] Thus although Pertini, too, was elected after an exhaustive series of ballots, it was eventually with the support of the DC, PCI, and the lay parties together. Cossiga, indeed, was elected on the very first ballot with 752 votes out of 977.[19]

The recent history of elections to the presidential office underscores the fine line which has to be trodden between the original selection on a partisan basis, and the subsequent occupation of the office as an impartial umpire. The difficulties inherent in this—that a president is compromised by the circumstances that led to his election—are ever present, and are compounded by the manner in which even broadly based elections like Pertini's and Cossiga's get sucked into the daily partisan battle. In both cases, the sub-plot of political manœuvring both before and during the election had short-term ramifications for relations between the three main parties.

Nevertheless, almost all occupants—and certainly the last two— have given the appearance of putting party affiliation firmly behind them from the day they were elected. They are assisted in this by the immediate physical separation from day-to-day politics which they experience by occupation of the Quirinale Palace, and by the substantial official machinery in which they are enveloped. Italy is a country much attached to official procedures and to formal (if not always smooth-flowing) ceremony, and it is the president of the republic, above all others, who must bear the brunt of this.[20]

The president's most important tasks are those of nominating the prime minister after an election or a coalition crisis, or, if the crisis is beyond resolution, of deciding when to dissolve Parliament and hold fresh elections. As we have seen in Chapter 3, it is a convention of the constitution that the president will do all in his power to avoid a premature dissolution. Whether he has any discretion in nominating a new prime minister depends on political circumstances; but not infrequently, when the parties are divided—internally, or among themselves—there is no agreed name which emerges from the obligatory round of consultations held with party leaders. The 'exploratory' mandate he gives to an individual in these circumstances to investigate the feasibility of forming a government can then be influential over the eventual outcome. Moreover, the president's nominee may succeed in assembling a government, and be sworn in, but fail to secure a parliamentary majority. If so, and a premature general election has to be held—or indeed, if the coalition has fallen apart right at the end of its natural life, leading to the resignation of the government in anticipation of an election—then the president may have some discretion over whom he appoints as caretaker prime minister, and this again may have political implications. In this area, although each constitutional commentator seeks to lay down guide-lines, there are in fact no clear constitutional conventions, and, as may readily be imagined, it is the area that causes presidents their greatest difficulty in remaining above partisan politics.[21]

In addition to these powers the president performs a number of other roles. The most formal is that of promulgating laws, and in so doing confirming officially the regularity of the legislative procedure that has generated them. In this area, the president has little discretion, but does enjoy a temporary suspensive veto. He can refer a law back to Parliament before promulgating it—giving his reasons for doing so—but must act with care, and normally limit such actions to questions of legal-constitutional propriety, rather than of substantive policy merit, for Parliament can overrule the suspensive veto by simply confirming the legislation in its original form. Beyond that the president has several other formal roles. He authorizes the introduction of government bills to Parliament. He confers honours, grants pardons, accredits and receives diplomatic representatives, and at least nominally he presides over the High Council of the Judiciary, and over the Supreme Defence Council, and serves as commander in chief of the armed forces.

In addition, and seemingly innocuously, he may send messages to Parliament, and indeed may speak his mind, as 'representative of national unity' (art. 87), on whatever subject he sees fit. Until the arrival of presidents Pertini and Cossiga this last role was relatively underdeveloped. Since 1978, however, two different but combative personalities have occupied the Quirinale, with unpredictable results. Both were willing to speak their mind on controversial issues, and were not afraid to criticize parties and institutions across a wide field. Indeed in his last full year of office, president Cossiga took on both the legal system, criticizing the judiciary for its gross inefficiencies and virtually the entire party system, criticizing it for its inability to evolve towards a capacity to offer alternative governments to the electorate. What was achieved, either for the standing of the office of the presidency of the republic, or for the cause of institutional reform which he claimed to be supporting, remained to be seen as his period of office came to a controversial conclusion.

The constitutional court

The Italian constitutional court is a less controversial guardian of the constitution, and is widely considered to be one of the chief institutional successes of the republican order. It has developed a clear and fairly stable set of roles, serves as an important stimulant to the performance of the government, legislature, and the ordinary judiciary, and attracts relatively few serious critics. It has succeeded in preserving a careful balance in its composition, and this has enabled it to maintain its authority as impartial constitutional umpire, and as chief defender of the rule of law and the values underlying the 1948 constitution.

The court consists of fifteen judges, each elected for twelve years (reduced in 1967 to nine years), on a non-renewable basis. Five are chosen by the president of the republic, five by a joint sitting of the two chambers of Parliament, and five by the ordinary and administrative high courts (the court of cassation electing three, and the council of state and the court of accounts electing one each).[22] The judges can be selected from among the ordinary or administrative judiciary, from full university professors of law, or practising lawyers with twenty or more years of experience. Membership of the court is incompatible with membership of Parliament, local councils, or any public or private office. Constitutional court judges are guaranteed the same form of immunity from arrest and prosecution as are members of Parliament.

If these provisions were intended to keep the court's personnel out of politics, they have not entirely succeeded. As in many other areas of Italian public life, there has, in effect, been a form of political distribution of seats on the court, at least in the case of the five parliamentary nominees. This distribution has been allocated to a widening band of parties, including, from the 1960s onwards, the Communist Party. It does not mean that Parliament's nominees have been politicians (although some, prior to election to the court, have been in Parliament, and others have gone on to political careers subsequently). Nor, certainly, does it imply that parties have used their nominees to gain political influence over court decisions (although all parties value the connections that its nominees give to an institution that plays an important if concealed role in the legislative process). But the tendency, within Parliament, and to a lesser extent from presidents of the republic, to nominate academic lawyers, especially those with political affiliation, rather than politically neutral career judges, has ensured that political considerations are important in the selection process.[23]

Academics themselves have played a particularly important role in the court's development. The key post of president (elected from within the court on a renewable three-year term) has tended to be filled from among the academic group. The president assigns cases to particular judges for investigation and exposition to the rest of the court, he sets the timetable and the order of cases, and has the last (and hence potentially casting) vote. Moreover, the presence of academics has set the tone of much of the court's work, and has introduced into its activities a body of scholarly doctrinal interpretation of the constitution's more opaque passages.

The court's functions are defined chiefly in art. 134 of the constitution. The most important and time-consuming is that of deciding controversies over the constitutionality of ordinary legislation at both state and regional level, and of other acts having the force of law (decree-laws and delegated legislation—but not internal administrative or parliamentary regulations). Beyond this, the court resolves inter-institutional conflicts of competence between different branches of government (whether at national level, between state and region, or between region and region). It hears cases brought by Parliament against the president of the republic for treason or against ministers for crimes committed in office. And finally—a function not originally laid down in the constitution, but one which has become an important and politically delicate part of the court's role—it decides on the admissibility (and date) of referendums brought by popular initiative for the abrogation of existing legislation.

In determining the constitutionality of legislation, the court cannot subject laws to examination prior to their promulgation, as does the French constitutional council, nor does it have the power to hear direct appeals from individual citizens complaining of a violation of their basic constitutional rights, as does the German constitutional court. The Italian court's role is that of constitutional appellate court, hearing cases passed up to it from the ordinary courts. Where it finds that all or part of a piece of legislation is unconstitutional, it has immediate power to declare it invalid. Its role in this area has covered a very wide range of case types: family law, media law, the penal process, industrial relations, and so on.[24] It was an important part of the thinking of the Constituent Assembly that the constitutional court should be placed above the ordinary court system, and should take judgements about constitutionality out of the hands of ordinary judges. The need for this was confirmed during the 1950s, in the years before the constitutional court was established. During this time the court of cassation—the appeal court for the ordinary judicial system—was in effect the constitutional umpire, and its judgements, notably about the compatibility of pre-republican legislation with the 1948 constitution, proved to be remarkably conservative.[25]

The fact that the court's role is not, in practice, limited to the simple choice of confirming or striking down an item of legislation has assisted it in guiding the lower courts, and indeed in stimulating and cajoling Parliament into action in areas where legislation is lacking or internally contradictory, or where legislation is in conflict with the constitution but cannot, without drastic consequences, be immediately struck down. The court has various options available to it. It can, for example, accept a piece of legislation as constitutionally valid, but only under a certain interpretation—conceivably one different from that previously placed on it by a lower court, or different from that which Parliament originally intended. The court can also add riders to its judgements, indicating to Parliament what steps it considers necessary to rectify the constitutional position.

The constitutional court thus plays an important role in the wider legislative process. However, on its own there are limits to what it can achieve. Partly, this is because of the sheer physical limits to its own workload. It is capable of producing three or four hundred judgements in a year, but it faces a constant and large backlog of cases. As republican legislation has gradually replaced fascist and pre-fascist legislation, this problem ought to recede somewhat, but in practice the fragmentary, hurried, and often ill-drafted output of the Italian Parliament in recent years has prevented the problem from disappearing as rapidly as it should. Moreover, Parliament is often slow to respond to the prompting of the constitutional court. In the case of broadcasting, for example—an area where successive court judgements have had a major, but not always unilinear or even intended, impact on public policy—the court set out as early as 1974 the contents of legislation granting a public-service monopoly which it regarded as necessary if the constitutional prescriptions governing freedom of expression and the media were to be respected. It elaborated on these again in the early and mid-1980s, yet only in 1990 did comprehensive framework legislation emerge, addressing the full range of issues raised by the court. Although Parliament had, in the interim, produced a series of stop-gap legislative responses—most notably in 1975 and 1985—they had by no means addressed all the issues raised by the court. During the intervening years various principles—in particular those relating to political control of the public-service sector, and to the unregulated growth of the private sector—had been studiously ignored. The moral and legal power of the court, in short, is not enough to shame Parliament and government into action where the latter do not wish to act, or cannot find enough common ground to do so.[26]

6

Parliamentary Government

The Italian Conception of Parliamentary Government

Despite the counter-powers described in the previous chapter—constitutionally entrenched regionalism, direct democracy, constitutional review of legislation, etc.—the Italian Parliament is widely thought of as considerably more important, in relation to other parts of the political system, than are most European legislatures, and it is generally seen as the one major exception to the thesis of the long-term 'decline' of parliaments during the twentieth century.[1] If not unequivocally 'powerful', it is at least argued to be 'central' to the political process.[2] Intuitively, such judgements have some plausibility. The Italian Parliament, with its fragmented party system and its independent-minded members, appears to be a far more formidable obstacle to the concerted will of the political executive than in any other West European democracy.

Some caution has to be exercised in the use of terminology however. Judgements about the 'power' of a legislature are inevitably simplifications of complex reality. There is generally more than one dimension to such power and it is perfectly possible for a legislature to score well on some criteria and poorly on others. It may have a well-developed capacity to block or alter the executive's legislative proposals, but little capacity to scrutinize the work of the administration, or to maintain a clear grip on public-spending strategies. The concept of 'centrality' is equally ambiguous. The personnel of a legislature overlaps with members of the government, leaders of parties, and even some interest-group spokesmen, and it is frequently hard to establish in what capacity each individual is acting, and thus in what institutional arena a decision has really been taken. If centrality simply implies that Parliament is the cross-roads where pressures from the electorate, parties, the executive, and interest groups are played out, this does not take us very far. It does not tell us whether Parliament—as an institution, rather than as the main instrument for the exercise of majoritarian will—is capable of exercising any clear-cut leadership against other institutional actors. Parliament may appear to be central to the political system precisely because it lacks the structuring that comes from established lines of division between government and opposition, and from strong disciplined parties. If so, however, it may be exposed to a range of unmanageable and contradictory demands. Some commentators have argued that the Italian Parliament suffers from exactly such a weakness, and that it is therefore neither powerful nor central. On the contrary, its weakness generates a 'crisis of representation' in the wider political system[3]—a thesis we examine in greater detail below.

The ambiguity of concepts like 'power' or 'centrality' when applied to the Italian Parliament reflects more basic uncertainties over the principles on which it should operate, as the constitutional debates of the last decade have shown.[4] Post-war Italy has rarely contented itself with one conception of an institutional theory, and has certainly not done so in the case of parliamentary representation. There is, as a result, a decided lack of clarity over whether the primary focus of a representative's loyalty should be party or constituency. Moreover, the constitution appears to sanction a third principle: that the representative must, as art. 67 states, 'represent the whole nation and carry out his duties without the ties of a mandate'.[5] The resultant ambiguity has not been confined to arcane disputes between constitutional lawyers. It has applied very clearly to the reality of parliamentary life. Furthermore, since 1970, when enabling legislation introduced the appropriate machinery, Italy's referendum procedure has been in competition with the entire representative process. As we have seen, even though it permits only annulment, rather than direct popular initiative, the system has had an important effect on political life, settling some high-profile issues the parties were unable to handle themselves, but also, on several occasions, driving an awkward wedge between parties and their electoral supporters.

These ambiguities make it very difficult to identify the Italian legislature with any of the various conceptual styles—majoritarian and adversarial, pluralist and bargained, consociational[6]—which comparative political analysis normally deploys to classify representative institutions in parliamentary democracies. At one time or another arguments have been adduced to place the system in each. In the 1950s and 1960s, and again in the 1980s, Parliament appeared to operate on the majoritarian principle, although below the surface it might at times have been better described as pluralist, so lacking in cohesion was the parliamentary majority, and so open to concealed influence by the opposition. During the years of reconstruction, and again in the latter half of the 1970s, the internal compromises between government and opposition became more overt. Some saw in this the elements of a form of quasi-consociationalism both in Parliament and in the wider political system.[7]

Moreover, it was not just the interpretations of observers or politicians which changed. New types of working arrangement brought forth new formal rules of parliamentary procedure. The most important reform of procedure occurred in the early 1970s. As we shall see, it brought with it practices that consolidated a form of bargained interaction between government and opposition which outlived the period of most active coalition between the Communists and Christian Democrats. During the 1980s, in a series of stages through the decade, attempts were made to shift procedure back towards a more majoritarian emphasis, but the pace of change was slow, and it was only towards the very end of the decade that these attempts began to bear fruit.

Naturally, changes in the ground rules by which parliamentary government operates have been less the result of a disinterested search for institutional balance than of changing party strengths in a complex and ideologically divided party system. Parties in power prefer not to compromise with the parliamentary opposition, but may do so when they have little alternative, or they perceive some short-term advantage from doing so. Parties in apparently permanent opposition may sometimes prefer arrangements by which they gain at least some bargaining power *vis-à-vis* the governing majority. Whatever their real motives, each party will seek to clothe its objectives in the respectability of constitutional convention, although this is difficult because, almost by definition, it requires that the other side itself comes to support such objectives. The difficulty of reaching agreement in the Bozzi Commission on institutional reform testifies to the difficulty of arriving at this level of agreement. Moreover, what makes Italy unusual among parliamentary democracies is not so much the interspersing of periods of majoritarianism (or something like it) with periods of quasi-consociationalism, but rather the fact that this occurs in the context of a party system characterized by wide ideological distance.

In the light of such ambiguities, it is not surprising that interpretations of the role of the Italian Parliament have varied considerably. So too have the formal procedural rules governing its internal workings. To make sense of these complexities, the best place to begin is the role of parties. How the party system has affected the outlook and behaviour of the parliamentary class, and how changes in party relationships have changed Parliament's internal procedures, are the keys to understanding the institution's contemporary role.

Party in Parliament

Party plays an important role in parliamentary life, reflecting the wider primacy of party in the political system as it emerged after 1945. It is underpinned both by the electoral system and by parliamentary rules. Electoral law makes independent candidacies in elections impossible. Candidates must be elected on party lists, which require minimum local and national thresholds effectively precluding individual electoral initiatives. Public subsidization of politics also goes to parties rather than individuals, and parliamentary rules give quite generous research and clerical resources to party groups, rather than to individual representatives. The latter, though exceptionally well paid by European standards, have, until recently, officially had almost no office, research, or other facilities available to them *personally*.[8] Party groups, through their group leaders, also share control of the parliamentary timetable, and have special procedural rights, such as proportional membership of committees, the right to introduce amendments beyond normal time limits on such action, and the right to call for secret or roll-call votes on particular issues. (Note, however, that these privileges are less extensive in the Senate than in the Chamber.)

Admittedly, not all members of Parliament in practice belong to clear-cut party groups. The purity of Italy's form of proportional representation enables some local representatives to get into Parliament, and these—lacking the minimum size to qualify as a parliamentary group—are technically assembled in the so-called *Gruppo misto*. Moreover, representatives are not formally obliged to join the group on whose party list they are elected. Thus, in addition to occasional switching between parties, there has been, since 1976, a group known as the *Indipendenti di sinistra* (left independents) whose members—generally radical left-leaning intellectuals—have been elected on Communist Party lists, but who have made clear to the PCI and to voters in advance that they intend to sit in Parliament as independents, rather than as members subject to Communist-group discipline. For the Communist Party, the loss of group members is more than compensated for by the prestige which such names bring to its candidate lists.

These exceptions apart, most representatives join party groups, and are subject to group discipline. But what this means varies greatly between parties. It obviously does not entail that once a governing majority is constructed, it holds together with complete reliability for as long as the parties of which it is composed stay in agreement. Indeed, the so-called majorities which support government are very often not at all clear-cut. On occasions, there is no real majority. Even when there is, the boundary between government and opposition is frequently indistinct. Poor internal party cohesion, procedural peculiarities, high levels of absenteeism, and the strong local ties which condition the behaviour of many representatives all combine to weaken the cohesion of the majority. This does not necessarily mean that governments cannot maintain the formal *confidence* of the legislature; indeed, few governments fall on confidence votes, or fail to win them when first constructed. But it does mean that, often from the outset, support for particular government measures is flaky and unreliable. Over the life of the government this problem tends to increase, gradually wearing down the government's will to continue, and finally causing it to collapse.

In part, this syndrome is the result of procedural rules which assist both the opposition and dissident government back-benchers. These rules are examined later in the chapter. Proposals for institutional reform in recent years aiming to make governing coalitions more cohesive have tended to focus on such rules. However, they are not the primary cause of the problem. It is apparent, first, that the cohesion of different parliamentary groups is varied. The Communist/PDS group has tended to exhibit a high level of cohesion, reflecting the disciplined nature of its parent party, and the authority of the party organization over the parliamentary group. Real authority in the PCI/PDS lies in the central committee and the executive, not in the parliamentary group. Members of Parliament, a greater proportion of whom than in other parties are professional politicians relying entirely on the party for their livelihood, have tended to come into Parliament later in their careers, and (a small top leadership group apart) have stayed for a shorter period than in other parties.[9] The pressure towards centralized party control has thus been extensive, for such individuals cannot easily afford to fall foul of the party leadership. The Christian Democrat Party, in contrast, is generally thought to exhibit one of the lowest levels of cohesion,[10] and this clearly reflects the DC's faction-ridden internal life, and what has often been described as the 'entrepreneurial' character of Christian Democrat members of Parliament.

Several commentators have argued, however, that the causes of the problem lie less in the nature of individual parties than in the overall shape of the party system.[11] Their arguments have formed a powerful critique of the operation of the Italian Parliament. The central thesis is that the absence of alternation in power between government and opposition, itself the result of the Communist Party's strength, and the

Christian Democrat Party's centrality in the party spectrum, has undermined majority discipline. The governing parties, especially Christian Democracy, have known that, barring a cataclysmic electoral shift, the Communists could never come to power. They have therefore had less need of the unity, efficiency, and policy cohesion which might stem from majority discipline. Members of Parliament have not needed to be the collective bearers of clear-cut policy programmes. Given coalition government, such programmes would rarely have passed in an orderly or meaningful way. Instead, members of Parliament, at least on the government side, have become bearers of their own sectional demands: benefits for their constituencies, and resources for their personal electoral machines and their faction's organization. These tendencies have been especially marked in the south, where the traditional structure of political linkages, and the widespread occurrence of clientelism, have ensured that political representation is locally focused and fragmented in character.

On the other side of the political spectrum, so the argument continues, the improbability of coming to power discouraged the Communist Party from treating the parliamentary arena as a training ground for government. Thus the external party organization continued to dominate the parliamentary leadership. Furthermore, knowing it would not have to redeem its electoral pledges, the PCI could support demands on an indiscriminate basis. Although it did not do so through the same *individual* entrepreneurialism characteristic of the DC's representatives, the PCI too was inclined to press sectional demands which overlapped with those of the governing parties. Moreover, the structure of opportunities set by the internal rules of procedure in the Italian Parliament encouraged the Communist opposition to bargain with the government majority in ways that blurred the distinction between the two.

With parliamentary parties thus representing overlapping and highly fragmented interests, and with relatively little differentiation between government and opposition, the consequence has been a poorly institutionalized Parliament. It has lacked set mechanisms by which members are socialized into political life and clear-cut and stable operational rules by which it fulfils its various functions.[12] Admittedly, the main cause is not the lack of formal rules in themselves, for Parliament's internal regulations are spelt out in great detail and its internal committee articulation is long-standing. However—so the argument runs—the rules have operated in an unpredictable way, and the backgrounds and attitudes of members of Parliament have led them to undervalue important roles like the scrutiny of government legislation and administration, while over-emphasizing the servicing of their own constituencies and clienteles. Evidence for this is to be seen in Parliament's tendency to produce a mass of legislation which deals in detail with minor distributional issues, without properly addressing broad policy issues. Thus, it is said, Parliament fails to set the broad framework for public policy, dealing in disproportionate detail with technical issues which would be better left to administrative discretion and delegated legislation.

The issues raised by this critique, as summarized in the preceding paragraphs, are clearly complex ones requiring careful scrutiny. The sections which follow deal with its various aspects.

Parliamentary Outlooks and Legislative Behaviour

The parliamentary class

While there is rather little detailed evidence on the nature of the Italian parliamentary class,[13] some broad features stand out clearly. The largest element within the membership of the Italian Parliament is from middle- or lower middle-class backgrounds: teachers—both primary and secondary—party and trade-union officials and organizers, and independent professionals (lawyers, doctors, etc.). It is notable that much of the upper middle-class (senior managers, entrepreneurs, and landowners on one side, and the so-called 'state bourgeoisie' of judges, higher public officials, and diplomats on the other) is relatively under-represented in the Italian Parliament. The one element of the latter category which is not under-represented is probably university professors. The shift from senior levels of the state bureaucracy to a political career, common in France, is rather rare. Likewise, and in contrast to the pattern in Britain, few who have made a successful career in business seem to feel the need subsequently to assert themselves in politics.

Moreover, while members of Parliament are quite well educated (three-quarters have some form of tertiary-level education) they are on the whole upwardly mobile, coming from family backgrounds more modest than their own. Within this broad picture there are of course variations between the parties, with the Communist Party bringing a larger group of working-class, or originally working-class, representatives than other parties.[14]

A parliamentary career in Italy has in fact normally been the preserve of those who have worked their way up from the grass roots. In recent years, the tendency to place prestigious names on party electoral lists has changed this somewhat, bringing in even more academics, and a few entrepreneurs and media personalities, but the impact remains limited, and the individuals are generally there primarily for decorative purposes. Most parliamentarians begin their political careers early, as politicians in local government, or as paid officials in parties or unions, building up a local base from which to make the transition to the national stage. Only a few individuals can come to politics in mid-career and still hope to exercise real influence. The local base is vital in most cases; only a very few (two or three at most) of the national leaders in each party can afford to stand outside their home constituencies as well as in them.[15] Otherwise, the preference-vote mechanism described in Chapter 4 makes a strong local base absolutely indispensable.

Origins that make rather few MPs part of a flexible mobile social élite thus combine with an electoral mechanism—the preference vote—which, as we have seen, is not unlike the US primary system in its divisive effects on parties, to force members of Parliament to spend a great deal of time cultivating their local base. They need to maintain a network of loyal local-government allies and party workers, and this does not mean simply attending meetings, socializing, and being seen, but intervening actively on behalf of constituents with the bureaucracy, or, in Parliament, through the promotion of locally directed legislation. To be sure, this is part of an MP's role in most democracies, and there is no index which demonstrates beyond doubt that Italian MPs spend more time on these types of activity than do their counterparts in other parliamentary systems. It is nevertheless clear that constituency pressures are very powerful, and that they dominate role-perceptions for large numbers of Italian MPs until they reach a fairly advanced stage of their careers.[16] This has traditionally made it very difficult for Parliament to develop a reservoir of policy expertise similar to that which is said to characterize, for example, the German Bundestag. Except where policy expertise has coincided with constituency interest (in which case it is likely be used primarily for that end), it has been unlikely to help representatives further their careers, whether in parties of the governing coalition, or in the opposition.

Constituency pressures are reflected in the highly contested use of the preference vote in elections. As we have already seen in Chapter 4, this competition is especially marked among governing parties, which enjoy favoured access to the resources members of Parliament seek to distribute to their clienteles. It is also particularly marked in the south, where such political links are most widespread. Constituency pressures are also reflected in the clear neglect of ordinary parliamentary business in favour of party activities and local political work. As we shall see later in the chapter, absenteeism in the Italian Parliament is rife, frequently making it difficult to achieve a quorum, and often leaving the government exposed to defeat. And since governments rely on several party-group leaderships to secure attendance, absenteeism cannot easily be solved by tighter discipline unless this is co-ordinated across several parties. In any case, the link between the government and group leaderships in the Italian Parliament is a more difficult and tenuous one than in most European legislatures.

The origins of MPs, together with the pressures placed upon them by electoral competition, thus tend to create a parliamentary class which is provincial, if not parochial, in outlook. Proponents of the thesis of the failed institutionalization of the Italian Parliament claim that this factor is important in explaining why Parliament's concerns are not focused primarily on issues of broad public policy of national importance, but on the small change of political life—the distribution of benefits on a very localized and fragmented level. This is reflected, they argue, in the hyperactivity of the Parliament, which produces a vast, but ill-directed, quantity of legislation.

Legislative output

Certainly, by comparative standards, the quantity of individual items of legislation is high,[17] although, as Table 6.1 indicates, over the post-war years, and particularly since the 1970s, the absolute volume of Italian legislation has shown a tendency to decline quite substantially. The standard explanation for legislative hyperactivity is that a large proportion of legislation concerns minor matters (so-called *leggini*) or micro-sectional legislation, the scope of which is limited to local communities (special grants or subsidies, for example) or small groups within society (limited categories of welfare recipients or public employees). Such legislation, it is argued, reflects the attempts of MPs to service their own or their party's electoral clienteles. It also reflects the impossibility of agreeing upon clear-cut government programmes which will produce winners and losers in large aggregated groups of the electorate. In the absence of such agreement, and indeed in the absence even of agreement on clear-cut decisional rules defining the respective roles of government and opposition, the Italian Parliament falls back on an exaggerated form of incrementalism in its legislative work. This, in turn, crowds out major reform, and concentrates the attention of members of Parliament on minor issues of immediate concern to their supporters. In other political systems, these issues would be subsumed in more uniform framework legislation, or would be dealt with by administrative discretion.

TABLE 6.1 *The legislative output of the Italian Parliament*

Parliament	Laws[a]	Constitutional laws	Annual average[b]
I: 1948–53			463
1948	106		
1949	437		
1950	508		
1951	470		
1952	576		
1953	219	1	
Total	2,316 (28)	1	
II: 1953–8			379
1953	79		
1954	395		
1955	340		
1956	413		
1957	367		
1958	302	1	
Total	1,896 (60)	1	
III: 1958–63			359
1958	43		
1959	296		
1960	345		
1961	382	1	
1962	437		
1963	290	2	
Total	1.793 (28)	3	
IV: 1963–8			353
1963	64	1	
1964	266		
1965	340		
1966	298		
1967	412	2	
1968	385		
Total	1,765 (89)	3	

TABLE 6.1 (*contd*)

Parliament	Law[a]	Constitutional laws	Annual average[b]
V: 1968–72			210
1968	18		
1969	238		
1970	214		
1971	357	1	
1972	12	1	
Total	1,765 (66)	2	
VI: 1972–6			282
1972	64		
1973	338		
1974	240		
1975	297		
1976	189		
Total	1,128 (108)		
VII: 1976–9			222
1976	34		
1977	295		
1978	258		
1979	79		
Total	666 (136)		
VIII: 1979–83			215
1979	46		
1980	277		
1981	238		
1982	261		
1983	141		
Total	963 (169)		
IX: 1983–7			198
1983	24		
1984	238		
1985	258		
1986	207		
1987	66		
Total	793 (136)		

Parliament	Law[a]	Constitutional laws	Annual average[b]
X: 1987–92			215
1987	42		
1988	193		
1989	242		
1990	226		
1991	241	I	
1992	124		
Total	1,068 (187)	I	

[a] Converted decree-laws in brackets; on the use of the decree-law, see above, pp. 149–50.
[b] Legislatures I to IV and X lasted their full five years; the others lasted four, except the VIIth, which lasted only three. Since Italian general elections have always been held in the spring or early summer, it is legitimate to calculate the annual legislative output by dividing the total output for the relevant legislature by the (round figure) number of years it lasted, even though some *calendar* years straddle two legislatures. Output in the second six months of those years in which general elections are held is understandably low, as goverments take time to gear up their legislative programmes.

Sources: Legislatures I to VIII: Camera dei deputati, *La Camera dei deputati dalla I alla VIII legislatura* (Rome, 1985), 14–19. Legislatures IX and X, data supplied by Dr de Benedetti, of the Ufficio informazione parlamentare e relazioni esterne, Camera dei deputati.

Summary judgements of this type, on the output of an entire legislature, are difficult to assess. All democratic systems produce a variety of different types of legislation, some of it very narrow in application, other parts very broad. The claim that the Italian Parliament is defective because of a high output of minor distributional benefits must be based upon some hypothetical standard of what is the appropriate balance between different types of legislation, upon some objective method of assessing what constitutes micro-sectional legislation, and upon some clear model of the impact that it has on the rest of the legislature's activities.

The argument that micro-sectional legislation reflects the ubiquity of clientelism in a system where there is little possibility of agreement on broader and more programmatic legislation is partly valid, but not the complete story. Micro-sectional legislation is also encouraged by the legalism of Italian politics. Indeed, the outlook of the administrative courts (council of state, court of accounts, and regional administrative tribunals) may be said positively to *require* that much Italian legislation is of the micro-sectional type. The problem is rooted in the Italian legislative tradition, and has its origins well before the promulgation of the post-war republic; legislative output actually reached its *peak* in the years 1910–30.[18]

The drafters of the post-war constitution recognized that this habit posed a serious risk that the legislature would be swamped by the promotion of *leggini*. To avoid this danger they included a provision (art. 72) by which certain types of bill[19] could complete all stages in the restricted environment of committee, without reference back to the whole house for article-by-article plenary examination and final approval. They sought, in other words, to recognize that legislation varies in nature, and that it could be perfectly proper for less important and politically uncontroversial bills to be assigned to the less partisan and less public environment of committees, where they may be dealt with most efficiently. At least in theory, the device could be justified on the ground that it released the energies of the plenary sessions for legislation dealing with broad policy.

The effects of art. 72 were more profound than originally intended, however. By recognizing such a need, the constitution actually facilitated the use of the device for clientelistic purposes. Precisely because the Italian Parliament could cope, albeit with difficulty, with an enormous mass of legislation, the voices raised in favour of reforms that would give procedural priority to government legislation (the so-called *corsia preferenziale*) were never heeded, and to this day government legislation takes its chance with that promoted by ordinary back-benchers. Members of Parliament were thus encouraged to exploit the committee route to promote their own proposals, and there is little doubt that this fostered the culture of individual activism and bargaining which has established such profound roots in the contemporary Italian Parliament.

A further twist to art. 72 added a further peculiarity. The committee-only route can be overridden at the request of the opposition. Strictly one-fifth of the proportionally selected committee, or one-tenth of the whole house, can request that a bill is referred back to the plenary session. This gave the opposition considerable concealed power in the legislature, since it could, if it so desired, choke the work of the whole chamber by demanding that all legislation be subject to the full legislative procedure. It also facilitates what has often been regarded as undesirable collusion between government and opposition.[20]

A further complication in judging the impact of high legislative output on the wider political system arises in assessing the impact of the trivial on the substantive. If it could be shown that the Italian Parliament generates a satisfactory amount of substantive legislation, the high output of micro-sectional legislation might be best read as complementary rather than damaging. Unfortunately, there is no simple measure of 'satisfactory', and different observers use different definitions.[21] However, it is evident from the main research conducted on this subject, and from the quantity of generalized reform legislation reaching the statute book, especially in recent years, that there is still a substantial output of non-trivial legislation, at least in *absolute* terms, if not also when seen as a proportion of the total legislative output. Post-war Italian history, especially that of the 1970s and 1980s, is littered with grand schemes for reform that have passed through Parliament, even if not all have achieved their aims when implemented. They are at least as numerous as lamentations over the absence of reform itself and include the establishment of a national health service, the introduction of regional devolution, major reforms to the higher civil service, to the broadcasting system, to the criminal code, to the process of southern development aid, to budgetary procedure, to parliamentary procedure' to the co-ordination of the central executive achieved through the prime minister's office, to provincial and local government, to the co-ordination of European Community politics, to the Church–State Concordat, to wage indexation, to the banking system, and so on. The list is formidable, at least on paper, and casts some doubt on the argument, mainly constructed on the experience of the early post-war decades, that Parliament is incapable of passing major reform.

The problem with legislation, in fact, is often far more that it is of poor quality (short, badly drafted, inadequately reconciled with existing statutes, etc.), and that the administrative system fails to make it work, than that it does not exist in the first place. If so, the charge that permissive quantities of micro-sectional legislation are detrimental to the overall performance of the Italian Parliament must, for the last two decades, be based on the idea that the trivial is damaging the quality of the more substantive, rather than precluding it altogether.

If in their anxiety to promote micro-sectional legislation members of Parliament are distracted by them from the task of careful examination of government legislation, this danger could materialize quite regularly. However, attempts to demonstrate it by direct examination of how MPs view their role and spend their time have not come up with conclusive evidence.[22] As with other multi-faceted occupations, MPs can often be heard complaining that the balance between their various activities is wrong.[23] What is clear, however, is that plenary sessions are frequently ill attended and ritualized, and committee sessions are often dominated not by detailed consideration of major items, but by horse-trading over trivia. There have certainly been recurring problems of absenteeism which suggest that MPs spend more of their time looking after constituency concerns than is desirable for the effective working of the legislature, and this problem seems to have grown worse in recent years. Finally, there is an evident problem of follow-up in relation to much legislation. Often, it *empowers* a minister and his department to take a particular action or pursue a particular policy, but for a variety of reasons—most often a change of government—action is delayed, or renegotiated, or simply ignored. Unlike overspending or *ultra vires* administrative action, departmental *in*action does not readily fall foul of the administrative, financial, or constitutional control mechanisms of Italian public law. It is therefore up to Parliament to be vigilant, a matter on which there is often rather little political return for busy members of Parliament with their minds on local and constituency pressures.

As we shall see at the end of this chapter, Parliament is not unaware of its own shortcomings in these areas. Indeed, it has been actively setting in motion internal reforms to improve its capacity for information-gathering, and for committee scrutiny of administrative action. However, it is unclear whether voluntarism is enough without changing the underlying structure of incentives which MPs face in securing re-election and building power bases in their own party.

Parliament and the Budgetary Process

Undoubtedly, the most serious consequence of the large quantity of micro-sectional legislation, and more generally of the culture of bargained Parliamentary interventionism which it has fostered over the years, is the difficulty of developing a rational and planned approach to public expenditure, and particularly one which will keep the public-sector borrowing requirement in bounds. In the last decade, this has come to be seen as the central problem in the policy-making process, and the one which causes governments their greatest difficulty in relations with Parliament. The problem is a complex one, involving difficulties on both the revenue and expenditure sides of the budget. It touches on the way in which public funds are spent, and the value for money which the public receives. And it is heightened by the weaknesses of Parliament's own budgetary procedures, and by artificial distinctions between budget and off-budget public expenditure.

The nature of the problem

As we have seen in Chapter 2, the proportion of gross domestic product accounted for by public spending increased substantially in the first three decades of the post-war era, rising especially rapidly from the early 1970s onwards.[24] Subsequently, it stabilized, but at a level which made allocative spending decisions the key element of the political agenda. Moreover, although in the 1980s total public spending was beginning to stabilize as a proportion of GDP, the budget *deficit*, and hence the public-sector borrowing requirement, remained stubbornly high. Indeed the total stock of accumulated debt rose in a seemingly inexorable manner to reach 100 per cent of GDP by 1990.[25] The cause was the problem of debt servicing. In the 1970s, high inflation and low, or negative, *real* interest rates kept the gross deficit in bounds. In the 1980s, however, with inflation lower, but interest rates remaining high, the burden of interest payments on the national budget increased significantly. The ratio of the primary (i.e. net-of-interest) deficit to the gross deficit thus deteriorated. Moreover, anxiety about the long-term consequence of a major overhang of public debt gave borrowers a preference for short- and medium-term government bonds, relative to that for longer-term instruments. This too pushed up interest rates and hence the cost of financing the deficit.

The levelling off in the growth of public expenditure has not therefore reduced the contentiousness of the issue. On the contrary, the pressures on spending that have been generated by the budget-deficit problem, and by the apparent inability of the ruling majority to solve the problem by increasing revenue, have intensified distributional conflicts. Whatever judgements are made about given allocative patterns on the expenditure side of a government budget, there is a strong case against financing them through a growing debt burden. It is, in effect, a major reallocation against future generations of voters who have played no part in the decision. The high interest rates it generates are a burden on industry—especially on its international competitiveness. And in so far as a major objective of public policy in recent years has been to integrate the Italian economy, including its financial system, into the European economy, it is a barrier here too, since it exacerbates the difficulties of maintaining stable exchange rates and open capital markets.[26]

There is thus wide agreement, extending to economists and politicians on the left, that the high budget deficit is undesirable. However, neither among those favouring measures to solve the problem by increasing revenue, nor among those favouring measures to reduce expenditure or obtain better value from it—let alone across the boundary between these two approaches—is there much agreement on a remedy. To a large extent this reflects the fragmentation of the representative process. Revenue enhancement, for example, could most profitably be applied in the area of fiscal evasion. Incomes, goods, and services escape taxation, both direct and indirect, by the widespread informality of the black economy, and the inefficiency of tax-gathering mechanisms. Pay-as-you-earn employees, in contrast, cannot easily evade taxation, and, as in the 1970s, their tax liability can rise substantially through the effects of fiscal drag.

Even in the 1980s, when, on grounds of minimal equity, pay-as-you-earn groups could be squeezed no further, the political difficulties of heavier and more effective taxation of small businesses, professionals, and the self-employed remained a major barrier to reform. Specific categories had to be tackled by specific measures, on occasions by imputing bitterly resented hypothetical average incomes to members of such categories where individual assessment was especially unreliable. It is here that the disaggregation of the representative process, both through parties, and through the interest-group universe, has had its most serious consequences on decisional effectiveness. The capacity to organize and apply parliamentary pressure shown by groups such as shopkeepers, farmers, artisans, hoteliers, restaurateurs, taxi-drivers, and various types of producers' association, has been considerable and, so it is widely argued, has increased substantially in recent years.[27]

On the revenue side, then, what prevents the effective aggregation of choices and selection of priorities before the legislative stage of the budgetary process is the plethora of well-organized *private* groups. Interests on the expenditure side are rather different, with a disproportionately large group found among public-sector employees, and beneficiaries of various types of income and welfare transfer, both in cash (pensions, unemployment and redundancy pay) and in kind (health services, transportation, etc.). The power and political combativeness of these groups, however, appears to be no less strong than that of the private-sector opponents of revenue reforms. In some cases, where groups of public-sector workers have the direct ear of a minister, and can deliver disciplined bodies of votes for his faction or his party, it is even stronger.

The problem for Parliament, then, is one of permeability. It appears to lack the protection from a very diversified and articulate range of interests that would be afforded by a more programmatic form of party government, with a clearer vision of budgetary constraints and spending strategies, and greater protection against short-term sectional pressures. This problem is exacerbated by two other factors: first, an administrative and parliamentary tradition that places more emphasis, in budgetary matters, on procedures and legal controls than on economic management; and secondly, a wide range of procedural opportunities enabling lobby representatives to amend, add to, or strike out important parts of draft legislation.

Budgetary procedure

Parliament's budgetary procedures are determined in broad outline by art. 81 of the constitution.[28] Its main aim is to separate the process of overall budgetary authorization (the approval of an annual budget) from individual decisions to raise revenue or spend money. It thus prevents the annual budget authorization itself from imposing new revenues or expenditures, and requires that all new legislation containing spending commitments shall identify the mechanisms for covering the expenditure. The intention of the first requirement was that revenue-raising and spending proposals should be considered on their own merits, separately from an overall budget authorization. Art. 81 was thus supposed to prevent the budget becoming a spending omnibus, in which revenue or spending measures could be slipped surreptitiously into a budget law without being given the attention each was thought to deserve. The purpose of the second provision was to prevent irresponsible overloading of government funds, and precisely the recourse to deficit spending which, as we have just seen, has become such a burden in recent years.

The problem with this approach was that it did not reflect the pattern of government revenues and commitments in the modern, interventionist, welfare state, where public expenditure accounts for almost half of GDP. In such a state, revenues and spending commitments cannot neatly be divided into single calendar years, nor quantified with exact precision. Nor, for obvious reasons of economic management, is it desirable that the very real expansionary and deflationary consequences of spending, revenue-raising, and borrowing requirements should not be considered in terms of their overall impact on the economy. To do so annually may not be sufficient; circumstances may change over the short term, and adjustments may need to be made. Many advanced democracies find it necessary to introduce interim mini-budgets between annual finance bills. But the desirability that such issues should be seen as a whole, and that the budget should be more than the mathematical summary of a series of decisions taken in isolation from one another, is an undeniable one in a modern industrial economy.

In Italy, however, until 1978, the annual budget was indeed little more than a summary of all the spending commitments already entered into through pre-existing spending authorizations. These accumulated over many years (and at different times of the year). The budget also included an estimate of the revenue accruing from taxes, tariffs, and sales, etc. The requirement that each spending authorization should be covered by a source of revenue had little meaning. General revenue funds could be expected to vary in a variety of ways, which made creative accounting forecasts a fortuitous source of cover.[29] In any case, a large part of public expenditure, including the budgets of state enterprises and other public agencies, which were specifically designed to be run on semi-autonomous lines, was not included in the annual budget. While this had much to recommend it if it encouraged operational independence and flexibility, it also implied that public decisions having significant macro-economic effects could be taken without Parliament being able to consider them in the overall context of public-spending policies. And if the bases of the calculations contained in such off-budget programmes proved unfounded, they might also entail significant *future* claims on public resources (as in the case of loss-making enterprises, investment projects which ran seriously over budget, or programmes that entailed unquantifiable future costs).

The constitutional bar on raising new revenue or entering into new commitments in the annual budget thus rendered the budgetary exercise meaningless. Worse still, it had a cumulatively pernicious effect in discouraging budgetary responsibility. Each decision, taken in isolation, was not seen in Parliament as a choice among priorities, precluding some other possible choice, but as a simple decision on whether to spend. The growth of spending commitments that developed during the 1970s through the expansion of welfare programmes (health, pensions, and education in particular), and through transfers and subsidies to industry, while not in itself *caused* by these procedural features, nevertheless facilitated the understandable tendency of individual members of Parliament to seek to insert their own particular claims or client-demands into spending authorizations.

Attempts at reform

The realization that this growth, if left unchecked, made a nonsense of overall expenditure planning, had serious macro-economic conse-quences, and dramatically expanded the public-sector borrowing requirement led Parliament to launch a major reform of its procedures in the shape of the 1978 budget and finance law reform (law no. 468, 5 August 1978). The reform introduced three new principles. The first was that spending authorizations should no longer take the form of separate expenditure bills scattered throughout the financial year, but should be consolidated into a single finance bill, passed at the same time as the annual budget. The second was a recognition that public expenditure could only be controlled effectively, and real choices made by Parliament, if the long-term consequences of spending decisions were taken into account. Hence the introduction of a rolling budget forecast (*bilancio pluriennale*), stretching three to five years ahead, as the background for annual decisions. The third, linked to the second, was that each budget should be presented in two versions. One was the so-called *bilancio di competenza*, covering revenue and expenditure which the government is legally authorized to receive/incur, but which, because of lags in the collection of income or the implementation of expenditure, may not *actually* take place until a later financial year. The other was the *bilancio di cassa*, covering revenue and expenditure which the government expects to receive/incur during the course of the given financial year, even if it pertains to a previous year. The annual budget is presented in both these forms, while the rolling budget forecast comes only in the *competenza* version.

The significance of this third procedure lay in its recognition of the importance of the budget-deficit problem. The *bilancio di cassa* gave only a time-slice view of a long term process, and hence an ultimately inaccurate view of the eventual structure of revenues and expenditures a government was committed to in a given financial year, but since it reflected the state of a government's financial balances, it was a far more accurate guide than the *bilancio di competenza* to the borrowing requirement at any particular moment. It was thus the key to an important economic variable. When coupled with an innovation introduced the previous year (1977), by which the Treasury minister was required to make a quarterly report to Parliament on the progress of public spending through the financial year, it should, in principle, have assisted Parliament in seeing the overall consequences of its actions.

In practice, however, the 1978 reform had effects rather different from those intended. Instead of introducing greater rationality into the budgetary process by concentrating expenditure proposals into a single annual finance bill, it actually encouraged members of Parliament to subject the bill to a regular bombardment of amendments which frequently changed its parameters quite drastically from those originally presented by the government, and in ways which made the control of the borrowing requirement increasingly difficult to manage. Indeed, the fact that the finance bill, unlike ordinary legislation, was guaranteed to pass provided a reliable channel through which members of Parliament could pilot a range of (individually) minor spending decisions. Before 1978, as discrete items of legislation, each would have had to take its chance separately in the lottery of a heavily over-extended parliamentary timetable. As amendments to the finance bill, they could be slipped through in the systematic horse-trading that came to characterize the autumn budget cycle. Once members of Parliament understood this, and it only took them a year or two after the 1978 reform to do so, the cycle became an unedifying, and for the government's beleaguered parliamentary managers anarchic, scramble of favours exchanged across factions, parties of the majority, and not infrequently across the boundaries of government and opposition.[30]

What in Britain in the 1980s took place in the exclusive secrecy of the cabinet subcommittee known as the Star Chamber, in Italy occurred in the full glare of parliamentary business. Which approach is more democratic is unclear, but there is no doubt which system contains spending and deficit pressures more effectively.

Even the procedure by which the annual finance bill was divided into sections (corresponding roughly to the areas of competence of one or a small group of ministries) proved to have unfortunate side-effects. Each section was devolved for detailed parliamentary scrutiny to the relevant parliamentary committee. This encouraged special interests (who in any case needed little encouragement) to focus their pressure increasingly on the committees, and thereby further fragmented what was meant to be Parliament's opportunity to bring to the analysis of public-spending policies a coherent, overarching, rationality.

The unsatisfactory aspects of the 1978 reform have engendered various attempts to rework and improve it over the last decade, most notably through efforts to get Parliament to be more honest with itself about the nature of its budgetary calculations. This has involved, in particular, agreeing at the outset of the finance bill's parliamentary passage to a fixed ceiling for the public-sector borrowing requirement, and establishing a series of stages leading to better and more realistic appraisal of the yields of particular tax measures, and the costs of particular spending commitments.[31] By the later years of the 1980s, some of these efforts were beginning to bear fruit, and indeed were codified in a further piece of framework legislation (law no. 362, 23 August 1988) updating and replacing that of 1978. The start of the budget cycle was brought forward into the summer, through the publication each July of an economic and financial planning document emanating from the Treasury. This document was prepared to bring to Parliament's attention the full implications of the accumulated effect of public-spending policies, before members of Parliament launched their own amendments to the government's draft finance bill. The ordering of the various stages of the budget cycle was further modified to ensure that Parliament *first* approved (or modified) the government's estimates of fiscal yield and expenditure commitments from existing legislation, and only subsequently proceeded to considerations of new expenditure. In this way, it was hoped, the previous (self-deceiving) tendency for Parliament to cover new commitments by retrospectively adjusting forecasts of the yield on existing tax legislation could be blocked.

Exactly how much these procedural changes have affected parliamentary behaviour is difficult to judge, although it is worth noting that from 1987 onwards the primary (i.e. net-of-interest) deficit began to decline, albeit slowly. While this was mainly attributable to enhanced revenue, some impact was at long last beginning to be felt on the expenditure side as well. Nevertheless, at over 10 per cent of gross domestic product the budget deficit remained in 1990 well above the EC average, even towards the end of an extended upswing in the business cycle, which generated particularly high tax receipts. Parliament's difficulties in evolving a rational approach to budgetary politics through institutional and procedural reform thus underline the extent of the problem faced by would-be reformers. Changes to the budgetary process can, at least to a degree, expose the dubious forecasts of revenue and expenditure on which Italian budgets are constructed, but they cannot prevent determined members of Parliament in the budget committees of the two chambers from constructing such forecasts. The fact that budget-deficit ceilings solemnly agreed to at the start of the budgetary cycle are not respected at its conclusion, or that revenue estimates built on assumptions about yields from taxes or asset sales do not stand up to close scrutiny, embarrasses few deputies or senators for very long. The government itself, which is the chief critic of such practices, engages in them too. The budgets for 1991 and 1992, as written by the government even before amendment by Parliament, contained highly optimistic estimates for expected receipts from privatization policies, which few took seriously, and which, at least for 1991, quickly proved unfounded.

The main difficulty in budgetary reform is that there is no real sanction against Parliament—or the government—for failure to meet self-imposed budget-deficit targets. Politically, the concept of the budget deficit appears to be little understood outside élite circles, and it is possible that rather few Italian voters understand what the implications of the outcome of the annual budgetary cycle hold for the economy as a whole. Whatever costs the deficit brings, they are spread so broadly as to be largely invisible. The governor of the Bank of Italy and the court of accounts can draw attention to the deficit and its causes in their annual reports. The president of the republic can, as President Cossiga threatened towards the end of his period of office, refuse to counter-sign a finance law that he interprets as unconstitutional according to the dictates of art. 81, but he would have a hard time justifying the execution of such a threat. Ultimately, if the government cannot control its own members of Parliament, and cannot agree within its own ranks on higher taxation or lower spending, the budget deficit will continue until its wider costs become sufficiently pressing and visible that Parliament can prevaricate no longer.

Structural Features

While the root cause of parliamentary fragmentation is political and behavioural, structural and procedural factors are not unimportant. The relationship between behaviour and procedure is still two-way. Members of Parliament develop perceptions of their role, and of their power *vis-à-vis* the executive and party-group leaders, which both shape and reflect the structure of procedural opportunities available to them. Such opportunities abound in the Italian Parliament. The regulations of each chamber are determined internally—a prerogative jealously guarded from government interference. Parliamentary regulations have frequently been the target of fierce inter-party rivalry. When the fragility of the government majority has lasted for some considerable period, as during the 1970s, the opposition has directed its attention not just at substantive legislation but also at the rules of procedure, aiming to change them in a way that would give it a lasting position of strategic influence. Benefits acquired in this way tend to prove difficult to dismantle, partly because they assume a quasi-constitutional aura, and seem to require all-party consensus to amend, and partly because it is not just the opposition that benefits from them. Back-benchers on the government side—especially those in the smaller parties of the majority—will often be loath to relinquish weapons that give greater meaning to their role than would be the case were discipline tighter, majorities more compact, and rules of enforcement stricter.

We have already seen the impact of some of these procedures. One of the most long-standing is that by which committees have the power to legislate *in sede deliberante*, i.e. without reference back to the whole house after the committee stage. This procedure is enshrined in the constitution itself, although in reality, as the preceding discussion has demonstrated, it draws its political significance not just from the way it has conditioned representatives to see their role, but also from the fact that Italian legal institutions require that legislation is detailed and specific. If governments could resist such imperatives (as they have on occasions attempted to do) by legislating in more general terms, the resort to the use of committees for this purpose would be less necessary. The fact that they normally cannot do so gives the opposition behind-the-scenes leverage over both government and private-member legislation.

A more recent change, the reform of the regulations governing the Chamber of Deputies, approved in 1971, provides a further illustration of the consequences of enforced consensualism.[32] Among the innovations introduced by this reform was the principle that the three-month rolling parliamentary timetable should henceforth be agreed, not by decision of the President of the Chamber, but, wherever possible, on the principle of 'unanimity' by a committee of party-group leaders. Even when this was not possible, and where in consequence the timetable was approved by a straight vote on recommendations from the President of the Chamber alone, the fact that, from 1976 onwards, that office was occupied by a Communist (first Pietro Ingrao, then Nilde Iotti) testified to the degree of consociationalism which the 1970s brought to parliamentary procedures. The reform also opened up various possibilities for obstruction by relaxing the limits on amendment, extended debate, etc. As we shall see below, the consequences of these procedural changes lived on in Parliament throughout the 1980s, and for many years defied the efforts of successive governments to reverse them.

Before considering attempts at reform, however, it is necessary to look in greater detail at the two structural features which stand out most clearly in comparison with most parliamentary systems: perfectly co-equal bicameralism and the procedure for secret voting, widely used to the detriment of government legislation until its reform in 1988.

Bicameralism

Unlike almost all other European legislatures, the Italian Parliament is based on completely co-equal bicameralism. The Senate and the Chamber of Deputies perform identical functions. Governments must win and retain the confidence of both, legislation must pass both in the same form, and both have a full range of committees for legislation, and for scrutiny and oversight. The original purpose of this was to ensure that the second chamber really could perform the checking and revising role ascribed to it. It was to be elected at different times, and on a somewhat different basis (the voting age for the Chamber was 21, lowered in 1975 to 18, while that for the Senate was, and remains, 25). There was also a different age qualification for election (25 in the Chamber; 40 in the Senate).

In practice, the composition and political complexion of the two chambers have remained almost identical, since a constitutional amendment brought the duration of each chamber into line at five years each, and elections have always been held simultaneously. This was probably fortunate. The pathways to votes of confidence in the government, and to the approval of government legislation, are already strewn with so many obstacles that, under conditions of co-equal bicameralism, the system would almost certainly have ground to a complete halt if there had been significantly different majorities between the two chambers. Admittedly there are subtle differences in tone, and, since each chamber is in charge of its own procedures, there have been some important procedural differences. The Senate, with a higher average age, and the curiosity of its small number of life senators (ex-presidents of the republic, and other highly distinguished personalities), has a calmer, more authoritative, and less partisan tone. But the impact of this on political life is small. The real problem is that the revising and checking benefits of a second chamber have been purchased at a high price: the duplication in a second chamber of almost all of the technical obstacles and political difficulties considered in this chapter.

The secret vote and parliamentary regulations

The most serious such obstacle, until its virtual abolition in 1988, was the secret vote, a device unique among modern parliamentary democracies. The procedure has a long history in Italy, stretching back to the Piedmontese constitution (*Statuto albertino*) which Italy adopted after unification.[33] Art. 63 of the *Statuto* made secret voting the norm, a practice seen as necessary to free deputies from religious pressure and interference in a society still deeply divided between Catholic universalism and the principles of the lay state. The 1948 constitution, in contrast, left it to each chamber to determine its own internal regulations and voting procedures, except in the cases of votes of confidence and no confidence, for which open roll-call voting was made obligatory. The decision not to abolish entirely a procedure which ostensibly conflicted with the principle that voters have a right to know how their representatives have voted stemmed from a desire to prevent monolithic party organizations controlling the behaviour of their representatives in Parliament. As we have seen, art. 67 of the constitution sought to affirm the principle that a member of Parliament cannot be subject to the mandate of organizations external to Parliament itself.

The Chamber of Deputies subsequently adopted the regulations of its pre-fascist predecessor, and made secret voting mandatory for the final reading of the full text of all bills. The Senate left the question of the final reading to be determined case by case. In reality, however, the vote on the final bill was less likely to cause problems for the government majority than votes on individual articles within it. Voting down a full text actively desired by the government would indicate a complete breakdown of a parliamentary majority, and such a breakdown would normally already have entailed the withdrawal of one or more parties from the coalition long before the final vote on important legislation. It would also often be a costly activity, since to get rid of elements which government back-benchers actively disliked they would have to vote down other parts of the bill which they actively supported. Voting on changes to individual articles of the text, in contrast, was a much sharper and more subtle instrument of back-bench control, and here the secret vote, while not mandatory, was given ample scope by the provision in both houses that requests for its use would have priority over the normal procedure (raising of hands) and over roll-call votes. All that was necessary to obtain a secret vote was a request by a minimum number of representatives. The precise ruling has varied somewhat over time, and between the two chambers, but the necessary number of deputies has always been pitched low enough to allow the Communists to call for a secret vote, and often has allowed combinations of minor opposition parties to do so as well.[34] Back-benchers of the government majority intent on rebellion, who cannot, for obvious reasons, call for a secret vote themselves, can thus generally count on the connivance of opposition members to detect a split in the government ranks.

The secret vote became an increasingly painful thorn in the government's flesh in the 1970s and 1980s. The fragility of ruling coalitions, the growth of factionalism in the Christian Democrat Party, and the enhanced tensions over public expenditure all combined to make parliamentary management more difficult than earlier in the post-war era. At just this time, moreover, the reform of the procedural regulations of the Chamber of Deputies (discussed above) was beginning to make its impact felt. Among its innovations, the reform introduced an initially little-noticed provision by which, even when governments made particular articles of draft bills issues of confidence (i.e. cases in which the open roll-call would be used) there would still be a secret vote on the final bill, even when the bill itself consisted of only one article. The latter condition applies to many decree-laws, the use of which, as we have seen in the previous chapter, increased dramatically during the 1970s. It opened up the extraordinary possibility of two votes on exactly the same text: one, the confidence motion, an open roll-call; the second, the 'final' vote on the full text, by secret ballot.

The growth in the number of decree-laws which the government felt obliged to present to Parliament, in the face of increasing difficulties in pushing its legislative programme through, was both cause and effect of a deteriorating relationship between the two branches. The more governments sought to force issues in Parliament by making them the subject of decree-laws, which by definition had to be dealt with inside their sixty-day expiry limit, the more willing Parliament became to reject them, either on the procedural grounds that the requisite urgency to justify a decree-law did not exist, or on the substantive grounds that it disapproved of what the government proposed.[35]

The result was an intensifying conflict between successive governments and their own back-benchers, expressing itself most clearly in secret votes, particularly those dealing with the conversion of decree-law into ordinary law. On three notable occasions such issues led directly to the downfall of the government. The first occurred in September 1980, when the then prime minister Francesco Cossiga made an issue of confidence out of the conversion into ordinary law of a previously issued decree authorizing a package of short-term economic measures. The vote of confidence was obtained easily, but in the (secret) substantive vote on the measure itself the government was defeated, forcing Cossiga to resign. Two years later, Giovanni Spadolini's government was defeated, and subsequently forced to resign, in a secret vote on whether a particular decree-law satisfied the necessary criteria of urgency. In 1986, the procedure claimed its third government when the then prime minister Bettino Craxi resigned after defeat in yet another secret vote, having just won a vote of confidence on exactly the same issue by a margin of over 100.

Not surprisingly, throughout the 1980s, as governments encountered more and more difficulties with the procedure, pressure mounted for its modification. Government defeats linked to confidence votes were only the tip of a large iceberg. During the 1983–7 legislature Craxi suffered a constant series of reversals in secret votes. His first government (August 1983–July 1986) was defeated 134 times; the second, which lasted only eight months, was defeated a further 21 times.[36] The votes touched on all types of issue, but the majority involved amendments to the details of government spending plans. The same problems beset the Goria government in 1987–8.

From 1983 onwards, therefore, a growing awareness of the consequences of the secret vote, particularly for the government's ability to keep within its spending and deficit targets, generated demands for reform, and led to several, initially abortive, attempts to rewrite the relevant parts of parliamentary regulations.[37] Finally, in 1988, a major curtailment of its use in both chambers was agreed. Under the new rules, the secret vote is now limited in effect to constitutional and electoral issues, and questions of personal morality and family law.

The change should in the long term assist the government's management of its parliamentary majority, but the experience of the De Mita government immediately after the secret-vote reform suggests a note of caution. For the most notable consequence was a drastic decline in attendance in Parliament. Dissident deputies responded to the removal of what many regarded as the main instrument which gave purpose to their presence in Parliament by simply failing to attend—frequently making the chambers inquorate, a problem which the inadequate whipping system had few powers to remedy. Parliament frequently works little more than a two and a half day week—representatives arriving in the capital on Tuesday morning, and departing on Thursday afternoon. There is, moreover, a long-standing convention that Parliament does not sit during party congresses (of which there are on average five per year, each lasting a week), during national holidays, election campaigns (at least one or two per year), and cabinet crises (which may last up to three or four weeks). Thus any further systematic decline in attendance by deputies aiming to influence the government by the indirect mechanism of further pressure on the timetable poses serious problems.

To be sure, absenteeism is a rough and ready instrument, far more difficult to co-ordinate than the secret vote. What it indicates, however, is that while procedurally the secret vote was a great irritant to the government's parliamentary managers, it was not the root cause of its problems and was in some respects a safety-valve for back-bench frustrations.[38] Without it, a government might find cruder weapons deployed against it, as the fate of the short-lived De Mita government suggested to many observers.

Structural Reform in the 1980s: Successes and Failures

After four decades of post-war evolution, it would be surprising if the accusations of weak institutionalization levelled against the Italian Parliament on the basis of its early operation could be sustained as effectively as in the past. Parliament has over time developed procedures, patterns of operation, and internal structures which clearly influence profoundly the behaviour of those who become members of the legislature, and which make it a central institution in the political system. There can be little doubt that Parliament has developed a characteristic style of legislative activity, and of legislative interaction with other institutions, which is significantly different from that of legislatures in other European democracies. In many respects the style of activity, with the strongly individualistic entrepreneurialism of many representatives, is closer to the American Congress than to a parliamentary system.

The accusation that Parliament lacks autonomy from the political parties is at best a partial truth. Parliament is better understood as an arena in which pressure from parties mixes with that from the government (itself by no means a cohesive and unidirectional pressure), from interest groups, and from the local interests to which representatives as individuals must always be responsive. Against this complex background, the procedural rules examined in this chapter (bicameralism, the secret vote, the role of legislative committees, the proportionalist basis on which posts and influence over the timetable are distributed) have all contributed to a syndrome in which, for better or worse, individuals and back-bencher groups *count* in the decision-making process, see their involvement as legitimate and desirable, and fiercely resist attempts to weaken it.

At the same time, the negative dimensions of the Italian legislative culture have not been lost on members of Parliament. For many years it has been recognized that the complexity of the system can produce random and unpredictable results. Indeed, as the government–opposition divide became less clear-cut, and Parliament became a correspondingly more important arena, so, during the 1970s, these dangers grew. More parties were involved in decisions, and (within the ruling coalition) minor parties became more influential. Under such circumstances what was 'institutionalized' was a style of decision-making more unsatisfactory than in the earlier post-war decades, when party control was probably stronger. Not surprisingly, therefore, the 1980s have seen an extensive but uncertain search for remedies. In some areas, this has brought some partial successes. The Italian Parliament has made a conscious attempt to devote less of its time, especially in committee activity, to detailed bargaining over minor legislation. The sheer number of items of legislation approved fell, from an average of over 400 per year in the first three legislatures to an average of just under 300 per year in the three legislatures elected between 1976 and 1987. More significantly, the proportion of bills approved in committee (i.e. items approved under the accelerated procedure by which reference back to the whole house is unnecessary) also fell from the early post-war years.

Furthermore, the balance in committee activity between the legislative role on the one side and that of scrutinizing government departments and policies, holding hearings, and approving policy resolutions on the other has undoubtedly changed, with more time spent on oversight and control activities.[39] The mechanism of investigative inquiries (*indagini conosciativi*) was introduced in the early 1970s, to allow parliamentary committees to question witnesses, commission research, and produce reports in particular policy sectors.[40] Parliament has also established more bicameral committees of administrative supervision. Four new ones (dealing with southern development, industrial restructuring, intelligence and security issues, and the Mafia) were established from the mid-1970s onwards, and one of the two pre-existing ones, dealing with parliamentary supervision of the broadcasting system, was substantially strengthened. There was also an attempt to introduce greater rationality into the budgetary process, through the creation of an annual budgetary cycle which would force members of Parliament to look at the overall public-spending and borrowing context in which they were making their demands.

These successes have been quite limited, however. The 1978 reform of the budgetary process did not achieve its intended effects. Indeed, much of the decline in the quantity of micro-sectional legislation over recent years has probably been bought at the expense of the coherence of the budgetary process. Amendments, codicils, and exemptions are still easily added to the finance bill, and to other items of legislation. Often, under the intense time-pressures that build up in the complexity of the legislative process, it is impossible to make accurate assessments of the implications of such modifications. The huge increase in the number of decree-laws the government has presented to Parliament in recent years has only added to this pressure.

As for the growth of investigation and scrutiny, there must remain doubt as to its impact, as there is in most parliamentary systems. Even in systems where the legislature is faced with a coherent executive, capable of absorbing and reacting to legislative demands, the effectiveness of parliamentary scrutiny is often rather limited. In Italy, as we shall see in the following chapter, the executive is anything but coherent, and the impact of reports, resolutions, and parliamentary inquiries is limited because responsibility is hard to pinpoint, and few people are in the same positions long enough to be made publicly accountable. At the level of public utterances, if not also in the privacy of parliamentary committees, party rivalries remain strong, and it is for this reason probably unrealistic to suppose that investigative committees can generate an all-party consensus about the direction of policy or the performance of the executive. If party-driven government majorities cannot do this, the likelihood that special forums and procedures inside the legislature can do so seems small.

It may therefore be concluded that reforms such as the 1978 budgetary reform, the growth of investigative activities, and even the abolition of the secret vote are in themselves insufficient. The legislative process needs to be made more efficient and more transparent, and the pressures on the timetable need to be eased, and this can only come about with a more cohesive government majority. Without a reduction in the complexity and uncertainty of the legislative process, and its pressured urgency, there is probably little prospect of improving the permeability of the Italian Parliament to special interests. Parliament may be central to the political process, but it is too exposed to the pressures of a multiplicity of parties and interests. In a sense, it can be said to be in the hands of parties, but not sufficiently protected by them from sectional pressures. Only a more cohesive majority can enable it to develop greater programmatic purposiveness, and this throws the emphasis back on to institutions beyond Parliament itself.

7

The Political Executive

The Problem of Policy Co-ordination

Policy co-ordination is a central concern for Italian governments. How co-ordination is obtained varies considerably across liberal democracies. The emphasis may be on the chief executive (presidential or 'prime-ministerial' government); it may be on collegiality (collective cabinet responsibility); or it may be on bureaucratic and administrative (as opposed to either of the above two 'political') mechanisms, entailing a self-confident, policy-evangelistic administrative class with a high level of self-endowed legitimacy to carry out the co-ordination mission. Naturally, however, co-ordination may not be achieved to a very high degree at all; policy-making may be segmented, with policy communities taking decisions in relative isolation from one another. Indeed, much recent research on policy-making in Western Europe points to an increasing *sectorization* of the policy process.[1]

Conventional wisdom has it that Italy falls squarely into this latter category, suffering from a chronically low level of policy co-ordination compared to most of Western Europe. Evidence of successful or failed co-ordination is of course more anecdotal than systematic, since there are few generalized measures against which to judge it. However, we have already seen in the preceding chapter that one standard is the ability of government to co-ordinate spending policies so as to meet, and not regularly overrun, its own budgetary targets. Certainly, on this score, the evidence suggests Italy does indeed suffer from a low level of effective co-ordination.

This chapter and the next examine how the mechanisms of policy co-ordination outlined above work in the Italian context, and the efforts which have been made in recent years to make them more effective. This chapter analyses the political executive: prime minister and cabinet (Council of Ministers).[2] In Chapter 8 we examine the administrative machine, the legal tradition which underlies it, and the sociology of the civil service and the wider public sector.

At an abstract level, political executives may be said to perform three principal functions: formulating a programme; securing, where appropriate, its translation into law; and overseeing its implementation by the public administration. In Italy, each of these is complex, and its outcome often unpredictable. The formulation stage is not the semi-automatic product of party programmes or manifestos. It begins only when the government itself is being constructed. The programme has to be manufactured, through a series of highly formal stages. Indeed, given its complexity and its frequency, the formulation process may almost be described as an institution in its own right, with set procedures, stages, and rules about consultation.[3] It is generally long drawn out, and ends only with the successful passage of votes of confidence in both houses of the Parliament. Its high level of formalism conditions the role played by the Italian executive. Its complexity generates a sense of contractual obligation, vigilantly supervised by the contracting parties. Observance is generally measured in legislative terms and this in turn emphasizes the role of law, as against policy formulation and programme management in a broader sense.

The formidable difficulties a government encounters in its second function—translating its programme into legislation—have been examined in the previous chapter. The essential point is that a formal vote of confidence supporting the programme is only the beginning of a long and demanding battle. In it, the government has few of the procedural weapons available in other liberal democracies. All too frequently, it is forced to yield in ways which feed the tensions eventually bringing about its own downfall. And if the legislative stage is difficult, the implementation stage is equally so. Coalition government and intra-party factions cut across most of the collegiality which is supposed to derive from the cabinet system. The bureaucracy is highly segmented, and infused by a legalism making policy co-ordination difficult. Moreover, segmentation feeds back to the legislative stage. The translation of a programme into detailed legislative proposals has to be done mainly at the departmental level. If the ability of the executive to transmit its collective purpose to the departmental level is weak, its legislative programme will be distorted.

The Prime Minister

Prime-ministerial authority

The formal powers of chief executives are rarely defined with precision. In systems regulated by written constitution the general provision that the chief executive 'conducts, and is responsible for, the general policy of the government' is often ambiguous, especially where the constitution also sanctions the principle of individual ministerial responsibility for the work of departments. Comparison of the constitutional and legal powers of the Italian prime minister with those of his counterpart in Britain reveals little to explain the fundamental political weakness of the Italian prime minister. Indeed art. 95 of the constitution, from which the above quotation is drawn, puts in writing what is a mere unwritten convention in Britain.

Clearly, more intangible variables are at work. The strength invested in the office of prime minister is closely linked to perceptions and expectations of the office held by cabinet colleagues, members of Parliament, and voters. Once a particular level of prime-ministerial authority becomes part of the accepted conventions of a system, it is likely to shape what forms of behaviour are acceptable in the relationship between prime minister and cabinet colleagues, and the way in which voters judge that behaviour. How such expectations are built up, however, is very difficult to establish. In the Italian case there is little evidence that the electorate has ever been significantly attracted to demands for 'strong leadership', despite the fact that by comparative standards almost all Italian prime ministers of the twentieth century have been rather weak figures.[4]

A pervasive scepticism about the motives and morals of all professional politicians seems to have made voters reluctant to believe that investing power decisively in any one of them would be desirable or effective. Italy's one unequivocally strong leader in the twentieth century—Benito Mussolini—made much of the need for strong leadership, and in the political confusion of the early 1920s demands were briefly heard for the smack of firm government, but a mass popular base played little part in his rise to the post of prime minister. A few of his predecessors in liberal Italy—most notably Giovanni Giolitti—had at times worked the patronage potential of the government machine so well that they were able to construct reasonably durable parliamentary coalitions, but their authority over political colleagues, like their rapport with the mass public, was always tenuous.

Through fascism itself, Italy was further inoculated against the pretensions of strong leadership. Admittedly De Gasperi, who served as prime minister uninterruptedly from 1945 to 1953, played the role—not unlike Adenauer—of forceful, conservative, patrician democrat, combining the virtues necessary to work his country's passage back to democratic respectability. Like Adenauer, he was well suited to this role, and by later standards was given quite generous powers by his party and coalition colleagues to play it.[5] Yet as chief executive and as party leader De Gasperi was always far more constrained than Adenauer, as the eight governments over which he presided in as many years confirm.

In any case, a broad consensus soon developed in the Christian Democrat Party that leadership was to be collegial rather than individual. Whether this would have been true if any other party had been in office is uncertain, but the question did not arise. The leadership of the DC was shared between prime minister, party secretary, senior government ministers (some of whom had been, and expected again to be, prime minister), and prominent faction leaders. Shared leadership clearly suited the DC factions even if it did not always work to the party's electoral benefit. It was a guarantee of mutual tolerance, and while it stemmed more from self-interest than from any disinterested theory of the superiority of collective over personal leadership, it was in line with the institutional caution which Mussolini's excesses had generated.

Thus neither the political class, nor the mass public, has been accustomed to *perceiving* the prime minister as the dominant figure in government. He rarely if ever personifies a particular thrust in public policy, and has rarely sought to establish a direct and personal link with mass public opinion. In Italy there has, until recently, been little interest in the poll-ratings of prime ministers (or indeed party leaders), and the tendency to assess them in terms of their utility to the electoral standing of the party and the re-election chances of members of Parliament has not been marked. This is not to say that there has not been a good deal of personalism in Italian politics. In constituency electoral contests there clearly *has* been, and national prominence can benefit a politician in his home base considerably. But nationally, the coat-tails effect for a prime minister's party is generally perceived to be weak. Normally, he represents at most a political formula, and his main task is to negotiate agreement on the detailed legislative implementation of that formula between the factions and parties of which it is composed. Even relatively 'strong' prime ministers are strong only in so far as they can assemble an effective alliance and then hold it together. Their skill is one of negotiation not policy enforcement: reconciling differences, distributing concessions, balancing one group against another, and sometimes just playing for time. Rarely have they led from the front or adopted a public stance on a policy issue before that issue has been resolved inside the government.

The prime minister is therefore as much a chairman as a policy leader, and has relatively little power to influence the careers of ministers in his government. Cabinet reshuffles without cabinet crises (the latter being as risky to the prime minister as to ministers) are unusual. If the composition of the cabinet changes, and individuals move up or down the hierarchy, they do so largely because of changing fortunes within their party, not because of the patronage of the prime minister. Whether in public or in private, a ministerial challenge to the prime minister over policy is not a fundamental break with convention or with expectations of coalition solidarity. It may actually benefit rather than harm a minister's standing with his party colleagues. Members of the government have even been known, on rare occasions, to vote against government policy in Parliament.

There is thus in Italy rather little sense that a cabinet stands or falls together, and that the political fortunes of the prime minister are critical to a party's level of public support, or to its chances of staying in office. When there is no taboo against challenges to prime-ministerial authority and when the consequences of such challenges are accepted by both voters and politicians, a major weapon in the normal armoury of a chief executive is missing.

Styles of prime-ministerial leadership

This view of prime-ministerial leadership was the conventional wisdom for a large part of the post-war era. However, within the broad constraints outlined above, there have always been significant differences in prime-ministerial style, and these variations have been particularly marked during the 1980s. They are determined in the first instance by variations in the cohesion of the coalition over which the prime minister presides—variations which are themselves the result not just of relations between parties, but also, and in some ways more importantly, of conflicts inside the dominant party in the coalition.

Some coalitions are clearly little more than administrative conveniences for conducting the essential routine of government in the absence of a parliamentary majority for a particular programme. Others are built on single-party (Christian-Democrat) governments, enjoying the highly contingent support of other parties—as in the case of the so-called National Solidarity governments from 1976 to 1979, which depended on the support of the PCI. Others still are more firmly rooted, with a clear programme, and with all parties to the agreement formally present in the cabinet. Their long-term prospects may nevertheless remain uncertain if some parties have entered with a degree of reserve, sometimes declared very publicly, and are ready to withdraw at an opportune moment. Their contingent support does not necessarily mean they are uncommitted to the political formula itself, but they perceive no undesirable side-costs in attempting to win for themselves a bigger share of power (more cabinet seats, more acceptable policy outcomes, etc.). Finally, there is the strongest category of coalition, sometimes said to be based on broad 'political' agreement, as opposed to that constructed on policy alone, in which all parties are not only implicitly committed to the government through full cabinet membership, but have also made clear, long-term, and explicit commitments to it as an enduring political formula.

The latter type has become rather rare, however. It was essentially the product of Cold War politics in the 1950s and 1960s, when the need to stand firm against the alleged threat from the PCI generated a clear exclusion of certain types of alliance. The political climate of the 1980s has been very different, and even when, as in the case of the Craxi governments, the coalition has been enduring, the commitment of the contracting parties has been in recurring doubt.

A prime minister's public authority, ability to speak on behalf of his government, and capacity to influence choices made within it clearly vary according to which of the above coalitions he presides over. Prime ministers heading pre- or post-election caretaker governments have almost no substantive policy-making power at all. Notable figures who have played this role include Leone (1963 and 1968), Cossiga (1979–80), and Fanfani (1982–3 and 1987). Often, such prime ministers cultivate an air of disengagement from the day-to-day conflicts of ordinary party politics, and it is no coincidence that Leone and Cossiga subsequently became presidents of the republic, and that Fanfani, by the 1980s, was a respected *eminence grise*, and president of the Senate.

Prime ministers who head governments based on agreed programmes are naturally better placed, although here too their real authority is dependent on the conditions under which the programme has been launched, the forthcoming political calendar, and, for Christian Democrat prime ministers, the strength of their own faction within the party. The prime minister who scores well on each of these is relatively well placed to exert pressure on his cabinet colleagues and his government's back-benchers. He may even venture occasionally to lead from the front in areas where his cabinet is undecided, and he can expect at least a minimum of support from party secretaries and parliamentary group leaders.

However, such circumstances are rare. In recent years the Christian Democrat Party has been internally divided, and its parliamentary group correspondingly difficult to con... fortunes have been under dramatic threat, as... the early 1980s, has it had the sort of cohesion that... to back a strong prime minister, and in the latter perioo... were so great that it lost the office of prime minister entirely— the Republican Party, and then to the Socialists. Moreover, regio... and European elections, and increasingly referendums, now regularly punctuate the intervals between parliamentary and local elections. With enhanced electoral volatility, each becomes a traumatic and disturbing political event. As a result, governments enjoy few breathing spaces when intra-coalition relationships are calm and manageable, and prime ministers can concentrate on the conduct of longer-term policy.

In fact, it is necessary to go back to the Andreotti governments of 1976–9 to find a Christian Democrat prime minister who could be said to have a reasonably firm grip on the office. Even then, circumstances were unusual. Andreotti exercised considerable control over his cabinet, and was even able to appoint to key cabinet posts technocrats who, having no power base of their own, were unusually committed to particular cabinet policies. Yet the obverse of control over his own party—chastened as it was by electoral difficulties—was dependence in Parliament on a broad coalition which included the Communists.

Of the five subsequent Christian Democrat prime ministers (Cossiga, Forlani, Fanfani, Goria, and De Mita) two (Cossiga and Fanfani) were stop-gap occupants of the office, falling into our first two categories. One, Giovanni Goria, was a middle-ranking technocrat with only the narrowest of bases in the party, who was manipulated into office at the temporary convenience of other coalition leaders. Although his government was based on an agreed coalition pro- gramme, its first finance bill suffered the indignity of a series of devastating parliamentary defeats, and Goria fell in barely eight months.

In the 1980's, therefore, only Forlani and De Mita represented Christian Democrat prime ministers from the very top echelons of the party leadership. The former had been party president immediately before taking office; the latter party secretary and effective leader for the previous seven years. Both could be said to represent the strongest candidate the DC could field. Yet Forlani's government collapsed within nine months of its formation under the enormity of the P-2 masonic lodge scandal, while De Mita, having taken office just as his grip on the party machine was slipping, found party colleagues in and on the back-benches no more pliable than did the unfortunate Goria, and he too lost office in little over one year.

Prime-ministerial authority in the 1980s

The record of recent Christian Democrat prime ministers, and the fact that the office was occupied for nearly five years by incumbents from the minor parties, might suggest that, in the 1980s, the prime-ministerial role has even declined in importance, and has received rather little attention. For three reasons, however, this has not been the case.

First, the two minor-party prime ministers, Spadolini and Craxi, proved in their different ways to be unexpectedly forceful figures. In part, this reflected the fact that it is easier for a prime minister to force issues in cabinet as leader of a small but cohesive party than as one leader among several in a large but divided party. His public profile and political authority come across more clearly to the electorate, and where his views are contested by cabinet colleagues the conflict can be turned into a more clear-cut party conflict. As long as his party is electorally in the ascendant, or thought to be, and his adversary's is not, he can afford to turn a conflict with cabinet or Parliament into a public and partisan issue.

This consideration is linked to a second, which is that electoral volatility, the decline of strong party organization, and the weakening of political subcultures has, to some degree at least, increased the importance of issues and personalities in Italian politics. As traditional channels of communication are weakened, so new ones, including particularly a more pluralist mass media, become available to politicians with a sophisticated understanding of popular political presentation. The potential of this to Italian prime ministers is considerable. Traditionally, they have not sought to use personal popularity as an internal weapon in cabinet or against back-benchers. In the 1980s, and especially with the Craxi government, this began to change. The degree of success it has met is questionable, as we shall see below, but that it has been consciously adopted is itself a significant development.

The third new factor complements the first two. Enhanced intra-coalition competition between the lay parties and the Christian Democrats has, since the late 1970s, made Italian governments increasingly difficult to manage. Hardly a coalition is born which does not have the unmistakable imprint of provisionality upon it. We have already seen that this generated a continuing debate about constitutional reform, culminating, in the 1983–7 Parliament, in a major parliamentary commission of inquiry charged with finding enough common ground between the parties to launch a far-reaching overhaul of institutional arrangements. An important element in this debate was the political executive. It focused attention on the prime minister and his political authority, and enabled successive holders to argue for a strengthening of his role, at least in legal and institutional terms. It justified three different prime ministers, Spadolini, Craxi, and De Mita, in presenting to Parliament a major bill, little changed across the three administrations, setting out the terms of the reform. And significantly, whereas in previous decades the fate of such bills was to disappear into parliamentary committees never to be heard of again, in the 1980s each prime minister made more progress than the last, until in August 1988 such a reform, discussed later in the chapter, was finally approved.

For various reasons, therefore, the role of the prime minister has been more controversial in the 1980s than ever before, and interpretation of it more complex. On one side, there has been an emerging acceptance that the chief executive should have greater political power, and there have been strenuous attempts by the incumbents to exploit this new climate in their dealings with cabinet and Parliament. On the other side, the results to date have been ambivalent. The Socialist Party has found in Bettino Craxi a leader both able and willing to play a high-profile prime-ministerial role, but the benefits, whether to his party or to policy co-ordination in government, have been modest. The Christian Democrat Party meanwhile has only slowly responded to the need to change its leadership structure to enable prime-ministerial leadership to emerge. In the middle of the decade it showed signs of doing so, but shied away at the very moment that its new champion, Ciriaco De Mita, was ready to assume office.

The unsatisfactory fate of these two figures, rivals throughout the decade for coalition leadership, illustrates the constraints on prime-ministerial power discussed thus far. Craxi's period as prime minister was certainly different from that of most of his predecessors. He frequently sought to lead from the front, and consciously courted controversy. On several occasions he turned issues into stand-or-fall resigning matters, with the clear implication that if he did not get his way complete political deadlock would ensue. In thinly disguised populist criticism of the inadequacies of the existing political order he contrived at different times to attack Parliament, the judiciary, the constitutional court, and the president of the republic. On controversial issues of policy such as the wage-indexation question, he took stands not shared by all, or in some cases even the majority, of his cabinet. In the delicate aftermath of the *Achille Lauro* hijack, when US and Italian troops had confronted each other on a Sicilian air base, he adopted a streak of injured national pride quite out of tune with Italy's normally compliant relationship with the United States. Indeed a high-profile conflictual style seems actually to have helped Craxi stay in office. Through it, he was able to retain the initiative. Any coalition crisis became a plebiscite on his own forceful style of leadership.

Craxi's self-declared *decisionismo* was, however, more style than substance, and was highly selective. He was evidently rather uninterested in the details of policy, which he tended to leave to his under-secretary, Giuliano Amato. Certainly, he had an astute sense of when to give way, and the policy record of his government may come to be seen as rather thin—especially in the critical area of controlling the public-sector deficit.[6] In reality, his aims were linked more to party than policy. The prime minister's office was above all a very visible platform from which to continue the campaign for his party's electoral recovery, and given the expected brevity of his government when he assumed office, this was perhaps to be expected. In fact his longevity in office owed less to his policy success than to the Christian Democrats' unwillingness, after their heavy electoral set-back in 1983, to call his bluff, bring him down, and face an election.

Whether, as Craxi hoped, the Italian electorate really had become more sensitive to appeals for strong personalized leadership is thus difficult to judge, but if so the process has been slow. Craxi's personal standing with the electorate clearly rose during his tenure, but in the 1987 general election the PSI vote rose only to 14.3 per cent. The 3 per cent increase over 1983 was a success for the PSI, but hardly the fundamental realignment Craxi hoped his personalized leadership would bring. The 'Craxi effect', in short, proved somewhat disappointing, suggesting that even if the Italian electorate was responsive to the appeal of *governabilità*, it did not perceive Craxi to have brought it about in any large measure.[7]

The impact on the Christian Democrat Party was correspondingly ambiguous. Initially, the party seemed to accept that an era of more personalized leadership was emerging, and that it would need to find a single leader capable of competing with Craxi on his own terms. But the closing of its ranks did not last long. De Mita's attempts to stamp his own authority on the DC met little success. He was not helped by the fact that, compared to Craxi, his own personal appeal was modest.

Moreover, many in his party, at the grass roots, especially in the south, were adamantly opposed to the internal party reforms with which he was trying to consolidate his leadership. Such was the store of resentment he engendered that by the time that he eventually won his own term as prime minister, in 1988–9, his authority over the DC had waned dramatically. A condition of it backing him as prime minister, in fact, was that he relinquish the party secretaryship, but once that office was gone there was little to protect him in difficult times.

Thus, at the end of a decade that might have augured an era of stronger prime ministers, and certainly saw a shift in prime-ministerial style in a more personalized direction, there came, at least temporarily, a reversion to type. The years 1987–9 saw three different Christian Democrat prime ministers (Goria, De Mita, and Andreotti) follow one another in rapid succession. Craxi had used the office to establish prime-ministerial positions on particular policy issues, and had challenged other members of his government to defy him and pay the electoral penalty. Yet what this seemed to suggest was that it was easier for the leaders of small cohesive parties to play this role than for Christian Democrats, whose real enemy is the capriciousness of party factions and recalcitrant back-benchers. When the Christian Democrats resumed control over the prime minister's office in the 1987–92 Parliament, it was Andreotti rather than De Mita who proved the longer lasting and more successful prime minister, but only because his personal style was anything but *dirigiste*, and because he was willing to return to the role of conciliator played by earlier Christian Democrat prime ministers, and to rely for the construction of his parliamentary support base on the patient alliance-building skills of his party secretary Arnaldo Forlani and his powerful Budget minister Paolo Cirino Pomicino.

The prime minister's office

Irrespective of his underlying political strength, and its variations over time, the Italian prime minister, like chief executives everywhere, needs organizational and administrative support to carry out his co-ordinating role. He needs sources of policy advice, including advisers whose perspective is wider than, and independent of, that which he can obtain from individual departments of government. Yet he needs links with departments, to influence and co-ordinate both the preparation of government legislation and the administration of policy. This is especially important where, as in Italy, there is no independent cabinet-co-ordinating machinery operating alongside the prime minister's own machine. As we shall see later, the secretariat to the Italian

Council of Ministers, such as it is, operates *inside* the prime minister's office, and reports to him.

Staffing

The Italian constitution stipulates that the structure and staffing of the prime minister's office (henceforth known as the PCM—*presidenza del Consiglio dei ministri*) 'will be determined by law'. In practice, until the 1988 reform (and indeed thereafter, since implementation was much delayed) the issue was determined by a combination of pre-republican legislation, administrative decree, and the style and resourcefulness of incumbent prime ministers. There was no independent budget for the PCM, and most of its staff were on secondment from other branches of the state machine, on whose payrolls they remained. This is not to say that many had not been effectively permanent, especially at lower levels, but it did mean that there was no systematic approach to recruitment, nor any clear pattern or objective in the turnover as staff entered and left the PCM. Only those at the very top of the machine—heads of the internal departments and a few others—were recruited as close political collaborators of the prime minister. For others (including many at quite senior level) the motive for recruitment was often personal advantage or convenience (better bonuses and overtime opportunities, etc.) or just a different working environment. On this basis, in fact, despite the lack of a formal budget, the PCM grew over the years to be a substantial bureaucracy in its own right, with over 6,000 staff. However, the great majority were engaged in activities which have little relevance to the core functions of overarching policy co-ordination with which we are concerned here. They worked in departments of the PCM which had been attached to the office over the years, such as the unit supervising publishing, the press, and authors' rights (SIEPLAS), or the departments of ministers without portfolio concerned with sectoral sub-branches of policy such as southern development or science and technology.[8] Admittedly, these latter departments had some nominal responsibility for cross-departmental co-ordination, but in reality, especially since they were headed by ministers without portfolio whose subordination to the prime minister was no greater than that of any normal minister they quickly became small departmental ministries in their own right, in all but name.

To a large extent, despite the reform described below, the PCM as a whole continues to operate along these lines. For those who work in closest contact with the prime minister the situation is somewhat different. They tend to be individuals with whom the prime minister, or more often his *capogabinetto* (chief of staff), have had some close working contact in the past. Most of them come and go with each successive administration. While they too are normally recruited through the public sector, where transfer and secondment raise few problems, they are generally drawn from rather more prestigious and mobile levels within it than their more permanent subordinates. Notable in this connection are the *consiglio di stato* (council of state), *corte dei conti* (court of accounts), ISTAT (Central Statistical Institute), the *ragioneria generale* of the Treasury (the élite of financial controllers which supervise expenditure in individual ministries), and the universities.

The three key figures who work most closely with the prime minister, and largely control access to him, are the *capogabinetto*, the under-secretary (*sottosegretario di stato*) to the PCM, and the *segretario particolare* (the personal secretary). The *capogabinetto* is normally the key administrative figure in the PCM, and its chief executive. Unlike the under-secretary, he is not an elected politician. He is generally a senior figure from the council of state or an equivalent body, although he will often have had some close working connections to the prime minister at some point in the past. The under-secretary, in contrast, is a politician. His formal role is to monitor the detailed legislative work of the government as a whole, to represent it in the Chamber of Deputies, and to negotiate with parliamentary committees over government bills. His other main task—to act as secretary to the Council of Ministers—complements this. The under-secretary's informal role is to act as close political confidant and adviser to the prime minister. Finally, the personal secretariat deals with personal political arrangements—links with the prime minister's party, other politicians and parties, personal affairs, etc. It is headed by a close political colleague, generally brought in from the prime minister's party machinery, who has probably played a rather similar role when the prime minister was party secretary or faction leader. In theory separate, the roles performed by members of this inner group are in practice intermingled. Close daily contact, the need for flexibility in responding to events, the sense of common pressure and purpose generated within the innermost circle, all tend to break down clear lines of division. In fact, during the Craxi governments from 1983 to 1987, the role of key organizer and administrator within the PCM seems to have been played more by the under-secretary (Professor Giuliano Amato) than by the *capogabinetto* (an official from the council of state).[9]

Departments

Below the top triumvirate, the PCM is normally divided into some combination of the following functional departments:

- secretariat to the Council of Ministers;
- legislative office;
- economic and social affairs section;
- press office;
- programme monitoring department;
- office of the diplomatic counsellor;
- office of the military counsellor;
- ceremonials department;
- information and archiving;
- personnel and administration.

Most of these departments are headed by one or more individuals who come and go with the prime minister, but in those concerned with routine administration (information, personnel) departmental heads may remain over several different administrations. Some constitute minor bureaucracies in their own right, with quite substantial middle- and lower-level staff in post on a virtually permanent basis. To some degree this bureaucratizes the PCM as a whole, creating an environment in which department heads often have to look downwards to routine administration rather than upwards to the support needs of the prime minister himself.

In addition to these administrative divisions, there are other departments, nominally under the authority of the prime minister, which, for all practical purposes, constitute ministries in their own right, and indeed are headed by ministers without portfolio who enjoy cabinet rank. These departments have grown up over the decades to carry out certain specific tasks: southern economic development; relations with Parliament; relations with the regions; science and technology; civil protection; administrative reform; urban-area co-ordination; European Community co-ordination. Several of them cover areas of policy action which clearly spread across the responsibilities of numerous ministerial departments, and this was no doubt the original purpose of giving them departmental status within the prime minister's office. Their formal role is indeed one of co-ordination. However, precisely because they have evolved into (in most cases relatively ineffectual) quasi-ministries, the heads of which see themselves as little more beholden to prime-ministerial will than full ministers, they appear to bring little of substance to the overall co-ordinating role of the PCM.[10]

Beyond this stands a further range of departments, even less linked to the central policy-co-ordinating role of the chief executive, and which appear, over the years, to have been housed under prime-ministerial authority for reasons of pure administrative convenience. These include the agency regulating press, information, arts, and authorship questions; the Central Statistical Institute; and the intelligence and security services. These are, of course, very large agencies indeed, but while under nominal prime-ministerial control, they too are not part of the co-ordinating role we are considering here.

The formal departmental structure set out above does not, of course, correspond neatly to any set of functional divisions in the prime minster's normal activities. It simply reflects some types of expertise (diplomatic, military, legal, economic, and social), and some of the research and technical services (legal drafting, information about legislative progress, international events, financial and commercial data) of which he is likely to have immediate and recurring need. How these services are used on any particular occasion will depend upon the enterprise the prime minister is engaged upon.

In fact, much of the real work of the PCM in co-ordinating government legislation and administration in pursuit of the coalition programme, and in preparing the prime minister for meetings and visits, is carried out by *ad hoc* advisers and committees assembled for specific purposes and disbanded once their work has been completed. Most of the key members of such committees tend to be outsiders. Academics—especially economists and jurists—figure very prominently among such outside advisers, reflecting the high status of the academic expert in the Italian establishment, and the correspondingly lower status of the civil service itself.

The formal structure, moreover, fails to communicate the style of the work carried out by the prime minister's office. In this connection, it is important to underline the role of the legislative office, which reflects the ubiquity of law and the legal outlook in the political process, and the high priority accorded to legislative co-ordination among the prime minister's list of tasks. To a large degree, in fact, the collective purpose of the government in Italy is expressed through its legislative programme. The area of executive discretion is limited; the court of accounts, the constitutional court, the administrative court system, and indeed Parliament are zealous guardians of the principle that executive action must be clearly sanctioned by law. General enabling legislation is correspondingly rare. Hence the need to legislate in fine detail is ever present. Moreover, the pressure on the parliamentary timetable is considerable since government legislation has to compete with that from parliamentary sources on equal terms, and faces a persistent challenge from the back-benchers of the government majority.

Prime-ministerial leadership, as we have seen, has traditionally been built upon cautious and somewhat legalistic organizational pillars. It entails a *reactive* not a *proactive* conception of co-ordination, couched in legislative rather than policy terms: a programme is constructed, often by contracting parties among whom the prime minister himself is not the senior partner, and the prime minister's office is there to ease the bargain and the adjustments through into legislative shape, being equipped primarily to that end. In contrast, the emphasis it has placed on policy analysis and administrative co-ordination has been correspondingly weak. The incentive to do so, until the arrival of a prime minister like Craxi seeking to lead from the front, was limited. There was no institutionalized cabinet secretariat which maintained permanent links with key departments. Those with the closest links, moreover, were the legal experts in the legislative office, who tended to focus more on the technical and legal aspects of legislation than on the merits of policy.

Reorganization and reform in the 1980s

It was the awareness of the contingent nature of the PCM machinery, of the lack of institutional memory, and of the heavy learning costs imposed on each prime-ministerial team as it grappled anew with the problem of setting up its machinery that led during the 1980s to a renewed effort to legislate on the matter. The first serious attempt came during the 1981–2 Spadolini government. Spadolini and his *capogabinetto*, Professor Andrea Manzella, an administrative expert and close adviser, were unable to push their draft bill through Parliament before their government fell. Nevertheless, Spadolini issued pro tem a decree reorganizing the internal departmental structure along lines similar to those set out in the bill.[11] Doing so before legislation was in place had many limitations—not least the lack of a proper budget, a new mechanism for staffing and recruitment, and a new formal definition of the prime minister's role. Nevertheless, the experiment drew parliamentary attention to the urgent need for reform, at a moment when the debate on institutional matters was taking off.

The changes tested under Spadolini in the advice system available to the prime minister and the co-ordinating capabilities of the legislative office proved worthwhile experiments. An Economics Department was established, under Professor Mario Arcelli, which gathered together a substantial phalanx of largely unpaid and part-time senior university economists.[12] It probably generated a rather patchy level of commitment, after the early enthusiasm of a new government had passed, and it appears that the individuals within it worked largely in isolation from one another, on issues connected to their own academic specialities.[13] Certainly the section operated less like a collective economic think-tank than was originally intended. Nevertheless, as a first experiment in the systematic channelling of economic advice up to a prime minister independently of the departmental administrations, it did at least raise questions about how such units could be built, and how they might mesh with policy advice coming from departmental ministers and the official administrative machinery. Previously, such questions had hardly ever been raised—either in the PCM or elsewhere in the administration.

The second major new unit to be established was the so-called *programme-monitoring* department under Professor Alberto Zuliani. It was to be responsible for tracking the government's policy performance in a way similar to that envisaged for the British Central Policy Review Staff when the latter was first established under Lord Rothschild in 1970,[14] but with the significant difference that it was attached to the prime minister rather than the cabinet as a whole. It was given new electronic data-network capabilities (the *ufficio informatico*), providing Palazzo Chigi with news services, market analysis, information on parliamentary business, etc.[15] The underlying idea was extraordinarily ambitious: a unit divided into three sections—two to monitor the government programme and the public administration's implementation of it, and one to act as the research service and data base. It was to have a professional staff of nearly fifty, and would become, in effect, the nerve centre of the PCM and the focus of the planning, legislative, and administrative phases of the entire policy process.

Not surprisingly, the scheme was too ambitious to be implemented. The caretaker government of Fanfani, which had no programme to monitor anyway, disbanded it overnight. Subsequent reorganizations separated out the various functions identified by Zuliani into discrete departments. Nevertheless, like the Economics Department, it too served a useful purpose in identifying functional needs of prime ministers, and it underlined the need to create a co-ordinating centre with a wider remit than the old legislative office.

The legislative office itself was not ignored, however. Under the direction of a member of the council of state, Professor Vincenzo Caianiello, it became the centre of a network of part-time legal consultants drawn from the various legal services operated by the state (court of accounts, court of cassation, council of state, attorney-general's office, the administrative court system, university law departments, etc.). The aim was to build links to agencies whose advice could be of use to the government in anticipating the complex (and often unintended) legal consequences of its legislative proposals. But the purposes of the office were political as well as legal and institutional; strategically placed academics, known to have the ear of the opposition parties in Parliament, were used to try to help smooth the path of its legislative programme in Parliament.[16]

Under Craxi, some of these innovations were continued, but in a more improvised and less systematic manner. Craxi's conception of the prime minister's role was more pragmatic and overtly party-political than Spadolini's grand design. As was to be anticipated from a leader whose party was enjoying a rising level of electoral support, and whose first aim was to maintain that momentum, Craxi's concerns focused on the external projection of the prime-ministerial personality, rather than on the details of low-visibility legislative and administrative co-ordination. He thus found a use for the research capabilities of the *ufficio informatico*, which was further developed during his administration, but he did not resurrect the full panoply of the programme-monitoring department. Craxi also slimmed down the Economics Department, turning it into a council of advisers on economic and social affairs, containing some of those who had advised Spadolini.

As during the Spadolini governments, the structure of the PCM under Craxi was determined largely by administrative decree. Despite his nearly four years in office, Craxi too was unable to persuade Parliament to pass the stalled bill on the reform of the PCM. However, in 1988 the arrival of De Mita in Palazzo Chigi[17] signalled the return of a prime minister with a similar level of concern for organizational and administrative questions to that displayed by Spadolini. As a result, the first major item approved by Parliament under De Mita was the reform of the PCM (law no. 400, 23 August 1988), finally encapsulating in law the fruits of the organizational experiments undertaken during the decade.

The 1988 law is a complex document only the last two sections of which concern the internal organization and finance of the PCM.[18] The new structure (renamed the *general secretariat* and headed by the prime minister's 'general secretary' rather than his *capogabinetto*) is given its own permanent staffing, and the capacity to hire either full- or part-time outside advisers paid directly out of its own budget. A maximum of 169 administrators and 1,781 lower-level posts (security staff, drivers, clerical posts, etc.) are to be brought on to the secretariat's permanent staff, alongside 95 and 884 respectively from these two categories who will continue to serve on attachment from other departments of government. A further 104 part-time advisers and experts may also be brought in to service special committees and working parties set up at the discretion of the prime minister and his senior staff.[19] In short, the reform envisages a formidable advisory machinery, even if, in terms of policy co-ordination, it is only the 300 or so administrative-grade staff that concern us here.

The key role in the new structure is accorded to the general secretary, who is assigned a broad range of co-ordinating tasks, the most important of which is to co-ordinate the activities of a new 'committee of experts for the government's programme'. Its brief combines that of the programme-monitoring office and the Department of Economics under Spadolini, and the council of economic and social advisers under Craxi. The six-man committee is backed up by consultants and advisers, by an economics and social affairs staff, and by the research and statistical services of the *ufficio informatico*.

Within the legislative office, the new law establishes a special unit to co-ordinate the codification of existing legislation, to act as a warning device alerting the government machine to the effects of new legislation, and to make proposals for revision where clear incompatibilities exist. Also established is a new unit for administrative co-ordination, divided into six sections (general, economic, social and labour, the environment, public services, and special and emergency affairs). The unit is entrusted with the task of drafting administrative directives to government departments in pursuit of general policy guidelines. The mounting concern over legislative and administrative complexity is evident in the establishment of these two units. Obscure, contradictory, or misunderstood legislation, and over-extended lines of administration, have, as we shall see in the next chapter, become a serious impediment to the government's ability to achieve its policy objectives.

Assessing the long-term impact of the reform is difficult, but a number of observations are in order. By defining a clear-cut structure, with a permanent staff, and institutionalized budgetary procedures, the new law should eventually go some way to solving the perennially high learning costs that prime-ministerial staffs face as a result of their own impermanence and high turnover. However, there will remain an interface between outsiders (the secretary-general, the committee of experts, outside consultants, heads of offices like the legislative office, and the co-ordination units) on the one side, and permanent staff on the other. In a system with high prime-ministerial turnover, this will still impose a substantial initial learning cost on the former group, and much will depend on how rapidly and flexibly the permanent staff can be adapted to meet the needs of their incoming superiors. In this respect, the evidence that the pre-existing staff will eventually be frozen in post, i.e. transformed into the permanent staff of the office, is probably rather discouraging.[20] At the least, it would have been desirable to recruit senior-level staff according to a pattern which brought in a range of administrative skills and experience from different areas of Italian administration. Many of those in post at the time of the reform had been in the PCM for some years and, it may be supposed, had developed routinized outlooks which will not fit well with the new roles the prime minister's office is seeking to assume.

Beyond these questions is the more general one of the appropriateness of a co-ordinating structure which serves the prime minister alone, and yet does not follow the German pattern of clear-cut secretariats which shadow the work of individual ministries. In the absence of such a mechanism, and particularly given the brief tenure of most prime-ministerial teams, there may have been a case for a reform which also institutionalized a co-ordinating mechanism which, working closely alongside the prime minister's office, nevertheless served the cabinet as a whole, and drew in senior officials on a rotating basis from the departments which it was trying to co-ordinate. This model—immediately recognizable as that of the British cabinet secretariat—is discussed further in the following section.

The Cabinet (Council of Ministers)

After all that has been said in this chapter and others about the fragmentation of representation in Italy—factionalized parties, divided leaderships, weak, unstable coalitions, powerful back-benchers in Parliament—it will come as no surprise that the cabinet is not thought to be an effective centre for policy co-ordination. The level of collegiality is extremely low, as are expectations of the cabinet's role in formulating or reviewing overall government strategy, or making policy in particular sectors. Indeed, given how much doubt there exists over the viability of the principles of collegiality and collective responsibility in all modern systems of government, even in countries which formally subscribe to the 'cabinet government' model, it would be astonishing if it applied to Italy. All the factors which are claimed to work against it elsewhere are present in Italy as well: unwieldiness; the size of the decision agenda; the technical complexity of issues on it; the natural tendency for ministers to focus on departmental concerns; the need to devolve decision-making to more limited and technically competent arenas, etc.[21]

In addition, the same political fragmentation which for so long prevented any reform of the powers of the prime minister has permanently impeded reform of the distribution of departmental responsibilities. Italian ministries have retained the same basic functions throughout the post-war years, and this despite a programme of regionalization during the 1970s that stripped several of them of major administrative roles. The only changes have been additions (the Ministry for State Participations, the Ministry of Tourism, the Ministry of Cultural Heritage, the Ministry of the Environment, the Ministry for Scientific Research), but apart from the failed attempt to elevate the Ministry of the Budget and Economic Planning to an economic-overlord role in the 1960s, it has proved impossible for would-be reformers to rationalize the structure by, for example, integrating separate departments into superministries.

The resulting fragmentation may readily be seen from the following list of departmental and non-departmental ministries of central government in 1991.

PRESIDENCY OF THE COUNCIL OF MINISTERS

i Full departmental ministries

Foreign Affairs	Defence
Treasury	Interior
Finance	Budget
Education	Health
Justice	Industry
Labour	Agriculture
Public works	State Participations
Posts and Telecommunications	Transport
Foreign Trade	Merchant Shipping
Environment	Cultural Affairs
Tourism and Entertainment	University, Science, and Technology

ii Non-departmental ministries within the presidency of the Council of Ministers headed by ministers without portfolio

Regional affairs and institutional matters
Social affairs
Urban affairs
European Policy Co-ordination
Civil defence co-ordination
Public services (public-sector productivity improvement)
Special southern development policies
Migration
Relations with Parliament

Most anomalous is the persistence of three separate departments with responsibilities for economic affairs: the Treasury (dealing with monetary policy and the authorization of public expenditure), the Ministry of Finance (tax revenue), and the Ministry of the Budget and Economic Planning (preparation of public expenditure planning).[22] Other departments are so specialized, and in most cases small, that their existence scarcely seems to justify a cabinet seat. Tourism, Foreign Trade, Merchant Shipping, Public Works, Scientific Research, all constitute departments in which the emphasis is on managerial and regulatory, rather than policy-making, roles. Several of the tasks assumed by the ministers without portfolio also seem to fall into this category. The departments vary hugely in size, moreover. The Ministry of Education has a complement of over a million; at the other end several ministries employ fewer than 500 staff. The consequence is a formidable range of departments and (since each departmental minister and each minister without portfolio has by right a seat in the cabinet) a large and unwieldy Council. The 1988 De Mita government had no fewer than twenty-one ministers, nine ministers without portfolio, and a deputy prime minister.

Inevitably, therefore, the cabinet operates as a formal plenum, and most commentaries on it focus on its more obvious formal/legal roles. These include approval of the government programme and other policy commitments which the government intends to put to Parliament, approval of draft government bills to be submitted to Parliament, approval of decree-laws, delegated legislation, and regulations, and approval of administrative directives to government commissioners in regional government.[23] The cabinet's capacity to act as the arena of intimate discussion, debate, and collective approval is undermined, moreover, not just by size and political fragmentation, but by the conventions which have grown up in response to these factors. Through such conventions, decisions involving the preparation of legislation, the conduct of most aspects of foreign policy, the process of appointment of senior officials in public enterprises, and the co-ordination of regional administration are left largely to single departments, or at best small groups. The cabinet itself merely registers decisions taken in these arenas. If there is dissent, or if departmental ministers decline to act on coalition agreements, the disagreement is resolved in some other context—between party secretaries, for example—or it simply remains as a source of intra-coalition tension until the next coalition crisis, when it will again be tackled through inter- and intra-party negotiation.

The council of the cabinet

One partial solution to this problem would be to bring all party secretaries into the cabinet. For many years there were periodic calls for this, especially from incoming prime ministers anxious to bolster their government.[24] Leaders who had to share personal responsibility for cabinet decisions could less easily wear a government down by constant dissociation from its actions. De Mita himself sought to take such a principle one step further in 1988, by persuading the Christian Democrat Party to allow him to hold the office of prime minister and secretary of the party simultaneously. Unfortunately for him, he managed to win only a temporary reprieve, being forced, on assuming the premiership, to agree to step down as secretary at the next DC congress, some months later.[25] More generally, during the 1980s neither leader of the two main parties of the coalition, the DC and the PSI, has been willing to serve in the cabinet when the other is prime minister.

Nevertheless, the 1980s has seen one important innovation in this respect. On assuming office in 1983 Craxi announced the formation of a council of the cabinet (*consiglio di gabinetto*).[26] This was to serve as a form of inner cabinet, bringing together eight of the most senior or strategically important members of the cabinet: the prime minister and deputy prime minister, together with the holders of the Treasury, Defence, Foreign Affairs, Interior, Budget, and Labour portfolios.[27] Although endowed with none of the formal decision-making powers given to the full cabinet, it was intended to be a forum in which major problems of policy and strategy could be resolved, in a way that would commit both the full cabinet (since it was representative of its main figures) and also the main parties (since it contained senior figures from each of them, even if it did not, as Craxi had originally hoped, contain the formal *leaders* of all parties). In short, it was intended in a single forum to combine the functions of meetings both of party leaders and of the cabinet.

In this sense, of course, it was not an inner cabinet as the term is sometimes used in the British context. Its members were not close and trusted confidants of the prime minister, chosen by him freely, but representatives of important power centres with whom he had to establish agreement. Nevertheless, it seems that under Craxi the experiment was a relative success. The council of the cabinet did become a significant centre for decision-making. Major strategic questions seem to have been discussed much more at this level than at official cabinet level. Furthermore, the 1988 reform gave the council full legal status as a standing committee, the composition of which was to be established by each prime minister in consultation with his cabinet.[28]

For constitutional purists, it should be admitted, as for enemies of the aggregation of power around the prime minister and around a more united cabinet, the advent of the council of the cabinet was a dubious departure. Although it had no formal powers, it was seen in practice as likely to usurp the deliberative role of the cabinet itself, and to introduce a formal inequality between ministers, according to whether or not they were part of the inner circle. Undoubtedly, in this formal sense, it was a violation of the constitutional principle of collective responsibility. However, since that principle had itself long since been consigned to the dignified rather than the efficient part of the constitution, the loss could hardly be seen as a serious one. Now enshrined in formal law, if not in the constitution, the council of the cabinet seems destined to remain a significant part of the machinery of the political executive, except in circumstances when the prime minister is a caretaker lacking a substantive political majority behind him.

Interministerial committees

Another mechanism for government co-ordination, with a longer but less happy history, is the interministerial committee.[29] These committees were established with the perfectly sensible aim of freeing the cabinet of much technical business and of co-ordinating activity in specified policy areas. They are not, however, analogous to cabinet committees in the British sense, since they have a formal/legal status and legally defined powers to act on their own behalf on a wide range of administrative matters. They are composed of all ministers having an interest in the policy area in question. Top civil servants very occasionally attend, but without voting rights, and do so more in a consultative than an active role.

Much the largest is CIPE (Comitato interministeriale per la programmazione economica), which deals with economic planning. Nominally chaired by the prime minister (in practice by the Budget and Planning minister), it includes all ministers in the area of economic policy—in fact the majority of the cabinet itself. When established in 1967, it was supposed to assume an overseeing role in relation to other interministerial committees, such as that for prices, and for credit and savings. However, it also acquired numerous administrative tasks: approving levels of industrial subsidies, incentive schemes, and loans; overseeing development plans in given sectors such as shipbuilding or hospital construction, etc. These tasks tended to swamp its agenda, and the CIPE ended up as a forum which to a large degree registered decisions taken lower down the system—either in its component ministries, or even in the public-sector agencies nominally under ministerial supervision.

Little changed after the 1977 reform of the interministerial committee system, when some of CIPE's various tasks were hived off to three new committees covering industrial policy, food and agriculture, and overseas commercial policy. In practice, this seems to have further fragmented economic decision-taking by introducing yet another tier between the overall government programme and the executing ministries and agencies. Indeed, in so far as the detail of most policy is made at departmental level, and can only be altered by deliberate cabinet intervention—which in practice means prime-ministerial intervention, or, more recently, that of the council of the cabinet—then the multiplication of intervening levels of authority between top and bottom, each with a degree of formal executive power of its own, probably weakens control and co-ordination from the centre, rather than strengthens it.[30] Indeed, what has tended to happen over time is that each department of state has pressed—not always successfully—to obtain an interministerial committee for which it performs most of the servicing operations. This attempt to win influence with other departments underlines an additional way in which the co-ordinating purpose of the committee system is under mined by centrifugal pressures.

Bureaucratic co-ordination

The reason *why* cabinet intervention in practice has to mean intervention by the prime minister or the council of the cabinet is that it cannot be performed by the cabinet's own secretariat. More generally, what the cabinet lacks in political cohesion is not compensated by a strongly institutionalized process of *bureaucratic* co-ordination. We have already observed that the secretariat to the cabinet is directly responsible to the prime minister, and a part of his support staff. The secretariat is, in fact, a modest institution, quite unlike its British counterpart. The head of the office (who works for a politician, the under-secretary at the PCM, and who does not even attend council meetings, since only politicians are permitted to be present) is certainly not, as in Britain, on a par, in terms of status, with top officials elsewhere in the ministerial hierarchy. He occupies a small office on the fourth floor of Palazzo Chigi, and his role is largely administrative: the formal circulation of agendas and decisions.

There is thus no permanent, institutionalized body which, through tradition, substantial staffing, and established legitimacy (and indeed a role partially independent of the prime minister) integrates ministers and senior civil servants into a committee-based policy framework which substitutes, to a degree, for the lack of political collegiality. Naturally, the long-term effect of such a framework on the distribution of power at the centre may be difficult to predict. In Britain it is often argued that it has strengthened the prime minister at the expense of cabinet, and there may be an element of truth in this. However, whether the co-ordination thus achieved is driven by prime-ministerial or cabinet impetus is less important than the potential co-ordinating benefits it might bring. For what is clearly lacking in Italy is an effective procedure for bringing in to the centre of the system selected senior staff with departmental experience, whose explicit function is administrative and legislative co-ordination, and who can do so through a mechanism with a strong institutional memory.

In Italy, members of departmental administrations *are* recruited to the PCM, as we have seen, and their previous links and experience *can* sometimes be valuable, but when this happens, it is more by chance than design. There is no systematic turnover designed to maximize its benefits, nor have there, until recently, been policy-area secretariats similar to those in the British Cabinet Office. The 1988 reform, which has established the new legislative and administrative co-ordination units (discussed above), may provide some partial rectification of this, but had not done so during its first two years of operation. Perhaps even more fundamentally, bureaucratic co-ordination runs up against the nature of the administrative class itself. It can be made effective where there exists a policy-evangelistic, self-confident, administrative élite, but it is far less likely to work if that élite does not wish to see itself and its role in these terms. This, as the following chapter demonstrates, is a very important constraint indeed in the Italian context.

Conclusion

What emerges most clearly from the experience of attempts to reform the co-ordinating capacities of Italian central government in the 1980s is the difficulty arising from the brevity and provisionality of most governments. The high turnover provides little time for changes to gel, and for new routines to be established. This is seen most clearly in the differing prime-ministerial styles of the four most important chief executives of the 1980s: Spadolini, Craxi, De Mita, and Andreotti.

Two—Spadolini and De Mita—were organizational innovators, interested in the structure of the PCM and genuinely concerned to make it congruent with the functional needs of the office. However, each was followed by prime ministers—Craxi and Andreotti—who were best described as pragmatic improvisers.

Andreotti, in particular, showed little taste for implementing the new reform legislation.[31] No new 'committee of experts' to replace De Mita's was appointed, and some other heads-of-department posts were left vacant for some time. The process of recruiting permanent staff, moreover, was slowed down. At times the major co-ordinating centre even appeared to be not the PCM at all, but the Ministry of the Budget. Its incumbent, Paolo Cirino Pomicino, a close political colleague of Andreotti's, and formerly president of the Budget Committee of the Chamber of Deputies, was an influential figure among Christian Democrat parliamentarians, underlining Andreotti's belief that what counted was effective management of the Christian Democrat back-benches, rather than what he may have regarded as the *dirigisme* of the 1988 reform law. The latter was based on a conception of the PCM as the directing centre of government. Andreotti's return to Palazzo Chigi marked a return to the low-key bargaining characteristic of most earlier Christian Democrat prime ministers.[32]

The interest of this is not whether or not Andreotti was more successful but that, in placing the emphasis so firmly on parliamentary management, he could radically weaken a structure so recently put in place. To a less marked degree, the same occurred in the transition from Spadolini to Craxi. It also occurs when a prime minister with a reasonably cohesive majority gives way to a caretaker prime minister with no majority and hence no real programme to pursue. In the face of such a pattern, it is almost impossible for new roles and structures to become institutionalized, and to shape the expectations and behaviour of those who occupy office. It is a problem, too, for the cabinet and the council of the cabinet. Cohesive cabinet government depends upon a stable inner group capable of working together in pursuit of a reasonably well-defined strategy over a sustained period. If the council of the cabinet is important under one prime minister, but fails to include key figures in the next, the locus of power is unstable. And if the composition of the cabinet itself shifts too frequently, its associated committee structure cannot build up a clear operating pattern.

This is not to dismiss the consequences of reform during the 1980s as of no importance. The 1988 legislation, in particular, is likely to be of enduring importance even if it has got off to an uncertain start. In the hands of a prime minister wishing to make use of it, it now offers considerable possibilities. What it does demonstrate, however, is the difficulty not just of making policy, but also of attempts to build up institutional memory and practice to *facilitate* the making of policy, in the face of the exaggerated short-termism of coalition relationships.

8

The Administrative System

Administrative systems are the tools for transforming political intentions into policy output. Their effectiveness depends on many different factors. Political scientists have tended to focus on the way in which the public sector is structured, the quality and productivity of public employees, and their role in the policy-making process, especially the role of those towards the top of the hierarchy. Overlying these more technical questions are broader issues: on the one hand, does the community obtain value for money in the resources it invests in its public sector? on the other, can (and perhaps also to what degree *should*) elected politicians control permanent and professional civil servants?[1]

In most European states the expression 'public administration' covers a range of different structures and administrative styles. As the regulatory, welfare, and productive functions of government have grown, so many different administrative formulae have been adopted. Some involve a very close and formal relationship between political power and administrative action. In other cases, agencies are given a high degree of administrative and commercial discretion. Some agencies at the very centre of government perform a supervisory or policy-making role; others are more like line agencies, performing tasks and providing services with extensive field networks throughout the national territory. Some enjoy a monopoly in their field of activity (defence, security, law and order); others operate alongside, or compete with, private suppliers in essentially market conditions. Corresponding to this functional and structural diversity, the personnel of the administrative system contains a range of functions, levels, professional status groups, and labour relationships. At the top stands the administrative élite of bureaucratic policy-makers and public-sector managers. Lower down are functional specialists—engineers, technicians, doctors, scientists—paralleled by lower-level line management, then clerical officers, police officers, soldiers, and auxiliary personnel, and finally, possessing various levels of skill, ordinary manual workers and their equivalents.

Italian Administrative Heterogeneity

The departmental model and its diversity

Italy is no exception to this picture of modern administrative heterogeneity. We have already seen in Chapter 6 the very fragmented range of ministerial departments: twenty-one in all, with generally a further six to nine ministers without portfolio in charge of what in some cases are, in all but name, separate ministerial departments. We have also seen, in the division of responsibility for economic management between three separate ministries, the long-unresolved problems caused by the overlapping competences of different departments. This is significant not just at the level of overall macro-economic management, but also at the sectoral level. Thus 'agriculture', for example, is administered not only by the Ministry of Agriculture, but also, among others, by the Ministry for Industry and the Ministry of State Participations (in the agro-business and food-processing sector), by the Ministry of Foreign Trade (agricultural imports and exports), and by the department in charge of southern development (agricultural credit and infrastructure). Similarly 'industry' involves the Ministries of Industry, State Participations, Foreign Trade, Tourism, Southern Development, etc., and the same dispersal is characteristic of transport, health, regional economic and social aid systems, etc.

For many years there has been discussion of departmental regroupings, but political pressures, and the need to avoid upsetting delicate inter- and intra-party balances by downgrading particular departments and upgrading others, has always made this difficult.[2] Among the few successes of recent years have been, first, the identification of environmental issues as a cross-departmental subject important enough to merit its own department (the Ministry for Environmental Protection was established by the first Craxi government (law no. 349, 8 July 1986)), and secondly, the according of a higher priority to technology, research, and scientific education with the establishment in 1989 of the Ministry for the Universities and Scientific and Technological Research (law no. 168, 9 May 1989). Hiving off certain departmental functions to regional government in the 1970s increased the need for a restructuring in several other areas. Over a longer period of time, the development of a European Community tier of administration involving Italy has had the same effect. Much economic regulation and some direct economic intervention now comes from Brussels and crosses the boundaries of various Italian departments. The problem of co-ordinating national departmental responses to Community activities is not unique to Italy, but it is especially serious there, as we shall see in Chapter 10.

These pressures, and others—particularly for greater consultation and participation—have not left the traditional departmental structure itself unaltered however. Indeed, they have given rise to a considerable range of departmental styles. Thus some departments are small central planning departments which operate through managerial agencies. The Ministry of Posts and Telecommunications supervises two such agencies, one for postal services, the other for telephone services. The Ministry of Transport operates the railway system through Ferrovie dello stato, the state railway network.

At the centre, most departments are built on a common structure consisting of a series of directorates-general, ranging in number from two to twelve, corresponding to functional divisions in the activities of the department. However, two (Defence and Foreign Affairs) have a single civil servant at their head—the secretary-general—who plays a role similar to that of a British permanent secretary, although strictly he is not senior to the heads of each directorate-general. The other departments have no single senior civil servant; each directorate-general has a senior manager (*dirigente generale*) responsible directly to the minister and his personal *cabinet*. Departments also vary according to the importance attributed to particular units of administration. Some departments give a major co-ordinating role to the legislative office within the personal *cabinet* of the minister, and (paradoxically, given that the *cabinet* normally consists of trusted confidants of the minister, coming and departing with him) the office in some cases has a permanent staff.[3]

In several cases—particularly in economic and technical ministries—there are institutionalized consultative committees, giving a voice to interest groups, professional bodies, or outside academic experts, who sit alongside civil servants in advising particular directorates or the minister himself. These committees, enshrined in law, have grown considerably in recent years and have seen their functions expand. There is also a clear trend towards the institutionalization of national councils, which include representatives of regional government and local authorities as well as interest-groups and experts. These councils are responsible not just for giving technical advice, but for establishing sectoral plans for development, and for co-ordinating different policy initiatives across national territory. This sectorization of policy-making, along with the increase in the number of actors involved, further illustrates the general tendency towards the dispersal of power to formulate policy to a wider number of participants, and hence away from the core executive.[4]

A further variation on the departmental model lies in territorial decentralization. Some departments have clear networks of territorial field agencies throughout the country (Interior, Treasury, Finance, Education, Labour, Industry). During the twentieth century, the complexity of territorial decentralization has gradually increased. Local activities of central government were originally controlled, as in France, through the provincial prefecture (the local representative of the Ministry of the Interior). As the number of ministries at the centre increased, and as each established its own field agencies, this prefectoral control has gradually weakened. The introduction of a uniform tier of regional government in the 1970s brought a further development in this direction as administrative functions formerly carried out at national level have been transferred to the control of elected regional authorities. The four main departments which have lost local functions as a result of this regionalization process are Agriculture and Forestry, Public Works, Health, and Tourism and Entertainment.

Government beyond the departmental ministries

Beyond the ministries themselves, there is even greater diversity. A wide range of special agencies has grown up since the beginning of the century. Common to all is a greater degree of managerial and budgetary autonomy from the sponsoring ministry than any internal directorate-general in an ordinary ministry possesses. A frequent aim has been to liberate management from costly and time-consuming legal and administrative controls to which all state administration is subject, and to give it greater flexibility in commercial decisions, personnel policy, etc. However, the precise level of autonomy varies considerably with agencies at different removes from ministerial control.

The first group consists of the so-called 'autonomous administrations'. These include, *inter alia*, the National Forestry Commission, the National Road-Building Agency, the National Aviation Authority, the State Monopolies Board, the telephone system, and (the two largest) the postal service and, until a 1985 reform of its legal status, the railways (FFSS).

In recent years the administrative formula of the autonomous administration has been especially controversial. Although 'autonomous', they have been under close ministerial supervision. The minister heads the administration's board and retains responsibility for its policy. As in the case of British public corporations, it has proved extremely difficult to define a satisfactory boundary between general policy—for which the minister retains responsibility—and day-to-day management. Thus for example in the mid-1980s the then director-general of the state railways, Mario Schimberni, former head of Montedison, the private-sector chemicals conglomerate, campaigned hard but unsuccessfully to transform the status of FFSS from an autonomous administration to a private commercial company (albeit one in which the state remained the dominant, indeed only, shareholder). The reform that did emerge (law no. 210, 15 May 1985), while paving the way for the injection into the financing of state railways of some stricter criteria for public subsidization of transport, underlined what has become an increasingly thorny issue for recent governments: the relaxation of party control over major public enterprises (FFSS employs around 200,000 workers[5]), and the extent and type of deregulation, or indeed of privatization.[6]

The second group is the so-called 'state-holdings' corporation, of which the prime example is IRI. Originally IRI was seen as an imaginative adaptation of a fascist legacy into a sophisticated tool of industrial policy facilitating state-led entrepreneurship in areas where private industry was slow to act and reluctant to yield monopoly powers.[7] Through it, the state could take an equity stake—usually a controlling one—in private-sector companies managed according to the rules of the market. IRI was the largest of the three main holding corporations. Like the others it was responsible to the sponsoring ministry—the Ministry for State Holdings. But after great success in the 1950s and 1960s, IRI and its chief counterparts, ENI (energy and chemicals) and EFIM (manufacturing industry in the south), came under increasing political control, as appointments to managerial positions were made on party criteria, and pressure mounted to use the state-holdings sector to hold down unemployment. The financial performance of the sector declined steadily, leaving Romano Prodi, IRI president during the 1980s, with a long dour struggle against an accumulated debt burden throughout the latter half of the 1980s.[8]

Beyond the autonomous administration and the state-holdings formula, there are several other kinds of functional decentralization. The full range of non-departmental public agencies in Italy is vast: somewhere in excess of 40,000 in all.[9] Some, like the autonomous agencies and the state-holdings formula, carry out commercial activities. Thus, in the banking sector (the majority of which is non-private), although several banks are run through the IRI-formula (including Banca commerciale and Credito italiano) others (including Banca nazionale del lavoro, Banco di Sicilia, and Banco di Napoli) are owned directly by the state, even though they are not subject to public law in the same way as a ministerial department. ENEL, the state electricity-generation corporation, has the same status. Other agencies have a redistributive and social-security function, dealing with pensions, insurance, etc., the most notable being INPS, the pensions and social-security conglomerate. This category in fact contains a great range of organizations, from the major pensions funds down to local-level welfare and relief organizations, and those servicing very specifically defined categories of citizen. Finally, there are agencies with supervisory and tutelage functions, of which much the most important, enjoying very great prestige both in Italy and abroad, and a high level of independence from government, is clearly the Bank of Italy, discussed below.

The consequences of administrative heterogeneity

Assessing the consequences of Italy's formidable administrative heterogeneity is difficult because of the problem of disentangling consequences which are purely the result of structural or organizational factors from the more general problems of productivity, staffing, morale, and legalism considered later in this chapter. There is little doubt, however, that administrative complexity discourages *generalized* solutions to these latter problems. Any government elected on a platform of 'value for money in the public sector' finds itself confronted with major problems in applying such a policy across the range of highly specific statutory regulations, budgetary systems, personnel policies, and so forth which govern not just government beyond the ministries, but even the supposedly more uniform ministries themselves. Indeed, the one serious attempt to get to grips with these problems—the regionalization reforms of the 1970s, considered in Chapter 9—was driven by a belief that wherever possible such problems were best tackled at subnational level. The same problem confronts any attempt to exercise serious parliamentary scrutiny of the budgetary policies and activities of the public sector. Budgets are highly disaggregated, and are presented in very different forms, some integrated in departmental allocations, others in special appendices—a state of affairs which greatly complicates the task of even determined members of the budgetary committees.

In fact, however, the problem is less the inability of the political class to get to grips with the problems of the public sector than its unwillingness to do so. Both the central ministerial apparatus and, in a different way, the non-departmental agencies are politically sensitive institutions. The ministries themselves are not actively politicized. No spoils system operates, nor is promotion on the basis of party affiliation widely available. As we shall see later in the chapter, conventional wisdom has it that quite the opposite is the case. The senior civil service, it is said, has traded security for policy-influence, with senior civil servants appointed on the basis of seniority and merit, but enjoying a relatively modest influence on policy. However, as a political lobby, the personnel of ministerial departments, especially but not exclusively the larger ones, is formidable when questions of departmental organization, salaries, training, and promotion issues are on the agenda. As Table 8.1 shows, in 1987 the Ministry of Education employed over 900,000 teachers; the autonomous agency under the Ministry of Defence employed a further 250,000; the Finance and Interior Ministries each employed over 100,000. Governments are extraordinarily reluctant to take on groups that wield considerable power, both indirectly in the form of non-co-operation and directly, in the form of organized groups of voters capable of using the preference-vote mechanism to great effect.

Outside the ministerial apparatus, the picture is different. Overt politicization of the top echelons of the various categories of non-departmental organization is widely practised and more or less openly acknowledged. The presidents of major institutions such as IRI, ENI, the public-broadcasting network RAI-TV, Alitalia, the largest banks, and so on are all openly referred to by their party affiliation. However great their merits and managerial talents, they need party backing to be appointed, and will find some difficulty resisting party pressure when it is applied in earnest. Indeed, the irony of the principle of government by special agency is that organizations deliberately placed outside the tightest forms of public accountability to allow flexibility and responsiveness to particular circumstances have as a result been invaded by party control. From pricing, investment, and employment decisions of the major state-holdings corporations, down to the purchasing and hiring policies of the smallest local health unit, policy is at least potentially subject to party supervision and influence.[10]

The worst aspect of this is probably not corruption, at least in the sense that only a small proportion of what happens is, in any clear sense, unlawful.[11] Rather, the consequence is a serious waste an misallocation of public resources, as the agencies in question, very clearly identified in the minds of their clients and employees with party control, *expect* policy to be shaped to their own benefit, and hold parties responsible for policy much more directly than if the agency in question were a politically neutral administrative department. Partisan control of special agencies clearly generates strong political lobbies. In

TABLE 8.1 *Employees in departmental ministries and independent agencies of Italian central government in 1990*

	Civil servants	Teaching staff	Military personnel	Total
Presidency of the Council of Ministers	4,469	72	—	5,931
Foreign Affairs	7,034	6	—	7,040
Agriculture	4,132	—	5,784	9,916
Environment	226	—	—	226
Culture	24,987	—	—	24,987
Budget	367	—	—	367
Foreign Trade	546	—	—	546
Defence	55,323	320	248,728	304,460
Finance	66,455	80	56,694	123,229
Justice	39,509	—	25,535	72,245
Industry	1,505	—	—	1,505
Interior	139,734	156	—	139,890
Public Works	4,452	—	—	4,452
Labour and Social Security	16,238	—	—	16,238
Merchant Shipping	1,167	—	905	2,072
State Holdings	132	—	—	132
Posts and Telecommunications[a]	5	—	—	5
Education	193,974	970,452	—	1,164,426
Health	5,161	—	—	5,161
Treasury	16,774	—	—	16,774
Transport	5,999	—	—	5,999
Tourism	432	—	—	432
Higher Education and Research	49,046	52,449	—	101,495
Total	637,827	1,023,535	337,646	2,007,528

[a] The Ministry of Posts and Telecommunications is in practice a shell holding ministry for the Amministrazione delle poste e telecommunicazioni (PPTT), the agencies delivering post and telecommunication services. The employees of these agencies (239,215 in 1990), while public employees, are subject to different legal status and contractual arrangements from civil servants proper. Hence the small size of the Ministry's personnel.

Source: Istituto centrale di statistica, *Annuario statistico italiano* (Rome, 1991), 253.

this sense, it may be truer to suggest that the parties are captured by the lobbies than that the agencies are captured by the parties. Other things being equal, the Christian Democrat Party might be better placed, and electorally more popular, if it had a freer hand when taking broad decisions affecting public spending and the management of the public sector. That things are not equal, as we have already seen, reflects a fear that what the DC does not occupy, other parties of the centre will, or, within the DC itself, what one faction does not occupy, another will, with significant consequences for the internal balance of party power. When leaders arise who attempt to adopt a different, more aggregated, approach to the making of public policy, as in the case of the De Mita premiership in 1988–9, the potential for rebellion within the party by those with most to lose is considerable, as De Mita's own fate suggests.

The Legal Context of Italian Administration

Law has a profound impact on Italian politics and administration. Indeed, there are few countries in Europe where the law plays such an invasive and complex role in the administrative system as in Italy. As we have already seen, the policy-making process in Parliament and in the Council of Ministers is dominated by an emphasis on the technical details of legislation. Law, legal categories, and most fundamentally legal controls dominate the thinking and procedure of senior civil servants. The law is generally complex, fragmented, obscure, and difficult to interpret.[12] It has generated a set of professional skills and a legal establishment with a far higher profile than in the United Kingdom. A legal training is a key resource in the public administration, and the power to interpret the law sets the judges of the council of state—the main administrative court—at the pinnacle of the administrative system. The importance of the law in administration has generated a vast, somewhat pedantic, and to outside observers often parasitic profession of interpreters of public law—be they in the departments of the major state universities, or in the agencies responsible for checking, controlling, and judging the actions of public servants.

The origins of this state of affairs lie in the post-enlightenment view of the needs of administration in the centralized, liberal state. Through it the concept of the *stato di diritto*—the state based on law—came to replace the state based on feudal privilege. Traditional ascriptive authority, unbounded, or bounded only by convention, and varying from area to area within a national territory, thus gave way to a centralized system of rational-legal authority. The task of defining and limiting political and administrative power was gradually achieved both through constitutionalism—entrenched civil and political rights, the separation of powers, judicial review of the constitutionality of legislation—and through an articulated body of administrative law. Subjecting the exercise of public power to tight legal controls had the advantage not just that it was a guarantee against arbitrary executive action, but also that it gave explicit authority to the actions of even the lowest level of officialdom and provided a uniform system of administration throughout the national territory. Hence administrative procedures came to be regulated by a complex series of laws, decrees, and regulations.

The centrality of administrative law need not necessarily have had detrimental effects. It would not have done so if legislation were clearly drafted, regularly reviewed and codified, and scrutinized for contradictions and overlaps, if the civil servants themselves kept sight of broad managerial objectives, and did not lose their way in punctilious efforts to stick to the full and detailed letter of the law, and if public employees did not become rigidly litigious in imposing the law in matters related to employment and career progress. However, these conditions in turn require that the legislature should refrain from using the law in a fragmented and piecemeal way, distributing finely targeted benefits, obligations, and regulations on limited groups of citizens, and setting out in great detail procedures which limit the discretion of the civil service to achieve the objectives it has been set. As we have seen in Chapter 6 the cast of mind of the Italian legislator has exactly this particularistic, micro-sectional bent. Parliament sets up the administration to operate in particular ways, so that, even assuming the administrative system genuinely wants to escape from its excessive legalism, it has great difficulty doing so.

Backing up the system of administrative law, there is, as we have seen in Chapter 5, in any case a mechanism for the dispensing of administrative justice, in the shape of the *consiglio di stato* (council of state) and the *corte dei conti* (court of accounts), which is distinct from the ordinary court system and further underlines the importance of legal and procedural propriety. In addition to its consultative role, the council of state has, since 1971, been the court of appeal of a system of regionally based administrative courts of first instance (*tribunali amministrativi regionali* or TAR). There has been an explosive growth in recourse to the council and the TAR over the last twenty years, with the number of judgements handed down increasing five fold since the 1971 reform. Striking, in this connection, is the high proportion (40 per cent) which involve matters of public-sector employment.[13] The court of accounts has an even more immediate impact in proceduralizing the activities of the administration. Its checks are both 'preventive' (approval in advance) and *post facto*. It approves state contracts, disbursements, matters of personnel administration, etc., and it conducts an annual audit on the state accounts, on which it reports to Parliament. The court of accounts plays a complex role. Its procedural requirements are detailed, it frequently takes issue with the administrations under its supervision. It is a punctilious and demanding task-master, and it has engendered much post-war debate about the continuing need for detailed preventive controls of the type it exercises—particularly since they do not appear to be demanded by the constitution itself. On the other hand, its *ex post* reports to Parliament are sophisticated analyses not just of procedural aspects but also of the general shortcomings and internal contradictions of government policy.[14]

In recent years, the procedural administrative justice dispensed by the council of state and the court of accounts has been increasingly supplemented by the intervention of the penal justice system, especially in the investigation of corruption in planning decisions, but also in cases of alleged negligence. The latter class of action has been particularly controversial, since it is often aimed at general administrative inefficiency, failure to implement programmes, spend funds, make appointments on time, etc. As such, it has a political as well as judicial air to it, as confirmed by the tendency to focus such cases on administrators increasingly higher up the public service, and on those who are directly appointed by political parties. It has inevitably engendered allegations of political bias on the part of some members of the penal justice system, less, it should probably be added, to defend civil servants than to defend the reputation of politicians. In 1987, it became a *cause célèbre* when, in a referendum, immunity of the judiciary from civil actions for damages was abolished—a move widely read as a warning by the politicians to the penal judiciary to tread carefully.[15] At any event, the increasing involvement of the judiciary in this area has had the inevitable effect of further entrenching legalism into the behaviour of the civil servants, and even of making them advocates of the strict procedural controls of the court of accounts, behind which they can effectively shelter.

The controls on administrative action imposed by the various judicial agencies are, of course, far more strict and precise than those imposed by Parliament, the other mechanism by which, traditionally, administrative systems have been supervised and held to account.

Under normal circumstances the constraints on the time of parliament-arians—even those who specialize in particular areas and serve on specialist committees—and their relative lack of professional expertise in legal or financial investigation makes this an unsuitable mechanism for detailed scrutiny. This could, of course, be beneficial if it persuaded members of Parliament to direct their attention to the broad lines of public policy, forcing senior civil servants to defend and explain their policies. In reality, however, Italian civil servants have avoided the challenge of the public spotlight, preferring instead to hide behind ministerial responsibility. And parliament itself has tended to pay little attention to the very large numbers of annual reports on the state of policy implementation which it now tends to build in as a condition in much legislation. Indeed, rather than limit itself to *ex post* judgements, based on such reports, Parliament has, on occasions, tried to build a direct style of parliamentary intervention in administrative matters, rather along the lines of the links between Congress and the administrations in the USA in recent years. The fine tuning of the annual state budget by the various sectoral commissions which consider it during its parliamentary passage exemplifies this type of direct parliamentary involvement.

Clearly, the more Parliament conceives of its role as a *co-participant* in government, rather than a body whose role is to scrutinize and supervise the activities it has entrusted to the executive, the more it will produce detailed legislation binding both civil servants and ministers in very precise ways. It is not what is traditionally understood by parliamentary oversight, and it is not conducted at the higher level of aggregation that should arguably be achieved in a body which stands between the detailed activities of the administration and the general concerns of the electorate. Its principal effect, in fact, is to add to the legalism for which there are already ample impulses elsewhere in the system.

Public-Sector Personnel

It is often supposed that Italian public administration is overstaffed. In international terms, it is difficult to verify this. While different methods of defining 'public administration' make comparison very difficult, Italy does not appear to be out of line with the European Community average: indeed, if anything, it is probably slightly below the average in terms of total numbers employed.[16] The real problems are more subtle: a maldistribution of the Italian public-sector work-force, with overstaffing common in the south, but serious personnel shortages in the north; relatively poor quality staff; low morale and a poor system of training, career-management, and incentives; and high levels of unionization making personnel management difficult.[17]

TABLE 8.2 *Public-sector workers in state, local government, and independent agencies, 1990*[a]

Departmental ministries[b]	2,008,000
Aziende autonome[c]	281,000
Insurance funds	63,000
Enel[d]	113,000
Other public agencies	131,000
Regional authorities	81,000
Provincial authorities	69,000
Municipal authorities	593,000
Municipal enterprises[e]	158,000
Local health units and public hospitals	629,000

Note: Figures rounded to nearest 1,000.

[a] The approximately 4.1 million workers listed here do not exhaust the range of agencies which may be said to be part of the 'public sector'. The above categorization—the most frequently cited—comes from the national statistical institute. The categorizations adopted in Italy vary widely, and there is no clear 'outer limit' to the public sector, because the so-called state-holdings groups, such as IRI or ENI, are agencies which may take either controlling or minority stakes in notionally private-sector commercial enterprises. In law, the workers in such enterprises are subject to private-sector regulation that applies in any other private commercal enterprise; in political terms, however, the state may be said to have a considerably greater responsibility to such workers than it has towards others in the private sector. Another agency which is still *de facto* part of the public sector (albeit earmarked for future privatization by legislation in 1991) is the state railways (*ferrovie dello stato*), which employs over 200,000 workers.

[b] Includes teachers, professional military personnel, the judiciary, as well as officials and industrial civil servants (*impiegati civil e operai*).

[c] Posts and telecommunications, highway authorities, public monopolies (tobacco, salt, etc.), forestry, etc.

[d] State electricity authority.

[e] Includes local transport, and other notionally commercially provided services whose employee status is separate from legislation governing direct municipal labour.

Source: Istituto centrale di statistica, *Annuario statistico italiano* (Rome, 1991), 252.

Most of the approximately 4.5 million 'public-sector' workers are career employees, although a significant group, about half a million, fall into the category of representatives of political parties, nominated for a fixed period of office (and on varying terms, some full-time, most part-time) to administer nationally or locally owned public agencies. Approximately half of all the 4.5 million employees are employed directly by central, regional, and local government, and half by other agencies with greater operational independence—the so-called para-state sector of public enterprises and services. Within the former category around 900,000 arc teachers (out of a total employed directly by the centre of 1.6 million) and 700,000 are employees of regional and local government. Within the second category (the parastate) there are around 600,000 workers in the national health service, and 1.2 million workers distributed between wholly owned corporations like the railways, posts, electricity, etc., and enterprises owned under the 'state-participations' formula.

The recruitment, status, contracts, and management of employees throughout such a vast range of activities is an academic study in itself, most aspects of which cannot be dealt with in any detail here. In this chapter we are mainly concerned with civil servants (*impiegati civili*) in the administrative system most closely connected to policy-making and enforcement within central government. This group—the approximately 400,000 employees of the central ministries—excludes functional specialists like teachers and career military personnel. Within it about 100,000 are employed in Rome and the remainder in field agencies throughout the country.

Social background

At the top end of the public administration hierarchy, the single most striking feature of the Italian civil service is that, unlike the top echelons of the British or French administrative system, the Italian higher civil service has not traditionally been drawn from a dominant social élite. Low pay, slow promotion prospects, and low status have all helped to make the civil service, even at its senior levels, a preserve of those who see themselves to have relatively few other options for employment but the state. The northern middle class, the most 'modern' social group, are not attracted to a civil-service career, and do not have the same need for job security found in the south.

This has not always been so. In the nineteenth-century liberal state the majority of senior civil servants were Piedmontese, while the south lacked an administrative tradition. During the twentieth century, however, there has been a gradual change. Southerners, especially the many law graduates from the big southern universities, have acquired the basic educational skills necessary for work in public administration, while the relatively southern location of Rome as the country's capital has helped them to realize their ambitions at the centre as well as locally. Fascism also contributed to the problem. It set a trend, continued in the post-war era, of bypassing the civil service by coping with new problems through the establishment of special party-dominated agencies parallel to but separate from the civil service proper. The natural consequence was to leave civil servants excluded and demoralized, making the career less attractive to those who had alternatives to which to turn. As a result, over 60 per cent of senior civil servants are of southern origin.[18] Given the dualism of Italian society and economic development, the consequences of this are far-reaching. Educational standards in the south are lower; contact with the 'can-do' flexible, managerial outlook of the northern entrepreneurial world is minimal; aspirations are for status and security, rather than risk-based opportunity.

All this would not be so serious if the civil service itself could provide a system of career training which could mould its recruits into an efficient managerial élite. Indeed, southern underdevelopment could even offer some compensatory advantages in comparison with societies with more even levels of development. In all advanced societies, public-sector recruitment and retention of high-calibre staff has become an increasing problem as public-spending restraint has made a public-sector career comparatively less attractive than one in the private sector. A territorial reservoir in which the recruitment of able staff took place in a less competitive labour market could actually be a benefit. But few Italian observers have taken comfort in this prospect. With the possible exception of Rome itself—an increasingly modern city with high educational standards among the middle class—such a potential advantage may still be outweighed by the general cultural poverty of the south. However potentially able the southerner, the argument runs, he or she is still likely to lack the attitudes, aspirations, and experience available to those from the north.

Worse still, once having joined the civil service, recruits are rapidly socialized into a system conditioned by several decades of solidly southern domination. Pre-recruitment and in-service career training is poor. And with Italy's rigid compartmentalization of career structures there is almost no cross-fertilization between the civil service and business or even the more business-orientated parts of the public sector. Mid-life recruitment from the private sector is almost unknown; transfer out from the service to business or politics is rare. Unlike in France where recruitment to the civil service is, in virtue of rigorous selection procedures, professional training systems, and high prestige, a desirable route to a range of attractive careers in both the public and private sectors, recruitment in Italy is recruitment to a closed world. The southern preference for security and predictability has ensured that its employees would have it no other way.

Recruitment, pay, unionization

In principle, all recruitment to the civil service is by open public examination, and is to immediately vacant posts in specific departments. The principle has however been disrupted in recent years by frequent exceptions. Some of these have been demanded by the civil-service unions to encourage upward mobility. They include the reservation of a proportion of newly created posts for internal promotions, and special legislation enabling those hired initially on temporary contracts to be made permanent without an open competition. On other occasions the considerable complications, time, and expense of special open competitions can be avoided by hiring those who in previous competitions had not obtained posts but had been declared employable.

All posts have specific entry qualifications, which are naturally more detailed for more specialist posts (doctors, scientists, etc.). Nominally, however, other than the thin layer of top-level managers (the so-called *dirigenza*) there is only a single class of civil servants. But it is divided into eight functional divisions, and since these include everything from doormen, through clerical officers and typists, to graduate heads of section, the concept of a single omni-comprehensive class is little more than a nominal concession to the egalitarianism that swept the public service with the unionization of the 1970s.[19]

A more significant, and probably more disabling, concession in this direction is the very low level of pay differentials across the wide range of activities in that class. Once in, in fact, civil servants are neither over-paid nor over burdened. They work generously short and concentrated hours leaving time, especially at lower levels, for a second job in the black economy.[20] Pay levels, job for job, are well below those in the private sector, making recruitment for specialized technical qualifications very difficult. Morale has also been seriously undermined by the many years in which real earnings have been affected by special supplements, minor differences between those on the same grade in different departments, unevenly spread overtime opportunities, and special allowances (for which the Ministry of Finance has the best reputation for generosity). In the 1970s, a growing trade-union consciousness led to efforts to combat these anomalies. Differentials were reduced, but as union representation on the council of administration in each ministry gradually gave unions more influence over personnel policy, an increasingly contractual and often obstructive attitude to work practices developed.[21]

In view of these difficulties, it is not surprising that public-sector productivity has been lagging far behind that in the private sector in the last decade. A study by the research institute FORMEZ on sixteen divisions of various Italian ministries and their field offices, as well as a number of local-government agencies, found extraordinarily low levels of productivity.[22] It suggested that, at least by the criteria set by its own methodology, central-government productive efficiency was only 36 per cent of that potentially attainable, and in regional government only 21 per cent.

The administrative élite

The top echelons of any society's administrative system constitute the area where politics fuses into administration. The nature of that connection has a profound effect on the ability of the political class to transmit its will to the administration and translate ideas into policy output. But few politicians will expect the dividing line to be a clear and distinct one in which their own role is to make policy, and that of the administration, including its top levels, merely to implement it. On the contrary they will expect senior officials to be pro-active: to anticipate, to plan, to research, to test, and generally to act as policy consultants and advisers.

An administration which from the top down is the passive instrument of the politician's will is unlikely to serve him well. The administration is, after all, likely to be the minister's best source of advice and expertise in the area with which it deals—probably far more knowledgeable than his party's research facilities. It is also important that it does not overburden him with managerial decisions. It has to have the flexibility and discretion to find operational solutions to the problems posed by the minister's policy objectives. Here too, the boundary between the responsibility of the minister and that of the senior civil servant is not easy to define. In an administrative system as dominated by legalism as that in Italy, where Parliament, administrative courts, the Ministry of the Treasury, and the court of accounts are ever ready to contest administrative action, it may be difficult for the system to cope with a very high level of civil-service involvement in the policy-making process, and with a high level of operational discretion invested in the hands of the civil service rather than the minister.

More fundamentally still, allowing the senior administrators into the policy-making process opens up the risk of bureaucratic capture. The more ministers rely on civil servants, the more they risk accepting the departmental conventional wisdom in any given policy area. To avoid this, they can adopt one of several strategies. They can use a spoils system by which, with every change of government, the top layer of the administration is stripped out and filled with partisan loyalists. Alternatively, they can foster a spirit of political neutrality in the administration, by which civil servants are involved in policy-making, but nevertheless have a clear sense that their prime duty is to serve ministers, and, albeit with the right to warn and advise, to defer to their choices on the key issues of policy. If the first approach is close to the American model, the second is close to the British. Between the two there is a third way, resembling most closely perhaps the French model, in which the civil service is notionally permanent and neutral, but in which partisan loyalties among individual civil servants are often clear and more or less accepted. Ministers do not remove all the senior civil servants on coming into office, and even those who are moved cannot be sacked outright. Rather ministers surround themselves for the duration of their tenure with a *cabinet* of generally fairly young but high-flying civil servants who assist them in their relations with the top officials in their department. The *cabinet* does not control the department; its role is to advise rather than to command and manage. When ministers move on, members of the *cabinet* may return to their original departments, move with the minister to a new ministerial *cabinet*, or leave for jobs elsewhere—in politics, or elsewhere in the public or private sector.

It is widely accepted that Italy's own mechanisms for coping with these problems have not proved satisfactory. On the whole, it has opted for political neutrality, tempered by a *cabinet* system of ministerial advisers drawn largely from the civil service. But the strict legalism of the system, together with the cautious and conservative mentality of recruits to it, have ensured that senior civil servants are fastidious guardians of a rigid dividing line between policy and administration. They have chosen not to become involved in the policy-process, and have been resistant to the development of a managerial and entrepreneurial outlook. They have expected, and received, full respect for their neutrality in that ministers, who formally have to approve all senior-level appointments, have rarely interfered with the internal seniority system by, for example, fostering fast-stream promotions of very bright or very politically committed candidates. The *cabinet* system, meanwhile, is also infused with the legalistic outlook. It spends a large part of its time negotiating the technical details of legislation with other departments, with the prime minister's office, and with Parliament. This is reflected by the key role played in the *cabinet* system by members of the council of state, the chief function of which is to provide the government with advice about legal and technical aspects of its legislation. A significant proportion of the membership of the council may be found serving in ministerial *cabinets* at any one time. Certainly councillors of state form one of the most prestigious and able groups within the administrative system, but while the more politically sensitive of them become semi-permanent advisers to the minister, even their outlook is infused with the background from which they are drawn.

Attempts to improve on this state of affairs have proved disappointing. In 1972, a new function—the *dirigenza* or management—was established at the top of the service. Its purpose was to create a group of senior managers who would assume wider roles than previous top officials, unburdening the minister of a range of decisions which previously only he could take—in particular the approval of contracts and spending plans up to certain limits. The group—about 6,000 strong—was originally intended to be selected from the upper tier of the main grade civil service as and when individuals showed managerial aptitudes. There was to be much emphasis on training, with one means of access to the *dirigenza* being a *corso-concorso* (competitive-entrance training programme) run by the higher school of public administration, which new entrants would have to complete successfully for a public-sector management career. There would be three levels of *dirigente* ('primo', 'superiore', and 'generale'), but the primary aim was less to create a hierarchy of career grades *above* that of the civil-service main grade, than to create and emphasize a *functional* role—management, within the broader and multi-functional administrative class.

The implementation has worked out very differently. The *dirigenza* has been incorporated into the hierarchy of career steps. Without becoming a *dirigente* a civil servant can aspire to no more than head of section. To head the next level up, the division, one must be selected for the *dirigenza*. To become a director-general, the highest level of all, one needs to rise to the status of *dirigente generale* (of which there are around a hundred). In short, the *dirigenza* has become part of the regular career grade system. The pre-career and mid-career training for management that was supposed to be the hallmark of the role has, by and large, been disappointing. It took from 1972 until 1985 to establish the first *corso-concorso*, which, when finally established, was grossly under-resourced, and selection for which was to be by the receiving ministry, nipping in the bud any prospect of creating a unified civil-service outlook transcending departmental loyalties.

Neither fast-stream promotion, nor a downgrading of seniority as the main criterion for promotion, have materialized. The government retains the power to nominate internal promotions within the *dirigenza*, but has rarely used its discretionary powers to interfere with promotion patterns based on seniority. When it has tried to do so, or to bring in outsiders, it has generally been greeted with resolute protests from the trade-union representatives. In any case, the incentives are modest for outsiders to use the *dirigenza* recruitment system for lateral mid-career transfer in. Those qualified to participate in the 'mid-career' competitions—academics, independent professionals like lawyers with five years' practice experience—will almost always be earning salaries well in excess of salaries awaiting them if they are successful.

Most fundamentally of all, the creation of the *dirigenza* seems to have done little to alter the real relationship between ministers and civil servants. The decree regulating the managerial group assigns to it the task of contracting for supplies and purchasing, approving projects, taxation agreements, subsidies, etc., introducing new technologies and systems, running and updating personnel policies, deploying labour resources, training, and so forth. These might seem the very essence of the modern role of the public-sector manager, but in the absence of real career incentives, including financial rewards and incisive training programmes, and in the absence of a steady and progressive change in the nature of the group required to carry them out, such plans are bound to be little but pious hopes.[23]

Equally striking is how quickly the tasks assigned to the managerial group can become meaningless in an administrative context dominated by legalism.[24] The civil servant who is used to being given clear but limited tasks, and is reluctant to take the initiative for fear of exceeding his powers and incurring sanctions for doing so, will want clear guidelines about the objectives he is supposed to achieve in his new managerial role. So will his trade union, and any administrative court which becomes involved if his superiors should try to take sanctions against him for poor performance. In any case, the politicians themselves have been reluctant to devolve managerial power, and have rarely set out the overall planning directives and priorities foreseen in the original legislation on the *dirigenza*, even though such directions are essential in giving managers operational criteria against which to judge themselves and be judged. The highly political implications of personnel questions inside the public sector have made ministers reluctant to relinquish control of such issues. In this connection, of course, the 1972 legislation coincided with the start of a period of increased unionization in the public sector, and thus an environment in which such issues assumed an increasing political sensitivity.

In the absence of clear guidelines and genuine managerial autonomy, therefore, civil servants can hardly be arraigned for operational inefficiency, as indeed the court of accounts recognized in 1985 in annulling the transfer of a civil servant claimed to be incompetent, on the grounds that he was not given a clear indication of what his shortcomings were, and hence could not defend himself.

The administrative élite in Italy is thus a still largely closed and compartmentalized world. Horizontal recruitment is rare even from other ministries, let alone from outside the service. Senior civil servants have little knowledge of other departments, and cross-fertilization of ideas between departments is modest. Most civil servants face a long dour struggle to get as high as possible in their own departments. Those who reach the top do so late in their career—almost always into their fifties—stay in office a relatively short time, and are already in many cases past their most vigorous.

Very few mainstream civil servants make the passage to elected political office, even though there is no formal ban on party membership or political activity. In general, and with the exception of those who become part of the *cabinet* system, senior civil servants have preferred to avoid overt partisan involvement on the grounds that this would interfere with established, seniority-based, promotion systems. As Cassese has argued, civil servants have traded political influence for predictability and security in their relationships with politics. There are, of course, exceptions to this—Ruggiero Ruggieri, former secretary-general to the Ministry of Foreign Affairs, became Minister of Foreign Trade in the Goria government and its successors after 1987—but they are rare.

Regulation and Service Provision beyond Ministerial Departments: Three Examples

As we have seen, the range of administrative formulae adopted across the public sector, and the problems they generate, vary considerably among agencies that lie outside the traditional ministerial model. It is impossible in a single chapter to give more than a few examples of this diversity. In what follows, three cases have been chosen for illustration: the Bank of Italy, the national health service, and the judicial system. Each has considerable political importance although only the first is regarded as a relatively satisfactory agency in reaching the objectives set for it. The ratio of two 'problem' cases to one relative success should not, of course, be taken as a reflection of the system as a whole.

The Bank of Italy

Italy's central bank is a key element in the Italian institutional landscape. It has a major influence on macro-economic management, and it has been indispensable in sustaining Italy's reputation in international financial circles throughout the post-war era. It cannot wield the influence of the Bundesbank, both because of the inherently weaker political and economic infrastructure it has to work with, and because it does not have the same constitutional underpinning. Nevertheless, both in Italy and abroad, it has established a reputation for determined defence of the lira against inflationary pressures, and for a sophisticated and professional approach to monetary management. It plays a major behind-the-scenes role in influencing the thinking of government ministers and senior civil servants, if not also members of Parliament. Such is its reputation, in fact, that it can almost claim a degree of intellectual deference to its thinking in senior policy-making circles. This is certainly not to claim that the Bank always gets its way, but its reputation for political independence, clarity of analysis, and fixity of purpose singles it out as a very unusual institution by Italian standards.

It has a broader range of roles than its counterparts in most other industrialized countries. It has responsibility for monetary policy, management of the country's foreign exchange controls, supervision of the credit system, advice to the government on interest-rate policy and on broader economic issues. It is Italy's representative on a range of international organizations such as the Group of Ten, the European Community's Monetary Committee, the IMF, the Bank for International Settlements, etc. The Bank also manages all state payments and receipts through the Treasury current account, and it regularly finances the government through the overdraft on that account.[25]

The formal power structure of the Bank reflects the subtle balance between autonomy and co-operation with the government. The Bank is a public-law institute whose capital is divided among several public institutions: savings banks, public-law banks, public pension funds, and insurance companies. It is run by its seventeen-strong *consiglio superiore* (high council), which nominates the top management and the four members of the 'directorate' (governor, director-general, and two deputy directors-general). The latter are then formally appointed—for indeterminate terms of office—by the government. However, the government itself has almost no real choice in this area. All recent governors have come up through the Bank's career structure, and almost all members of the directorate have had experience in the Bank's prestigious research department. To change this practice would be taken as a signal to the outside world that the government intended to increase its influence over the Bank. Given the pressure to enhance the autonomy of central banks generated by trends towards

European monetary union, such interference looks increasingly unlikely.

While constitutionally the Bank of Italy enjoys no special autonomy from the government, in practice it enjoys wide discretion in monetary and credit matters. It is normally the initiator of major decisions connected to bank regulation and other policies in the financial sector. These decisions are formally taken by the interministerial committee for credit and savings (CICR). Although this is chaired by the Treasury minister, the governor plays a major role in the committee, most of whose decisions coincide with the Bank's proposals. On occasions, the governor has been known to dissent from the government over the latter's budgetary strategy, but the government generally seeks to maintain a good working relationship with the Bank—and, just as important, seeks to be seen to be doing so. It thus rarely replies directly for fear of getting involved in open conflict with the governor. A good working relationship between the governor and the Treasury minister is an essential condition for effective monetary policy. Through its open-market operations the Bank has a profound influence on market rates and therefore on the outcome of the Treasury auctions. Changes in the official discount rate are in principle decided by the minister after a formal proposal by the governor, but in fact they are largely predetermined by action in the market by the Bank of Italy. If a serious conflict were to develop between the two, the governor would, strictly, have to resign, but this has never arisen.

A minister who wants to exert a real influence on the Bank has to take the initiative at an early stage in the policy process. He can in principle do so by nominating a special joint Bank–Treasury committee to work on a particular subject. This approach was used by Treasury Minister Andreatta to negotiate the so-called 'divorce' between Bank and Treasury (i.e. the end of the Bank purchases of all unsold Treasury bills) in 1981.[26] It was again used by the Treasury Minister Amato in 1987 to prepare the reform of the government securities market. Normally, however, the governor himself initiates policy and the Bank would not accept joint committees as a permanent method for decision-making on monetary policy and banking supervision. Once the Bank has reached an internal decision approved by the directorate, there is very little the minister can do.[27]

The real strength of the Bank lies in its 200-member research department. Significantly, there is no comparable research office at the Treasury, and the minister normally accepts that he has to rely on the Bank for both information and expertise, especially on the Bank's own econometric model of the Italian economy, leaving most initiatives squarely in the Bank's hands. The research department regularly monitors problem areas. In recent years it has been the Bank that has been in charge of the two key issues of Italian monetary policy connected with European integration: preparing Italy's financial system for internal-market liberalization, and coping with foreign-exchange liberalization ahead of European monetary integration. Tommaso Padoa-Schioppa, head of the research department, has also played a leading role at European level, and was a key figure in the Delors Committee on monetary union.

The reputation of the Bank staff has made it much the most prestigious point of access to public service. It is without question one of Italy's élite corps. Access is difficult and highly selective. Training is rigorous, and the Bank makes much use of prestigious overseas universities in its training programme. On rare occasions some of its high-calibre personnel do transfer to other parts of the public sector. Rainer Masera (to IMI—the largest of the public special credit institutes) and Stefano Micossi (to ENI) are two leading figures who have done so. The Bank is, of course, too small to compare in this way with the French Grand Corps, and there is no significant entry from the Bank to the political class. Nor has it made much of a breach in the principle of the vertical separation of Italian careers. However, this enables the Bank to retain its separation from politics, and maintain itself as an island of excellence in a public administration system where excellence is not always in abundant supply.

The national health service

The Italian Servizio santità nazionale (henceforth SSN) was established in 1978, to create a system of universal health insurance for the entire population. Previously, while some form of publicly provided health care had covered over 90 per cent of the population, the system was compartmentalized in a variety of ways that divided the recipients into categories of the population receiving different levels of care, under different institutional arrangements. The consequences for consistency in provision and co-ordination between levels of the system were serious. The SSN was supposed to change this through consolidation, rationalization, and democratization: free and equal provision through consolidation of the insurance funds and hospital schemes, with control devolved to local units of administration under the supervision of representatives from elected local authorities. It was to restore a degree of professionalism to a public service in which general practitioners had gradually been overwhelmed by the bureau-cratization of the insurance funds and the preference of their patients for specialist care. Under the SSN general practitioners were to take over responsibility for health education and preventive medicine, and were to monitor patient progress even during receipt of specialist care, while playing an important part in controlling costs through judicious and efficient prescription and referrals policies.[28]

In reality, the SSN provided few incentives to doctors to assume these responibilities. It had to contend with widespread hostility to the reforms from most categories of doctor. The expansion of the public health-care system over the previous two decades had led to growing concerns about professional standing and identity, as public-service doctors increasingly lost status as unionized and frequently full-time employees of the state. The arrival of the SSN seemed only to confirm this trend, even though the possibility of private practice remained open to most doctors for whom it was worthwhile.

The problems of the new service were compounded by its participatory elements. Health-care provision was to be divided up into local units of a population size between 50,000 and 200,000, known as *unità socio-sanitarie locali* (USL). They were to be run by managers (6,000 across the country) nominated by a general assembly of delegates from the municipal authorities in the territory of the USL. By universal consent they proved to be profoundly unsatisfactory. They were immediately colonized by the political parties, who filled them with individuals with little managerial competence, expertise, or understanding of cost controls, but a voracious appetite for the exercise of political patronage in purchasing and job-creation. Within three years of its inauguration, the public health bill had risen from 4.5 to 5.5 per cent of GDP.[29]

From its birth, the SSN faced three forms of pressure to spend: doctors who were unwilling to co-operate voluntarily in efforts to contain costs; local politically appointed managers who saw in the service a new reservoir of patronage; and an egalitarian philosophy of universal free provision on an open-ended basis. The problem was compounded by the absence of mechanisms to monitor spending. Checks and controls which had been condemned under the old system of mutual insurance funding as time-consuming and expensive were dismantled, leaving the service with no way of identifying what doctors were doing, especially in the field of prescriptions and tests.

The last decade, from the point in the early 1980s when governments began to realize that the system was out of control, has witnessed a long battle of attrition by central government to regain control over the system. This has involved a three-pronged attack. First, the steady abandonment of free universal provision through so-called 'ticketing': a percentage contribution paid by the patient for pharmaceuticals and, in recent years, also for some tests and other services. This has risen gradually to as much as 50 per cent of the cost of the item, while the range of prescriptions which appear on the list of SSN-approved pharmaceuticals has been cut back and divided into categories according to level of necessity to patients. Prescriptions now run from 'free' through a range of subsidy-levels to 'full-price'. The ticketing policy was fiercely resisted by the opposition and the trade unions, however, who fought a rearguard action in favour of particular categories of beneficiary in what rapidly became a complex hierarchy of entitlements to exemption according both to the medical problem and to income. In 1986 they even forced the government to reduce the 'ticket' temporarily, before irrefutable evidence of the highly price-sensitive nature of patient demand led to further increases in 1988 and 1989.[30]

Central government's second line of attack on cost-escalation in the service focused on doctors. In the first half of the 1980s it involved a largely confrontational approach—attempting to limit the autonomy of doctors (especially at the general practice level) over what could be prescribed, and what procedures had to be followed before patients could be referred on up the system for more specialized and expensive treatments. In the later part of the decade confrontation gave way, at least to some degree, to incentives to co-operate, especially through the incorporation of doctors at various levels in the planning and administration of health services, frequently at the expense of politically appointed administrators. The latter were the targets of the third prong of the attack. Central government has gradually sought to limit the autonomy of the political appointees running the USL, by imposing stricter accounting regulations, placing executive control in the hands of professional managers, and by establishing performance criteria overseen by regional governments, whose overall health funding has become increasingly cash-limited. Larger hospitals have been taken out of the hands of the USL altogether.

None of the problems described in these paragraphs would be unrecognizable to those administering public health-care systems in most West European states. Rising demand for medical services, together with growing medical costs, especially through higher technological capabilities, and an ageing population, have forced all governments to face searching questions about universal medical provision. They have had to do so against medical and paramedical staff who have become increasingly unionized on one side, and increasingly resistant to the bureaucratization of health administration on the other. They have experimented with cash limits, cost controls, contracting out of services, etc. What is striking in the Italian case is: first the speed with which the political system has passed through the cycle of espousal of the principle of free universal provision, leading to escalating costs, to a steady erosion of this principle as charges and means tests have gradually been restored;[31] secondly, the extent to which central government, as paymaster, has had difficulty in winning the active co-operation of any of the actors involved—whether doctors or administrators—in containing costs, or indeed in supplying basic information about prescription, referrals, and treatment policy; and thirdly, the extent to which decentralization and democratization have increased this loss of control.

None of these problems is easily solvable. The standard of public provision in health care remains low, and the coalition is constantly under electoral pressure to improve it. Both the Socialist Party and the Christian Democrat Party have groups strongly resistant to funding cuts. Moreover, the extent of regional-government co-operation is patchy, with a few regions attempting to impose some order on the system within their areas, but others, especially in the south, largely ignoring government exhortations to co-operate.[32] Efforts to take control of USL out of the hands of party nominees and 'professionalize' the management under politically neutral, performance-orientated executives has proved difficult. There is little tradition of non-partisan public-agency management outside the formal ministerial bureaucracy in Italy, and party influence is difficult to eradicate, especially where health-service unions with whom the management has to deal exert considerable leverage through the parties. In the health sector this general problem is compounded because, even if central government can socialize local health management into its way of looking at financial performance and efficiency, management itself still has to impose this on the doctors. Experience in Italy, as in other countries, suggests that the more doctors see local managers as agents of cost-cutting financial controls imposed from the centre, the more they resist.

The administration of justice

The provision of justice, like that of health, is universally regarded as one of the major failings of Italian administration. The problems of the judicial system reflect many of the themes recurrent in the development of the twentieth-century Italian state.[33] First, the whole system has to be seen against a social reality, especially in the south of the country, inimical to the basic principles both of the observance of the law, and of the effective prosecution of its transgressors. Secondly, as in other areas of the administration, the system is manned by personnel who for many years after the fall of fascism continued to reflect authoritarian values and attitudes. Thirdly, the system is endowed with a set of rules and procedures built on conflicting philosophical foundations—on the one hand, punctilious observance of rules of procedure, on the other, a substantial, if gradually diminishing, body of illiberal law inherited from the fascist regime. And finally, the judicial structures themselves are seriously under-resourced for their allotted tasks, and the resources they do enjoy are badly distributed.

The diversity of law-and-order problems confronting the judiciary has grown steadily over the years. On the one hand there are problems common to most European states: the prevention and detection of the rising level of ordinary crime (robbery, theft, rape, and other forms of physical violence, etc.) and the problems of the speed, cost, and efficiency of civil justice, especially in business and commerce, as society becomes more litigious and law-orientated. On the other, there are many problems which, while not absent elsewhere in Europe, have assumed a peculiar intensity in Italy. The best known and most spectacular is the problem of the Mafia and other networks of so-called 'organized' crime in the southern half of the country, linked especially to corruption in the provision of public works and to trade in illegal drugs.[34] But there are several others including the long-standing issue of political terrorism, the detection and suppression of large-scale fraud in the financial sector, and the control of political corruption. The last of these, which shades from outright and systematic illegality to minor cases of personal impropriety, has, despite its apparent ubiquity, proved exceptionally difficult for the judiciary to detect and bring to court.

As in many other judicial systems, the most fundamental problem has been that of balancing the defence of civil liberties against the measures needed to fight the ever increasing scope and complexity of the law-and-order problem. As the difficulties have grown—especially in the area of organized crime and financial fraud—so this balance has become harder to find, and the search for it more public and controversial. Indeed, as public opinion has come to play a more significant role in legal policy-making, there have been dramatic swings of public mood towards the judiciary. On the one hand, the judicial system is seen as responsible for the low level of detection and the glacially slow pace at which legal proceedings unfold. Investigators, public prosecutors, and judges are also often accused of political bias and arbitrary and high-handed exercise of the extensive powers vested in them. On the other hand, a temporary upsurge of public outrage and sympathy can quickly develop when a judicial investigator is assassinated by the Mafia, when powerful figures from the world of organized crime go free for lack of clear evidence, when senior judges transfer the investigative phase of a case involving important business or political figures out of the hands of an apparently over-zealous junior, or when, as frequently occurs, Parliament declines to lift the immunity from prosecution of one of its members.

Public suspicion of the legal system is fed by the corporate identity which the *magistratura* (the generic term for the judicial class) has come to assume. As a single, self-governing corps, administered, as we saw in Chapter 5, by the High Council of the Judiciary, it encompasses various types of legal figure. It includes trial judges (at various levels, from those sitting in single-judge local courts, through the tribunals and assize courts hearing more serious cases, up to the appellate courts, and the court of cassation) but it also includes public prosecutors (*pubblico ministero*). Until the new criminal code introduced in 1989, it also included examining magistrates (*giudice istruttoria*), whose role has now been suppressed. At the lowest levels, moreover, it has traditionally been the *pretore* (the trial judge) who conducts the investigation, directs the police, and gathers and assesses the evidence. Even at the higher court levels, the fact that investigator and prosecutor are from the same judicial corps as the presiding judges, and often work alongside them in the same offices, has exposed the judiciary to charges of systematic collusion and the violation of the fundamental principle of the separation of the roles of judge and prosecutor.

These problems are exacerbated by the extensive powers the judiciary traditionally enjoyed in investigating cases: powers which were undoubtedly greater than those enjoyed by the judicial and investigatory bodies in most other European states, particularly since, until the reform of the criminal code in 1989, the capacity of defence lawyers to gain access to the nature of charges, and to prosecution evidence—and at times even to their clients—was extremely limited. Such powers were used to deprive individuals of their liberty, property, and social status for extended periods of time. More than half of the Italian prison population in recent years has actually been awaiting trial rather than serving sentences—often for some years. And at the end of the whole process those same individuals can be, and frequently are, found guilty of no crime whatsoever.

In 1987, resentment against the inefficiency of the judiciary and high-handed use of judicial power resulted in a referendum which deprived judges and prosecutors of their immunity from civil liability for the consequences of their actions.[35] One result was the rapid approval of the long-awaited new penal code, together with various other items of reform legislation. However, it was accompanied by amnesties to clear some of the backlog of cases pending and give the new legislation a chance to work. It also coincided with major increases in organized crime in Sicily, Sardinia, and Calabria, as members of the Mafia under investigation benefited from liberties facilitated by the new criminal code which, to all appearances, left them freer than before to intimidate witnesses, the police, and judicial authorities. In such circumstances, and especially in the aftermath of some spectacular Mafia attacks on judges and reform-minded politicians, opinion swung sharply back in favour of the judiciary. Accusations that police and judges fighting organized crime have been betrayed by the government (either through overt collusion between politicians and organized crime, or simply through inadequate public funding) have again become widespread.

Such public controversy has made effective reform extremely difficult. The judiciary itself is not without political influence, despite frequent charges that politicians have betrayed it. Indeed it enjoys influence in the political parties (including the PCI/PDS), in parliamentary judiciary committees, and in the Justice Ministry, where the senior administrative group is drawn largely from the judiciary. (The legislation which replaced that abrogated by the 1987 referendum was considered by many as almost equally protective.) The judiciary is thus well placed to defend its own interests as a group in the administration, and even—there being no bar on party affiliation— in the parties and in the legislature. These, and recurring accusations of political bias, have made efforts to establish an all-party technical consensus on judicial reform especially difficult.

Even the introduction of the new criminal code, finally replacing in full the 1930 Rocco Code, has been widely seen as inadequately prepared. On paper, it seems to provide greatly improved prospects both of respect for civil liberties, and of swifter dispensation of justice. It replaces the old inquisitorial system with an adversarial approach yielding better rights for the defence, and it introduces a range of plea-bargaining devices to speed up judicial procedure. Its implementation, however, has been severely damaged by shortcomings in the recruitment and training of new judicial personnel, and the provision of new buildings and equipment. At the time of its introduction, in fact, there was a backlog of no fewer than 2.7 million criminal cases. Court buildings were, quite literally, falling down. The 8,000-strong judicial corps was well over 10 per cent below official strength, as were the ranks of ancillary staff. Plans to recruit new staff were set to take at least three years. In the Naples area, 21 members of the judiciary and 86 auxiliaries had to do the work of a hypothetical complement of, respectively, 46 and 160—work which included, at the moment at which the new code was introduced, a backlog of 36,000 criminal proceedings, added to each month by nearly 90,000 new reported crimes.[36] Given such inadequacies, and given a judicial corps whose morale was reaching historically low levels even by the depressed standards of the wider Italian public sector, it looked, at the start of the 1990s, increasingly unlikely that legislation like that pushed through by the Justice Ministry in 1989 could make a real impact on the Italian judicial crisis.

Conclusion

Italy's administrative system constitutes a problem for effective policy-making and democratic choice which is no less intractable than the problems of policy aggregation and leadership at the political level. A properly functioning democracy needs agencies that can turn policy choice into efficiently delivered output just as much as it requires parties to make those choices in the first place. For years, the administrative system has been identified as a major distortion in the use of economic resources. For a country as prosperous as Italy, the resulting quality of public services—education, health, social security, justice, transport—is exceptionally low. The administrative history of the last three decades is littered with schemes of reform, some of which have been struck down by Parliament, but others of which, having been turned into legislation, have failed abysmally to achieve their ends. The absence of a strong and prestigious state tradition makes public employment comparatively unattractive as a profession, and the abilities, commitment, and morale of those in public service have suffered correspondingly. Against such deep-rooted handicaps, it has always been unlikely that the good intentions of legislative reformers would be sufficient to improve administrative performance dramatically. The fragmentation of party representation, the electoral power of public-sector workers, and the attachment to detailed administrative law make it difficult for the political authorities to tackle the problems of the administrative system in a systematic way. Efforts at reform run up against the corporate power of public-sector unions, the fragmentation of administrative agencies, and the oppressive restraints of legal traditions. In recent years, the urgency of reform has increased sharply. The budget-deficit problem, and the difficulty of resolving it by increased taxation, have made it more necessary than ever to improve the productivity of the public sector and reduce the level of public expenditure. The failure to do so lies at the heart of the disillusion so clearly felt by many voters towards the governing parties. Yet as long as those same parties remain heavily tied to the votes of the four million public-sector workers (and their many more dependants) the likelihood of effective action remains disappointingly low.

9

Regional and Local Government

The Limits of Italian Devolution

Italy has a three-tier structure of elected government below the national level, consisting of regions, provinces, and municipalities (*comuni*). As we have seen in Chapter 5, the constitution defines the role of each and, in a minimal sense, guarantees local autonomy.[1] Without constitutional amendment, the authorities cannot be abolished, their general powers cannot be altered, and, without complex legislative procedures, their boundaries cannot be changed. However, the reality of territorial devolution is more complex than the constitution suggests, and reflects the problems of adjusting to the legacy of the centralized unitary state against the background of a strong national party system.

Modern Italy developed from a particularly centralized state tradition. In the nineteenth century there were enthusiastic advocates of federalism, but the fear that devolution would strain the fragile unity of the new state proved the dominant concern. Fascism was even less sympathetic to local autonomy, undoing what little devolution had developed in the latter years of the liberal state. Moreover, in a society with uneven levels of wealth and social infrastructure there was a strong case for giving the centre powerful tools of redistributive intervention. Even after World War II this consideration continued to influence arrangements. Both the massive injection of development funds through the *Cassa per il mezzogiorno* and the inclusion of southern development as a major aim of the successive attempts at indicative economic planning enhanced the power of the centre against the locality.

These factors had the most marked effect on the regional tier of government. Although the case for regional government was written into the post-war constitution, it took until 1970 to get the fifteen so-called 'ordinary' regions going (five 'special' regions around the periphery were established earlier).[2] Even after the first ordinary regional assemblies had been elected, it took several more years to draft regional constitutions, transfer administrative responsibilities, and work out financial arrangements.

The regional tier of government is thus still evolving. Formal powers granted by the constitution are not underpinned by legal and administrative clarity, or financial autonomy. What local authorities can do is subject to intervention from the centre, and long wrangles in the constitutional and administrative courts. Regional and local authorities are reliant on the centre for funding, and many activities depend on the willingness of the central government to delegate administrative activities to regional government. This is most notable in the case of the national health service established in 1978, which now accounts for by far the biggest single item of regional expenditure. Decentralization of special regional funds for such purposes has thus not greatly added to the devolution of decision-making *powers*, merely to the devolution of the *administration of centrally-determined policies*.

Devolution has also been affected by variations in size and resources between authorities, especially at the municipal level. The majority of municipalities are far too small to be effective. A few—the big cities—are so large that they are remote from the neighbourhood, let alone the citizen. Attempts to overcome these drawbacks have complicated the simple three-tier picture. In some areas where municipalities are unable to provide certain types of service, inter-municipal consortia have been established to do so properly. The scope of some is restricted to a single activity. Others, such as the *comunità montane*, servicing the hill and mountain areas, play several roles. Unlike the three main tiers of local government, however, they have not been directly elected, but are run by nominees of the participating municipal councils. A further innovation—in the major urban conurbations—is the *circoscrizione*. These have been established at the discretion of the municipality, and are found mainly in the north. They come in two forms: those elected directly, which tend to be endowed with certain decisional powers over local services, and those appointed by the municipal authority, which generally have only consultative status.

Adjustments have also been necessary at the regional level—particularly in Trentino-Alto Adige, which straddles the linguistic divide between the Italian- and German-speaking Tyrol. It contains two provinces—Trento and Bolzano—which are more or less congruent with the two cultural communities. The Italian majority in this region was for many years the source of great disaffection in the province of Bolzano, even generating a sporadic terrorist threat. As a result, in the early 1970s the region was for all practical purposes split into two, by devolving the powers of the region to the two provincial authorities, henceforth known as the 'autonomous provinces' of Trento and Bolzano.

The powers allocated to regional and local government are not extensive by international standards. Italian regionalism is distinct from strong forms of co-ordinate federalism in various ways. Fewer powers are devolved, there are virtually no areas of 'exclusive' (as opposed to 'concurrent') legislative powers attributed to the regions, financial autonomy is extremely limited, and there is no formal representation of regional authorities in the legislature. The proportion of the civil service employed by regional authorities is small (76,000 in 1986, compared with 61,000 in provincial administration, 529,000 in municipal administration, and 3.4 million in the public service in total, including central government, the health service, the military, etc.).[3]

Provincial and municipal authorities also operate over a fairly limited range. They have only modest discretionary roles in the provision of big-spending services like education, housing, or health. In many of the services that they do provide, they are constrained to co-operate with central government, by which they are strictly supervised. In particular, given their limited financial autonomy, most of their investment projects have to be funded from a central-government investment fund, the *Cassa depositi e prestiti*.

Local politics in the national political system

Constitutionally and administratively, then, Italian local government is subject to quite tight limits. Rarely do either practitioners or observers of the system profess themselves very satisfied with it, or express much confidence that it achieves the aims set for it. From a sociological standpoint, however, political life at local level is generally *considered* quite important, and not just by politicians themselves. It absorbs much energy and activism. It is quite widely followed by the media and the public. In the major urban centres, especially the regional capitals, public office brings politicians high visibility and high status. The outcome of regional and local elections is followed closely. Coalition politics at local level—especially control of the major cities like Rome, Milan, Turin, Naples, and Palermo—is an important element in national political bargaining.

Part of the reason for this lies in the symbolic importance of the local community in Italian society. Although migration and improved transport and communications have made the country more homogenous and territorially integrated, the diversity inherited from Italy's late national unification is still marked. For many Italians, identification with the distinctiveness of the locality remains pronounced. Regions, cities, and towns have their own traditions, culture, and sense of identity. National politicians thus need a strong local base; experience in regional or local government, along with office-holding of a quasi-full-time nature in provincial party organization, thus constitute the two most important routes into Parliament and national politics.

This creates an interdependence between local and national politics. National politicians cannot afford to ignore their local bases. To get elected and re-elected, most need to maintain strong local links, preferably having been born and raised in the area. They are expected to act as champions for the locality—delivering grants, new public works projects, special legislation, publicly subsidized business projects, and so on. In a centralized political system the extraction of benefits from the centre is a prime obligation for national representatives, and explains why strong local distinctiveness coexists with the dominance of national parties. National representatives are better placed to serve the locality if they are part of a party which is strong (preferably in government) at the centre.

What applies to whole parties also applies to individual politicians. The latter get elected by winning more preference votes[4] than their fellow candidates on their party's list. They are thus in constant competition with local rivals. To win preference votes within their party's overall electorate, they need, unless they are very prominent figures in national government, to maintain a network of local supporters who will gather together this army of preferences. Local government, and the networks of contacts it provides, is one important source of such support.

The system of subnational government is thus closely tied in to national politics by a series of vertical connections and exchanges. Local politicians have a degree of leverage which they can use to extract benefits from the centre in the many areas where they lack the resources to take action on their own initiative. This makes local political life important, even if the institutions of local government themselves dispose of relatively little real decisional autonomy.

Whether it enhances local democracy, or leads to the efficient use of public resources, is a more doubtful matter. It clearly encourages local politicians to become political entrepreneurs, maximizing benefits on behalf of their localities.[5] If local politicians engage in credit-claiming not on the basis of how they dispose of local taxpayers' money, but on how large a slice of central-government funds they can obtain for their locality, there is a serious risk that too little attention is paid to how those funds are eventually used. If the paymaster is central government, not local taxpayers, voters will not perceive a linkage between what they pay as locally contributing taxpayers, and what they receive in local benefits. Both local voters and elected officials will tend to see local government as the agency of the centre, and the political incentives to imaginative or efficient use of local resources will be correspondingly reduced in scope.

The Region

The regional structure

The formal structure of Italian regional government can be described quite simply. Each regional authority consists of an assembly, directly elected at five-year intervals by proportional representation. The assembly varies in size from thirty members in the smallest regions up to eighty in the largest.[6] It enacts regional legislation and elects an executive (*giunta regionale*), which runs the regional administration. The key figures are the members of the regional *giunta*, and especially its president, together with the president of the assembly, and leading members of the assembly committees covering the main policy sectors.

The organization of the assembly and the *giunta* follow the pattern of central government. Taking, as an example, the structure of the Lombardy region in 1990, one finds that the assembly is subdivided into six rather heterogeneous standing committees covering the main policy areas dealt with by the *giunta*: overall regional development; planning and budgetary affairs; institutional, educational, and cultural affairs; social security; the economy and land use; the environment and energy. It has a range of support services including a research and library service, a press office, a legislative office, and an administrative office.

The Lombard regional *giunta* consists of a president, deputy president, and no less than fifteen *assessori*. The latter, the equivalent of ministers, run the administrative departments of the region. They are grouped into four main categories:

1. financial, budgetary, administrative, and legal affairs;
2. territorial and planning issues (transport, environment, planning controls);
3. social services (health, social security, education and training, cultural affairs);
4. productive activity (employment, agriculture, forestry and fishing, commerce, tourism, sport, energy and civil defence, industry and the artisan sector).

The departments are articulated into internal *servizi* (services) equivalent to the directorates-general in national ministries. Each is headed by a *dirigente regionale*, from the managerial corps of the regional civil service. In 1990 the Lombardy region's departments reported the existence of a formidable bureaucracy of over 100 separate services.[7] Interestingly, however, and again paralleling practice at national level, there is no overall regional executive management, answerable to a chief executive. A regional chief executive would weaken the tight political control which parties seek to maintain over the operation of regional government. There is, instead, a regional-level *cabinet* system like that at national level, and the president and deputy president of the *giunta* are themselves managerial chief executives, co-opting politically selected officials to work alongside them in a *cabinet* drawn largely from the regional managerial corps.[8]

In all regions, the administrative system also includes a range of consultative and managerial committees, bringing together administrators and interest groups, professional practitioners, etc., in the area in question. In Lombardy in 1990 thirty were listed as formal permanent standing committees, and at any one time numerous other *ad hoc* working groups will be in operation. Their remit is extensive, ranging from atmospheric pollution, through exhibitions and fairs, to women's affairs, music, the theatre, and the media.

The region is also the location of the office of the regional *ombudsman*,[9] and of the regional control committee (*comitato regionale di controllo*). The latter supervises the legality of the affairs of the provinces, interprovincial consortia, local health-service bodies and hospitals within the region's boundaries. Reversing the flow of supervision, the region is itself subject to supervision from the centre. This is exercised through the government control commissioner and his regional control committee. The long arm of administrative and financial justice also reaches down from the centre to the regions. The *tribunale amministrativo regionale* (TAR) is in effect a decentralized version of the council of state, responsible for administrative justice, while local offices of the court of accounts oversee the financial probity of regional government.[10]

Competing versions of the regional model

If the formal structure is relatively easy to describe, the philosophy underlying it is elusive. As in other areas of Italian government, constitutional and political ambiguities and changing political circumstances have provided scope for appeal to widely differing philosophical assumptions about the regional role, offering a close parallel to the fundamental dissensus over the respective roles of Parliament and government at national level.

At one end of the scale there is a top-down philosophy—driven by the aims of administrative decentralization—that reflects the unitary state. In this conception regions are mechanisms for implementing *national* policies. They are not seen as needing large government bureaucracies in their own right, or exclusive legislative areas of competence. Policy agendas being set by the national level, regional government is seen as an essentially *reactive* activity. A clear-cut ruling majority, with an overall political strategy at the regional level, with co-ordination between sectors of its policy programme, is, on this reading, at best unnecessary, and at worst potentially even subversive of the integrity of the state. Regional governments are primarily local representatives assembled to adapt national framework legislation to local purposes.

At the other end of the scale there is a bottom-up, quasi-federalist view that each region is a discrete community, with different political patterns, aspirations, and needs. Such a vision implies a series of regional political systems each with its own resources, its own administrative system, and, if not a distinctive party system, then at least one in which local branches of national parties do not always follow patterns of coalition-formation worked out in Rome. This outlook also implies a clear-cut regional programme or political strategy, integrating policy across several different sectors. At the limit, it requires not only that the region should have control over its own local affairs, but also that it has a legitimate right to be represented, *as a region*, at national level.[11]

The conflict between these outlooks has never been fully resolved. The constitution itself seems to support the former outlook.[12] Art. 117 seems to imply a reactive philosophy of administrative decentralism, establishing firmly that legislative power for the ordinary regions is to be shared or concurrent, rather than exclusive. The regions are to enjoy no absolute areas of autonomy. Admittedly, the five regions on the periphery (Sicily, Sardinia, Val d'Aosta, Trentino-Alto Adige, and Friuli-Venezia Giulia), are endowed, through art. 116, with 'particular forms and conditions of autonomy' over and above those of the ordinary regions. In practice, however, even for these regions, the main difference was simply their earlier establishment.[13]

The centre-dominated view of the regions was further bolstered by the advent of the post-war interventionist state. The planning of economic activity and territorial development, including the allocation of resources between sectors, and across the national territory, became the major concern. In reality, rather little of Italy's post-war development has been 'planned', but this did not stop much lip-service being paid to the principle, right across the political spectrum. For the regions, the planning vogue implied their subordination to a grand national design. Even if regionalism was conceived as a way of making planning more 'democratic', more efficient, or more responsive to local needs, it nevertheless implied a decidedly secondary role for regional authorities.

By the time the ordinary regions were set up, however, the emphasis had shifted. The shift was linked to the change in political context—most notably the increasing power of the Communist Party, which saw in the regional tier of government an opportunity both to increase its own political strength (it assumed power in several of the new regional authorities) and to press home its case that the regions could be the testing ground for the broad quasi-corporatist alliance of political parties which it sought. This new outlook was shared by the Socialist Party, which, from the late 1960s, was moving steadily towards a more left-inclined position. It was also shared by a broad segment of élite opinion frustrated by the inadequacies of the centralized state, and attracted by the notion that decentralization could provide answers to Italy's more intractable policy problems, particularly in the area of service provision.

The genealogy of these ideas is complex, and cannot be traced here. They doubtless involved the drawing of a good many unjustified conclusions about the link between institutional reform and administrative and policy efficiency, which contributed to later disappointment with the regional ideal. What was clear, however, was that they pointed in the direction of greater political autonomy for the regions than previously, and this is reflected in the statutes of the ordinary regions, as they were drafted in the early 1970s. The idea that the region should establish *general* political objectives of its own, and hence that it constituted a distinct political community, was widely present. The same outlook pervaded the legislation that fleshed out the devolution process between 1975 and 1977. Decree 616, 24 July 1977, the most important part of this process, established that the region could not only set overall purposes and values in its own policy process, but had a role to play, separate from national political parties and the national Parliament, in formulating *national* policies. This was recognized in the establishment of a plethora of sectoral consultative committees incorporating the voice of the regions in the policy-making process at national level. At the apex the *Conferenza permanente stato-regioni*, a standing consultative committee of national and regional government, was established as a formal channel through which the regions had access to government on a wide range of policy issues. The planning ideal was not therefore abandoned, but was henceforth to entail a more decentralized process, in which the regions could participate at the formulation stage, as well as that of implementation.

Planning and participation, in fact, were seen as the vital accompaniment of decentralization and the watchwords of Italian institutional reform in the 1970s. Government, so the argument went, had to be opened up to the demands of new social actors, and more self-aware local interests. The region was the appropriate level of aggregation at which to achieve these improvements, and was to become the model for the type of participatory, assembly-dominated system which the parties of the left sought to establish. The regional constitutions reflected this in the emphasis placed on the administrative as well as the legislative role of the regional assembly and its committees. It was also reflected in the emphasis on the involvement of provincial and municipal government in the writing of general policy programmes for the region, and the decentralization of the execution of those policies to provincial and municipal administration. Regional government was to be government with a light touch, and a minimum of bureaucracy. In its most developed ideal, the region represented the new aspiration of the 1970s for rational, integrated planning of policies and resource use. Policy would be implemented by the administrative agencies closest to the citizen—particularly the province, the municipality, and the *quartiere*. With a high level of participation, policy would emerge in a consensual form from a harmonious circuit of co-operation, with lines of communication and control running up from the base through the regions to the centre, as much as down in the classic chain of command of the old unitary state.[14]

The reality, not surprisingly, has proved somewhat different. The ideal set out above was essentially an ideal generated on the left, but in the years during which the regions have been fully functioning—effectively since the late 1970s—the power of leftist ideas has been on the wane. The electorate of the PCI/PDS has diminished steadily from its 1976 peak, and with it the party's influence in regional and local government. The PSI has become considerably less disposed to form alliances with the PCI/PDS while the end of the grand coalition in 1979 has drawn an even clearer line under the end of 'National Solidarity' and of the need, or willingness, of the Christian

Democrat Party to co-operate with the Communist Party in Parliament.

As a result, the emphasis on assembly-dominated government at regional level has declined. The fashionable watchword of political discourse changed in the 1980s from 'participation' to 'decisionismo'. Effective government seemed increasingly incompatible with participatory government based on broad inter-party agreement, and with this change the planning ideal has faded rapidly. Resource constraints on public policy, at both national and lower levels, have grown tighter, and the ideology of co-ordinated public intervention has suffered steadily diminishing credibility. Admittedly, the growth of public expenditure has been only halted, not reversed, but as competition for resources has increased, and spending lobbies have become more vociferous and demanding, resource allocation has been marked more by piecemeal incrementalism than consensus-based long-term planning.[15]

Legislative and administrative powers

Art. 117 of the constitution specifies seventeen headings under which the region may legislate: municipal boundaries; urban and rural police forces; fairs and markets; public charities, health, and hospital assistance; vocational training and financial assistance to students; local museums and libraries; urban planning; tourism and the hotel industry; regional transport networks (excluding railways); regional roads, aqueducts, and other public works; lake navigation and ports; mineral and spa waters; extractive industries; hunting; inland fisheries; agriculture and forestry; and artisanship.

The thinking that shaped this list has become increasingly outdated over the four decades since the constitution was drafted, and major shifts have occurred in what subnational authorities can do, and what the appropriate level of aggregation for a particular function or service is thought to be. The role of public activity has changed, political expectations have altered, and technology has made possible different forms of intervention. The state is now engaged on a far wider front than in the early post-war years. *Ad hoc*, locally based functions of public charity in education, health, and others areas have been transformed into the full-blown assistance of the welfare state. Economic-development planning has become fashionable, even if it is not always successful. Pressures on land use have steadily increased, as have those on the environment generally. Economies of scale have made it advisable to undertake certain activities on a national scale;

conversely problems of administrative congestion have suggested strongly that some forms of administration and implementation be decentralized.

Flexibility in responding to these changes is facilitated by the constitution. In addition to the general powers allocated under art. 117, it adds an additional category of regional legislative power ('other matters indicated by constitutional laws'). More importantly, however, it grants the central state the power to take back, as well as to delegate. Regional legislation is to be constrained 'within the limits of the fundamental principles decided by the State', and the region is free to legislate *provided that such legislation is not in contrast with the interests of the Nation, or of other Regions*. The result has been an endemic conflictuality between state and regions, and much litigation before the constitutional court.[16] Such a principle gives the centre an important advantage in its relations with regional government, although, as we shall see below, the relationship is not entirely one-sided, and in terms of sheer legislative volume the regions have not been backward.[17]

At the administrative level there is also considerable uncertainty about what powers the regions possess. Art. 118 of the constitution gives the regions administrative authority in the seventeen policy sectors identified above, but qualifies this by making exceptions for any function declared, by national law, to be administered instead through the province or municipality. It also allows the centre to confer administrative functions on the regions in any additional area of policy. Through this power, during the 1970s, several new administrative responsibilities, especially in the area of health and transport, passed to the regions.

It is thus very difficult to give a precise account of the region's administrative powers. They vary over time, between policy areas, and according to the political situation at national level. The extension of administrative responsibilities has pushed the system towards a form of administrative devolution similar to that found in the Federal Republic of Germany. But this occurred by default, not design, and is accepted only reluctantly by both national government and the regions. The former often behaves as if it would prefer no real regional devolution at all; the latter periodically chafe at the restrictions that the lack of real legislative autonomy imposes.

Financial powers

With few resources of their own, regional governments have been unable to determine distinctive fiscal stances and expenditure patterns. The principle laid down in art. 119 of the constitution—that the regions should enjoy sufficient 'own fiscal resources' to fulfil the normal tasks assigned to them by the constitution—has been interpreted in a narrow sense. Most of the roles performed by regional government have been specially assigned tasks, with earmarked funding coming not from 'own fiscal resources', but from special transfers from central Treasury funds.

This was clearly established in the 1970 regional finance legislation (law no. 281, 1970) which set the precedent for earmarked funds for specific activities. It limited the size of 'own resources' to approximately 5 per cent of total regional spending. The remaining 95 per cent, coming in the form of transfers from the centre, is divided into three categories: the so-called 'common fund', the fund for regional development plans, and 'special contributions'. Transfers under the first category are calculated on the basis of territory and population, but with a redistributive element to take account of various socio-economic indicators of development levels. In principle, such transfers should involve a level of funding at least no lower than that of the cost of functions carried out by the centre before regionalization. However, inflation in the 1970s rapidly eroded its real value.[18]

In 1976 the problem was rectified by linking the size of transfers to the level of Treasury tax yield at central level. This gave a measure of protection to the regions, enabling them to plan activities over a longer time-horizon. By the early 1980s, however, the long recession, and consequent decline in central-government tax receipts, persuaded the government that it needed tighter short-term control over regional finance. The linkage with Treasury tax yield was abandoned, and the annual finance laws approved by Parliament have been the effective determinant of regional income ever since. In any case, even before this, other developments were working to limit the autonomy of the regions. The level of central funding for both the common fund and that for regional development was gradually cut, and commitments to allow regional governments to retain a part of the yield of local income taxes were abandoned. Meanwhile, the regional basis of the new national health service, while itself a rational response to the urgent need for territorial planning of the allocation of health resources, had further negative consequences for regional financial autonomy. Funding for the service was calculated on an inadequate formula of historic cost. More seriously, it was financed through a special fund which further increased the size of the third category of regional funding—that earmarked for very specific purposes—relative to that of the more general categories of transfer. The almost contemporary establishment of a special regional fund for national transport, the details of which were also determined at the centre, further entrenched such a principle.

During the 1980s, the consequences of these developments proved self-reinforcing. More than 80 per cent of regional financial income was destined for the three sectoral funds dealing with health, transport, and agriculture—all areas where the regional authorities had no effective autonomy. Moreover, forward budgeting in these sectors at the centre was invariably based on unrealistically tight estimates of future expenditure on the ground—estimates that had little credibility for any of the actors involved. This generated widespread expectations that operating deficits would in the end be covered by the centre through additional grants, soft loans, etc. As such expectations were regularly fulfilled, the problem of effective accountability grew steadily worse. Central government, under pressure from the electorate, from regional employees, and from regional lobbies operating through the national parties, rarely had the courage to resist.[19]

The affairs of regional government have thus tended to divide into two categories—a modest sector of real regional responsibility, and a much larger sector in which grandiose regional budgets and policy plans are a fiction, because spending is determined by, and ultimately covered by, national taxpayers. In the latter sector the region itself plays at best a passive, administrative role. Regional governments, dependent on central funds, have had little chance to develop their own distinctive spending priorities and, in any given area, too little reason to limit their propensity to spend, lacking, as they do, a direct responsibility to voters paying for their services through local taxes. Every regional government seeks to persuade its voters that it is doing a good job, but regional elections are rarely seen as verdicts on their performance, rather than on the national performance of parties and coalitions. And the knowledge that ultimately regional choices and priorities count for little only reinforces this attitude among voters.

Party mediation and regional acquiescence

It would be wrong to imply that the relationships described in the foregoing paragraphs amount to an unambiguous imposition of central power on reluctant regions. There is a degree of conscious acquiescence by many regional governments, particularly those in the south. The reason is simple. The redistributive elements favour the poorer regions at the expense of the richer.

In almost all funding formulae used in Italian regional government, there is a substantial redistributive component.[20] The system of regional finance adopted in 1970 compounds two different principles:

the provision of resources to regional government according to size, population, etc. (redistributively neutral); and the channelling of special funds to areas in need of special assistance. Arguably, these are two quite separate activities, and the resources required to attain policy goals in each should be kept distinct. As long as they are not, the less-developed regions probably have an interest in not reopening the basic formula adopted over twenty years ago. For in the process of allocating funds to the regions, there is a long-established 'one region, one vote' principle, which benefits the south against the north. Against the winning coalition of the Ministry of Finance, and regions from Lazio southwards (sustained by southern Christian Democrats, and under-written, incidentally, by the ideology of the Italian left), the richer northern regions of Lombardy, Emilia, Piedmont, Liguria, the Veneto, and Tuscany stand little chance of changing the basic system, particularly given their own political divisions.[21] The political periphery (the prosperous north) is thus not synonymous with the economic periphery (the south and the islands).

Such a system has become solidly entrenched by the large number of arenas in which regional pressures can be brought to bear at the centre. The legislation which has imposed obligations on regional authorities, and supplied the funding for them, has generally established new mixed regulatory and allocative committees consisting of representatives of both the state and the regions.[22] Such arenas—in total they probably number over one hundred—play a key role in smoothing out the complex and often uncertain relationship which has developed between centre and regions. The centre may dominate in financial terms, but the legal ramifications of its activities are frequently uncertain. This, when allied to party pressure, and the desire on the part of the centre not to get bogged down in long legal wrangles, often results in a set of bargains in the joint state–region arenas that gives the regional authorities considerable leverage. The processes involved are not always predictable or edifying, but equally they are by no means overwhelmingly weighted in favour of the centre. The model of state–region relationships can thus best be defined as 'centralised collegiate decision-making'. It is centralized in so far as quite detailed decisions are taken *at the centre*, but it is collegiate in that the regions have won for themselves extensive rights to representation in the taking of decisions.

A factor which assists regions in this relationship is the party system. If the national government were composed of a single, centralized party, the balance would lie overwhelmingly in favour of the centre. But in Italy governments are complex coalitions. The boundary between parties of government and those of opposition is indistinct, with the latter always able to exercise at least some influence over government policy. The parties themselves are internally diversified hierarchies in which leaders have to respond to pressures from the rank and file. Such arrangements have a powerful impact on the state–region relationship. The parties act as channels through which regions and regional party leaders can bring pressures on the centre. The distribution of resources to the regions is thus an important element in national coalition bargaining. It may not be very efficient— indeed it is one more burden on a system of national coalition bargaining that is overloaded, slow, and prone to sub-optimum compromises—but it helps hold the regional system together, and provides a mechanism for ironing out what might otherwise become hopelessly tangled and conflictual relationships.

The future of regional government: enhancing regional performance

The essential problem for Italian regions lies in overcoming the ambiguity in which they languish and the lack of a clear agreement on their relationship to the centre and to local government. Their role has been established by trial and error, party bargaining, and legal controversy, and reflects changing balances of coalition power at the centre, and changing priorities in national government.

This does not mean that the regions have failed. Admittedly, when the reality is compared to the heady aspirations of two decades ago, there is much disappointment. In many regions administrative efficiency does not seem to have improved over the era of direct rule from Rome, although in a society where legal and constitutional theorists rather than analysts of policy processes dominate the study of regional government, assessments of overall regional performance are almost non-existent, as indeed are effective performance criteria.[23]

However, regional government appears firmly entrenched in the political system, and, even if it is not congruent with the long-standing importance of the municipality, or with the power structure of the political parties, it has established itself as a significant administrative link in the chain running from state to community. It is also a frequent testing ground for new approaches to policy and administration. However much dissatisfaction there is with regional autonomy and regional performance, then, it is difficult to imagine the Italian state dispensing with this intermediate level of political identity. Certainly, few politicians are ever heard arguing seriously for the abolition of regional government, or even for a reduction in its powers.

What is needed to consolidate the regionalization process is an increase in the chain of accountability between regional authorities and the regional electorate. This link is weak because those who benefit from locally produced services are not those who pay for them. Any system of administrative decentralization incurs such a risk, and it is not just in Italy that the problem arises. But it is especially acute there, because regional governments are given such little opportunity to experiment in the allocation of resources, because the immediate paymaster is central government not the local taxpayer, and because local voters tend to vote in regional elections as well as national elections on the basis of national party performance.

How this state of affairs might be improved upon is difficult to say in detail, but there is clearly a need for regional authorities (like all other tiers of Italian public administration) to curb their own administrative costs, and for some restriction on the range of activities in which they engage, particularly in extending subsidies to a multifarious range of minor economic activities, whether directly, or through municipal government. Focusing on the provision of a few major services (health, transport, environment) and taking more explicit responsibility for them, it is argued, will increase the meaning of regional government for ordinary voters, and hence make the electoral link more direct. This in turn requires central government to give regional governments greater discretion in the allocation of resources between budget heads, including the major ones such as health and transport. Central government also needs to encourage efficient resource-usage by resisting more resolutely pressures from regions for supplementary finance when budget ceilings prove inadequate. However, these latter imperatives take us back to the relationship between legislature and executive at the centre, for as we have seen, in determining its budgetary choices national government is subject to extensively brokered intervention from a fragmented legislature. Ultimately, administrative efficiency and fiscal responsibility in the regions, like that at the centre, depend on the establishment of strong and effective government in Rome.

Local Government

The provinces and municipalities

Below the regional level there are two further tiers: provinces and municipalities. The province, equivalent to the French department, was originally the basic unit of field administration inherited from the Piedmontese state, and still retains this administrative role. There are provincial prefectures, tax offices, educational inspectorates, etc. However, it is also an elected authority, albeit with relatively few functions.

The municipality (*comune*) is the lowest tier. The category covers an enormous range; 94 are provincial capitals, just over 100 more have a population in excess of 300,000, but nearly 7,000 have fewer than 5,000 inhabitants. The functions of the municipality are quite extensive, and make it far more important as a unit of local government than the province. Its share of public expenditure is nearly ten times that of the province, and its share of public employees is considerably greater. Indeed, while the municipality's overall expenditure, as a proportion of total public expenditure, is slightly smaller than that of the region, its long history of importance in the political system, and the number of employees it disposes of, make it in some respects more important than the region too.

The province

The provincial council is elected by proportional representation based on a single-member unit, similar to that used for the Senate. Councils range in size from twenty-four to forty-five members, according to population. They elect a *giunta* (executive) headed by a president who serves as head of both the executive and the provincial council. Their functions were for much of the post-war period relatively few in number: psychiatric hospitals, provincial roads, some parts of the water-supply system, community health, some minor social services, and the maintenance of certain types of public building. Indeed, in the late 1970s and early 1980s there was some discussion of abolishing the province altogether as a directly elected tier of government. In the last decade, however, the fortunes of the provinces have revived somewhat.[24] This has mainly been the result of the tendency of regional governments to devolve the administration of regionally defined policy to provincial governments in various areas: agriculture, commerce, tourism, and transport.

In the local government reform of 1990 (law no. 142, 8 June 1990—on which see below), these roles were recognized systematically in a new formulation dividing the activities of provincial authorities into two groups: areas in which the province plays a formal administrative role, and areas in which it is assigned a purely planning role. The former includes environmental protection, local transport networks, public health, and some activities in the area of education and training, as laid down in regional and state legislation. The latter mainly involve the task of intermediation between municipalities and regions in land use and development planning. This mediating role was already clear some years before the 1990 reform. The gap between region and municipality proved, for many purposes, too large, and, in reconciling competing claims for regional resources, the province showed itself to be a useful level of aggregation in formulating plans for transmission upwards, and indeed executing projects which had been decided by regional authorities, but had to be administered at a level closer to the end users than the region itself. Moreover, for the nine newly designated 'metropolitan areas' (on which see below), the province—or at least the *territory* (and electorate) of the province—becomes, in effect, the main unit of subregional government, taking over from the provincial capital's municipal administration.

How effective these reforms will prove to be remains to be seen. While the province is in many respects the 'natural' unit of aggregation between region and locality, the roles it will have to perform will be grafted on to a provincial administrative framework that has not, in the past, been a byword for efficiency.[25] Both for the province and the municipality problems of excessive legal and procedural checks on administrative action are considerable. The 1990 legislation seeks to remove some of these, but at the same time it replaces them with others, in an effort to increase the standing in local policy-making of permanent expert officials at the expense of elected politicians.[26] Whether such officials, whose traditional attitude to their elected masters in local government was one of extreme deference, and of zealous respect for legal and procedural correctness, will display the confidence to make use of the more flexible legal framework for local government remains to be seen.

The municipality

Structure

Like the region, the municipality is run by a directly elected council. The method of election depends on size. In municipalities with fewer than 5,000 inhabitants, voters generally choose between pre-formed coalition lists, casting four out of five of their preferences for candidates on the same list. Some *panachage* is allowed, but it does not normally prevent the emergence of fairly solid ruling majorities. In the larger municipalities, however, voting is by single-party lists, with proportional representation and individual preference-voting similar to that in the Chamber of Deputies.

The municipal council varies in size—from 15 members for the smallest to 80 for the largest—as does the executive (*giunta comunale*), elected by the council, which can have as few as 4 or as many as 16 full *assessori* (elected officials heading particular departments of the municipality—effectively local-level ministers). Both the council and the executive are presided over by the mayor (*sindaco*), who is majority leader and chief executive. The relationship between council, executive, and mayor, especially in the larger communities, is formalized and politicized, with majority and opposition divisions, and an executive that depends on the continuance of a relationship of political confidence analogous to that at national level.

The structure of the municipality is internally quite complex, and derives from the multiplicity of roles it performs. Just under half the 1.1 million staff employed in the municipalities are directly employed. (Note, however, that although they are employees of individual municipalities, their conditions of service tend to be uniform, and subject to national-level labour contracts.) These employees carry out the basic regulatory functions like local commercial licensing, local policing, urban development control, building regulations, basic public health and social services. They also provide most school buildings, local public infrastructure provision, and (modest levels of) subsidized housing. The remainder of the municipal labour force is employed indirectly in what are, in all but a few cases, wholly owned, but notionally separate, service agencies under indirect municipal management (transport, water, gas, and electricity utilities, cleansing services, milk distribution centres, slaughter houses, public-hoarding advertising, and so on).

These various activities are grouped under the direct or indirect control of municipal departments, administered by one or more *assessori*, and generally supervised by a committee of the council. Despite this supervision, in the large authorities the *assessore* enjoys considerable administrative discretion, and the real centre of affairs lies in the municipal executive (grouping together mayor and *assessori*) rather than in the council, which is too large and unwieldy and, in some cases, inexpert to exercise regular control.[27]

The mayor

The key individuals in municipal politics are the mayors. Few Italian politicians would consciously seek to hold senior office in the provincial or even the regional level in preference to the post of mayor of the provincial capital city. Mayors of major urban areas like Milan, Turin, Rome, or Naples are important national political figures with as high a level of public visibility as many ministers. Traditionally the mayor was elected by the council, by an exhaustive secret ballot, which in practice often resulted in his being elected on a plurality rather than an absolute majority of the council. When mayors were elected on minority votes, this led to later trouble when they could find themselves short of majorities in votes on, for example, city budgets (which require an absolute majority). Coalitions at local level have, as a result, tended to be very brittle, and long political crises have been common. Since 1990, however, as discussed below, a reform has introduced the principle of an open ballot, in which the mayor, the *assessori*, and their proposed programme must be approved in an open ballot, within sixty days; if there is no absolute majority, the council is dissolved and there are fresh elections.

The mayors play a dual role. They serve as political heads of the coalition running the municipality, but also serve as administrative representatives of the government, on whom certain statutory duties are conferred. In the smaller municipalities, for example, where there is no separate commissioner of police, they have ultimate responsibility for public order, and everywhere mayors are responsible for urgent issues of public health and for dealing with other emergencies. They also have responsibility for the register of births, marriages, and deaths, the electoral register, the holding of elections and censuses, and the keeping of military-service registers.

Politicization of local government agencies

Service agencies like local transport, cleansing, water utilities, although only indirectly run by the municipality, are highly politicized. The administrators who run them are appointed on a partisan basis. This is not to say that they are unqualified for the jobs they perform—indeed the law requires that at their appointment there has to be a public declaration of their fitness and qualification for office. Nevertheless, holding office for renewable fixed terms, they cannot ignore the importance of party contacts. Politicization of managerial appointments is thus the norm, and large numbers of party card-holders are in turn recruited into the agencies they run. For many, such party affiliation is doubtless an act of career convenience rather than ideological conviction, but this matters little to the parties, since they are primarily looking for solid blocks of voters and party workers who have a personal interest in keeping in office the party through which they acquired their jobs.

Over time, this aspect of municipal government has become a prominent feature. The more managerial posts and seats on the boards of directors of municipal agencies that a party controls, the more powerful it is judged to be. Sharing the spoils has become a virility symbol and, not unnaturally, a source of enormous dissension in municipal governing coalitions.

The larger municipalities (the roughly 200 with populations of more than 30,000 inhabitants) thus supply the bulk of the local political class, and are the proving ground in which young politicians acquire skills of political entrepreneurship, and develop the contacts and personal networks that enable them, through the preference-vote mechanism, to make the transition to the national stage. Once there, however, they continue to need the support of local politicians from among whom they have sprung, and this gives the municipal politician—especially the mayor—a mechanism for bargaining with the national level for resources.

As already suggested, such linkages are just as significant in understanding municipal government as are variations in the policies and programmes pursued by different coalitions. The latter are not unimportant, especially, for example, in the area of urban planning issues, where there is considerable scope for using development licensing to affect the social composition, mix of usage (between for example residential and business accommodation), and general environmental quality of particular urban areas. But policy variations are limited, at municipal as at regional level, by the key issue of funding. The municipalities, like the regions, are not the masters of their own budgets, and have little discretion to vary the allocation of resources between different activities. Over many years, obligations have been laid down by national law, and even where some flexibility is permitted, expectations of what should be provided, and how, have become rather rigid.

The municipal reform of 1990

These concerns, together with others resulting from the overlap of functions between regions and municipalities, and most of all from the combined effects of diseconomies of scale and the inequities in service provision that stem from the enormous variations in the size of the municipalities, have generated a series of attempts over the years to reform the structure of municipal government. They have been paralleled by mounting concerns over party behaviour at local level—especially in the larger cities—reflected particularly in the instability of ruling coalitions, and the enduring struggle for political patronage through control of jobs, licensing powers, building contracts, and so on. Such concerns exactly parallel the debate over the aggregative capacities of political parties and the instability of government at national level.

Earlier in the chapter, we referred to efforts to bring city administration closer to the citizen through the creation of the *circoscrizione* in the larger cities, and, at the other end of the scale, efforts to mitigate the effects of the small size of many municipalities through various types of *consortium*. The experience of the *circoscrizione*—which began on an informal and experimental basis many years ago, and was permitted explicitly by a reform in 1976 (law no. 278, 8 April 1976)—has probably been more successful than efforts to promote the consortium. The highland communities (*comunità montana*) have had some successes with the consortium approach, but tend to lack necessary financial and technical resources, and are often unable to persuade the regional authorities in which they are located to devolve functions down to them, to yield economies of scale to the municipality. The other main type of consortium—the so-called *comprensorio*—has been even less satisfactory. It has stemmed from the efforts by the regional governments to create an intermediate tier of administrative activity between itself and the municipalities more rational in scope and function than the existing province. It was thought to be especially suitable for large and distinct communities (quasi-provinces) inside existing provinces. However, it has proved extremely difficult to operate in the absence of a more general administrative reform persuading or requiring all units involved in the relevant territory—municipalities, provinces, and field administrative units of central government—to co-operate. Frequently, key units of administration like education districts or local health units (*unità sanitaria locale* or USL, on which see Chapter 8) have not corresponded with the territory of the *comprensorio*, making a co-ordinated approach to social-service provision particularly difficult.

For all these reasons, a more general reform of local government—both municipalities and provinces—was prepared during the latter years of the 1980s, and finally approved in 1990 (law no. 142, 8 June 1990). The legislation divides into four main areas.

1. Measures empowering municipalities and provinces to write their own local 'constitutions' (*statuti*) which will regulate the internal organization of the local administration, co-operation with other municipalities and provinces, and internal decentralization and citizen access. Linked to this are measures by which the municipality is encouraged to improve citizen participation, access to information, and redress of grievances. Although not explicitly presented as such, the aim is a form of 'citizens' charter' intended to increase grass-roots pressure for better, and more responsive, public services. The reform

proposes consultative referendums on local issues, a *difensore civico* (local ombudsman) to identify and deter maladministration, open access to municipal information and records (with confidentiality restricted largely to the area of personal privacy), and mechanisms of consultation not just for territorial units within the area of a municipality, but also for particular interests such as sporting associations, pensioners, etc.

2. A more rational division of territory, through mergers between municipalities, new forms of inter-municipal association, and the designation of *aree metropolitane* (urban conurbations). The three main provisions in this connection are: first, financial incentives to encourage the merger of smaller municipalities (and a bar on the creation of new ones through subdivision if this results in municipalities of fewer than 10,000 inhabitants); secondly, the designation of the provinces of Turin, Milan, Venice, Genoa, Bologna, Florence, Rome, Bari, and Naples as *aree metropolitane*; and thirdly, other measures to encourage new forms of convention, consortium, and association between municipalities. The biggest innovation involves the conurbations, which will henceforth become two-tier authorities, with the most important functions (territorial planning, transport, environment, water resources, energy, health services, school-building programmes, commercial regulation) run by the metropolitan council (with its own executive and 'metropolitan mayor'), while residual functions are devolved to the municipal councils within the metropolitan territory. The main aim is to develop a more balanced approach to the development of major urban conurbations than was possible in the past, when smaller municipalities on the edge of larger ones tended to be swamped by the less-desired features of their larger neighbours, such as the deprived residential areas, refuse disposal and recycling plants, prisons, etc.

3. Measures to encourage more durability and cohesiveness among the party coalitions running local government. As we have seen above, the chief measures in this connection are the requirements that the mayor, executive, and coalition programme be approved within sixty days, by open (as opposed in the past to secret) ballot in the council, and that, once installed, the coalition can only be removed collectively (no votes of no confidence in individual *assessori*) by a motion winning an absolute majority of the council, and nominating a new mayor, executive, and programme.[28]

4. Measures to encourage a more managerial outlook among local-government officials. In this area, the major change involves the figure of the municipal secretary (*segretario comunale*), who traditionally played

the role of secretary to the council and the executive and main official channel of access to the Ministry of the Interior and the provincial prefect. To the secretary's legal and political role is now added that of general manager of the municipal administrative machinery. Senior management (*dirigenti*) within that machinery are also given wider responsibilities than in the past, and the possibility is envisaged of bringing in individuals from the private sector on a temporary basis.

It is, of course, too early to say how successful this major reform will be. Some parts have immediate application, and following the local elections of 1990 it was notable that the process of electing mayors and forming governing coalitions was, under the threat of automatic dissolution and fresh elections after the sixty-day time limit, far easier than following previous municipal elections. However, much of the reform depends for its effectiveness on follow-up legislation by national government, regions, and municipalities. National government has to rewrite local-government finance legislation and redeem its pledges on financial incentives for municipal restructuring. Regional and local governments have to co-operate in redrawing boundaries, reorganizing local administrative structures, and introducing the elements of public participation and citizen access required in the legislation. They also have to find the political will and self-discipline to grant local service deliverers more managerial autonomy to improve productivity and quality, and this means a tougher approach to the financial performance of agencies themselves. Moreover, national variations in the quality of local administration and in local political culture make it likely that the impact of the 1990 legislation will for many years be very uneven. Nevertheless, the reform does show that local government can be a testing ground for ideas (the constructive vote of no confidence, for example) upon which politicians at national level have to date been unable to agree. In that sense at least, the 1990 legislation, while containing much that *enables* rather than *requires* local government to act, may come to be seen as a significant innovation.

Beyond that, the reform puts more clearly on the public agenda issues connected with the quality of public services closest to the citizen, and sets out ways in which grass-roots pressure may help in persuading politicians and administrators to improve their performance. As we observed earlier in the chapter, in connection with regional-government performance, this circuit of political responsibility and accountability at local level is the key issue. If local democracy is to mean anything, it must be based on a constitutional or statutory grant of political (and where appropriate fiscal) autonomy *from the centre*, recognized by the electorate as well as the political class. In Italy, local government depends more on contingent political leverage exercised by local politicians *at the centre*. This may give regional and local governments collectively (i.e. through their various national associations: the conference of regional presidents, the national association of Italian municipalities, etc.) some influence on allocative decisions taken in national consultative committees. But this influence is rarely durable, and where national government makes concessions in an incremental, piecemeal way (for example by financing activities for limited periods only) the outcome of any particular bargain is contingent and reversible. Such a relationship encourages local voters to believe that real power lies with the centre, and therefore to discount the possibility that local politicians are responsible for locally administered policies.

10

The European Community Dimension of Italian Government

The European Community and National Politics

Over the last three decades, the European Community has added a significant dimension to the domestic political systems of its con stituent states. In Italy, especially, Community affairs are no longer simply a part of the foreign-policy processes. Although Italy's membership of the Community, like that of all other states, is based on a contingent treaty commitment which could in principle be reversed, there seems no possibility of this occurring. Italians appear as close as any EC national group to developing a 'European' dimension to their sense of citizenship. It is not yet shared by all other EC member states, of course, but whether Community membership is rooted in citizenship and identity, or merely contingent foreign-policy choice, it increasingly affects the autonomy of national and subnational governments. Community law is almost universally accepted as superior to national law, and in its area of competence the Community's Court of Justice is the highest court of appeal. Although the financial transfers between national level and Community level are still small (little over 1 per cent of Community GDP) major areas of national public policy are constrained by Community decisions. Italy's external trade relations, not only with her EC partners, but also with third countries, are largely determined by the Community.

Increasingly, domestic macro-economic management is also constrained by developments in the wider European economy. Much of this is less the result of formal EC obligations than of the *de facto* Europeanization of the Italian economy, in which trade with EC partners has become a major element of domestic demand. However, the economic constraint is also formalized in Community institutions—most notably the European Monetary System—which, after a decade of modest success in stabilizing European exchange rates, began, at the end of the 1980s, to accelerate towards the goal of full monetary union. Italy's desire not to be excluded from this process has been a powerful (although still in 1991 not yet a sufficient) impetus to bring domestic inflationary pressures into line with those of her EC partners. It has affected policy in numerous areas: the labour market, supply-side structural rigidities in commerce, distribution, financial markets, etc., and most of all in the area of the domestic budget deficit.

The acceleration of European integration under the impetus of the 1985 internal-market programme, and associated institutional reforms to Community decision-making—most notably the Single European Act—have also played a major role in locking Italy into the Community political system. The internal-market programme aims to remove, or at least harmonize, national regulations in areas like public procurement, industrial standards, financial-market rules, state aids to industry, differential tax regimes, barriers to the free movement of people and goods, etc.[1] The Single European Act marks a recognition that such barriers can only be removed by greater use of majority voting in the Community's Council of Ministers, and the abolition of the national veto. The wider use of majority voting implies a corresponding loss of sovereignty for national legislatures, and this has been met by a modest increase in the decisional powers of the European Parliament. It is not at present possible to see how this latter process will develop, but if taken far it would create a political authority with a claim to representative legitimacy which further undermined the autonomy of the national level.[2]

Finally, in the most fundamental area of 'high politics'—defence and foreign policy—the Community dimension has also eroded national sovereignty. Here too, it may be argued, *de facto* pressures have to date been greater than *de jure* ones. The mechanisms of European Political Co-operation are still based on a consensualism that leaves member states free to opt out where they wish. The concept of a *defence* dimension to the Community has yet to assume any concrete reality. Yet in practice Community members find it increasingly difficult to avoid acting in unison. The changing international context that has come with the end of the Cold War and the decline of communism have been the most important influences in this process. For at least a decade before the upheavals of 1989–91, the Community was aware of the need for foreign-policy co-ordination to maximize the impact of its member states in international affairs, and of the long-term need to assume a larger share of the burden of its own defence. The dramatic changes in Eastern Europe both accelerated this process and made the Community conscious of the political strength its economic power as a trading block could give it. Perhaps most important of all, the Community offers a context in which the reunification of Germany, and that country's growing political and economic strength, can be accepted by its discomfited neighbours to both its east and its west.

The European Community's political system can therefore be seen as a significant level of government affecting political decisions in Italy. In some respects, linkages up to the Community level from national level are as important as those downwards to subnational level discussed in the previous chapter. This does not mean that Italian politics can only be understood after an exhaustive analysis of European Community policy process, but it does mean that the linkages between Italy and the Community cannot be ignored. How Italians conceive of their European identity, how they formulate Community policy, how the national administrative system meshes with the Commission in Brussels, and how it implements Community policy once made are vital questions. They affect how far Italian interests are taken into consideration in shaping Community policy, and how far Italian policy and administration are affected by European standards and values. Just as important, though not something which can be explored here, is the reciprocal question of the impact on Community policy-making made by Italian administrative styles and outlooks, Italian standards of respect for, and implementation of, EC law, and Italian attitudes to the expenditure of European Community funds.

Italy's European Commitment

Early membership and institutional congruence

Italy's original membership of the Community was more a political act of faith than a reflection of the country's real economic strength. Italy was the earliest of several countries—later to include Greece, Spain, and Portugal—to suppose that, in societies with initially fragile democracies and weak institutional arrangements, democracy could be consolidated, and institutions galvanized, by close association with the stronger and more advanced democracies at the core of the Community. The gamble paid off. Like the decision in the late 1940s to liberalize the Italian economy and opt for a market mechanism in an open trading system, joining the Community at its outset—when stronger economies such as the British remained outside—proved a wise choice. The Community proved more successful than could have been expected in 1958. The EC became one of the cornerstones of a West European order based on economic interdependence, on successful social-market economies, and stable and peaceful relationships between formerly hostile states. If 'Mediterranean' status endowed a country with the aura of economic underdevelopment and political instability, association with the European Community provided Italy with a symbolic, but psychologically important, protection against such a status.

Fortunately, the first decade of Community membership coincided with the dramatic growth rates achieved during the peak years of the Italian economic miracle. The growth performance may not, in reality, have been primarily attributable to the EC, but for business leaders, and subsequently politicians and the mass public, Community membership was a guarantee that the open-market-economy path which Italy had embarked upon would be adhered to, and therefore that a stable framework for economic decisions and business planning could be counted on.

The 1970s confirmed this. Although a bleak time for Community development in any other area than enlargement, and a difficult decade for Italy both politically and economically, the country's EC membership was an important stabilizing factor. Community loans eased the country through its external-payments difficulties. Politically, there was a widespread—and, in the light of subsequent developments, almost certainly correct—belief that EC membership represented the best hope of generalized regional solutions to these difficulties. To have yielded to the strains placed on Italian democracy would have isolated the country from its Community partners (for whom liberal democratic values were a *sine qua non* of EC membership), and thus put the country beyond reach of these collective solutions.

The strength of this commitment was confirmed in December 1978, in the decision of the Andreotti government to place the lira within the newly formed exchange-rate mechanism of the European Monetary System. Given the gap between Italian and German inflation rates, this move was riskier for Italy than for most ERM participants. Had it failed completely, as did the 'Snake' in the early 1970s, it would have signalled to participants in the labour market that the monetary authorities were willing to underwrite inflationary wage settlements by repeated devaluations. Yet despite some bumpy realignments, and, until 1990, despite wider margins of fluctuation than for other members of the scheme, Italian participation proved a qualified success.[3]

The Italian approach to the Community has thus been that 'tying one's hands in advance' by agreeing to be bound by rules that are not immediately beneficial can work as an important disciplinary mechanism.[4] In Italy, it is seen as a strategy that works. Initially it assisted the country to consolidate its own democratic framework; subsequently it has forced it to keep its inflation and external trade balance performances under tighter control than structural features of the Italian economy might otherwise have allowed.

Italy's positive attitude within the European Community stands in sharp contrast with that of the United Kingdom, a country similar in size and economic importance within the Community. Unlike Italy, Britain joined fifteen years after the Community was established, when its structures and policies were already established, after a long, agonizing debate about the merits of membership, and after one (French-inspired) rebuff on the grounds of alleged unpreparedness to yield sovereignty. In contrast, Italy, as a founder member of the European Community, and as a country where perceptions of Community membership are largely positive, is one of the strongest advocates of European integration. Italians appear to share a widespread perception that the yielding of sovereignty can be a gain rather than a loss, and to have little fear of tighter integration, whether political or economic.

This attitude may also stem from the congruence between the style of politics and public policy-making to which Italians have become used over forty years, and the style of Community institutions and decision-taking procedures. Italians may believe they understand the Community because its political system, like their own, is multi-tiered and pluralistic. There is no strong executive and no clear-cut majority–minority divide. As a result majorities in favour of given policies are in both systems fragile and pliable, so that many decisions need to be taken on the basis of a very broad consensus. Neither the Italian government nor the Commission-Council tandem can count on pushing legislation through in a form which resembles that in which it was introduced, or to a predictable timetable. Both systems are heavily juridicized and based upon marked elements of inter-institutional and territorial bargaining. Both display a great deal of ambiguity about the status of decisions and the point at which decisions have actually been taken.

Public attitudes and administrative performace

Support for the process of European integration is widely reflected in Italian public attitudes towards the Community. The Community's Eurobarometer poll has been monitoring attitudes towards integration across the Community for over two decades, and Italy regularly emerges as one of the EC member states where opinion is most favourable.[5] At the level of mass opinion, Italy is as near to the model *fédérateur* state as it has been possible to get. If European integration requires the creation of a domestic political climate supportive of integration, Italy's record is almost unimpeachable. The Italian government is under constant pressure from parliamentary opinion to be more committed to the integration process. In most states such pressure is non-existent; in a few it works in quite the opposite direction. The Italian *acquis* is shared by virtually all Italian parties, social movements, and interest groups. As a result, the Italian government's position is generally supportive of the Commission, the European Parliament, and those states (generally the Benelux members and Germany) pushing for faster integration, right across the range of Community initiatives.

However, public utterances are not the only form of *acquis communautaire* required of Community member states. European integration requires a measurable internal commitment from national governments and legislatures. The internal-market programme, and the accelerated rate of EC legislation requiring translation into national law, have in recent years underlined disparities between states in the process of implementing Community policy and ensuring that the writ of EC law applies evenly throughout the Community.[6] For Italy, this poses especially acute problems. Externally, Italian objectives are relatively clear, and fully supportive of rapid European integration in almost all areas, but internally the adjustments necessary to prepare the country for further European integration have come very slowly. The substance of Italy's commitment to European policy on the domestic front has been disappointing. This applies in several areas, but most notably in relation to the compatibility of domestic economic and budgetary policies with the demands of European Community developments, and in relation to the ability of the institutions to translate Community law into national law, and to guarantee the writ of Community law in Italian territory.

The first of these problems needs little elucidation here. We have already seen in Chapter 6 that the budget-deficit problem is a serious one. Although full monetary union across the Community has long been one of Italy's main objectives, Italy itself presents one of the biggest barriers in the path to monetary union as charted in the Community's timetable for union by the end of the 1990s laid down at the 1991 Maastricht European Council. Its budget deficit is far out of line with that agreed in the Delors Report on monetary union, and consistently reaffirmed by European central banks, and by the 1991

Council, as necessary for effective economic and monetary convergence. To date, Italian governments have been unable to make the internal fiscal and expenditure adjustments to remedy this problem, and if monetary integration cannot force the Italian political authorities into changes of policy, then a major goal of Italian policy will not be achievable. As a result, either monetary union will not be achieved, or Italy will be excluded from a system of monetary union extending only across an inner core of member states whose economies have already reached the required level of convergence.[7] Paradoxically, the Italian monetary authorities have tended to regard monetary union as the discipline which would force them (or rather force the overspending, under-taxing Italian parliament) to correct the budget deficit, but if the problem itself makes the country ineligible for submission to the discipline, the strategy cannot work.

The second problem is the inability of the institutions to translate Community law into national law, and to guarantee the writ of Community law in Italian territory. It is manifested in two very clear measures: the Italian government's ability to translate directives agreed at EC level in pursuit of the 1992 internal-market programme into Italian national law, and the level of Italian compliance with decisions of the European Court of Justice. Successive reports by the Commission have cast light on significant variations across the Community in the implementation process. Italy's poor performance is striking. As Table 10.1 shows, in autumn 1990, out of just over a hundred measures which should have been implemented, Italy had notified the Commission of only forty-three which had been passed into law—the lowest figure of any member state.

Italy's poorly developed ability to observe the letter of Community law is also seen in the number of infringement proceedings which have been initiated against member states since 1982—proceedings which end eventually, if not settled beforehand, in the European Court of Justice.[8] Recent reports on this matter show that in 1990 Italy had the highest number of 'letters of formal notice' of infringements, the highest number of 'reasoned opinions' issued by the Commission, and, at 159 since 1982, the highest number of references to the Court of Justice (the next highest was Belgium with 85, with the UK—new members apart—lowest with only 20).[9] Italy is also the only country in which over recent years there is a clearly discernible *rising trend* in the number of infringement proceedings. Most noticeable of all, the Italian performance in complying with Court of Justice judgements when these are delivered up against it is also far out of line with its Community partners. In 1990, Italy had the dubious distinction of

TABLE 10.1 *Implementation of the European Community's internal-market programme into national law by member states by October 1990*

	Measures notified	Measures not notified	Derogation	Not applicable
Belgium	72	32		5
Denmark	89	15		5
Eire	70	31	2	6
France	77	28		4
Germany	84	20		5
Greece	54	44	7	4
Italy	43	62		4
Luxembourg	67	35		7
The Netherlands	71	33		5
Portugal	80	20	7	2
Spain	75	27	5	2
UK	85	18	1	5

Source: Commission of the European Communities, *Implementation of the Legal Measures Required to Build the Single Market, Communication from the Commission to the European Parliament*, Com. (90)473, Final (Brussels, 5 Cct. 1990).

having no less than twenty-one Court of Justice judgements with which it still had to comply, on which proceedings had been initiated under art. 171 of the Treaty of Rome. [10]

The consequences of this systematic failure are potentially serious. Politically and diplomatically, it discredits the country among its EC partners. Commercially, Italy risks appearing as a country where the writ of Community commercial law does not run. If this were sustained over a long period, entrepreneurs considering inward direct investment, participation in equity markets, mergers, and acquisitions would have to add a risk premium when contemplating business in or with Italy. At the limit, even Italian entrepreneurs might begin to alter their perceptions of the relative merits of retaining core activities in Italy and diversifying abroad.

Making Italy's European policy

These difficulties reflect the complex institutional framework in which Italy's European policy is made. As we have seen in earlier sections of this book, Italian government is government by department, and the failure to rationalize departmental structures over time has generated major overlaps of competence between departments. Community policy in Italy is made in several different departments; in all at least fifteen out of twenty-one full ministries are involved. Monetary and fiscal policy affects the Treasury, the Finance Ministry, the Budget Ministry, and the Bank of Italy. EC trade policy affects the Ministries of Foreign Affairs, Foreign Trade, and Industry. Social affairs affect the Ministries of Health, Labour, Industry, and several others. If the structure of Italian ministries and the failure to rationalize it generate a lack of congruence with policies on the domestic front, they do so even more on the European front. Any particular area of Community policy has implications for several Italian departments—especially in the areas of the internal market, monetary policy, external trade, and social policy.

Italy is not, of course, alone, in facing such problems. All European governments were caught by surprise by the unexpected pace of the internal-market programme in the 1980s, and by the cross-departmental implications of much of that programme. The Single European Act and the *de facto* abolition of the national veto forced governments to accept that they would more often be defeated in their EC objectives in the Council of Ministers. Governments had to start establishing clearer priorities and better mechanisms for trading off concessions with other states against gains in priority areas. This has had to be done against a background of gradual 'Europeanization' of national administrations, generating direct links between Brussels and parts of the national administration (sometimes even parts of the subnational administrations), all of which has made *national* priority setting and *national* co-ordination more difficult. The response has varied widely. Britain and France, for example—the two states with the clearest sense of national interest in the EC—have long had well-established mechanisms for EC policy co-ordination. The Foreign Office and the Quai d'Orsay play major roles, but there is also an important co-ordinating mechanism linked closely to the centre of the executive machine: in the UK the European Unit in the Cabinet Office, and in France the Secrétariat Général du Comité interministériel pour les questions de coopération économique européenne.[11]

In the Italian case there existed in the early years of the Community successive versions of a grand interministerial committee grouping the ministers of Foreign Affairs, Industry, Agriculture, and Finance, and subsequently the Treasury and Labour ministers, together with others on an *ad hoc* basis. At the administrative level, its work came to be shadowed (and prepared) by a parallel committee of directors-general from the various ministries involved. Indeed, the interministerial committee itself gradually faded out, meeting only to resolve difficulties not capable of being resolved at the administrative level.[12] As a result, in practice the Ministry of Foreign Affairs (MFA) came to play the major role in administrative co-ordination of Italy's European Community policy. More than any other department, it had good lines of contact with Brussels through the Italian Permanent Delegation, the great majority of which, in the early years, came from its own ranks. It was responsible for monitoring new policy initiatives in the Community, acting as early-warning mechanism, and keeping a close eye on the positions of other governments. Moreover, as one of the most self-confident departmental corps, with a clearer sense of collective purpose and mission than almost any other part of the Italian public sector apart, perhaps, from the Bank of Italy, the MFA had the psychological foundations necessary for such a role.

Evidently, the MFA was not anxious, for reasons of departmental interest, to allow independent channels of communication to develop between national departments of government and the Community, or counterpart ministries in other national governments. They would clearly have undermined the Ministry's near-monopoly in handling Italy's external relations. The MFA was thus anxious to adapt quickly and effectively to the Community. The formal structure of the mechanism centred, and still centres, on the Directorates-General for Economic Affairs and for Political Affairs, with the emphasis, in normal circumstances, rather more on the former, but shifting to the latter in more 'heroic' times, including those recently which have seen major questions of European foreign policy and defence co-operation and major institutional changes on the Community agenda.

From an early stage, the Directorate-General for Economic Affairs thus came to play the key role in inter-departmental liaison. Other 'technical' departments, including the Bank of Italy, could still take the initiative when they alone possessed the requisite expertise, but the MFA and the Permanent Delegation in Brussels were rarely excluded from the process, and played a key role in fostering an élite of European specialists both within its own ranks and within other departments. It seems likely, indeed, that this socialization process worked to the MFA's benefit. The existence of specialist corps operating across departments with a keen sense of cohesion is unusual in Italy, and almost certainly gratifying in both a psychological and material sense for those involved. The chance to work in the Permanent Delegation in Brussels, on politically high-profile questions where one could be seen by ministers and senior directors-general, all flowed from participation in the European policy networks. As a form of patronage, it could act as a powerful incentive inducing departmental officials to co-operate under the MFA's leadership.

The structure is now long established.[13] Section I of the Directorate-General for Political Affairs deals with European Political Co-operation, the Council of Europe, and Western European Union. Section I of the Directorate-General for Economic Affairs deals with the Community's internal economic affairs. It includes a small number of personnel seconded to it from other ministries. Section V deals with the EC's external trade policy. Officials in these three sections (in total about a dozen individuals) work full-time on EC affairs, co-ordinated by a secretariat under a senior official. Other sections of the MFA are naturally involved, however, including the *cabinet* of the minister of Foreign Affairs himself (which is in any case frequently staffed to a large degree by Ministry of Foreign Affairs personnel) and the office of the secretary-general. Moreover, the directors-general not only of Political Affairs and Economic Affairs but also of Social and Cultural Affairs make a significant input, as does the legal office of the Ministry.

Beyond this, the reach of the Ministry stretches in three other directions. One, already mentioned, is the Permanent Delegation in Brussels. A second is the prime minister's office, where the department of the diplomatic councillor to the prime minister is an important point of reference for high-profile Community issues, or for political assistance in the resolution of inter-departmental conflicts.

The role of diplomatic councillor is almost invariably held by a serving member of the Foreign Ministry staff. A third, of more recent and gradual innovation, is the extension of this to all other ministries through the appointment of diplomatic councillors to the ministerial cabinets of all ministers. This network, while sometimes placing some short-term strains on the resources of the MFA itself, gives the latter an invaluable network across the whole gamut of the Rome administration. The MFA, in short, sees itself as having a modern responsibility for cross-departmental co-ordination similar to that, long established under the Napoleonic administrative tradition, assumed by interior ministries through the prefectoral corps, or by finance or treasury ministries through decentralized inspectorate agencies such as the Treasury Ministry's central accounting office, the *ragioneria generale dello stato*. Naturally, *advisers* cannot wield the same *statutory* powers as these more illustrious predecessors, but the purpose is nevertheless similar.

Reforming European Community co-ordination

A process of co-ordination is only as good as the departments being co-ordinated, and from a European Community point of view several Italian ministries, like their counterparts in some other states, have found considerable difficulty in incorporating a Community dimension into their planning and procedures. It has thus been necessary, in Italy as elsewhere, to stimulate departments to think in 'European' terms, to develop strategies for adapting to European legislation, to train personnel with the skills to negotiate in the complex technical committees operating alongside the Commission in Brussels, to prepare clear and trouble-free legislative proposals to translate Community directives into national law, and to steer those proposals through Parliament. These needs have become gradually more pressing since the start of the 1980s as the quantity and complexity of Community legislation has grown, and as Community spending programmes—regional funds, social funds, the so-called integrated Mediterranean programmes, and so on—have multiplied. Such tasks have not fallen within the natural range of aspirations or capacities of the Ministry of Foreign Affairs. The MFA is best suited to identifying the Italian interest on large but relatively non-technical issues. It has little expertise to deal with complex issues in the area of health, veterinary controls, product standards, public procurement law, and so on. It can partially compensate for its own shortcomings in these areas by co-opting experts from specialist ministries into the Italian Permanent Delegation in Brussels, but it still cannot take responsibility

for following these issues through their stages of domestic implementation, once agreed at Community level. In short, while the MFA may
be a good channel for the external projection of Italy's interests, it has
neither the resources to undertake the internal task of reform, nor an
immediate institutional interest in doing so.

Since 1980, therefore, a new mechanism has gradually been
developed to assist EC policy-making, in the shape of the *Department
for the Co-ordination of European Community Policies*. This department,
nominally responsible to the prime minister and headed by a minister
without portfolio, is charged with the task of co-ordinating the
activities of all ministries whose fields of competence lie at least partly
in the European area. The choice of the 'minister without portfolio'
approach to policy co-ordination is not necessarily the most efficient,
however. The device has a rather patchy history in post-war Italy, and
the European Co-ordination Department and its minister have been
no exception to this.[14] It is small, and lacks permanent staff,
administrative authority, and other resources with which to control the
ministries nominally under its co-ordinating powers. It is not a full
ministry in a legal sense, nor is there even a formal obligation on a
prime minister to appoint a politician, as opposed to an official, or
indeed the minister of Foreign Affairs himself, to head the Department, although the prime minister would probably be unwise not to
appoint a politician.

Politically, moreover, the post of minister for European Co-
ordination has rarely been held by a heavyweight. Most incumbents
need strong political backing from the prime minister to be successful,
but this is only likely to be forthcoming if the two are from the same
party, and mostly this is not the case. Moreover, although in formal
terms the Department is under the direct authority of the prime
minister's office, it has tended—like all agencies headed by ministers
without portfolio—to act as a ministry in its own right, albeit one
without an effective staff or structure.

The Department for the Co-ordination of European Community
Policies thus had great difficulty, during the 1980s, in establishing
itself as the real motor of Italy's European Community policy-making
machinery. Initially it did not even represent Italy in any external
arena, such as meetings of the European Council of Ministers. As its
first title—the Department for '*internal* co-ordination'—made clear, it
had to confine itself to internal issues mainly in the area of the
implementation into national law of Community directives. Only since
the mid-1980s has the European Co-ordination minister been allowed
to represent Italy in meetings of the European 'Internal-Market'

Council. Moreover, his Department has to carry out its allotted task with meagre resources. It is housed in cramped conditions which contrast extremely unfavourably with those of full ministries, or with the central sections of the prime minister's office. Until the 1988 reform of the latter, there could be no permanent staff on the payroll at the managerial level since, being a department of the prime minister's office, it had no budget, and no basis on which permanent staff could be recruited. The Department was thus staffed by the time-honoured principle of secondment from other parts of the public sector, but finding top-quality staff in this way, for a department with little prestige and an uncertain future, was not easy. Staff morale and self-confidence have inevitably suffered. Given how much the Department's success depended upon the capacity to persuade (rather than command) other ministries to follow its lead, these problems were a serious impediment.

The Department also sufers from the lack of close links with Italy's Permanent Delegation in Brussels. The latter is, for all member states, a vital link between the core EC decision-making machinery of the Commission and the Council of Ministers, on the one side, and national governments, on the other. National-government officials and ministers naturally come to Brussels on a regular basis for meetings in their areas of competence, but much of the preparatory work for such meetings, and all the regular monitoring of the Commission's managerial and administrative activity, are carried out by the Permanent Delegation.[15] Italy has a Delegation of some forty to fifty staff members. Just under half are from the Ministry of Foreign Affairs. Until recently, none were from the Department for European Co-ordination. Part of the reason for this seems to have been the chronic shortage of staff with which the Department has had to struggle, and part has been a deliberate policy of exclusion, encouraged by a Ministry of Foreign Affairs which sees itself as the sole legitimate organizer and co-ordinator of Italian interests outside national territory.[16]

Only in the late 1980s, in the wake of mounting concern about the growing backlog in the translation of Community directives into national law, did a more serious attempt to strengthen the Department get under way. It took the form of a series of new items of legislation: the 1988 reform of the presidency of the Council of Ministers itself (discussed in Chapter 7), various decrees issued in pursuance of that reform, and two successive laws—one in 1987, another in 1989—seeking to speed up the translation of EC directives into Italian law.[17] The 1987 legislation employed a number of devices to clear the backlog of EC directives. These included a new form of administrative delegation enabling individual departments to issue decrees giving force to Community directives. However, their main effect was specific to the list of directives appended to the legislation itself; they had rather little general applicability. The 1987 legislation also contained other strategies to improve co-ordination. It assigned to *CIPE*, the interministerial committee for economic planning, the tasks of setting out guidelines for Italy's overall Community policy, improving mechanisms for the rapid expenditure of Community resources accruing to Italy,[18] and monitoring the progress of the implementation into Italian law of EC directives. In this task, CIPE was to work closely with two other interministerial committees (CIPI—industrial policy— and CIPES—external trade policy). The minister for European Policy Co-ordination was made a member of all three interministerial committees. His Department was also given several other new tasks. These included regular stimulus to individual ministries to report on progress on EC policy initiatives in their area; regular reporting to Parliament and subnational government on EC matters; and co-ordination of the presentation to Parliament of bills implementing Community directives, particularly in the area of the internal market. Most ambitiously of all, the minister was to head, and his Department supply the secretariat for, a grand consultative committee composed of senior civil servants drawn from virtually all government departments, which would act as an administrative clearing house for the multitude of delays hitherto experienced in implementing Community law.

However, the legal complications of administrative discretion in implementing EC law proved greater than had been foreseen, and the inertia of Italian ministries proved far stronger than the drafters of the legislation allowed for. Moreover, the grand consultative committee proved such an unwieldy instrument that it never met. The 1987 legislation was thus enhanced, two years later, by the so-called *legge comunitaria*, which was based on the application of a different principle—the idea of a special timetabled parliamentary session—already tried in the field of budgetary politics. It introduced a fixed timetable for the annual passage of all outstanding Community legislation requiring translation into national law.[19] It required the government to submit a package proposal to Parliament between 31 January and 1 March every year, containing timetabled deadlines for legislative implementation, and granting the government the authority to complete the process through decree. This delegated authority covered not just new measures, but the power to remove from the statute book legislation incompatible with the supremacy of Community law. It complemented other recently introduced efforts to simplify the Italian legislative process and overcome the extreme legalism and rigidity of the public administration.[20]

As to the reform of the prime minister's office, this, as we have seen in Chapter 7, was a complex, multi-purpose document, only a small part of which dealt with European co-ordination, but it did at least have the merit of endowing the Department with a permanent status, even if not yet that of a full ministry. Moreover, by providing the prime minister's office with permanent staff and its own budget, the reform could eventually improve the resources available to co-ordinating agencies inside Palazzo Chigi, such as the European Co-ordination Department. However, the implementation of the reform has, as we have also seen, been painfully slow.[21] Part of the difficulty in its effective implementation has been that it has proved difficult and sensitive to recruit *new* staff with the requisite administrative experience into the prime minister's office. Those appointments which have been made have tended to convert into permanent staff those already inside the office on secondment. Two years after the reform few, if any, new staff had been allocated to the European Co-ordination Department. Certainly, staffing of the Department remains inadequate to the tasks allocated by the decrees setting out the Department's role and internal structure. Its internal structure, as described in the most recent decree issued by the prime minister's office,[22] consists of six main areas of activity: the internal market; fiscal harmonization; social and cultural activities, and links with local government; the integrated Mediterranean programmes; communications and new-technologies policy; and general and administrative affairs. Each of the six areas is itself divided into at least three subsections making a total of eighteen, a figure considerably in excess of the number of senior-level officials available in the Department. While such fundamental problems persist, the prospect of turning the Department into a powerful and authoritative co-ordinating mechanism across the range of Italian government departments seems remote.

Conclusion

In many dimensions of its linkages with the European Community, it would be unfair to single out Italy for special criticism. In all European states—even those like Italy apparently most committed to European integration—the political linkages between Community and state running through the European Parliament, as opposed to the administrative ones operating through the Permanent Delegation in

Brussels, and through national representatives in the Council of Ministers, are weak. This reflects the generally low saliency of European Community issues in national politics, and the low visibility and decision-making status of the European Parliament. Admittedly, in Italy voters in elections to the European Parliament tend to vote along lines decided essentially by national political issues,[23] and even the high-profile national political leaders who sit in the European Parliament do so mainly for reasons of domestic political prestige, and keep their seats (and their main political role) in the Italian Parliament. But in this respect Italy is little different from other EC member states.

The real problem for Italy is to ensure that its political system can cope with both the policy-making and administrative demands placed upon it by the process of integration. If it cannot, it will undermine the concept of a single internal market, and will be identified as an area of the Community in which normal internal-market rules do not fully operate. The problem, in turn, for the Community arising from this is to ensure that the EC's own policies are not, by default, undermined by Italy's difficulties in complying with them. If the Community cannot ensure this, its aims, particularly in the area of monetary integration, will be undermined by Italy's budget deficit. Either it will have to change its own self-imposed rules on the parameters national budget deficits, inflation rates, and interest rates must meet before each member state may participate in its planned common currency area, or it will have to accept that the Italian economy will be excluded from that area.

The lesson for Italy from these difficulties is clearly that major overhaul of administrative procedures, policy co-ordination, and national budgetary politics are all urgently required. The needs are widely recognized, and the hope is frequently expressed that the exigencies of Community membership will force such reform on the national political system. In the area of the budget deficit, such hopes may eventually be justified, because participation in a common currency area—which all major Italian social actors appear to agree is desirable—may one day become an all-or-nothing issue. Even in this area, however, the pressure on Parliament to reform its budgetary behaviour has so far been inadequate, and success may depend on a far wider change to the institutional order, generating more cohesive governments. As for the broader problems of independent departmental administrations, slow procedural adaptation, and the general difficulty of linking the strategic aims in Community policy-making of several different ministries, progress to date has been slow. Piecemeal reform, as we have seen, is having some effects, but here too, until wider political reform generates more cohesive governments, the political impetus to such reform may be crucially lacking.

CONCLUSION
The Limited Scope for Reform

Defining the problem

That Italy has established a system of liberal-democratic government that has survived numerous challenges, has been extended in various directions, and has enabled the country to integrate fully into the democracies of the European Community is clearly the most significant fact of post-war Italian history. By most formal standards, contemporary Italy has a sophisticated and complex democratic system. It has entrenched civil and social rights. It has extensive checks and balances against the abuse of majoritarian power. It has well-tried mechanisms giving citizens and interest groups access to those who govern. It has an articulated system of devolved power at regional, provincial, and local level. In long-term perspective, criticism of the way in which democracy in modern Italy now operates must be set against the background of those achievements.

Nevertheless, as the democratic system has been consolidated, critics of its practical operation (though not, on the whole, critics of democracy itself) have become increasingly vociferous, and a widely accepted case has emerged for some change in the balance between, on the one hand, the system of democratic openness and procedural guarantees, and, on the other, government stability and programmatic purposiveness. The outcome of the 1992 general election—a clear defeat for the main parties of the political establishment—is best interpreted in this vein.

The case for institutional reform rests upon the changed circumstances in which Italian democracy functions. While democracy was fragile, there was a fear that the system would lose support, and lapse into divisive conflicts over alleged authoritarianism in government, unless political life stuck fairly closely to procedures that were at least in a formal sense both politically liberal (i.e. restrictive of the use of executive power) and inclusive of a wide range of parties. In recent years, however, the prevailing fear has begun to run in the opposite direction: that democracy may lose support *unless* it can cut through its power-dispersing, liberal-guarantee mentality in order to deliver greater purpose and direction in government policy. Moreover, as the scope of government has grown, so has the need for greater allocative efficiency in the use of public resources. Here too, more selectivity seems to be required in the construction of government programmes. Such allocative efficiency can only be achieved at the expense of many of the public-sector employment lobbies and state-dependent beneficiaries which have grown up in Italy's highly bargained system of open and inclusive pluralist democracy.

The most fundamental problem of the contemporary Italian political system may thus be said to stem from its poor *aggregative* capacities. The democratic framework allows for the extensive articulation of political demands, but it is less satisfactory in combining these demands into an effective programme. Government policies are constructed on the basis of incrementalism and inclusion, rather than clear choice and selectivity. This problem is present in both political parties and formal institutions of government. It begins in the complexities of interest-group representation, with both public- and private-sector interests articulated on a highly disaggregated basis. It is manifest in the party system, where not only is the number of parties high, but so too is the internal fragmentation of some of the most important individual parties—most notably the Christian Democrats. It is reflected in Parliament, especially in the lack of discipline and cohesion of the governing coalition. It is highly visible even in the Council of Ministers, where individual ministers make few efforts to conceal differences of view with their colleagues. And it is present in the administrative world, where the division of decision-making into discrete policy communities is marked in relation to most other European societies.

The consequences of this failure of political aggregation are widely lamented. The unimpeded access to party leaderships, members of Parliament, the government, and the bureaucracy enjoyed by a wide range of interest groups may be desirable in principle, but in practice overloads the decision-making process, preventing any clear link between electoral choice and policy output. The articulation of such demands in a complex society needs to pass through an effective filtering mechanism that reconciles competing claims, places them in priority order, and ensures that that ordering receives some form of electoral endorsement. Such a filter needs to ensure that open access does not facilitate or encourage the artificial creation of state-dependent interests and lobbies. Moreover, the low barrier to the entry of new political movements and parties encourages the fragmentation of representation, giving a further premium to interest articulation over interest aggregation and co-ordinated policy response. Extensive legal and constitutional checks and guarantees, when deployed against a government with only weak capacities to aggregate interests and pursue a programme, further undermine the coherence of government policy.

Defining the remedy

Setting out the problems in this way might seem to make the remedies self-evident. Government needs to be better protected from the undifferentiated demands of society. It requires the time granted by greater coalition stability to devise long-term solutions to policy problems. It requires enhanced cohesion, more stable and authoritative leadership, and a changed relationship between itself and the parliamentary majority on which it is built. This almost certainly requires in turn some reduction in the number of parties, and some increase in the internal cohesion of those that remain. In short, it almost certainly requires electoral reform, and, as the debate of the last decade has shown, the biggest obstacle to electoral reform is the interests of the parties which would have to implement it. This obstacle defeated the Bozzi Commission in the 1983–7 Parliament, as it defeated the party and government leaders of the 1987–92 Parliament.[1] And the 1992 general election showed the difficulty of doing so through the ballot box. An electorate which seemed to want less party fragmentation in Parliament, and more cohesion and purpose in government, ended up voting into being a Parliament more fragmented by some way than any of the previous ten legislatures, and one in which agreement on the creation of an enduring governing formula, let alone decisive institutional reform, seemed likely to be extremely difficult.

However, the problem posed by the fact that different parties propose different types of electoral reform is not the only difficulty. Even if the parties were forced to agree on new institutional rules behind a veil of ignorance about the balance of party advantage which would result, it is far from clear what the precise effect of given procedural reforms would be. It is one thing for political scientists to conceptualize the defects of the system in particular ways; it is quite another to deduce the implications of that conceptualization for institutional reform. How any particular electoral system interacts with a given party system depends on the political conditions in which it is introduced. The debate on the impact of electoral systems on party system format has generated few firm conclusions among exponents of comparative politics. For every tentative generalization there are numerous counter-examples. In Italy itself, the case of the preference-vote mechanism is a cautionary tale in this regard. Introduced as a means of weakening the expected hold of strong party organizations over who was elected to Parliament by offering voters a role in this process, the device proved to have profoundly deleterious consequences for party cohesion. It encouraged candidates to inflate party membership rolls with faction-followers, and to use the patronage potential of the public sector to create reserves of loyal supporters ready to concentrate their preference votes on particular candidates.[2]

If this uncertainty applies to relatively minor elements of the electoral system, it also applies to the effects of its central characteristics—most notably the degree of proportionality. The pure proportionalism of the Italian system has often been singled out as its most undesirable property, and one which has had a particularly damaging effect in the last ten to fifteen years, as the hold of the major parties has declined, and new political movements have sprung up. Certainly, from the point of view of government stability, it seems undesirable that the entry threshold for new political parties is low. As new movements spring up—especially short-term protest movements—they can field candidates and gain entry to Parliament all the more easily when the threshold is as low as it is in Italy. To the extent that they gain votes at the expense of the parties of the governing coalition, they undermine the coalition's cohesion and resolve.

This has become an increasingly serious problem since the mid-1970s. Until then, the party system showed, if anything, a tendency towards rationalization behind the two largest parties. Over the last fifteen years, however, what might be described as a 'new fragmentation' has emerged, increasing the fear of electoral losses on the part of the established parties. By the 1992 election, this tendency had become very serious. A group of parties none of which existed before 1968 had, by the early 1990s, over 20 per cent of the popular vote. To this extent, in so far as it is legitimate to suppress spontaneous developments in the electorate in the interests of the cohesion of the governing coalition, the case for some limits on the extent of proportionality has increased substantially.

How might such suppression be achieved, assuming it to be a legitimate goal? If the aim is to dilute but not abandon altogether the proportionality principle, one method is through the introduction of a threshold of representation like that in Germany or Sweden. These countries have requirements that parties obtain a given percentage share of their national electorate (respectively, 5 and 4 per cent) for participation in the proportional distribution of parliamentary seats. An alternative method of partial dilution would be through a reduction in the size of Italian constituencies, and the abolition of the system of 'remainders'. The latter, in Italy, are notionally 'wasted' votes, which either fail to secure parties any seats at constituency level (because the party has failed to reach the quota required for even its first seat in a given constituency), or which exceed the quota, but are insufficient to reach it a second or subsequent time to win further seats. Such remainders are aggregated at national level to increase proportionality, and naturally benefit the smaller parties, which in all but the largest constituencies do not reach the quota required to win even one seat.[3]

However, the case for reducing the extent of proportionality is by no means straightforward. First, a threshold could not so justifiably be raised against parties with marked concentrations of territorial strength. Exclusion thresholds may be legitimate when targeted against parties with electoral support spread evenly and thinly across the nation. They are harder to justify when aimed against parties that secure representation outright in particular constituencies or regions. That form of exclusion would disenfranchise very large numbers of voters in such constituencies, even if it did not do so nationally, and these voters are likely to form a group with a special, potentially even violent, sense of grievance at such exclusion. Secondly, small parties always have the option of presenting joint slates of candidates to overcome the threshold. Admittedly, this might not help new movements since they would be less willing, and probably less able, to merge their identity with another party. Even for established parties, a joint list of candidates may alienate some voters from each party, and attract few new ones to replace them. Nevertheless, it remains true that the precise route by which small parties might be excluded through higher exclusion thresholds is an uncertain one. Electoral coalitions may quite easily overcome such a barrier.

This is one reason why some proponents of electoral reform advocate not simply a limitation on the extent of proportionality, but a more drastic step: a move straight to the so-called 'first-past-the-post' system used in the United Kingdom, based on single-vote, simple-plurality, single-member constituencies. Certainly, this system would encourage voters to line up behind three or at most four of the largest parties, although it is most unlikely that it would simplify political life to a straight *two-party* system. This is because, apart from the DC, even the largest Italian parties do not get very large shares of the vote. The system could thus quite easily generate a Christian Democrat landslide majority, while dispersing votes to several different opposition parties. In the most recent (1992) Italian general election, the second largest party, the PDS, won a mere 16 per cent of the vote. It would thus be very difficult for the PDS (even without the handicap of being a former 'communist' party) to dominate the opposition, and hence act as a magnet for voters looking for an alternative single-party government. It would be no easier for the third largest party, the PSI, to do so either, even if a degree of bipolarity in the system might be expected to generate some redistribution of votes between the parties of the centre-left.

However, an even more fundamental objection to the thesis that pure proportionalism is the root cause of party-system fragmentation and weak government is that frequently it does not really seem to be small parties—whether those in the coalition or those outside it—which generate the instability in Italian coalitions. More powerful factors, it may be argued, lie, first, in the conflict inside the governing coalition between the two largest parties and, secondly, in the tensions *inside* the largest of these two: the Christian Democrat Party. The fact that there can be no alternation in power, and hence that almost irrespective of how badly these inter- and intra-party tensions reflect on the coalition, that coalition cannot be removed from office, further weakens the disincentives to indiscipline within government ranks. Indeed, even if the first-past-the-post system did result in a Christian Democrat majority government, it is far from clear that this would lead to stable, effective, and purposive government. It would depend on the nature of both the Christian Democrat Party and the state of the opposition. If the DC were faced with a divided opposition, then a simple-plurality, single-member electoral system could make the party even more complacent about the dangers of being voted out of power than under the existing system.

Moreover, a more far-reaching impact of introducing a 'first-past-the-post' electoral system in Italy than the reduction in the number of parties, even if that also occurred, could well be a form of entrepreneurial constituency individualism similar to that practised in the United States. Italian parties, especially those in government, have weak programme-building capacities and loose ideological identities. At the local level there is already a great deal of personalism, most notably in the southern half of the country, and this might well increase with single-member constituencies, particularly if electoral volatility and declining partisan identification were to increase. Senators and deputies could well run the same sort of highly personal and individual electoral campaigns operated by their American counterparts. The fact that in Britain this sort of individualism does not result from single-member constituencies is only in part attributable to the cohesion and discipline imposed by a parliamentary system of government (as opposed to the separation of powers present in the United States). It also depends on a range of other historical and contextual variables determining the way in which both candidates and voters perceive the meaning of elections, and these might well not apply to a modern Italian electorate unused to strong party discipline and programmatic purpose.

These considerations underline the importance of identifying exactly what problems electoral reform is intended to remedy. The ills that are said to stem from *partitocrazia* are often defined with too little precision. The term is generally associated with over-mighty party rule, but even if Italian parties are *strong vis-à-vis* Parliament and government, they are extremely weak as bearers of coherent programmes. In many respects, as in the United States, they are merely *arenas* in which real interests compete for power and resources. Under the existing electoral system that competition is not limited to party congresses or party executives (and resolved there through the production of a coherent programme); it spills out into all other political arenas in which parties are present, and is exacerbated by the combination of multi-member constituencies, party lists, and preference voting. The costs of *partitocrazia* might thus best be countered by a *strengthening* of parties rather than by their weakening. The goal would be to limit conflict over political resources (jobs, spending programmes, etc.) and give parties stronger programmatic identities in the eyes of voters, thereby ensuring that the latter choose programmes rather than individual candidates.

It could thus be argued that the aim of electoral reform should be less to water down the purity of proportional representation than to encourage alternation in government, or the serious prospect of it. This would force the governing parties to act with greater discipline and cohesion, on pain of being removed from office altogether. Such a goal lies at the heart of proposals for reform aimed at the creation of some form of 'pledge' by the parties of a governing coalition to the electorate, increasing the extent to which the electorate feels it has 'chosen' a particular government and its policies, and thus committing those parties to see the programme through.

The form such a pledge might take varies. For some, it is best achieved by making a proportion of seats in Parliament dependent on the outcome of a second ballot. This would take place after the majority of seats had been allocated in a first ballot based on proportional representation. In such a system, parties or coalitions of parties would compete against one another, and the coalition winning the largest number of votes (above a given threshold) would earn a premium of additional seats. The runner-up too would receive a premium, albeit much smaller. Such a system, it is claimed, would enhance coalition stability not just by increasing the number of seats available to the governing majority, but, more importantly, by forcing parties to co-operate together, and to differentiate themselves into competing groups: 'government' and 'eligible opposition'. Voters would then have a clear choice in elections. Under some proposals, moreover, they would be given a chance to pronounce on the outcome of a political crisis, since, if the coalition which won the majoritarian premium should collapse, Parliament would be dissolved.

This form of second ballot is clearly very different from that employed in French parliamentary elections. There, if no candidate wins an absolute majority, there is a second-ballot run-off. Candidates that obtain a given percentage in the first ballot (currently 12.5 per cent of the electorate) may run, although the system contains clear incentives to parties to conclude stand-down agreements, and this in turn, particularly when added to the polarizing effects of a directly elected executive presidency, provides a key incentive to government-opposition bipolarity, even though in numerical terms the system remains multi-party. The French system has its proponents in Italy too, and, as in the case of the 'majority-premium' version of the second ballot considered above, the aim is to increase bipolarity, and hence give the voter a clear choice between programmes, and the opportunity to cast a fresh electoral verdict in the event of a government crisis. Whether, without the direct election of an executive president, it would have the effect it appears to have had in France is, of course, much debated, as is the nature of party alliances and the extent to which parties which had participated in second-ballot arrangements (or indeed in first-ballot ones) would feel obliged to pursue such alliances throughout the life of a Parliament.

Partly because of doubts about the disciplining effects of such arrangements, other observers have explored the possibility of reinforcing the government through some form of indirect or even direct electoral investiture of the head of government, or the head of state. Several possibilities have been advanced. One, linked to the proposal discussed above for a second ballot allocating a premium of seats to the largest coalition of parties, simply adds the name of a proposed prime minister to the proposed coalition (rather as in the case of Germany's informal 'chancellor candidacies'). If the chosen prime minister were subsequently brought down by his/her coalition majority, a general election would automatically be held. Parliament could not chose a new government and prime minister without further electoral ratification of the change. Other proposals entail a closer parallel with Germany, making the parliamentary vote of confidence in an incoming government a vote of confidence in a prime minister and his/her programme. Some also advocate a 'constructive vote of no confidence' by which the prime minister can only be removed from office if Parliament can agree simultaneously on his/her replacement.

Just because the probability of such arrangements working in Italy's fragmented parliamentary spectrum is limited (it has never been established that post-war Germany's political stability owes much to such arrangements either), the debate in Italy on direct election has focused more on the president than the prime minister. Here too, however, there has been much ambiguity in the proposals advanced, since few Italians seriously entertain the possibility of abandoning a parliamentary system in favour of a fully presidential one, based on the separation of powers. Yet if a directly elected president is to preside over a semi-presidential system such as that in France, the retention of a prime-ministerial government and a parliamentary majority requires the sort of congruence between presidential and parliamentary majorities that even France, in the last decade, has been unable to guarantee. The prospect of such congruence being delivered by Italian voters in the electoral conditions of the 1990s thus seems remote. What role might be available to a directly elected Italian president is thus unclear, although it should be noted that one observer—Giovanni Sartori—has advanced an imaginative, albeit ambiguous, hybrid scheme by which government would, during the life of any Parliament, automatically change from a parliamentary to a presidential basis after two successive (parliamentary) governments had lost their majorities.[4]

The limits of institutional reform

It is evident from even the cursory outline of the debate on institutional reform provided here that, among academics as among practising politicians, there is little agreement about the sort of electoral reform that would introduce greater cohesion, purpose, and discipline in parliamentary majorities and governments. The socio-psychological conditions under which political actors feel constrained to act in a cohesive and purposive manner are complex, and it is by no means clear that they can be generated by institutional engineering at the electoral level alone. In the debate on reform attention has been concentrated so much at that level because it seems the central one in giving a programmatic government the authority to govern effectively: to contain public spending, to improve fiscal yields, to increase public-sector productivity, to enhance the quality of public services in areas such as health, education, justice, and so on. Only authoritative governments, liberated from daily pressures to compromise their objectives coming from parliamentary back-benchers and party secretariats, it is supposed, can deliver this sort of improvement in the quality of government output.

However, in order to put itself in such a position of authority, a government needs some form of explicit electoral backing. It requires the legitimation of a clear electoral mandate, and it is far from certain that any of the proposals alluded to above can provide this in contemporary Italy. The process of interest representation is fragmented not just because the party system is fragmented, but also because the interests to be represented are themselves fragmented. The only thing that unites the electorate appears to be a sense that the country is not well served by its existing political class and party system. But between north and south, public sector and private sector, between moderate left and moderate right, the employed and the self-employed, core workers and the young and ageing unemployed, taxpayers and welfare beneficiaries, and so on, there is no clear political project. Indeed, as the distinction between left and right has become more blurred, and as the politics of anti-system extremism is undercut by a growing consensus over the desirability of maintaining market-economy rules in a European Community framework, the scope for a mobilizing policy programme seems to be becoming narrower.

The general election of 1992 underlined this point clearly. An electorate evidently dissatisfied with the performance of the governing parties generated desertions not just from the four parties of the governing coalition but also from the main party of the opposition; yet that electorate signally failed to find a clear outlet for its dissatisfaction. The beneficiaries of the protest—northern leagues, Sicily's *Rete*, the Greens, *Rifondazione comunista*, and a range of other forms of protest—could not possibly form the basis of an alternative political élite to the established parties. The dispersal of votes in so many directions emphasized the fact that a dissatisfied electorate is not necessarily one with a clear idea of what it wants. Indeed, in the campaign for referendum-driven institutional reforms led by Christian Democrat Mario Segni, there was clear evidence that such campaigns of anti-establishment dissatisfaction could be conducted on behalf of the establishment itself!

In short, there is no party or individual capable of giving a clear lead. This is not to say that institutional reform will not be forthcoming. In the wake of the 1992 election it looked more likely than at any time over the previous decade that the governing parties themselves would finally take a lead. But the beneficiaries of such reform, in the short term and in the absence of a credible counter-élite, were likely to be the established parties themselves. And such parties, as previous coalitions had shown, straddle too many of the diverse interests identified above to be capable of making clear choices. Beyond a diffuse desire for better government, the electorate is incapable of making these choices for the parties. And behind their own diffuse desire to respond to the demand for better government, government ministers continue to be subject to a wide range of back-bench, constituency, and party pressures. As for the back-benchers and party officials themselves, they are unlikely to feel any great pressure from constituency party members or from voters to alter their ways in order to help government leaders. Their behavioural traits seem too deeply conditioned by the cultural style of four decades of party and parliamentary brokerage to change on the basis of new electoral rules. Things might alter if Italy could generate a new political party whose parliamentary and local leaders were socialized into different habits. This, and the personal leadership of de Gaulle, was what helped change parliamentary behaviour between the Fourth and Fifth French republics. But in Italy, the leagues notwithstanding, there is no such new party in sight. Reforms must therefore cope with the existing political class, or at best with one which is slowly renewing itself, but in which the existing generation's survival profoundly affects the climate in which the new generation is socialized into parliamentary life.

Even a successfully renewed political class, moreover, has to come to terms with public-sector personnel who, in Italy's rigid labour market, are highly unlikely to be prepared for an administrative revolution paralleling one in Parliament and the parties. The sorts of reforms that a purposive and responsible programmatic government might pursue—more cost-effective and better-quality public services especially—entail a thoroughgoing change in attitudes to training, job-security, incentives, flexibility in the deployment of resources, etc., that takes many years to work through, and certainly does not come automatically in the wake of one-off institutional reform of the type so widely discussed in recent years. This is not to say that progress is not being achieved towards these goals. As we have seen in Chapter 8, there has been a range of experiments with new administrative formulae. But, in comparison to most European administrative systems, the Italian public sector remains relatively backward.

The conclusion must therefore be that even if the profound shock of the 1992 election jolts the political class into institutional reform, the results to be expected from such reform are likely to be slow to emerge, and for the foreseeable future quite modest. The features of the Italian system of government as laid down since 1945 are now deeply ingrained, and reflect an electorate which, while enjoying a high if unevenly distributed standard of living, contains within it many contradictory needs and pressures. Those pressures are no longer, as they were in 1945, so powerful, and so much in opposition to one another, that a complex and bargained system of pluralist intermediation unlike any other in democratic Europe is necessary. But, even if no longer potentially violent, such pressures remain sufficiently diffuse and complex to make clear electoral choice difficult, and its effective implementation improbable. There are many worse fates than the politics of bargained pluralism that Italy has practised for the past four decades. The *dirigisme* of more purposive systems further north in Europe is by no means without its costs. But Italians who nevertheless anticipate the imminent arrival of some of that *dirigisme* may discover that it takes more than a new electoral law or a constitutional amendment to bring it as far south as Rome.

Notes

Introduction

1. Camera dei deputati/senato della repubblica, *Relazione della Commissione parlamentare per le riforme istituzionali*, IX legislature, doc. XVI-*bis*, no. 3, vols. i, ii, iii (Rome, 1985).
2. See David Hine, 'Thirty Years of the Italian Constitution: Governability and Constitutional Reform', *Parliamentary Affairs*, 34/1 (1981), 63–80.
3. See Joseph LaPalombara, *Democracy: Italian Style* (New Haven, Conn. 1987).
4. Ibid. 229–57.
5. Sidney Tarrow, 'Italian Politics and Political Change: "Eppure si muove." But where to?', *West European Politics*, 11/3 (1988), 311–24.
6. See LaPalombara, *Democracy*, 160–5.
7. Alessandro Pizzorno, 'Uno schema teorico per un analisi dei partiti politici italiani', in Paolo Farneti (ed.), *Il sistema politico italiano* (Bologna, 1973), 241–60.

Chapter 1

1. For an introduction to this complex issue, see Giuliano Procacci, *History of the Italian People* (London, 1968), esp. chs. 2–6.
2. See P. Villani, "Gruppi sociali e classe dirigente all' indomani dell'Unità, in *Storia d'Italia: Annali*, i (Turin, 1978), 881–978.
3. See Martin Clark, *Modern Italy, 1971–1982* (London, 1984), esp. chs. 2 and 6.
4. See A. C. Jemolo, *Church and State in Italy 1850–1950* (Oxford, 1960); also Clark, *Modern Italy*, 81–8.
5. On the historical origins of Italian public administration see Piero Calandra, *Storia dell'amministrazione pubblica in Italia* (Bologna, 1978), esp. chs. 1–6.
6. The left–right distinction is here used in its 'historic' or pre-class sense, to distinguish between political liberals and political conservatives. For a succinct account of parliamentary politics in this period see Clark, *Modern Italy*, 61–6.
7. On the origins of the Italian Socialist Party see Gaetano Arfè, *Storia del socialismo italiano, 1892–1926* (Turin, 1965), also Alexander de Grand, *The Italian Left in the Twentieth Century: A History of the Socialist and Communist Parties* (Bloomington, Ind., Indiana University Press, 1989).
8. On political Catholicism in liberal Italy see Jemolo, *Church and State*, 50–91.

9. See Francesco Gaetà, *Il nazionalismo italiano* (Naples, 1965).

10. The literature on the fall of the liberal state is voluminous. For an introduction see Adrian Lyttleton, *The Seizure of Power* (London, 1973).

11. See Denis Mack Smith, *Mussolini's Roman Empire* (London, 1976).

12. See P. Vannicelli, *Italy, NATO, and the EEC* (Cambridge, Mass., 1974).

13. See David Conradt, 'The Changing German Political Culture', and Giacomo Sani, 'The Political Culture of Italy: Continuity and Change', both in G. Almond and S. Verba (eds.), *The Civic Culture Revisited* (Boston, 1980), respectively 212–72 and 273–324.

14. Details on several of these episodes, and on the right in Italian politics more generally, can be found in Piero Ignazi, *Il polo escluso: Profilo del Movimento sociale italiano* (Bologna, 1989).

15. The Concordat and Church–state relations under fascism are discussed in P. Kent, *The Pope and the Duce* (London, 1981).

16. The first revision, indeed, was not until the Villa Madama agreement of 18 Feb. 1986. See Silvio Ferrari, 'The New Concordat between Church and State', in R. Leonardi and R. Y. Nanetti (eds.), *Italian Politics: A Review*, vol. i (London, 1986), 134–45.

17. On the origins of the Italian state-holdings trusts see M. Posner and S. Woolf, *Italian Public Enterprise* (London, 1967).

18. The literature on the resistance is extensive. As an introduction see G. Quazza, 'The Politics of the Italian Resistance', in S. Woolf (ed.), *The Rebirth of Italy 1943–50* (London, 1972), 1–29.

19. See de Grand, *The Italian Left*, 81–99; Francesco Catalano, 'The Rebirth of the Party System 1944–48', in Woolf (ed.), *The Rebirth of Italy 1943–50*, 56–94.

20. The PCI's strategic moderation had origins in the earlier history of the party. It was rooted in Gramsci's analysis of Italian history, of the strength of particular Italian social institutions, and of the case for the phased establishment of a working-class 'hegemony', rather than a head-on confrontation with bourgeois power. Togliatti's ideas of a new 'mass' party, different from the traditionally conspiratorial Leninist model, and adapted to a strategy of non-violent socialist transformation, were presented as a direct development of such ideas. On these issues see G. Bocca, *Palmiro Togliatti* (Rome, 1973); G. Amyot, *The Italian Communist Party* (London, 1981); Joan Barth Urban, *Moscow and the Italian Communist Party* (London, 1986).

21. This section describes historical events determining the building of the new party system. Readers unfamiliar with Italian parties should read it in conjunction with ch. 3, which takes an analytical rather than development approach.

22. On these events see Francesca Taddei, *Il socialismo italiano del dopoguerra: Correnti ideologiche e scelte politiche, 1943–47* (Milan, 1984), and de Grand, *The Italian Left*, chs. 6 and 7.

23. See M. de Cecco, 'Economic Policy and the Reconstruction Period, 1945–51', in Woolf (ed.), *The Rebirth of Italy 1943–50*, 160–4.

24. On these issues see Paul Ginsborg, *A History of Contemporary Italy: Society and Politics 1943–1988* (London, 1990), 72–8, and John L. Harper, *America and the Reconstruction of Italy, 1945–48* (Cambridge, 1986).

Chapter 2

1. The periodization suggested here is the author's own. Where breaks should be placed between periods is somewhat arbitrary. A clear break in development is visible around 1963, but where the second division (set in this chapter for the purposes of exposition at 1975) should be placed is more debatable, as will become clear in the text. The literature on Italian post-war economic development in English is not voluminous, but cf. K. J. Allen and A. A. Stevenson, *An Introduction to the Italian Economy* (London, 1974); Gisele Podbielski, *Italy: Development and Crisis in the Postwar Economy* (Oxford, 1974). In recent years there have been no major specialized works, but useful material relevant to the issues treated here is to be found in Robert J. Flanagan, David W. Soskice, and Lloyd Ulman, *Unionism, Economic Stabilization, and Incomes Policies* (Washington, DC, 1983), esp. 496–566. In Italian, in addition to the annual reports of the Bank of Italy and *Confindustria*, a basic guide to the economy and policy management is V. Valli, *Politica economica: I modelli, gli strumenti, l'economia italiana* (Rome, 1988).

2. See Fabrizio Onida and Gianfranco Viesti (eds.), *The Italian Multinationals* (London, 1988).

3. See Allen and Stevenson, *An Introduction to the Italian Economy*, esp. ch. 4, from which much of the data in this paragraph is drawn.

4. On the development of the Italian labour movement see, *inter alia*, Peter R. Weitz, 'Labour and Politics in a Divided Movement: The Italian Case', *Industrial and Labor Relations Review*, 28/2 (1975), 226–42; Ida Regalia, Marino Regini, and Emilio Reyneri, 'Labour Conflicts and Industrial Relations in Italy', in Colin Crouch and Alessandro Pizzorno (eds.), *The Resurgence of Class Conflict in Western Europe since 1968*, i (national studies) (New York, 1978), ch. 4; and Miriam Golden, *Labor Divided: Austerity and Working-Class Politics in Contemporary Italy* (Ithaca, NY, 1988).

5. Allen and Stevenson, *An Introduction to the Italian Economy*, 117.

6. Ibid. 58.

7. On the history and development of Italian public enterprise see M. Posner and S. Woolf, *Italian Public Enterprise* (London, 1967); S. Holland (ed.), *The State as Entrepreneur* (London, 1972).

8. Podbielski, *Italy*, 137.

9. See esp. Paolo Saraceno, *Risultati e nuovi obbietivi dell'intervento straordinario* (Rome, 1970), and A. Graziani, *L'economia italiana: 1945–70* (Bologna, 1972).

10. On the Centre-Left see Paul Ginsborg, *A History of Contemporary Italy: Society and Politics 1943–1988* (London, 1990), 254–97.

11. Flanagan, Soskice, and Ulman, *Unionism*, 515.

12. On the reform programme of the Centre-Left see V. Parlato (ed.), *Spazio e ruolo del riformismo* (Bologna, 1974), and G. Tamburrano, *Storia e cronaca del centro-sinistra* (Milan, 1971).

13. Podbielski, *Italy*, 38.

14. On the build-up of labour tensions in the mid-1960s see Flanagan, Soskice, and Ulman, *Unionism*, 518–22.

15. See Michele Salvati, *Alle origini dell'inflazione italiana* (Bologna, 1979), 65–75.

16. See Regalia, Regini, and Reyneri, 'Labour Conflicts' ch. 4.; P. Lange, G. Ross, and M. Vannicelli, *Unions, Change, and Crisis: French and Italian Union Strategy and the Political Economy, 1945–80* (London, 1982), 97–206; D. Grisoni and H. Portelli, *Le lotte operaie in Italia dal 1960 al 1976* (Milan, 1977).

17. See Lange, Ross, and Vannicelli, *Unions, Change and Crisis*, 132–6.

18. See Federico Mancini, 'Lo Statuto dei lavoratori dopo le lotte operaie del 1969', in Enzo Bartocci, *Sindacato, classe, società* (Padua, 1975), 303–41.

19. See T. Treu (ed.), *L'uso politico dello Statuto dei lavoratori* (Bologna, 1975), also Lange, Ross, and Vannicelli, *Unions, Change, and Crisis*, 135–52.

20. See M. Golden, 'Neo-corporativismo ed esclusione della forza-lavoro dalla rappresentanza politica', in G. Pasquino (ed.), *Il sistema politico italiano* (Rome, 1985), 208–31, and her *Labor Divided*.

21. As is confirmed by the regular warnings inherent in successive reports on the Italian economy both by the OECD (see esp. OECD Economic Surveys, *Italy*) (Paris, 1975 and 1977), and the governor of the Bank of Italy (see Banca d'Italia, *Relazione annuale*, published annually following the governor's annual spring report).

22. On the leverage thus given to the PCI see, *inter alia*, Stephen Hellman, 'The Longest Campaign: Communist Party Strategy and the Election of 1976', in H. R. Penniman (ed.), *Italy at the Polls: The Parliamentary Elections of 1976* (Washington, DC, 1977), 155–80; cf. Joseph LaPalombara, 'Two Steps Forward, One Step Back: The PCI's Struggle for Legitimacy', in H. R. Penniman (ed.), *Italy at the Polls, 1979: A Study of the Parliamentary Elections* (Washington, DC, 1977), 104–40.

23. See Regalia, Regini, and Reyneri, 'Labour Conflicts', 110–116.

24. Renato Brunetta, *Spesa pubblica e conflitto* (Bologna, 1987).

25. The literature on this subject is extensive. See Carlo Carbone (ed.), *Classe e movimento in Italia 1970–1985* (Romei, 1986), esp. chs. by L. Gallino, 'L'evoluzione della struttura di classe in Italia'; A. Pizzorno, 'I ceti medi nei meccanismi del consenso'; M. Paci, 'Mercato del lavoro e struttura sociale'; A. Bagnasco, 'La struttura di classe nelle tre Italie'. See also P. Sylos Labini, *Le classi sociali negli anni '80* (Rome, 1986).

26. See Bruno Contini, *Lo sviluppo di un economia parallela: la segmentazione del mercato del lavoro in Italia e la crescita del settore irregolare* (Milan, 1979).

27. See Ernesto Longobardi, 'La politica fiscale', in Ugo Ascoli (ed.), *Welfare state all'italiana* (Rome, 1984), 119–52.

28. See ch. 6, pp. 180–7; also Brunetta, *Spesa pubblica*.

29. On perceptions of public policy in the sphere of macro-economic

management during this period see esp. Flanagan, Soskice, and Ulman, *Unionism*, 539–56.

30. The classic statement of this fear, from the Communist Party leadership, was the three articles written by the then party secretary, Enrico Berlinguer, in the wake of the Chilean coup: 'Riflessioni sull'Italia dopo i fatti del Cile', reprinted in E. Berlinguer, *La questione comunista* (Rome, 1975), 609–39.

31. On these issues see Ida Regalia, 'Le politiche del lavoro', in Ascoli, *Welfare state*, 53–86.

32. On these issues see Flanagan, Soskice, and Ulman, *Unionism*, 546–56; Peter Lange, 'Crisis and Consent, Change and Compromise: Dilemmas of Italian Communism in the 1970s', in Peter Lange and Sidney Tarrow, *Italy in Transition: Conflict and Consensus* (London, 1980), 110–32.

33. In the latter half of the 1980s, the growth of the small-firms sector may have been somewhat less rapid, as the major corporations themselves recovered their dynamism (although the 1991 census of production was incomplete at the time of publication). Moreover, given the areas in which small firms predominate—generally 'intermediate technology' sectors like leather goods, footwear, and textiles—they are susceptible to competition from newly industrializing countries. A degree of product differentiation (design, style, specialization etc.) can protect Italian producers from this competition, but not indefinitely. On the 'third Italy' and small-business phenomenon see, *inter alia*, C. Trigilia, *Grande partiti e piccole imprese* (Bologna, 1986); A. Bagnasco, 'Borghesia e classe operaia', in Ugo Ascoli and R. Catanzaro (eds.), *La società italiana degli anni ottanta* (Bari, 1987); M. Paci, *La struttura sociale italiana* (Bologna, 1982); G. de Rita, 'L'impresa famiglia', in P. Melograni and L. Scaraffia (eds.), *La famiglia italiana dall'ottocento a oggi* (Bari, 1988).

34. This predisposition to ideologically improbable social alliances (the so-called *via emiliana al socialismo*) is a much-discussed feature of the PCI's post-war political and social strategy. See, *inter alia*, S. Hellman, 'The PCI's Alliance Strategy and the Case of the Middle Classes', in D. L. M. Blackmer and S. Tarrow (eds.), *Communism in Italy and France* (Princeton, NJ, 1975), 373–419.

35. See, on the events of Sept. 1980, A. Baldissera, *La rivolta dei quarantamila: Dai quadri FIAT ai COBAS* (Milan, 1988).

36. See Lorenzo Bordogna, 'The COBAS Fragmentation of Trade-Union Representation and Conflict', in Robert Leonardi and Piergiorgio Corbetta (eds.), *Italian Politics: A Review*, iii (London, 1989), 50–65.

37. *OECD Economic Surveys: Italy, 1990/91*, (Paris, 1991) (statistical appendix).

38. See Aldo Piperno, 'La politica sanitaria', and Antonio Tosi, 'La politica della casa', both in Ascoli, *Welfare state*, 153–80 and 239–64.

39. By 1987, 95% of Italian families owned a television set, 75% a car, 90% a washing machine, and 95% a refrigerator. See Istituto centrale di statistica, *Sintesi di vita sociale* (Rome, 1990), 35–49.

40. See Clemente Lanzetti, 'Le famiglie nei censimenti', and Angelo Saporiti,

'Le strutture familiari', both in Istituto centrale di statistica/Associazione italiana di sociologia, *Immagini della società italiana* (Rome, 1988), 107–36 and 137–59.

41. On the immigration question see G. Cocchi (ed.), *Stranieri in Italia* (Bologna, 1990); also Emilio Reyneri, 'L'immigrazione extra-comunitaria in Italia: Prospettive, caratteristiche, politiche', *Polis*, 5/1 (1991), 145–55.

42. Fondazione CENSIS, *XXIV rapporto sulla situazione sociale del paese, 1990* (Rome, 1990), 48–50.

43. Data drawn from Commission of the European Communities, *Fourth Periodic Report on the Development of the Regions*, Com. (90) Final (Brussels, 9 Jan. 1990). It is notable that while 7 Italian regions figured in the bottom 50 (with less than 85% of EC GDP) France, Britain, and Germany each had only 1 region in this category—excluding, of course, the former territories of the GDR, and the French overseas territories.

44. In this respect, the parallel with the economies of former Central and East European states is striking. In both cases the problem is one of transforming an already industrialized economy towards levels of factor productivity comparable to those of the successful market economies, starting from a base line of very wide divergence.

45. See Guido Corso, 'L'intervento per il mezzogiorno', Progetto CER-CENSIS, *Pubblico e privato: Secondo rapporto CER-CENSIS sull'economia italiana*, i: *Mutazioni, confini, intrecci, modelli* (Milan, 1987), 469–86.

46. In the nation-wide 'ordinary' regional elections of 1990 local party lists began the run of remarkable successes that culminated in the general election of April 1992. See, on the 'league' phenomenon, R. Mannheimer, *La Lega lombarda* (Milan, 1991).

47. See Pizzorno, 'I ceti medi', 42–9; M. Paci (ed.), *Stato, mercato, e occupazione* (Bologna, 1985); F. Ferrarotti (ed.), *Mercato del lavoro, marginalità sociale, e struttura di classe* (Milan, 1978); F. Barbano (ed.), *Le frontiere delle città: Casi di marginalità e servizi sociali* (Milan, 1982).

48. See Corrado Barberis, *La società italiana: Redditi, occupazione, imprese* (Milan, 1985), 352–82.

49. Ibid. 10–11.

Chapter 3

1. See Gianfranco Pasquino, *Party Government in Italy: Achievements and Prospects*, The Johns Hopkins University Bologna Center Research Institute, Occasional Paper no. 48 (Jan. 1985).

2. See S. M. Lipset and S. Rokkan, 'Cleavage Structures, Party Systems, and Voter Alignments', in Peter Mair (ed.), *The West European Party System* (Oxford, 1990), 91–138.

3. As Prandi and Galli have shown in their analysis of electoral behaviour in the early post-war period, the continuity between the elections of 1919 and 1921 on the one hand, and 1946 and 1948 on the other, is striking. Despite the long fascist interlude and the 'resolution' of the church–state conflict, the organizational networks and the loyalties of the electorate

established before the March on Rome reappeared in 1945 on much the same lines. See A. Prandi and G. Galli, *Patterns of Political Participation in Italy* (New Haven, Conn., 1970).

4. See R. E. M. Irving, *The Christian Democrat Parties of Western Europe* (London, 1979).

5. For a succinct summary of the pillars on which Christian Democrat dominance in this region is built, see Percy Allum and Ilvo Diamanti, 'Ambiente sociale e comportamento elettorale nella provincia di Vicenza negli anni del primo dopoguerra', *Quaderni dell'Osservatorio elettorale*, 15 (July 1985), 65–140, but see also M. Caciagli, 'Erosione e mutamento dell'elettorato democristiano', in M. Caciagli and A. Spreafico (eds.), *Vent'anni di elezioni in Italia, 1968–87* (Padua, 1990), 3–30.

6. On the 'third Italy' see A. Bagnasco, *Tre Italie: La problematica territoriale nello sviluppo italiano* (Bologna, 1977), and C. Triglia, *Grandi partiti e piccole imprese* (Bologna, 1986).

7. See P. Allum, *Politics and Society in Postwar Naples* (Cambridge, 1973), esp. chs. 5, 8, 9.

8. See Sidney Tarrow, *Peasant Communism in Southern Italy* (New Haven, Conn., 1967).

9. The literature on this subject is now extensive. Two recent analyses, both with useful bibliographies, are F. Anderlini, 'Una modellizzazione per zone socio-politiche dell'Italia repubblicana', *Polis*, 1/3 (1987), 443–79, and R. Cartocci, 'Otto risposte a un problema: La divisione dell'Italia in zone politicamente omogenee', *Polis*, 1/3 (1987), 481–514.

10. Anderlini, 'Una modellizzazione', 474–6.

11. See ch. 4 below, for a description of the impact of the preference vote on party cohesion. In the referendum of 9–10 June 1991, the electorate voted (with 95% of voters supporting the change) to reduce the number of preferences each voter could cast to only one. Whether, as the promoters of the proposal argued, this would reduce internal conflict inside parties, and limit the struggle for political patronage, which the preference-vote mechanism is alleged to generate, remains to be seen.

12. The national constituency is however hypothetical rather than real; when its party composition has been calculated, its seats are allocated to candidates on party lists in the individual constituencies, in descending order of 'wasted' votes.

13. See Mogens Pedersen, 'Electoral Volatility in Western Europe 1948–77', in Mair, *The West European Party System*, 195–207.

14. See esp. M. Barbagli, P. Corbetta, A. Parisi, and H. M. A. Schadee, *Fluidità elettorale e classi sociali in Italia* (Bologna, 1979); P. Corbetta, A. Parisi, and H. M. A. Schadee, *Elezioni in Italia: Strutture e tipologia delle consultazioni politiche* (Bologna, 1988); Roberto Biorcio and Paolo Natale, 'Lo studio dei flussi elettorali: Questioni di principio e diagnostica delle distorsioni', *Polis*, 5/1 (1991), 121–38. The method used by proponents of this model identifies the characteristics of each polling station (past vote, social composition, etc.) in any pair of elections and, through

multiple regression analysis, claims to account for the degree of change imputed to each independent variable.

15. On changes in Italian turn-out, its cuases and effects, see Renato Mannheimer and Giacomo Sani, *Il mercato elettorale: Identikit dell'elettore italiano* (Bologna, 1987), esp. ch. 2; P. Nuvoli and A. Spreafico, 'Il partito del non voto', in Caciagli and Spreafico, *Vent'anni di elezioni in Italia*, 223–58.

16. Mannheimer and Sani estimated that among voters who in the 1983 general election had voted for one or other of the two major parties, Communists and Christian Democrats, a willingness to consider voting for the opposing party was limited to only 10% of the total 2-party vote of 23 million voters. Since this willingness was only hypothetical, and was almost equally divided between the voters of the two parties, it was improbable that direct 2-party competition could affect the distribution of support between the two in any dramatic way. See Mannheimer and Sani, *Il mercato elettorale*, 169–78.

17. In the same survey, Mannheimer and Sani estimated that nearly 6 million voters out of 16.3 million who had voted for either the Christian Democrats or Socialists were potentially open to the possibility of voting for the other party. And out of 15.2 million who had voted for either the Communists or Socialists, 5.3 million would be open to the possibility of voting for the other party. Ibid. 169–78.

18. See V. Capecchi, V. Cioni Polacchini, G. Galli, and G. Sivini, *Il comportamento elettorale in Italia* (Bologna, 1968).

19. Mannheimer and Sani, *Il mercato elettorale*, 89–101.

20. The evidence on secularization in Italian society is clear, taking the post-war period as a whole; this does not however automatically imply that the Christian Democrat Party itself has become a correspondingly less Catholic party. On this complex question see A. Parisi, 'Un partito di cattolici? L'appartenenza religiosa e i rapporti col mondo cattolico', in A. Parisi (ed.), *Democristiani* (Bologna, 1979), 85–152; also Robert Leonardi and Douglas Wertman, *Italian Christian Democracy: The Politics of Dominance* (London, 1989), esp. ch. 7.

21. Mannheimer and Sani, *Il mercato elettorale*, 92–3.

22. See A. Parisi and G. Pasquino, 'Changes in Italian Electoral Behaviour: The Relationships between Parties and Voters', *West European Politics*, 2/3 (1979), 6–30.

23. Altogether Craxi held office for 3 years and 9 months. The full list of governments since 1945 is set out in Appendix I.

24. See G. Sani and G. Sartori, 'Mass Constraints on Political Realignments: Perceptions of Anti-System Parties in Italy', in Hans Daalder and Peter Mair, *Western European Party Systems: Continuity and Change* (London, 1983), 322–3.

25. See also David Hine, 'The Consolidation of Democracy in Postwar Italy', in G. Pridham, *Securing Democracy: Political Parties and Democratic Consolidation in Southern Europe* (London, 1990), 62–83.

26. This is not always because they favour the dominant Christian Democrat Party. Many acts of presidential arbitration involve disputes over the allocation of power within the ruling Christian Democrat Party—an example of which was witnessed in the summer of 1987, following the general election of that year. President Cossiga's willingness to appoint as prime minister a Christian Democrat *other* than the DC's leading candidate for the post, Ciriaco De Mita, was seen as arbitration not merely between the DC and PSI (which latter had effectively vetoed De Mita's nomination) but also between pro- and anti-De Mita wings in the DC itself. It should be added that in the months leading up to the 1992 general election the behaviour of President Cossiga increasingly threatened to break up the consensus over the presidential role in avoiding a premature dissolution of the legislature, primarily because of his repeated threats to dissolve in the face of coalition disputes (even though these were disputes not leading to coalition breakdown) and policy inertia. On the role of the president, see ch. 5 below, and A. Baldassare, 'Il capo dello stato', in Giuliano Amato and Augusto Barbera, *Manuale di diritto pubblico* (Bologna, 1986), 471–508.

27. Thus in March 1987, when Bettino Craxi resigned, and a general election was agreed for the following June, there was controversy over who should head the government through the ensuing pre-election phase, the Socialists arguing (unsuccessfully) that as the outgoing prime minister was from the PSI Craxi should remain in office until the election.

28. In fact only the Christian Democrats were actually present in cabinet, with five other parties (PCI, PSI, PSDI, PRI, PLI) supporting then in Parliament. The literature on the Historic Compromise is extensive. See Paul Ginsborg, *A History of Contemporary Italy: Society and Politics, 1943–1988* (London, 1990), 348–405, and F. Cazzola, 'La solidarità nazionale dalla parte del parlamento', LABORATORIO *politico*, 2/2–3 (1982), 5–43.

29. See G. Pridham, *Political Parties and Coalitional Behaviour in Italy* (London, 1988).

30. There is in fact an unofficial manual—written by a former Christian Democrat politician—setting out the ground rules for coalition construction. See R. Venditti, *Il manuale Cencelli* (Rome, 1981).

Chapter 4

1. See Cleoffe Corona, *Il costo della democrazia: I partiti politici italiani costi e finanziamenti* (Rome, 1984).

2. See Carlo Chimenti, 'I partiti politici', in Giuliano Amato and Augusto Barbera, *Manuale di diritto pubblico* (Bologna, 1986), 291–302; also David Hine, 'Italy: Parties and Party Government under Pressure', in Alan Ware (ed.), *Political Parties* (Oxford, 1976), 91–4.

3. These issues are dealt with in greater detail in the comparative literature on party organization. See in particular A. Panebianco, *Political Parties: Organization and Power* (Cambridge, 1988), and J. Charlot, 'Political Parties: Towards a New Theoretical Synthesis', *Political Studies*, 37/3 (1989), 352–61.

4. M. Duverger, *Political Parties* (London, 1964), 17–40.
5. See ch. 7 for more detail on the roles of local-government officials; also Gianfranco Bettin and Annick Magnier, *Chi governa la città?* (Padua, 1991).
6. Although there is a conventional wisdom that participation rates have fallen from their early post-war levels, and that the fall has been especially serious for the Communist Party in the last decade, the absence of long-term data on participation rates makes it very difficult, as one recent study has suggested, to tell how far Italian parties have ever lived up to the ideals of mass-party activism which they set themselves, and against which participation is frequently, and quite possibly misleadingly, judged. On this see the essays by Gianfranco Pasquino, Piergiorgio Corbetta, Arturo Parisi, and Maurizio Rossi, under the collective title 'La partecipazione politica in Italia', *Polis*, 1/1 (1987).
7. For a more detailed discussion of this issue see David Hine, 'The Consolidation of Democracy in Postwar Italy', in G. Pridham, *Securing Democracy: Political Parties and Democratic Consolidation in Southern Europe* (London, 1990), 62–83.
8. On the organizational features of the PCI see, *inter alia*, D. L. M. Blackmer and S. Tarrow (eds.), *Communism in Italy and France* (Princeton, NJ, 1975); M. Barbagli, P. Corbetta, and S. Sechi, *Dentro il PCI* (Bologna, 1979); G. Amyot, *The Italian Communist Party: The Crisis of the Popular Front Strategy* (London, 1980); M. Barbagli and P. Corbetta, 'La svolta del PCI', *Il mulino* (Jan.–Feb. 1981), 95–130; M. Ilardi and A. Accornero (eds.), *Il Partito comunista italiano: Struttura e storia dell'organizzazione* (Milan, 1982); A. Accornero, R. Mannheimer and C. Sebastiani (eds.), *L'identità comunista* (Rome, 1983); L. Berlinguer, 'Partito di massa e forme snodate di organizzazione', *Democrazia e diritto* (Jan.–Feb. 1983), 19–40; A. Baldassare, 'Un partito nuovo di massa?', *Democrazia e diritto* (Jan.–Feb. 1983), 41–64; S. Belligni (ed.), *La giraffa e il liocorno: Il PCI dagli anni '70 al nuovo decennio* (Milan, 1983); S. Hellman, *Italian Communism in Transition: The Rise and Fall of the Historic Compromise in Turin, 1975–80* (New York, 1988); G. Pasquino, 'Mid-Stream and under Stress: The Italian Communist Party', in Michael Waller and Meindert Fennema (eds.), *Communist Parties in Western Europe: Decline or Adaptation?* (Oxford, 1988) 26–46; G. Pasquino (ed.), *La lenta marcia nelle istituzioni: I passi del PCI* (Bologna, 1988); C. Valentini, *Il nome e la cosa: Viaggio nel PCI che cambia* (Milan, 1990).
9. On the crisis of the 'mass-party' model see, *inter alia*, M. Fedele, 'Il partito di massa e l'equivoco dell'organizzazione', in Belligni, *La giraffa e il liocorno*, 125–41; G. Pasquino, 'Mass media, partito di massa, e trasformazioni della politica' *Il mulino* (July–Aug. 1983), 559–79; L. Morlino, 'The Changing Relationship between Parties and Society in Italy', *West European Politics*, 7/4 (1984), 46–66; S. Hellman, 'The Italian Communist Party between Berlinguer and the Seventeenth Congress', in R. Leonardi and R. Nanetti (eds.), *Italian Politics: A Review*, i (London, 1986), 47–68.

10. The consequences of the Historic Compromise strategy were, of course, felt not just in a fall in electoral support, but also in a substantial rebellion amongst party members as well. See Barbagli and Corbetta, 'La svolta del PCI', 95–130.

11. On the DC membership see Robert Leonardi and Douglas A. Wertman, *Italian Christian Democracy: The Politics of Dominance* (London, 1989), esp. 125–36.

12. F. Alberoni (ed.), *L'attività di partito* (Bologna, 1967), 33–4; M. Rossi, 'Un partito di "anime morte" ', in A. Parisi, *Democristiani* (Bologna, 1979), 13–60.

13. F. Anderlini, 'La DC: Iscritti e modello di partito', *Polis*, 3/2 (1989), 277–304.

14. Hine, 'Italy: Parties and Party Government under Pressure', 93.

15. Rossi, 'Un partito di "anime morte" ', 13–59.

16. Anderlini, 'La DC: Iscritti e modello di partito', 292–5; also Leonardi and Wertman, Italian Christian Democracy, 145–57.

17. Maurizio Rossi, 'Sezioni di partito e partecipazione politica', *Polis*, 1/1 (1987), 67–100. On the Socialist Party more generally, see F. Cazzola, 'Struttura e potere del Partito socialista italiano', in G. Pasquino (ed.), *Il sistema politico italiano* (Rome, 1985), 169–207; W. Merkl, *Prima e dopo Craxi: Le trasformazioni del PSI* (Padua, 1987).

18. See David Hine, 'Social Democracy in Italy', in W. E. Paterson and A. H. Thomas (eds.), *Social Democratic Parties in Western Europe* (London, 1977), 67–85; and David Hine, 'The Italian Socialist Party', in T. Gallagher and A. M. Williams (eds.), *Southern European Socialism: Parties, Elections, and the Challenge of Government* (Manchester, 1989), 108–30.

19. See esp. the long process of self-examination to which the party subjected itself in 1974–5, reported in Partito socialista italiano, *Il Partito socialista italiano: Struttura e organizzazione* (Venice, 1975).

20. See G. Pasquino, 'Modernity and Reforms: The PSI between Political Entrepreneurs and Gamblers', *West European Politics*, 9/1 (1986), 120–41.

21. David Hine, 'Leaders and Followers: Democracy and Manageability in the Social Democratic Parties of Western Europe', in W. E. Paterson and A. H. Thomas (eds.), *The Future of Social Democracy* (Oxford, 1986), 156–203.

22. See Barbagli and Corbetta, 'La svolta'.

23. On these events see Donald Sassoon, 'The PCI and the 1987 Elections', in R. Leonardi and P. Corbetta (eds.), *Italian Politics: A Review*, iii (London, 1989), 129–45. Occhetto became the PCI's full party secretary the following year, after the illness of his predecessor, Alessandro Natta.

24. The events of Aug. 1991 in the Soviet Union, however, were less kind to the party. Even though by that stage the Italian party had itself abandoned the Communist name, the thoroughgoing rejection of the CPSU not only by the Soviet peoples, but by Gorbachev, left the ex-PCI leadership in as distinctly uncomfortable a position as Gorbachev himself—former defenders of a now systematically discredited party.

25. See Amyot, *The Italian Communist Party*.

26. The picture was further complicated by a breakaway group from the Ingrao left, headed by Antonio Bassolini, which feared that the tactical alliance between the two leftist groups would isolate the left and reduce its influence in the new party. It thus abandoned the Fronte dei no, and presented its own motion at the 20th Congress, under the somewhat laboured slogan 'per un partito antagonista e riformatore' (roughly translating as 'radical and reformist'). It obtained 21,000 votes in the party's pre-congressional elections (about 5 % of those who voted).

27. Both the PCI and PSI had a common model in François Mitterrand's feat in relaunching the French Socialist Party in the early 1970s in such a way as to create, in voters' minds, a sharp break between the old SFIO and the Parti socialiste.

28. For a guide to these conceptual distinctions, and further analysis of the incentives to factionalism in different parties, see David Hine, 'Factionalism in West European Parties: A Framework for Analysis', *West European Politics*, 5/1 (1982), 36–53.

29. David Hine, 'Surviving but not Reviving: The Italian Socialist Party under Craxi', *West European Politics*, 2/3 (1979), 133–48.

30. See, *inter alia*, P. Scaramozzino, *Un'analisi statistica del voto di preferenza in Italia* (Milan, 1979); P. Scaramozzino, 'Il voto di preferenza nelle elezioni politiche ed europee del 1979 e nelle elezioni politiche del 1983', *Il politico*, 4 (1983), 641–75; R. d'Amico, 'Voto di preferenza, movimento dell'elettorato e modelli di partito: L'andamento delle preferenze nelle elezioni politiche italiane del quindicennio 1968–1983', *Quaderni dell'Osservatorio elettorale*, 18 (Jan. 1987), 91–147; R. d'Amico, 'La fisionomia dei partiti nel voto di preferenza', in Mario Caciagli and Alberto Spreafico (eds.), *Vent'anni di elezioni in Italia, 1968–87* (Padua, 1990), 259–94.

31. Despite a low (65%) turn-out because some parties discouraged voting, 95% supported the move to limit preference-voting to a single preference, in a result which was widely interpreted as a public condemnation of the factionalism to which most parties of government are prone.

32. Leonardi and Wertman, *Italian Christian Democracy*, 109–19.

33. Ibid. 119.

34. See the 3 articles by Gianfranco Pasquino, Carlo Marletti, and Giampietro Mazzoleni, under the collective heading of 'Politici spettacolo' in *Polis*, 6/2 (1990), 203–73; also J. LaPalombara, *Democracy: Italian Style* (New Haven, Conn., 1987), 88–116. On 'charismatic' leadership, see L. Cavalli, *Il capo carismatico: Per un sociologia weberiana della leadership* (Bologna, 1981).

35. See Judith Chubb, 'The Christian Democrat Party: Reviving or Surviving?', in R. Leonardi and R. Nanetti (eds.), *Italian Politics: A Review*, i (London, 1986), 69–86.

36. Giovanni Sartori, *Political Parties: A Framework for Analysis* (Cambridge, 1976), esp. 216–36.

37. See ibid. ch. 6, and Alfonso Prandi and Giorgio Galli, *Patterns of Political Participation in Italy* (New Haven, Conn., 1970), esp. 25–71.
38. See Paolo Farneti, *The Italian Party System* (London, 1985), 181–9. Other attempts to interpret the changing nature of the Italian party system are to be found in: I. Daalder, "The Italian Party System in Transition: The End of Polarised Pluralism', *West European Politics*, 6/3 (1983), 216–36; G. Pasquino, *Party Government in Italy: Achievements and Prospects*, The Johns Hopkins University Bologna Center Research Institute, Occasional Paper no. 48 (Jan. 1985); Mark Donovan, 'Party Strategy and Centre Domination in Italy', *West European Politics*, 12/4 (1989), 114–28.

Chapter 5

1. See A. Barbera, F. Cocozza, and G. Corso, 'Le situazioni soggettivi: Le libertà dei singoli e delle formazioni sociali: Il principio di eguaglianza', in G. Amato and A. Barbera (eds.), *Manuale di diritto pubblico* (Bologna, 1986), 201–90.
2. This was the essence of the case of those critics present in the Constituent Assembly like Piero Calamandrei who claimed that articles such as that assigning an obligation on the state to 'protect the health of the individual' would bring subsequent governments—incapable of fulfilling the obligation—into disrepute. See J. C. Adams and P. Barile, *The Government of Republican Italy* (Boston, 1972), 56.
3. See Barbera, Cocozza, and Corso, 'Le situazioni soggettivi.', 282–4.
4. Art. 67 of the Basic Law of the Federal Republic of Germany, for example, provides such protection through the constructive vote of no confidence, though the temporary survival of the executive which it guarantees has never been needed in the safety-net sense in which it was intended. Similarly art. 44 of the constitution of the Fifth French Republic ensures that although deputies and senators may propose amendments to any bill, the government may, at any time, insist on a single vote on its own text. Likewise art. 49 makes votes of censure especially difficult, since *inter alia* those who abstain or are absent are counted as being in favour of the government. See David Conradt, *The German Polity* (New York, 1986), 156–7; and Vincent Wright, *The Government and Politics of France* (London, 1983), 129–36.
5. Although the governing majority is not so weak that *in practice* it is unable to receive favoured treatment, it clearly does, as the large disparity in the success rate of government and private legislation demonstrates. See Paul Furlong, 'Parliament in Italian Politics', *West European Politics*, 13/3 (1990), 64.
6. In practice, however, governments in recent years have been in the habit of renewing decrees as many as 3 or 4 times, despite the implicit assumption in the Constituent Assembly debates that they should either be converted into law or lapse after 60 days. See David Hine, 'Thirty

Years of the Italian Constitution: Governability and Constitutional Reform', *Parliamentary Affairs*, 34/1 (1981), 63–80, and David Hine, 'Italy; Condemned by Its Constitution?', in Vernon Bogdanor (ed.), *Constitutions in Democratic Politics* (Aldershot, 1988), 206–28.

7. See Vincent della Sala, 'Government by Decree: The Craxi Government and the Use of Decree Legislation in the Italian Parliament', in R. Leonardi, R. Nanetti, and P. Corbetta (eds.), *Italian Politics: A Review*, ii (London, 1988), 8–24.

8. On these questions see G. di Federico, 'The Crisis of the Justice System and the Referendum on the Judiciary', in R. Leonardi and P. Corbetta (eds.), *Italian Politics: A Review*, iii (London, 1989), 25–49.

9. See G. Ghetti, *La consulenza amministrativa, i: problemi generali* (Padua, 1974).

10. See ch. 7, below, and also S. Cassese, *Esiste un governo in Italia?* (Rome, 1980), 33–58.

11. A referendum was also held in 1946 on the continuation of the monarchy, which confirmed (by 12 million votes to 10 million), the republican framework. (This was, of course, before the 1948 constitution itself had been promulgated.)

12. Unfortunately for the Italian government, although a large majority of Italian voters supported the proposal—as had been anticipated—no other state followed the Italian example, leaving the gesture a rather empty one.

13. On this issue see Sergio P. Panunzio, 'Riforme costituzionali e referendum', *Quaderni costituzionali*, 10/3 (1990), 419–61; also Pier Vincenzo Uleri, 'The 1987 Referendum', in Leonardi and Corbetta (eds.), *Italian Politics*, iii. 155–77. Since 1988 there has been much discussion of various types of positive referendum (*consultivo* or *propositivo*) which might extend the range of options beyond the present negative (i.e. repealing) mode.

14. A dramatic illustration of this was the referendum of June 1991, in which voters were asked to support a proposal to reform the preference-vote mechanism (on which see ch. 4) by removing those articles of electoral law which allow voters to express up to three or four preferences for candidates on a party list. The overwhelming support this proposal received—associated as it was in voters' minds with electoral corruption and party factionalism—suggested an electorate ready to support radical constitutional reform in a referendum. It concentrated the minds of politicians on electoral reform issues in a way no opinion poll could succeed in doing.

15. These arguments are set out in more detail in Hine, 'Thirty Years of the Italian Constitution', 63–68.

16. On this episode see Paul Ginsborg, *A History of Contemporary Italy: Society and Politics, 1943–1988* (London, 1990), 141–5.

17. On the first 3 ballots, candidates require two-thirds of the electoral college for election, thereafter an absolute majority.

18. Thus after 1985 the DC held the presidency of the republic (Cossiga), the PSI that of the Council of Ministers (Craxi), the PCI that of the Chamber of Deputies (Jotti), and the PRI that of the Senate (Spadolini).

19. Immediate political manœuvrings were not entirely absent from either of these elections however. Ironically, Pertini's most lukewarm supporters were from his own party, which saw in the agreement between Communists and Christian Democrats to elect him a continuation of the grand-coalition alliance that Craxi was at the time seeking to undermine. His election was, thus, *inter alia* a tactical defeat for the PSI itself. As for Cossiga, his election owed much to astute tactical moves by DC party secretary Ciriaco De Mita. He not only consolidated his own position inside the DC by securing agreement on a single nomination, but also helped his party through it, especially *vis-à-vis* the Communists. The PSI was squared by the offer of continued DC support for Craxi as prime minister, leaving the Communist Party with a *fait accompli* which, out of weakness, it preferred not to oppose.

20. The Italian taxpayer, indeed, pays a formidable amount to keep the president of the republic serviced, informed, advised, and in the public view. The item in the 1992 budget for the cost of the Quirinale ran to 208 billion lire (about $150 million), excluding the cost of overseas travel. (Note that the president himself receives a relatively modest (but tax-free) official stipend of some 20 million lire ($15,000) per month.)

21. On these questions see ch. 3 above, pp. 98–9.

22. In one of its roles—that of hearing cases brought by Parliament against the president of the republic for treason, or against ministers for crimes committed in the course of office—the constitutional court is supplemented by a further 16 'judges' known as *giudici aggregati*, chosen from a list drawn up every 9 years by Parliament, and composed of citizens meeting the criteria for election to the Senate. To date this procedure has only been used once, against ministers involved in the Lockheed affair in the 1970s.

23. On these questions see Paul Furlong, 'The Constitutional Court in Italian Politics', *West European Politics*, 11/3 (1988), 7–23.

24. For a survey of these categories see G. Zagrebelsky, 'La giurisdizione costituzionale', in Amato and Barbera, *Manuale di diritto pubblico*, 664–96.

25. Furlong, 'The Constitutional Court'.

26. For an account of these issues see E. Barendt, 'The Influence of the German and Italian Constitutional Courts on Their National Broadcasting Systems', *Public Law* (1991), 93–115.

Chapter 6

1. The literature on the general issue of legislative strength *vis-à-vis* the executive is extensive. See, as an introduction, Philip Norton, *Legislatures* (Oxford, 1988), esp. chs. 3, 7, 10, and 11.

2. Numerous Italian constitutional authorities refer to the so-called 'centrality' of parliament. For a survey see E. Cheli, 'La centralità parlamentare: Sviluppo e decadenza di un modello', *Quaderni costituzionali*, 1/2 (1981), 343–51.

3. See esp. G. di Palma, *Surviving without Governing: The Italian Parties in Parliament* (Berkeley, Calif., 1977), and 'Parlamento-arena o parlamento di trasformazione', *Rivista italiana di scienza politica*, 17/2 (1987), 179–203. Also G. Pasquino, 'The Debate on Institutional Reform', in R. Leonardi, and R. Y. Nanetti (eds.), *Italian Politics: A Review*, i (London, 1986), 117–33.

4. This debate reached its height in the work of the Bozzi Commission on institutional reform. See Camera dei deputati/Senato della repubblica, *Relazione della Commissione parlamentare per le riforme istituzionali*, IX legislatura, doc. XVI-*bis*, no. 3 (Rome, 1985). (The report of the Commission is contained in vol. i, the proceedings are contained in vol. ii, and the minority reports in vol. iii.) Chs. 4 and 5 of the main report cover the Commission's conclusions on Parliament. Their limited scope, and the views of the minority reports, demonstrate the difficulty of reaching a common diagnosis of the problem.

5. The constitutional court also sanctioned this latter principle of representation in an important judgement in 1975 (Corte costituzionale, *Sentenza n. 203*, 1975).

6. The typology suggested here is a simplification of a wide range of literature on the classification of liberal democratic systems, but, it may be argued, it accords reasonably closely with concepts contained in the mainstream writings. See esp. A. Lijphart, *Democracies: Patterns of Majoritarian and Consensus Government in Twenty-One Countries* (New Haven, Conn., 1984); A. King, 'Modes of Executive–Legislative Relationships in Britain, France, and West Germany', in Norton, *Legislatures*, 208–36; and the conceptual chapters by Pulzer, von Beyme, and Smith in Eva Kolinsky (ed.), *Opposition in Western Europe* (London, 1987), 11–71.

7. For a review of this literature see A. Pappalardo, 'La politica consociativa nella democrazia italiana', *Rivista italiana di scienza politica*, 10/1 (1980), 73–123.

8. Since 1988, however, members of Parliament have been entitled, through an addition to the annual parliamentary budget, to a sum of some 30 million lire p.a. (c. $20,000) for research expenses.

9. For more information on the different backgrounds and behaviour patterns of Communist and government members of Parliament see M. Cotta, *Classe politica e parlamento in Italia 1946–76* (Bologna, 1979), esp. ch. 3; and G. di Palma and M. Cotta, 'Cadres, Peones, and Entrepreneurs: Professional Identities in a divided Parliament', in E. Suleiman (ed.), *Parliaments and Parliamentarians* (New York, 1986), 41–78.

10. That the Christian Democrat Party in Parliament exhibits a low level of cohesion is beyond dispute, as the general problem of ensuring a safe parliamentary passage for government legislation demonstrates. It is however impossible to quantify the phenomenon in the way it has been done in systems with open parliamentary votes, because, painstaking content-analysis of plenary debate apart, there is no way of estimating the most important dimension of dissent, namely, indiscipline in the secret ballot, where, by definition, there is no record of how individual deputies vote.

11. See A. Predieri *et al.*, *Il parlamento nel sistema politico italiano* (Milan, 1975); di Palma, 'Parlamento-arena o parlamento di trasformazione', 179–203.

12. See di Palma, *Surviving without Governing*. Also di Palma and Cotta, 'Cadres, Peones, and Entrepreneurs', 41–78.

13. The main sources for this section are G. Sartori, *Il Parlamento italiano* (Naples, 1963); Cotta, *Classe politica e parlamento in Italia*; G. Pasquino, 'Ricambiamento parlamentare e rendimento politico', *Politica del diritto*, 5 (1976), 543–65; and M. Guadagnini, 'Il personale politico parlamentare dagli anni '70 agli anni '80: Problemi di ricerca e di analisi, ed alcuni dati empirici', in Centro studi di scienza politica Paolo Farneti, *Il sistema politico italiano tra crisi e innovazione* (Milan, 1984).

14. See Pasquino, 'Ricambiamento parlamentare e rendimento politico', 550.

15. In Italy a candidate may stand in more than one constituency, opting to represent whichever he/she chooses if elected in more than one. National leaders like Berlinguer, Occhetto, Andreotti, and Craxi have habitually done so.

16. See G. Pridham, 'Parliamentarians and Their Constituencies in Italy's Party Democracy', in V. Bogdanor (ed.), *Representatives of the People* (London, 1985), 151–65.

17. In the 1983–7 legislature, an average of 230 separate items of legislation per annum were produced. This was well below the 410 of the first legislature (1948–53) and the 390 of the second (1953–8) but was still very high compared even to the Federal Republic of Germany's legislature over the same period (1983–7), which produced an annual average of only 80. See, for Italy, Camera dei deputati, *Resoconti sommari della legislatura IX* (Roma, 1988); and for Germany, T. Saalfeld, 'The West German Bundestag after 40 Years: The Role of Parliament in a "Party Democracy" ', *West European Politics*, 13/3 (1990), 78.

18. See M. Bonanni, 'Il governo nel sistema politico italiano (1948–1982)', *Rivista trimestrale di scienza della amministrazione*, 1 (1983), 5–10.

19. Art. 72 of the constitution lays down that bills dealing with budgetary legislation, international treaties, constitutional laws, electoral laws, and delegated legislation cannot be approved in final form in committee.

20. There are numerous studies on this phenomenon. See, *inter alia*, E. Maestri, 'Partiti e sistema pensionistico in Italia: Un analisi dell'azione parlamentare della DC e del PCI, 1953–75', *Rivista italiana di scienza politica*, 14/2 (1984), 125–59; Franco Cazzola, 'Consenso e opposizione nel Parlamento italiano: Il ruolo del PCI dalla I alla IV legislatura', *Rivista italiana di scienza politica*, 2 (1972); Francesco d'Onofrio, 'Committees in the Italian Parliament', in John D. Lees and M. Shaw (eds.), *Committees in Legislatures: A Comparative Analysis* (Durham, NC, 1979), 61–101.

21. Di Palma, *Surviving without Governing* (ch. 2), for example, finds that on average 28% of government bills and 22.5% of private members' bills in his sample are 'national' in scope; 26.5% and 21% respectively are 'sectional'; and 45.5% and 56.5% 'microsectional'. He further discovers that the overwhelming majority of *all* legislation is either beneficial or

neutral (as opposed to depriving) in its effects, and on this basis concludes that legislation is 'highly fragmented, and disaggregated, and therefore essentially uncontroversial . . . and prospers on narrow transactions that do not penalize any political party, and co-opt even the opposition' (p. 93). In contrast, a study by Bonanni, derived from the classification of three Italian law periodicals which operate on a narrower definition of the 'micro-sectional', suggests that for the three periods 1948–53, 1953–66, and 1966–80, the figures for micro-sectional legislation are much lower: 32%, 26%, and 17% respectively (see Bonanni, 'Il governo nel sistema politico italiano (1948–1982)', 9). Bonanni's criterion of trivial legislation is derived from the two legal journals *Lex* and *Le leggi*, whose law reports exclude what the editors of these periodicals regard as 'trivial'. Which constitutes the more realistic definition is difficult to judge, although it is worth noting that even on di Palma's figures the quantity of non-sectional or micro-sectional legislation is considerable, and that in other legislatures a fairly high proportion of bills fall into the 'micro-sectional' category. See Saalfeld, 'The West German Bundestag', 78.

22. Di Palma's interviews with a sample of MPs from the major parties in 1971–2 did not elicit major differences in the self-perceived role of the MP, according to whether they were part of the governing parties (and hence enjoyed access to patronage resources) or part of the opposition. Instead different interpretations are placed by the author on the same response, according to whether an MP is a member of the governing parties or the opposition. See di Palma and Cotta, 'Cadres, Peones, and Entrepreneurs', 66.

23. As in the case of the Bozzi Commission, which laid great stress on the power of the preference-vote mechanism in focusing the attention of members of Parliament excessively on constituency pressures. See Camera dei deputati/Senato della repubblica, *Relazione della Commissione parlamentare per le riforme istituzionali* i. 74–5.

24. The OECD estimate of 'general government expenditure' (a figure which included debt interest servicing) as a percentage of GDP for 1990 was 53.3%. *OECD Economic Surveys: Italy, 1990/91* (Paris, 1991), 23.

25. Ibid. 28.

26. The literature on the economic consequences of the high Italian budget deficit is voluminous. For a succinct general introduction see L. Spaventa, 'The Growth of Public Debt in Italy: Past Experience, Perspectives, and Policy Problems', *Banca nazionale del lavoro Quarterly Review*, 37 (1984), 119–49. In Italian see F. Cavazutti, *Debito pubblico e ricchezza privata* (Bologna, 1986).

27. The literature on these issues is voluminous. The classic study is A. Pedone, *Evasori e tartassati: I nodi della politica tributaria italiana* (Bologna, 1979). See also E. Longobardi, 'La politica fiscale', in U. Ascoli (ed.) *Welfare state all'italiana* (Rome, 1984), 119–51; G. Pasquino, 'Rappresentanza degli interessi, attività di lobby e processi decisionali: Il caso italiano di istituzioni permeabili', *Stato e mercato* (Dec. 1987), 403–29; P. Trupia, *La democrazia degli interessi: Lobby e decisione collettiva* (Milan, 1989), esp. 173–83; Ministero del tesoro, *Rapporto sulla spesa pubblica in Italia* (Rome, 1986).

28. For a useful commentary in English on legal and constitutional aspects of the budgetary process, see V. della Sala, 'The Italian Budgetary Process: Political and Institutional Constraints', *West European Politics*, 11/3 (1988), 110–25.

29. The various ways in which the formal bar on introducing new spending or revenue into the budget could be circumvented are described in M. Scioscioli, 'L'esame degli emendamenti alla legge di bilancio', in Camera dei deputati, *Il Parlamento della Repubblica, Organi, procedure, apparati* (Rome, 1987), 111–25.

30. For an analysis of the effects of the 1978 reform in this respect see Paolo de Ioanna, 'Dalla legge n. 468 del 1978 alla legge n. 362 del 1988: Note sul primo decennio di applicazione della "legge finanziario"', *Quaderni costituzionali*, 9/2 (1989), 205–27. Representative of the annual drama of the budget cycle was the 1986 budget, subject to 1000 amendments, 600 separate votes, 4 votes of confidence, and no less than 20 formal defeats for the government (and many other moral defeats where it was forced to back down). See della Sala, 'The Italian Budgetary Process', 119–22. The 1987 budget was a little less fraught, but still, in the space of 5 days in November, the Chamber subjected it to no fewer than 455 votes.

31. See de Ioanna, 'Dalla legge n. 468', 205–18.

32. On the 1971 regulation changes, and more generally on the consequences for Parliament in the 1970s, see the collection of articles in *Città e regione*, 6/4 (1980), esp. A. Manzella, 'I regolamenti parlamentari del 1971: Quale riforma?', and S. Passigli, 'Crisi o centralità del parlamento?' 36–42, 5–11.

33. See F. Sparasci, 'Alcuni aspetti delle votazioni a scrutinio segreto nei lavori dell'Assemblea costituente', in Camera dei deputati, *Il Parlamento* 341–64.

34. See A. Casu, 'Voto segreto e voto palese nei regolamenti dal 1948 ai nostri giorni', *Rivista trimestrale di diritto pubblico*, 2 (1986), 553–93.

35. On the growth of the use of decree-laws in the 1980s see Vincent della Sala, 'Government by Decree: The Craxi Government and the Use of Decree Legislation in the Italian Parliament', in R. Leonardi, R. Y. Nanetti, and P. Corbetta (eds.), *Italian Politics: A Review*, ii (London, 1988), 8–24.

36. Data obtained from Camera dei deputati, Servizio studi, *Documenti: Dati sulle votazioni a scrutinio segreto nel corso di procedimenti legislativi in cui il governo è messo in minoranza durante la IX legislatura* (Rome, 1989).

37. The drafts of the proposed changes are reproduced in Camera dei deputati, Servizio studi, *Documentazione per le commissioni parlamentari: Voto palese e voto segreto*, 81, 2nd edn., x legislatura (Nov. 1988), 69–146.

38. See Pasquino, 'Rappresentanza degli interessi', 416.

39. See V. della Sala, 'Parliament and the Italian Legislative Process' (D.Phil. thesis, University of Oxford, 1990), ch. 6.

40. See C. Cesareo, 'Le indagini conoscitivi delle commissioni permanenti', in Camera dei deputati, *Il Parlamento*, 213–31.

Chapter 7

1. See J. J. Richardson, *Policy Styles in Western Europe* (London, 1982), esp. the concluding chapter.

2. The terminology employed in this chapter is an Anglicized version of Italian terms: the 'prime minister' in Italy is strictly 'presidente del Consiglio dei ministri', and the 'cabinet' itself is the 'Consiglio dei ministri'. A further confusion arises in the use of the Italian term 'gabinetto' (the politically appointed advisers surrounding an Italian minister) for which there is no direct translation in English, the Westminster model having no equivalent institution. In political science literature, English tends to use the words 'ministerial cabinet' (derived from the equivalent French institution).

3. Almost all textbooks on constitutional law include a substantial section on the 'formation of the government', emphasizing the procedural elements. See, *inter alia*, S. Merlini, 'Il governo', in G. Amato and A. Barbera (eds.), *Manuale di diritto pubblico* (Bologna, 1986), 448–50. See also G. Pridham, *Political Parties and Coalitional Behaviour in Italy* (London, 1988), which contains some discussion of the process, esp. in ch. 6, pp. 62–109.

4. There is no single historical survey of the role of the Italian prime minister, but useful material may be obtained from G. Pitruzzella, *La presidenza del Consiglio dei ministri e l'organizzazione del governo* (Padua, 1986). See also E. Spagna Musso (ed.), *Costituzione e strutture del governo: Il problema della presidenza del Consiglio* (Padua, 1979).

5. See E. Rotelli, 'La prima legislatura repubblicana ed il ruolo del parlamento', *Quaderni costituzionali*, 1/1 (1981), 98–100.

6. See David Hine, 'The Craxi Premiership', in R. Leonardi and R. Y. Nanetti (eds.), *Italian Politics: A Review*, i (London, 1986), 106–16.

7. For observations on this see David Hine, 'The Italian General Election of 1987', *Electoral Studies*, 6/3 (1987), 267–70.

8. On the role of the minister without portfolio see G. Guaglia, 'Quale ruolo per i ministri senza portafoglio?', *Quaderni costituzionali*, 9/2 (1989), 386–90.

9. The case for doing so would be that it is more appropriate to entrust an elected politician and close colleague with sensitive administrative and negotiating roles, even though they are often given to a public official on secondment. Amato—a member of Parliament since 1979—was by origin a professor of constitutional law, with long consultative experience of the top echelons of the administration. Craxi's problem in filling the prime minister's office senior posts raises a more general unanswered question: how 'politicized' are the top echelons of the Italian administrative hierarchy, and what are the implications of the answer for an alternative (i.e. non-DC) government? The problem has never been faced because there has never been real alternation in power. Even the arrival of Craxi as prime minister did not constitute real alternation, since the DC retained most of its ministerial portfolios. Yet Craxi clearly faced a problem at the start of his premiership in finding a suitable and willing figure from the normal sources to fill the post of *capogabinetto*. I am indebted, for insights

on this question, to an unpublished research paper by Renato Finocchio, 'I governi Craxi (1983/87)', produced for the Consiglio nazionale delle ricerche, Progetto finalizzato organizzazione e funzionamento della pubblica amministrazione (Sottoprogetto sulla presidenza del Consiglio dei ministri) (Rome, 1989).

10. Basic descriptions of the departments traditionally linked to the PCM can be found in the following sources: R. di Passio, 'La struttura della presidenza del Consiglio dei ministri', *Rivista trimestrale di scienza della amministrazione*, 4 (1976), 606–51; R. di Passio, 'Gli organi della presidenza del Consiglio dei ministri', *Rivista trimestrale di scienza della amministrazione*, 1 (1978), 71–112. For the period since the reform of the PCM in 1988 see below.

11. See *Ordine di servizio del presidente del Consiglio dei ministri del 23 agosto 1981, Gazetta ufficiale*, 251 (12 Sept. 1981).

12. Among those brought in were Professors Mario Arcelli (Rome), Antonio Pedone (Rome), Rolando Valiani (Rome), Franco Momigliano (Turin), Salvatore Vinci (Naples), Franco Cotula (Director of Research Services at the Bank of Italy), and various research officers from publicly funded research agencies such as ISPE (Institute for Economic Planning Research), the Bank of Italy Research Department, CNEL (the National Council for Labour and the Economy), and ISTAT (the Central Statistical Institute).

13. I am indebted, for these observations, to a working paper by A. Cagli, 'La struttura, l'organizzazione, ed il personale del governi Spadolini', unpublished research paper of the CNR, Progetto finalizzato organizzazione e funzionamento della pubblica amministrazione (Sottoprogetto sulla presidenza del Consiglio dei ministri) (Rome, 1989).

14. On the CPRS experience see Tessa Blackstone and William Plowden, *Inside the Think Tank: Advising the Cabinet 1971–83* (London, 1987). Also Peter Hennessy, Susan Morrison, and Richard Townsend, *Routine Punctuated by Orgies: The Central Policy Review Staff, 1970–83*, Strathclyde Papers on Government and Politics, no. 31 (Glasgow, 1985).

15. 'Funzione e struttura del dipartimento per l'analisi e la verifica del programma di governo', typescript memorandum dated Sept. 1981, supplied by Prof. Zuliani.

16. See G. Rolla, 'Il Consiglio dei ministri fra modello costituzionale e prassi', *Quaderni costituzionali*, 2/2 (1982), 393–412.

17. Accompanied, significantly, by Andrea Manzella—now serving as *capo-gabinetto* to a Christian Democrat—despite his own Republican connections.

18. The earlier sections of the law seek to define legal aspects of the respective roles of the cabinet and the prime minister, and are dealt with below. On the organizational changes see G. Pitruzzella, 'L'organizzazione amministrativa della presidenza del Consiglio', *Il foro italiano* (June 1989), 5: 371–83; S. Labriola, *Il governo della repubblica: Organi e poteri* (Rimini, 1989), 199–220; and L. Ventura, *Il governo a multipolarità diseguale* (Milan, 1988), 186–99.

19. Full details are contained in the appendix to the draft legislation. See Presidenza del Consiglio dei ministri, *Disciplina dell'attività di governo e ordinamento della presidenza del Consiglio dei ministri*, Collana di testi e documenti, Dipartimento per l'informazione e l'editoria, no. 1 (Rome, 1989).

20. The difficulty of doing other than making the existing staff (most of whom were strictly on temporary appointments from their parent government departments) into permanent staff was acknowledged by the minister for Regional Affairs and Institutional Reform in his report to the Constitutional Affairs Committee of the Chamber of Deputies (sitting of 28 Feb. 1989). See Camera dei deputati, Servizio studi, *Documentazione per le commissioni parlamentari: l'attuazione della l. no. 400, 23 agosto 1989: Disciplina dell'attività del governo e ordinamento della presidenza del Consiglio dei ministri*, no. 326, x legislatura (1989), 56–8 and 210–11.

21. For a review of these features, as they are said to erode cabinet government in Britain, see Colin Turpin, *British Government and the Constitution: Texts, Cases and Materials* (London, 1985). The literature on the Italian Council of Ministers is extensive, and much of it written from a juridical rather than political standpoint. Some of the more illuminating commentaries are M. Bonanni (ed.), *Governi, ministri, presidenti* (Comunità, 1978); E. Cheli, 'Il coordinamento delle attività di governo nell'attuale sistema italiano', *Studi parlamentari e di politica costituzionali*, 4 (1969), 4–33; Stefano Merlini, 'Presidente del consiglio e collegialità del governo', *Quaderni costituzionali*, 2/2 (1982), 413–37; Pitruzzella, *La presidenza del Consiglio dei ministri*; S. Ristucci, *L'istituzione governo* (Comunità, 1975); Rolla, 'Il Consiglio dei ministri'; E. Ruggieri, *Il Consiglio dei ministri nella costituzione* (Milan, 1981).

22. The Bank of Italy, moreover, may be seen, for all practical purposes, as a 'fourth' ministry in the field of economic policy, and in a certain sense the governor of the Bank of Italy is probably a more powerful minister than any of the other three. See ch. 8 below, pp. 245–8.

23. The full range of legal powers attributed to the Council of Ministers is to be found in law no. 400, 23 Aug. 1988 (art. 2). See Presidenza del Consiglio dei ministri, *Disciplina dell'attività di governo*. Until the approval of the 1988 legislation, the powers of the Council were regulated by the Zanardelli decree of 1901, and a fascist law dating from 1926, regulating the government's power to issue decrees and nominate senior administrative officials. See Merlini, 'Il governo', 432–69.

24. See G. de Vergottini, 'Riforma della struttura di governo ed introduzione del gabinetto ristretto', *Studi parlamentari e di politica costituzionale*, 5 (1982), 29–53.

25. See M. Caciagli, 'The 18th DC Congress: From de Mita to Forlani and the Victory of "Neodoroteism"', in F. Sabetti and R. Catanzaro (eds.), *Italian Politics: A Review*, v. (London 1991), 8–22.

26. See P. Capotosti, 'Consiglio di gabinetto e governi di coalizione', *Quaderni costituzionali*, 3/3 (1983), 585–610; G. Focaccia, 'Consiglio di gabinetto e organizzazione del governo', *Diritto e società*, 4 (1986), 721–57; Labriola, *Il governo*, 111–16.

27. The Ministry of Labour would not always fall into the category of senior
    Council of Ministers post, but during the Craxi government one of the
    most pressing issues was that of modifying the wage-indexation mechan-
    ism. Hence the inclusion of Gianni de Michelis, the Socialist minister of
    Labour. On the wage-indexation issue see Peter Lange, 'The End of an
    Era: The Wage Indexation Referendum of 1985', in R. Leonardi and
    R. Y. Nanetti (eds.), *Italian Politics: A Review*, i (London, 1986), 29–46.
28. See Presidenza del Consiglio dei ministri, *Disciplina dell'attività del
    governo*, 14.
29. P. Ciriello, *Ordinamento di governo e comitati interministeriali* (Naples,
    1981).
30. See Merlini, *Il governo*, 463–6.
31. A commentary on the implementation of the new law in its first 8 months
    is contained in Carlo Fusaro, 'La legge sulla presidenza del Consiglio dei
    ministri, primi adempimenti a otto mesi dall'entrata in vigore', *Quaderni
    costituzionale*, 9/2 (1989), 374–86. See also the collection of articles under
    the heading 'La legge sulla presidenza del Consiglio', *Il foro italiano* (June
    1989), 310–83.
32. These issues are explored in greater detail in David Hine and Renato
    Finocchi, 'The Italian Prime Minister', *West European Politics*, 14/2
    (1991), 79–96.

Chapter 8

1. For an introduction to these issues in comparative perspective see E.
   Sulieman (ed.), *Bureaucrats and Policy Making* (London, 1984), and E.
   Page, *Political Authority and Bureaucratic Power* (Brighton, 1985).
2. One of the most comprehensive plans was that of the Piga Commission,
   which recommended in 1981 a reduction in the number of ministries to
   15, particularly through the merging of those dealing with social and
   economic regulation into three superministries ('economic production
   and distribution', 'territory', and 'social services'). The Commission also
   recommended a regrouping of departmental responsibilities of existing
   departments, to avoid overlapping competences, and to spread responsibilities more evenly between departments. The report had the backing
   of the then prime minister, Spadolini, but its implications were too far-
   reaching to make significant progress in Parliament before Spadolini's
   government fell. See G. Pastori, 'La pubblica amministrazione', in G.
   Amato and A. Barbera (eds.), *Manuale di diritto pubblico* (Bologna, 1986),
   549–51.
3. The two main accounts of Italian public administration are S. Cassese, *Il
   sistema amministrativa italiano* (Bologna, 1983), and M. S. Giannini,
   Istituzioni di diritto amministrativo (Milan, 1982). A more succinct account
   can be found in G. Pastori, 'La pubblica amministrazione', 521–73. For a
   detailed account of the internal structures of the ministerial apparatus see
   E. Spagna Musso (ed.), *Costituzione e struttura di governo: La riforma dei
   ministeri* (Padua, 1984), vols. i and ii.

4. See L. Ventura, *Il governo a multipolarità diseguale* (Milan, 1988), esp. 156–66.

5. The other major employer in the 'autonomous administration' category was Posts and Telecommunications, which in 1987 employed some 237,000 workers. See Istituto centrale di statistica, *Statistiche sulla amministrazione pubblica* (Rome, 1989), 39–42.

6. On the privatization debate see S. Cassese, P. Bianchi, and V. della Sala, 'Privatization in Italy: Aims and Constraints', in J. Vickers and V. Wright (eds.), *The Politics of Privatization in Western Europe* (London, 1989), 87–100.

7. For an overview of the 'IRI-formula', see P. Bianchi 'The IRI in Italy: Strategic Role and Political Constraints', *West European Politics*, 10/2 (1986), 269–90. See also S. Holland (ed.), *The State as Entrepreneur* (London, 1972); and M. V. Posner and S. J. Woolf, *Italian Public Enterprise* (London, 1967).

8. See E. Gerelli and G. Bognetti (eds.), *La crisi delle partecipazioni statali: Motivi e prospettivi* (Milan, 1981).

9. The classic study of the 'enti pubblici' was a survey published in 1972, which put the figure even higher—at least at the time—at some 60,000. See Ciriec, *Gli enti pubblici italiani: Anagrafe legislative e giurisprudenziali dal 1861 al 1970* (Milan, 1972).

10. The literature on this subject is extensive, though by its nature impressionistic, since there is no precise identification of party affiliation for the many thousands of appointments subject to party nomination. See *inter alia* G. Tamburrano, *L'iceberg democristiano* (Milan, 1974); R. Orfei, *L'occupazione del potere* (Milan, 1976); F. Cazzola (ed.), *Anatomia del potere DC: Enti pubblici e 'centralità' democristiana* (Bari, 1979); A. Sensini, *L'inverno della repubblica* (Milan, 1983); G. Pasquino, *Degenerazione dei partiti e riforme istituzionali* (Rome, 1982); and G. Galli, *L'Italia sotterranea* (Rome, 1984).

11. Though corruption itself is also a serious problem. See F. Cazzola, *Della corruzione* (Bologna, 1988); also D. della Porta, 'Risorse e attori nella corruzione politica: Appunti su tre casi di governo locale in Italia', *Polis*, 4/3 (1990), 499–532.

12. The debate on 'delegificazione' is correspondingly voluminous, and just as difficult to penetrate! For an introduction in English see P. Caretti and E. Cheli, 'Statute and Statutory Instrument in the Evolution of European Constitutional Systems', in A. Pizzorusso (ed.), *Law in the Making: A Comparative Survey* (Berlin, 1988), 131–55; in Italian, see G. Demuro, 'La delegificazione', *Il foro italiano* (June 1989), 5: 355–9. An introduction to the Italian legal system in English is found in M. Capelletti, J. H. Merryman, and J. M. Perillo, *The Italian Legal System: An Introduction* (Stanford, Calif., 1967).

13. S. Cassese, 'L'amministrazione pubblica in Italia', *Rivista trimestrale di scienza della amministrazione*, 2 (1985), 25.

14. David Hine, 'Italy', in F. F. Ridley (ed.), *Government and Administration in Western Europe* (Oxford, 1979), 198–9.
15. See P. V. Uleri, 'The 1987 Referendum', in R. Leonardi and P. Corbetta (eds.), *Italian Politics: A Review*, iii (London, 1989), 155–77; also C. Guarnieri, 'Magistratura e politica: Il caso italiano', *Rivista italiana di scienza politica*, 21/1 (1991), 3–32.
16. See Istituto centrale di statistica, *Statistiche sulla amministrazione pubblica*, 22–4.
17. On these general problems see Cassese, *Il sistema amministrativa*; many of the issues dealt with in detail in this volume are summarized in Cassese, 'L'amministrazione pubblica in Italia'; including personnel questions pp. 16–20. Two recently published volumes of research on public employment give much up-to-date technical detail on the question: see G. Cecora (ed.), *Il pubblico impiego: Struttura e retribuzioni* (Bologna, 1991), and M. d'Alberti, *La dirigenza pubblica* (Bologna, 1990).
18. See Cassese, *Il sistema amministrativa*, 17. More information on this is found in *Questioni amministrativi e questioni meridionali* (Milan, 1977). See also B. Bilotta, 'La burocrazia italiana tra tre culture: Un'ipotesi sullo sviluppo della "meridionalizzazione" della pubblica amministrazione', *Rivista trimestrale di scienza della amministrazione*, 3 (1983), 85–101; also F. Ferraresi, *Burocrazia e politica in Italia* (Bologna, 1980).
19. See M. Rusciani, *Il pubblico impiego in Italia* (Bologna, 1978), and G. Lo Bianco and G. Cecora, 'Politica contrattuale nel pubblico impiego e possibile evoluzione del sistema delle relazioni sindacali', in Cecora (ed.), *Il pubblico impiego*.
20. The second job can also take precedence over the first; in recent years, the fraud squad have been in the habit of raiding workplaces to discover who is really at work, provoking much frantic telephoning and scrambling back in over the railings.
21. See Cassese, *Il sistema amministrativa*, 112–28.
22. G. Pennella (ed.), *La produttività nella pubblica amministrazione*, vol. iii of *La produttività in Italia* (Milan, 1987).
23. See d'Alberti, *La dirigenza pubblica*.
24. See Cassese, *Il sistema amministrativo*, 73–84.
25. For a description of these roles, and of the historical evolution of the Bank, see A. Finocchiaro and A. M. Contessa (eds.), *La Banca d'Italia e i problemi del governo della moneta* (Rome, 1986).
26. See E. Addis, 'Banca d'Italia e politica monetaria: La riallocazione del potere fra stato, mercato, e banca centrale', *Stato e mercato* (Apr. 1987).
27. This is not to suggest that relations have always been smooth beneath the surface. It is evident that, from the latter half of the 1970s, the Bank shifted some way from government thinking on a number of issues connected with monetary policy and the supervision of the banking system. There was, moreover, an episode in 1979 when Mario Sarcinelli, the director-general, was arrested by an investigating magistrate, and the governor himself arraigned on a corruption charge, in what subsequently appeared to be a right-wing conspiracy to deflect Bank of Italy

investigations into the Banco Ambrosiano (which collapsed in a major financial scandal 3 years later). The charges rapidly proved groundless. That any members of the government were involved in this extraordinary episode has never been demonstrated, but in taking the more active approach to banking supervision that the Bank was at the time developing, the risks of running up against financial and political interests was clearly demonstrated. On this question see G. Nardozzi, 'Autonomia della banca centrale e istituzioni di governo', in D. Masciandaro and S. Ristuccia, *L'autonomia delle banche centrali* (Milan, 1988), 228–32.

28. See A. Ardigò and F. Barbano (eds.), *Medici e socio-sanitari: Professione in transizione* (Milan, 1981).

29. See M. Ferrera, 'Italy', in P. Flora (ed.), *Growth to Limits: The European Welfare State since World War Two* (Berlin, 1987); also M. Ferrera and G. Zincone (eds.), *La salute che noi pensiamo: Domande sanitaria e politiche pubbliche in Italia* (Bologna, 1986).

30. For an up-to-date assessment of efforts to regain control of the SSN see M. Ferrera, 'The Politics of Health Reformism: Origins and Performance of the Italian Health Service in Comparative Perspective', in G. Freddi and J. Bjorkman (eds.), *Controlling Medical Professionals* (London, 1989), 116–29.

31. There is, moreover, a sizeable lobby composed of private insurance and health-care companies, supported by the Liberal Party, which would like a more radical system of 'opting-out' by which individuals could be partially or almost entirely excluded from SSN health-care provision, in return for a major reduction in contribution rates to the national system. National insurance contributions, it should be noted, are by no means standardized across all contributors, as the consolidation of the pre-1978 mutual insurance funds might have suggested. On the contrary, contributions, especially as between the employed and the self-employed, vary considerably.

32. On this see the special issue entitled 'Il farmaco nel servizio pubblico: Esperienze regionali', *Salute e territorio*, 52–3 (1987).

33. For an overview, see M. Capelletti, J. H. Merriman, and J. M. Perillo, *The Italian Legal System: An Introduction* (Stanford, Calif., 1967), and G. L. Certoma, *The Italian Legal System* (London, 1985). Note that neither of these works includes the reforms to criminal procedure introduced in 1989, and discussed in this section.

34. The literature on this vexed subject is extensive. For an introduction see Filppo Sabetti, 'The Mafia and the Anti-Mafia: Moments in the Struggle for Justice and Self-Governance in Sicily', in R. Nanetti and R. Catanzaro, *Italian Politics: A Review*, iv (London, 1990), 174–95; also Christopher Duggan, *Fascism and the Mafia* (New Haven, Conn., 1989); Pino Arlacchi, *Mafia Business: The Mafia Ethic and the Spirit of Capitalism* (New York, 1989); Diego Gambetta, 'Fragments of an Economic Theory of the Mafia', *European Journal of Sociology*, 29/2 (1989), 127–45.

35. G. di Federico, 'The Crisis of the Justice System and the Referendum on the Judiciary', in R. Leonardi and P. Corbetta (eds.), *Italian Politics: A. Review*, iii (London, 1989), 25–49.

36. See, on the 1989 reform and the problems of making it effective, Gherardo Colombo, 'The New Code of Criminal Procedure', in F. Sabetti and R. Catanzaro (eds.), *Italian Politics: A Review*, v (London, 1991), 55–68; also Donatella Stasio, 'La giustizia alla prova della verità: Come funziona la nuova procedura penale?', and Alessandro Criscoulo, 'Il nuovo codice di procedura: Quale futura per la giustizia penale', both in *Questi istituzioni*, 17/79–80 (1989), respectively 13–23 and 41–9.

Chapter 9

1. *Constitution*, title v, arts. 114–33.
2. These were Sicily, Sardinia, Vall d'Aosta, Trentino-Alto Adige, and Friuli-Venezia Giulia. The first 4 were established from the beginning of the new republic; the fifth was established in 1964.
3. Istituto centrale di statistica, *Statistiche sulla amministrazione pubblica* (Rome, 1989), 21.
4. On the preference-vote mechanism see ch. 4, pp. 130–2.
5. This is the substance of a classic study of Italian and French centre-periphery relationships by Tarrow, in which he emphasized how local politicians are 'essentially political entrepreneurs with a wide network of contacts in both local and national political systems who use their party affiliations to open up a network of contacts in seeking resources for their communities'. S. Tarrow, *Between Center and Periphery: Grassroots Politicians in Italy and France* (New Haven, Conn., 1977), 19.
6. Law no. 108, 17 Feb. 1968, lays down the following rules for the ordinary regions (the individual constitutional laws setting up the 5 special regions determine the electoral system for the others, on a basis essentially similar to that described below). Regions up to 6 million inhabitants: 80 seats; up to 4 million: 60 seats; up to 3 million: 50 seats; up to 1 million: 40 seats; under 1 million: 30 seats. The electoral system used is similar to that operating nationally. Multi-member constituencies based on provinces are assigned seats in proportion to size. Parties put up lists of candidates, winning seats roughly in proportion to the votes cast, albeit with penalties for the smaller parties. Voters also express non-transferable non-discriminatory preferences for between 1 and 3 candidates on the list of their chosen party, candidates with the most preferences being elected, up to the number of seats assigned to the party.
7. Information drawn from *Guida alle regione* (Rome, 1990–1), 3003–18.
8. On the general problem of low mobility in the regional managerial corps, and the unwillingness of the elected *assessori* to yield managerial functions to regional management, see Rosaria Deganello, 'La dirigenza nelle amministrazioni regionali e locali', in Marco d'Alberti (ed.), *La dirigenza pubblica* (Bologna, 1990), 91–118.
9. On the regional ombudsman, whose role is to investigate allegations of regional maladministration referred to him/her by the regional assembly, see the various entries under 'Difensore civico', in the *Annuario delle autonomie locali* (Rome, successive years).

10. On these issues, on which there is a vast juridical literature, see L. Vandelli, *I controlli sull'amministrazione regionale e locale* (Bologna, 1984).

11. This might imply that the region/state unit of government is represented in the national legislature, as, in their different ways, states are represented in the German Bundesrat or the US Senate. It has frequently been suggested, in discussions over modifications to the Italian Parliament, that the Italian Senate too should become, in effect, a chamber of the regions. The standing conference of regional presidents argued in its evidence to the 1983 parliamentary commission into institutional reform that the Senate should become an indirectly elected chamber of regional governments. (The commission rejected this view however. See Camera dei deputati/Senato della repubblica, *Relazione della Commissione parlamentare per le riforme istituzionali*, vol. i, IX legislatura, doc. XVI-*bis*, no. 3, pp. 15–26.) It should be noted, of course, that in principle there is already an element of regionalism in the Senate in so far as the electoral system for the Senate has a regional base, but representation is essentially proportional to population and party strength, and party loyalty is a far more powerful consideration, in the Senate, than is regional identity.

12. However, the constitution itself has been a source of much dissent on this question. See S. Bartole *et al.*, 'Le regioni, le province, i comuni', in G. Branca (ed.), *Commentario della costituzione*, i (Bologna, 1985).

13. The special regions have not enjoyed powers that differ significantly from the others. In theory, they are to have some of the exclusive legislative power appropriate to a federal system, but the very general aspiration of art. 116, when fleshed out with constitutional legislation for each region, proved very disappointing. Moreover, the jurisprudence of the constitutional court worked as a further limit on the autonomy of both the special and the ordinary regions. The main way in which the special regions differ from the ordinary ones, in fact, has been in the rather higher degree of financial autonomy afforded to them by the special statutes, compared to the 1970 national legislation governing the finances of ordinary regions. This has ensured that more of their financial resources derived from the state by transfer fall into categories giving the region itself some discretion over usage.

14. For a contemporary analysis of this view of the regions see Fondazione Olivetti, *Le regioni: Politica o amministrazione?* (Milan, 1973).

15. For a general survey of these developments see B. Dente, *Governare la frammentazione: Stato regioni ed enti locali in Italia* (Bologna, 1985).

16. On this subject see F. Sorrentino, 'Le fonti del diritto', in G. Amato and A. Barbera (eds.), *Manuale di diritto pubblico* (Bologna, 1986), 165–81; also G. Rolla, 'La determinazione delle materie di competenza regionale nella giurisprudenza costituzionale', *Le regioni* (1982), 100–30.

17. On average, each produces between 25 and 60 items of legislation per year, although a part of this consists of annual re-authorizations of finance under specific spending programmes.

18. See E. Balboni and G. Pastori, 'Il governo regionale e locale', in G. Amato and A. Barbera (eds.), *Manuale di diritto pubblico* (Bologna 1986), 604–6.

19. For an account of the problems of regional finance see D. P. Giarda, *Finanza locale: Idee per una riforma* (Milan, 1982), and by the same author 'Vicende e problemi della finanza regionale', *Quaderni regionali*, 9/1 (1990), 23–32.

20. Whether there should be is of course debatable. There is considerable anecdotal evidence, and a widespread belief, that northern regions make better use of capital investment funding than do southern ones. Certainly, in the areas of agriculture, transport, and health, the latter regions find themselves unable to make use of funds made available, with significant build-up of passive reserves. And in so far as the regional governments are there to produce services and social capital, if funds are allocated disproportionately to areas which make least efficient use of them, and indeed, by some criteria, even have less urgent need of them, then the funding formulae adopted entail some misallocation of resources. On this issue see Giarda, 'Vicende e problemi della finanza regionale', 23–32.

21. The one qualification to this picture is perhaps to be found in the emergence of the so-called 'league' phenomenon, considered in ch. 4. As explained there, these parties constitute a (to date at least) largely northern protest against what seems to be perceived as the cost of the (allegedly southern-dominated) system of central government in Rome for northern tax-payers. The message is confused with several others, however, including some overtly racist ones.

22. For a list of legislation establishing such mixed committees see S. Cassese, 'La regionalizzazione economica in Italia: Un sistema alla ricerca di un equilibrio', in *Studi in memoria di Vittorio Bachelet*, iii: *Amministrazione e economia* (Milan, 1987), 165–77. See also C. Desideri and L. Torchia, *I raccordi fra stato e regioni* (Milan, 1986).

23. Among the few studies in this vein see R. Putnam, R. Leonardi, and R. Nanetti, *La pianta e le radici* (Bologna, 1984); and R. Leonardi, *La regione Basilicata* (Bologna, 1987); S. Mannozzi and V. Visco Comandini, *Le funzioni del governo locale in Italia*, ii: *Verifica dell'effettività* (Milan, 1990); G. Maltinti and A. Petretto (eds.), *Finanziamento ed efficenza della spesa pubblica locale* (Turin, 1987).

24. See F. Merloni (ed.), *La nuova provincia nella riforma del governo locale*, Unione delle province italiane, Quaderni delle autonomie, no. 1 (Rome, 1988).

25. For a study of local-government administration showing the impact of problems of resource shortage at provincial and local level on administrative efficiency, see Mannozzi and Visco Comandini, *Le funzioni del governo locale in Italia*, ii.

26. See E. Barusso, *Il nuovo ordinamento delle autonomie locali: Commento alla legge 8-6-90 n. 142* (Naples, 1990).

27. See G. Bettin and A. Magnier, *Chi governa la città? Una ricerca sugli assessori comunali* (Padua, 1991).

28. Note that like any other 'constructive vote of no confidence' this procedure can do no more than hold a minority administration in office; it cannot by itself create a majority where there is none, and a mayor who survives because there is no agreement on a replacement still has the problem of getting his policies through a hostile council. His only weapon is the threat to resign and provoke fresh elections.

Chapter 10

1. On the 'relance' of economic integration under the impetus of the internal-market programme, see L. Tsoukalis, *The New European Economy* (Oxford, 1991).

2. On the political and institutional developments stemming from the Single European Act, and from later moves towards closer political integration culminating in the 1991 Maastricht European Council on institutional reform, see S. Hoffman and R. Keohane (eds.), *The New European Community* (Boulder, Col., 1991).

3. The cost—for Italy as, until recently, for France—has of course been the loss of some significant level of output, given the high interest rates needed both to control inflationary pressures and to compensate capital for the perceived higher risk of staying with the lira. However, the labour-market discipline of the ERM is widely believed, in Italy at least, to have had a powerful effect in contributing to the reduction of the inflation differential between Italy and the rest of the Community.

4. See F. Giavazzi and M. Pagano, 'The Advantage of Tying One's Hands', *European Economic Review*, 32 (1988), 1055–82, from which the expression comes. The authors' case is that EMS membership 'is an effective discipline for inflation-prone countries. . . . [it] brings potentially large credibility gains to policy-makers. . . . [it not only] attaches an extra penalty to inflation, in terms of real appreciation, but makes the public aware that the policy-maker is faced with such penalty, and thus helps to overcome the inefficiency stemming from the public's mistrust of the authorities.'

5. Taking the most general indicator—overall support for the integration process—and using the Eurobarometer scale (from 4 ('very much in favour') to 1 ('very much against')) the Italian average for 1973 to 1986 was 3.32 (bettered only by Luxembourg's 3.37). (See *Eurobaromètre*, 25 (June 1986), 52–3). In a series of surveys between autumn 1987 and spring 1989, Italian support for a 'European government by 1992' remained within the 68–77% range, against 49–56% for the EC as a whole (see *Eurobarometre*, 31, Annex 22).

6. It is impossible to list here the many areas in which this applies. An effective competition policy at Community level, for example, and genuinely free access to all national markets require a progressive reduction of public subsidies to industry and an end to restrictive practices in public procurement. The principles underlying monetary integration—especially as now enunciated by the Delors Report—

demand a progressive approximation of national policies of macro-economic management.

7. Under a third outcome, in which monetary union is allowed to proceed even though Italy (and perhaps other high-deficit countries) has not made the required changes to budget deficits, the cost will fall on the credibility and effectiveness of the monetary policy pursued by the European Central Bank under a united European monetary system. Admittedly, Italy is not the only country which could be seen as seeking to loosen the rigour of monetary policy as it is imposed, through the existing European Monetary System, by the strongest central banks—most notably the Bundesbank. On these issues see, *inter alia*, H. Sherman, R. Brown, P. Jacquet, and D. Julius, *Monetary Implications of the 1992 Process* (London, 1990) and M. de Cecco and A. Giovannini, *A Central Bank for Europe? Perspectives on Monetary Unification after 10 Years of the EMS* (Cambridge, 1989).

8. Commission of the European Communities, *Seventh Annual Report to the European Parliament on the Commission Monitoring of the Application of Community Law, 1989*, Com. (90)288, Final (Brussels, 22 May 1990).

9. Ibid. 45.

10. Only four other states shared the dubious distinction of appearing in this list: Belgium with six judgements, Greece with five, Germany with three, and The Netherlands with one. See Commission of the European Communities, *Implementation of the Legal Measures Required to Build the Single Market, Communication from the Commission to the European Parliament*, Com. (90)473, Final (Brussels, 5 Oct. 1990).

11. See H. Wallace, 'The Presidency of the European Council of Ministers: The Case of the United Kingdom', and P. M. Defrages, 'La Présidence du Conseil des ministres des Communautés européennes: Rapport sur la France', both in C. O'Nuallain, *The Presidency of the European Council of Ministers* (London, 1985), respectively 119–37, and 237–59.

12. See F. Pocur *et al.*, 'Italie', in H. Siedentopf and J. Ziller (eds.), *Making European Policies Work: The Implementation of Community Policies in the Member States*, ii (national reports) (London, 1988), 449–517; A. Papisca, 'La Présidence du Conseil des ministres des Communautés européennes: Rapport national sur l'Italie', in O'Nuallain, *The Presidency of the European Council of Ministers*, 167–71; and N. Ronzitti, 'European Policy Formulation in the Italian Administrative System', *International Spectator*, 22 (1987), 207–15.

13. See Papisca, 'La Présidence', 167–71; also A. Massai, 'Il coordinamento interno delle politiche comunitarie', *Quaderni costituzionali*, 2/2 (1982), 481–90; G. Grotanelli de' Santi and F. Francioni (eds.), *National and Supranational Powers in the Shaping of Community Policies* (Milan, 1984).

14. On 'ministers without portfolio' see C. Romanelli Grimaldi, *I ministri senza portafoglio nell'ordinamento giuridico italiano* (Padua, 1984), and G. Guaglia, 'Aspetti e tendenze della prassi costituzionale in tema di ministri senza portafoglio', *Rivista trimestrale di diritto pubblico*, 34/2 (1984), 422–75.

15. On the role of the Permanent Delegation see D. Lasok and D. W. Bridge, *Law and Institutions of the European Communities*, 4th edn. (London, 1989), 199–202.

16. Even during the Italian presidency of the Council of Ministers during the period July–Dec. 1990, this tendency to exclude the Department was still noticeable. One of the major tasks of the presidency during this period was preparing the two European Community inter-governmental conferences on political union and monetary union, due to be held the following year at Maastricht. This task was co-ordinated from the prime minister's office, but by the prime minister's diplomatic adviser, not by the Department, which latter appears to have played no role in the working parties of officials set up to co-ordinate the process. On the Italian presidency of 1990 see P. Daniels, D. J. Hine, and M. Neri Gualdesi, *Italy, the European Community, and the 1990 Presidency: Policy Trends and Policy Performance*, Centre for Mediterranean Studies, University of Bristol, Occasional Paper no. 3 (June 1991), esp. 17–38.

17. These are respectively law no. 183, 16 Apr. 1987, *Coordinamento delle politiche riguardanti l'appartenenza dell'Italia alle Comunità europee ed adeguamento dell'ordinamento interno agli atti normativi comunitari*; and law no. 86, 9 Mar. 1989, *Norme generali sulla partecipazione dell'Italia al processo normativo comunitario e sulle procedure di esecuzione degli obblighi comunitari*.

18. As in the case of public expenditure paid for from domestically-raised revenue, expenditure in Italy on projects financed by the European Community encountered numerous administrative and legal obstacles tending to delay action and to build up unspent passive balances. The establishment, in law no. 183, 1987, of a so-called *fondo di rotazione* (revolving fund) was intended to improve this problem.

19. Law no. 86, 9 Mar. 1989. For a commentary see N. Ronzitti, 'The Internal Market, Italian Law, and the Public Administration', *International Spectator*, 25 (1990), 38–44.

20. See L. Carlassare, 'Il ruolo del Parlamento e la nuova disciplina del potere regolamentare', *Quaderni costituzionale*, 10/1 (Apr. 1990), 7–52; also in the same issue E. Cheli, 'Ruolo dell'esecutivo e sviluppi recenti del potere regolamentare', 53–76.

21. See D. J. Hine and R. Finocchi, 'The Italian Prime Minister', *West European Politics*, 14/2 (1991), 74–96.

22. DPC 30 Apr. 1990, no. 150, 'Regolamento concernente l'organizzazione del Dipartimento per il coordinamento delle politiche comunitarie nell'ambito della presidenza del Consiglio dei ministri'.

23. See P. Daniels, 'Italy', in J. Lodge (ed.), *The European Parliamentary Elections of 1989* (London, 1989), 159–78.

Conclusion

1. For an extensive analysis of the range of failed proposals for institutional reform put forward in the 1987–92 legislature, see, Carlo Fusaro, *Guida alle riforme istituzionali* (Soveria Mannelli, 1991).

2. Ironically, moreover, the 1991 referendum, which reduced the number of preference votes castable by a voter to only one, quickly came to be seen as a leap in the dark rather than a corrective. The proponents of the referendum, and, it may be surmised, the vast majority of voters who supported the proposal, supposed that the reduction to one of the number of preference votes cast would also reduce the struggle to control public-sector resources, and the internal factionalism rife within the governing parties. In the aftermath of the referendum, however, commentators and party activists asked whether, on the contrary, it might not, in the long run, actually reduce further the cohesion of the parties, and further increase the struggle for public patronage. Candidates who had previously been elected through a faction's organization might now have to build their own personal machine.

3. Small parties in Italy—those winning below 5 per cent of the vote—rarely win parliamentary seats (either outright, or those assigned to a particular constituency after national aggregating) in any constituency which has fewer than 20 seats altogether.

4. See G. Sartori, 'Le riforme istituzionali tra buone e cattive', *Rivista italiana di scienza politica*, 21/3 (1991), 375–407.

Italian Prime Ministers and Governments since June 1945

Prime minister	Coalition	Duration
Parri	DC–PCI–PSI–PLI–PDL–Pd'A	June–Dec. 1945
De Gasperi I	DC–PCI–PSI–PLI–PDL–Pd'A	Dec. 1945–July 1946
De Gasperi II	DC–PCI–PSI–PRI	July 1946–Feb. 1947
De Gasperi III	DC–PCI–PSI	Feb.–May 1947
De Gasperi IV	DC–PLI–PSLI–PRI	May 1947—May 1948
De Gasperi V	DC–PLI–PSLI–PRI	May 1948–Jan. 1950
De Gasperi VI	DC–PSLI–PRI	Jan. 1950–July 1951
De Gasperi VII	DC–PRI	July 1951–July 1953
De Gasperi VIII	DC	July–Aug. 1953
Pella	DC	Aug. 1953–Jan. 1954
Fanfani I	DC	Jan.–Feb. 1954
Scelba	DC–PDSI–PLI	Feb. 1954–July 1955
Segni I	DC–PSDI–PLI	July 1955–May 1957
Zoli	DC	May 1957–July 1958
Fanfani II	DC–PSDI	July 1958–Feb. 1959
Segni II	DC	Feb. 1959–Mar. 1960
Tambroni	DC	Mar.–July 1960
Fanfani III	DC	July 1960–Feb. 1962
Fanfani IV	DC–PSDI–PRI	Feb. 1962–June 1963
Leone I	DC	June–Dec. 1963
Moro I	DC–PSI–PSDI–PRI	Dec. 1963–July 1964
Moro II	DC–PSI–PSDI–PRI	July 1964–Feb. 1966
Moro III	DC–PSI–PSDI–PRI	Feb. 1966–June 1968
Leone II	DC	June–Dec. 1968
Rumor I	DC–PSI–PRI	Dec. 1968–Aug. 1969
Rumor II	DC	Aug. 1969–Mar. 1970
Rumor III	DC–PSI–PSDI–PRI	Mar.–Aug. 1970
Colombo	DC–PSI–PSDI–PRI	Aug. 1970–Feb. 1972
Andreotti I	DC	Feb.–June 1972
Andreotti II	DC–PSDI–PLI	June 1972–July 1973
Rumor IV	DC–PSI–PSDI–PRI	July 1973–Mar.1974
Rumor V	DC–PSI–PSDI	Mar.–Nov. 1974
Moro IV	DC–PRI	Nov. 1974–Feb. 1976
Moro V	DC	Feb.–July 1976

Prime minister	Coalition	Duration
Andreotti III	DC	July 1976–Mar. 1978
Andreotti IV	DC	Mar. 1978–Jan. 1979
Andreotti V	DC–PSDI–PRI	Jan.–Aug. 1979
Cossiga I	DC–PSDI–PLI	Aug.–Mar. 1980
Cossiga II	DC–PSI–PRI	Mar.–Sept. 1980
Forlani	DC–PSI–PSDI–PRI	Sept. 1980–July 1981
Spadolini I	DC–PSI–PSDI–PRI–PLI	July 1981–Aug. 1982
Spadolini II	DC–PSI–PSDI–PRI–PLI	Aug. 1982–Dec. 1982
Fanfani V	DC–PSI–PSDI–PLI	Dec. 1982–Aug. 1983
Craxi I	DC–PSI–PSDI–PRI–PLI	Aug. 1983–Aug. 1986
Craxi II	DC–PSI–PSDI–PRI–PLI	Aug. 1986–Apr. 1987
Fanfani VI	DC	Apr.–July 1987
Goria	DC–PSI–PSDI–PRI–PLI	July 1987–Apr. 1988
De Mita	DC–PSI–PSDI–PRI–PLI	Apr. 1988–Aug. 1989
Andreotti VI	DC–PSI–PSDI–PRI–PLI	Aug. 1989–Apr. 1991
Andreotti VII	DC–PSI–PSDI–PLI	Apr. 1991–June 1992

Notes: 1. *Period of office*: During a political crisis, prime ministers are generally requested to stay in office until their successors are sworn in; the periods given thus often include some weeks of 'caretaker' rather than 'effective' stewardship.

2. *Coalitions:* Parties named are those holding office in the Council of Ministers; other parties are from time to time essential elements of the parliamentary coalition on which the government depends.

3. *Abbreviations*: DC: Christian Democracy; PCI: Communist Party; PSI: Socialist Party; PSLI and PSDI: early and subsequent initials of the Social Democrat Party; PRI: Republican Party; PLI: Liberal Party; the PDL (Democratic Labour Party) and the Pd'A (Action Party) were casualties of the Cold War polarization of Italian politics and did not outlive the 1940s.

APPENDIX II

Presidents of the Republic since 1946

1946–8	Enrico de Nicola
1948–55	Luigi Einaudi
1955–62	Giovanni Gronchi
1962–4	Antonio Segni
1964–71	Giuseppe Saragat
1971–8	Giovanni Leone
1978–85	Alessandro Pertini
1985–92	Francesco Cossiga
1992–	Oscar Luigi Scalfaro

APPENDIX III

Political Secretaries of the Christian Democrat Party since 1945

1945–6	Alcide De Gasperi
1946–9	Atillio Piccioni
1949	Giuseppe Cappi
1949–50	Paolo Emilio Taviani
1950–3	Guido Gonella
1953–4	Alcide De Gasperi
1954–9	Amintore Fanfani
1959–64	Aldo Moro
1964–8	Mariano Rumor
1968–9	Flaminio Piccoli
1969–73	Arnaldo Forlani
1973–5	Amintore Fanfani
1975–80	Benigno Zaccagnini
1980–2	Flaminio Piccoli
1982–9	Ciriaco De Mita
1989–92	Arnaldo Forlani

APPENDIX IV

Political Secretaries of the Italian Communist Party, 1945–1991

1945–64	Palmiro Togliatti
1964 71	Luigi Longo
1971–84	Enrico Berlinguer
1984–9	Alessandro Natta
1989–91	Achille Occhetto

APPENDIX V

The Italian Constitution: Articles 55–139

PART II
ORGANIZATION OF THE REPUBLIC

TITLE I
PARLIAMENT

Section I *The Houses*

Article 55

Parliament consists of the Chamber of Deputies and the Senate of the Republic.

Parliament holds a joint sitting of both Houses only in those cases set forth by the Constitution.

Article 56[1]

The Chamber of Deputies is elected by universal and direct suffrage.

The number of Deputies is six hundred and thirty.

Every voter who has reached the age of twenty five on the day of elections is eligible to become a member of the Chamber of Deputies.

Division of seats among the electoral districts is obtained by dividing the number of inhabitants of the Republic, registered at the last general census, by six hundred and thirty and distributing the seats in proportion to the population of each electoral district, on the basis of the quotients and the highest figures below these quotients.

Article 57[2]

The Senate of the Republic is elected on a Regional basis.

The number of Senators chosen through elections is three hundred and fifteen.

No Region elects fewer than seven Senators; save Molise which elects two, and Valle d'Aosta which elects one.

Division of seats among the Regions, according to the provisions set out in the preceding paragraph, is made in proportion to the population of the Regions at the last general census, on the basis of the quotients and the highest figures below these quotients.

---

[1] As amended by article 1 of the constitutional law No. 2 of February 9, 1963.

[2] As amended by article 2 of the constitutional law No. 3 of December 27, 1963.

Article 58

Senators are elected by universal and direct suffrage by voters over twenty-five years of age.

Voters over forty years of age are eligible for membership.

Article 59

A former President of the Republic is by right a Senator for life, unless he refuses to accept the nomination.

The President of the Republic may appoint as Senators for life five citizens who have brought honour to the country through their exceptional merits in social, scientific, artistic and literary fields.

Article 60[3]

The Chamber of Deputies and the Senate of the Republic are elected for a term of five years.

The term of each House may not be extended save by law and only in the event of a war.

Article 61

Election of the new Houses must take place within seventy days after the end of the term of the previous Parliament. The first sitting must be held not later than twenty days after the elections.

The powers of the previous Houses are extended until the new Houses meet.

Article 62

The Houses meet on the first of February and of October, unless it is a holiday.

Extraordinary summonings may be issued for each House upon the initiative of its President or of the President of the Republic or of one-third of its members.

When there is an extraordinary summoning for one House the other House is also convened by right.

Article 63

Each House elects its President and the members of the Presiding Officers Committee from among its members.

The President and the members of the Presiding Officers Committee of the Chamber of Deputies shall preside whenever Parliament meets in joint session.

Article 64

Each House sets it own Rules by an absolute majority of its members.

Sittings are open to the public; nevertheless, each of the two Houses and Parliament in joint sessions may decide to hold closed sittings.

[3] As amended by article 3 of the constitutional law No. 2 of February 9, 1963.

The decisions of each House and of Parliament are not valid unless the majority of the members are present, and unless they are voted upon by a majority of the members present, save where the Constitution requires a special majority.

Members of the Government, even if they are not members of the Houses, have the right, and when requested have the duty, to attend sittings. They have the right to be heard whenever they request it.

Article 65

The law determines cases of ineligibility for or incompatibility with the position of Deputy or Senator.

No person may be a member of both Houses at the same time.

Article 66

Each House decides as to the conditions for admission of its members and as to any subsequently arising causes for ineligibility and incompatibility.

Article 67

Each member of Parliament represents the country and carries out his duties without restraint of mandate.

Article 68

Members of Parliament may not be proceeded against for opinions expressed and votes given in the exercise of their duties.

No member of Parliament may, without the authorization of the House to which he belongs, be subjected to criminal proceedings, nor be arrested or otherwise deprived of his personal liberty, nor be subjected to warrants to search his person or his home unless he be caught in the act of committing an offence for which a warrant or an order of arrest is compulsory.

Similar authorization is required to arrest or keep in a state of detention a member of Parliament in order to execute even an irrevocable sentence.

Article 69

Members of Parliament receive an allowance which is established by law.

Section II *Drafting Laws*

Article 70

The legislative function is carried out by the two Houses.

Article 71

Bills may be introduced by the Government, by each member of the two Houses and by those organs and bodies which are entitled to do so by constitutional law.

Bills may be introduced by the people through a proposal supported by no less than fifty thousand voters, drafted in the form of articles.

Article 72

Every Bill submitted to one of the Houses is, according to its Rules, examined by a Committee and then by the House itself, which first approves it article by article and subsequently with a final vote.

The Rules provide for an abbreviated procedure in the case of Bills declared to be urgent.

They also lay down in which cases and in what manner the examination and approval of Bills shall be entrusted to committees including standing committees, so composed as to reflect the proportion of the Parliamentary Groups. In such cases as well, a Bill until it is finally voted upon, may be submitted to the House if the Government or one-tenth of the members of the House or one-fifth of the Committee demand that it either be debated and voted on by the House itself or be entrusted to the latter for its final approval only with a debate limited to the motivation of votes. The rules decide the ways in which the work of the Committees shall be made public.

The normal procedure for debating and voting on Bills is always applied by the House in the case of Bills of a constitutional and electoral nature for those delegating legislature, authorizing the ratification of international treaties and voting on budgets and expenditure accounts.

Article 73

Laws are promulgated by the President of the Republic within one month after their approval.

If the Houses, each with an absolute majority of its members, declare a Bill to be urgent, it is promulgated within the time laid down in the Bill itself.

Laws are published immediately after having been promulgated and come into force on the fifteenth day after their publication, unless the laws themselves provide otherwise.

Article 74

The President of the Republic, before promulgating a law, may request a new decision by means of a message to both Houses in which the reasons for such action are set forth.

If the Houses approve the Bill once more, it must be promulgated.

Article 75

A referendum is held to decide on the total or partial repeal of a law or of an act having force of law, if it is demanded by five hundred thousand voters or by five Regional Councils.

A referendum is not allowed in the case of fiscal or budget laws, amnesties or pardons, or laws authorizing the ratification of international treaties.

All citizens entitled to vote in the election of the members of the Chamber of Deputies have the right to vote in the referendum.

The proposal submitted to a referendum is approved if the majority of those eligible have participated in the voting, and if it has received a majority of valid votes.

The law lays down ways for carrying out a referendum.

Article 76

The exercise of the legislative function may be delegated to the Government only after having established principles and criteria, for a limited period of time and for specified objects.

Article 77

The Government may not, unless delegated by the Houses, issue decrees having the value of ordinary law.

When, in exceptional cases of necessity and urgency, the Governent issues on its own responsibility emegency executive decrees having force of law, on the same day it shall submit them to the Houses for conversion into laws. The Houses, even if they have been previously dissolved, are expressly summoned for this pupose and shall meet within five days.

Decrees lose effect as of the day of issue if they are not converted into laws within sixty days of their publication. The House may, however, regulate with laws legal questions arising out of decrees not yet converted into laws.

Article 78

The Houses declare the state of war and confer the necessary powers on the government.

Article 79

Amnesty and indult are granted by the President of the Republic on the basis of a delegated law enacted by the Houses.

Amnesty and indult are not applicable in the case of offences committed after the introduction of the Bill concerning the said delegated legislation on this matter.

Article 80

The Houses authorize by law the ratification of international treaties of a political nature or which provide for arbitration or definition of controversies by judgement or imply modifications to the territory of the country or financial burdens or changes in the law.

Article 81

The Houses vote on the budgets and the expenditure accounts submitted by the Government each year.

The law may authorize the Government for a maximum period not exceeding four months to use the budget before its approval.

No new taxes or new expenditures can be established by the law approving the budget.

In all other laws implying new or additional expenditures the means for covering them must be set forth.

Article 82

Each House may order inquiries into matters of public interest.

To this end, it appoints a Committee of its own members, so composed as to reflect the proportion of the different political groups. The Committee of Enquiry carries out its investigations and examinations with the same powers and the same limitations as the judicial authorites.

TITLE II
THE PRESIDENT OF THE REPUBLIC

Article 83

The President of the Republic is elected by Parliament in a joint sitting of the two Houses.

Three delegates from each Region, elected by the Regional Council in such a way as to ensure representation of minorities, take part in the election.

Only Valle d'Aosta is represented by one delegate.

Presidential elections take place by secret ballot with two-thirds majority of the Assembly. After the third ballot an absolute majority is sufficient.

Article 84

Any citizen over fifty years of age enjoying civil and political rights is elegible for election as President of the Republic.

The office of President of the Republic is incompatible with any other office.

The allowances and endowments of the President are established by law.

Article 85

The Presidential term shall be seven years.

Thirty days before the term lapses the President of the Chamber of Deputies summons the two Houses in a joint sitting together with the Regional delegates to elect the new President of the Republic.

If Parliament has been dissolved or it has to be dissolved within three months, the election is held within fifteen days of the meeting of the new Houses. Meanwhile the powers of the President are prolonged.

Article 86

Should the President be impeded in fulfilling his duties they are carried out by the President of the Senate.

In case of permanent incapacity or death or resignation of the President of the Republic, the President of the Chamber of Deputies provides for the election of a new President of the Republic within fifteen days, unless a longer period is required either because Parliament has been dissolved or because its term expires in less than three months.

Article 87

The President of the Republic is the head of the State and represents national unity.

He may send messages to the Houses.

He determines the day for the elections of the new Houses and for their first meeting.

He authorizes the introduction to the Houses of Bills proposed by the Government.

He promulgates laws and issues decrees having the value of laws and regulations.

He determines the day for calling a referendum in the cases laid down by the Constitution.

He appoints, in the cases laid down by law, the officers of the State.

He accredits and receives diplomatic representatives and ratifies international treaties, provided they be authorized by the Houses whenever such authorization is necessary.

He is the commander of the Armed Forces, presides over the Supreme Defence Council, which is constituted by law, and declares the state of war when the Houses so decide.

He presides over the High Council of the Judiciary.

He may grant pardons and commute punishments.

He confers the honours of the Republic.

Article 88

The President of the Republic may dissolve one or both Houses, having heard their Presidents.

Article 89

No act of the President of the Republic is valid unless it is countersigned by the Ministers who have submitted it and who assume full responsibility for it.

Acts having the value of law and such others as laid down by law have to be signed also by the President of the Council of Ministers.

Article 90

The President of the Republic cannot be held responsible for the acts carried out in the exercise of his duties, save in the cases either of high treason or of action intended to breach the Constitution.

In such cases he is impeached by Parliament in a joint sitting of the two Houses and with an absolute majority of its members.

Article 91

The President of the Republic, before taking office, shall swear before Parliament in a joint sitting of the two Houses an oath of loyalty to the Republic and to the Constitution.

TITLE III
THE GOVERNMENT

Section I *The Council of Ministers*

Article 92

The Government of the Republic consists of the President of the Council and of the Ministers, who together constitute the Council of Ministers.

The President of the Republic appoints the President of the Council of Ministers and the Ministers who are proposed by him.

Article 93

Before assuming office the President of the Council of Ministers and the Ministers shall be sworn in before the President of the Republic.

Article 94

The Government must enjoy the confidence of the two Houses.

Each House grants or withdraws its confidence by a motion in which reasons are set forth and which is submitted to a roll-call vote.

Within ten days of its appointment, the Government shall present itself to Parliament and ask for its confidence.

The contrary vote of one or both Houses on a proposal made by the Government does not necessitate resignation.

A motion of no confidence must be signed by at least one-tenth of the members in either House and can be debated only three days after its submission.

Article 95

The President of the Council of Ministers conducts and is responsible for the general policy of the Government. He assures the unity and consistency of the political and administrative programme by promoting and co-ordinating the activity of the Ministers.

Ministers are responsible collectively for the decisions of the Council of Ministers and individually for those of their own Ministries.

The law lays down the regulations pertaining to the Presidency of the Council of Ministers and establishes the number, competence and organization of Ministries.

Article 96

The two Houses in a joint sitting can impeach the President of the Council of Ministers and the Ministers for crimes committed in the exercise of their duties.

Section II *Public Administration*

Article 97

Public offices are organized according to the provisions of the law, so as to guarantee efficiency and impartiality of administration.

The competence, duties and responsibilities of public officers are laid down in the regulations of public offices.

To gain employment in public administrations citizens must take competitive examinations, unless otherwise laid down by law.

Article 98

Civil servants are exclusively at the service of the country.

If they are members of Parliament they cannot be promoted save by seniority.

Limitations to the right of registering as members of political parties may be laid down by law for judges, professional members of the Armed Forces while in service, police officers, and diplomatic and consular representatives abroad.

Section III *Auxiliary Bodies*

Article 99

The National Council of Economy and Labour is composed, according to the provisions of the law, of experts and representatives of professional categories, in such a way that numerical relevance and their qualifications be taken into consideration.

It is an advisory body to the Houses and to the Government for such questions and duties as are attributed to it by law.

It has the right to introduce Bills and may contribute to the drafting of economic and social laws according to the principles and within the limits laid down by law.

Article 100

The Council of State is a body with advisory functions on juridical-administrative matters; it also performs juridical functions in the administrative field.

The Court of Accounts exercises a form of preventive control on the legitimacy of government measures and of subsequent control on the management of the State budget. It takes part, in the cases and in the ways laid down by law, in the control of the financial management of those bodies to which the State contributes in an established manner.

It reports directly to the Houses on the results of the audit so executed.

The law ensures the independence of these two bodies and of their members *vis-à-vis* the Government.

Title IV
The Judiciary

Section I *Jurisdictional Organization*

Article 101

Justice is administered only in the name of the people.

The judges are subject only to the law.

Article 102

The judicial power is carried out by permanent judges appointed and regulated according to the provisions for the Judiciary.

No special or extraordinary courts may be created.

For dealing with specific matters, specialized sections may be established only within the normal judicial organs and properly qualified citizens, who are not members of the Judiciary, may participate in them.

The law lays down the cases and the ways in which the people may directly participate in the administration of justice.

Article 103

The Council of State and other bodies concerned with administrative justice have jurisdiction over the protection of legitimate interests against administrative action and, in specific fields laid down by law, they protect even subjective rights.

The Court of Accounts has jurisdiction over matters of public accounts and over other questions as specified by law.

Military tribunals in war-time have jurisdiction as provided for by law.

In peace-time their jurisdiction is limited to military offences committed by members of the Armed Forces.

Article 104

The Judiciary is an autonomous institution independent of any other power.

The President of the Republic is chairman of the High Council of the Judiciary.

The President and the Attorney General of the Supreme Court of Appeal are *ipso jure* members of it.

Of the other members, two-thirds are elected by all regular judges of different categories and one-third by Parliament in a joint sitting of the two Houses among full professors of law faculties and lawyers in practice for at least fifteen years.

The Council elects a vice-President from among the members chosen by Parliament.

The elected members of the Council hold office for four years and are not immediately re-eligible.

While they are in office, they may not be registered on the rolls of the legal profession nor be members either of Parliament or of a Regional Council.

Article 105

According to the provisions for the Judiciary, the High Council of the Judiciary is entrusted with the appointment, assignment, transfer, promotion and disciplinary measures concerning judges.

Article 106

The appointment of permanent judges is based on a competitive examination.

According to the laws for the Judiciary, honorary judges may be named either by appointment or by election to perform all the duties attributed to one-man courts.

On the proposal of the High Council of the Judiciary, full professors of law, and lawyers in practice, for at least fifteen years, registered in the special rolls entitling them to practise in the higher courts, may be appointed Councillors of the Supreme Court of Appeal for exceptional merit.

Article 107

Judges cannot be removed from their office. They may not be dismissed or suspended from their duties nor transferred to other courts or duties save by a decision of the High Council of the Judiciary made either for reasons of and with guarantees for their defence laid down by the laws and regulations of the Judiciary or with their own consent.

The Minister of Justice is entitled to undertake disciplinary action.

Only their different functions differentiate judges.

The Public Prosecutor is safeguarded by the guarantees laid down in the provisions for the Judiciary.

Article 108

The provisions for the Judiciary and every judicial office are established by law.

The law ensures the independence of the judges of Special Courts, Public Prosecutors attached to these Courts and other persons taking part in the administration of justice.

Article 109

The judicial police are directly available for the judicial authority.

Article 110

Without prejudice to the competence of the High Council of the Judiciary, the organization and operation of the services related to the administration of the laws are entrusted to the Minister of Justice.

Section II *Rules on the Administration of Justice*

Article 111

All judicial decisions must be motivated [i.e. justified and explained].

Appeals to the Supreme Court of Appeal are always allowed against sentences and measures concerning personal liberty delivered by ordinary or special courts, whenever there is a violation of law.

This rule may be disregarded only in the case of sentences passed by Military Courts in time of war.

Appeals to the Supreme Court of Appeal against decisions of the Council of State and of the Court of Accounts are only allowed for motives concerning jurisdiction.

Article 112

The Public Prosecutor has the duty to institute criminal proceedings.

Article 113

Jurisdictional protection of rights and legitimate interest before the organs of ordinary or administrative justice is always allowed against decisions taken by public administration.

Such jurisdictional protection may neither be excluded in nor be limited to special kinds of appeal or specific categories of administrative decisions.

The law lays down those jurisdictional organs which may annul decisions made by the public administration in the cases and with the legal consequences provided for by the law itself.

TITLE V

THE REGIONS, THE PROVINCES, THE MUNICIPALITIES

Article 114

The Republic is divided into Regions, Provinces and Municipalities.

Article 115

The Regions are constituted as autonomous territorial bodies with their own powers and functions according to the principles established by the Constitution.

Article 116

Particular forms and conditions of autonomy, according to special statutes approved with constitutional laws, are attributed to Sicilia, Sardegna, Trentino-Alto Adige, Friuli-Venzia Giulia and the Valle d'Aosta.

Article 117

Within the limits of the fundamental principles established by the laws of the State, the Region legislates in regard to the following matters, provided that such legislation is not in contrast with the national interest or with that of other Regions:

Organization of the offices and of the administrative bodies dependent on the Region;
Town districts;
Local, urban and rural police;
Fairs and markets;
Public charities, health and hospital assistance;
Artisan and professional training and school aid;
Museums and libraries of local bodies;
Town planning;
Tourist trade and hotel industry;

Tram and motor coach services of Regional interest;
Roads, aqueducts, and public works of Regional interest;
Lake navigation and ports;
Mineral and thermal waters;
Quarries and peat bogs;
Hunting;
Fishing in lake and river waters;
Agriculture and forestry;
Other matters indicated by constitutional laws.

The laws of the Republic may delegate power to the Region to issue rules for their implementation.

Article 118

The administrative functions pertaining to the matters listed in the preceding article belong to the Region, except those of exclusively local interest which, by the laws of the Republic, may be entrusted to the Provinces, to the Municipalities or to other local authorities.

The State may delegate by law the exercise of other functions of an administrative nature to the Region.

The Region normally exercises its administrative functions by delegating them to the Provinces, Municipalities or other local authorities or by administering them through their offices.

Article 119

The Regions have financial autonomy within the forms and limits laid down by the laws of the Republic, which coordinate this autonomy with the finances of the State, of the provinces and of the Municipalities.

The Regions are assigned their own taxes and quotas of State taxes, according to the needs of the Regions for necessary expenditure, so that their normal functions may be fulfilled.

The State assigns by law special allocations to single Regions for specific purposes and particularly for the development of southern and insular Italy.

The Region has its own public property in accordance with the laws of the Republic.

Article 120

The Region may not levy import or export duties on transit between Regions.

The Region may not adopt provisions which hinder in any way the free movement of persons and goods between Regions.

The Regions may not limit the right of citizens to exercise their profession, employment or labour in any part of the national territory.

Article 121

The organs of the Region are: the Regional Council, the Regional Government and its President.

The Regional Council exercises the legislative and rule making powers granted to the Region and all the other functions conferred on it by the Constitution and by law. It may propose Bills to Parliament.

The Regional Government is vested with executive power for the Region.

The President of the Regional Government represents the Region; he promulgates Regional laws and regulations; he carries out the administrative functions delegated to the Region by the State in accordance with the instructions of the central Government.

Article 122

The electoral system, the number and cases of ineligibilty and incompatibility of Regional Councillors are established by the laws of the Republic.

No one may be a member of a Regional Council and a member of either House of Parliament or of another Regional Council at the same time.

The Council elects from among its own members a President and a Presiding Officers' Committee to organize its work.

Regional Councillors may not be called upon to answer for opinions expressed or votes cast during the exercise of their duties.

The President and the members of the Regional Government are elected by the Regional Council from among its members.

Article 123

Every Region has a statute which, in accordance with the Constitution and the laws of the Republic, provides for the internal organization of the Region.

This statute regulates the exercise of the right to introduce Bills and referendum on Regional laws and adminsitrative acts and provides for the publication of Regional laws and regulations.

This statute is passed by the Regional Council by an absolute majority of its members and then approved with a law of the Republic.

Article 124

A State Official, residing in the capital of the Region, supervises the administrative functions exercised by the State and co-ordinates them with those of the Region.

Article 125

Control of the legitimacy of administrative acts in the Region is exercised, in a decentralized form, by an organ of the State in the manner and within the limits established by the laws of the Republic. In specific cases, the law allows control of merit in administrative acts but only to the extent of promoting, through a request for which justifications are given, their re-examination by the Regional Council.

Administrative tribunals having jurisdiction of first instance for administrative justice are established in the Regions in accordance with the laws of the Republic. These tribunals may have branches in places other than the Regional capital.

Article 126

The Regional Council may be dissolved when it performs acts contrary to the Constitution or commits serious violations of the laws or fails to comply with the request of the national Government to replace the Regional Government or its President, when they have committed similar acts or violations.

It may be dissolved when by reason of resignation or through the impossibility of forming a majority, it is no longer able to fulfil its duties.

It may also be dissolved for reasons of national security.

The President of the Republic dissolves the Regional Council with a decree, in which reasons are given after having heard the advice of the Committee on Regional affairs composed of Senators and Deputies and constituted in the way established by the laws of the Republic.

The decree of dissolution also contains the appointment of a Commission composed of three citizens eligible for the Regional Council, which establishes the day of new elections within a period of three months and provides for the day-by-day adminstration which falls within the competence of the Regional Government and provides for such decisions as cannot be postponed: such decisions are subject to ratification by the new Regional Council.

Article 127

Every law passed by the Regional Council shall be communicated to the State official who, except in the case of opposition on the part of the Government, must sign it within thirty days from its submission.

The law is promulgated within ten days from its being signed by the State official and becomes effective not earlier than fifteen days from its publication. If a law is considered to be urgent by the Regional Council, and the Government of the Republic agrees, then its promulgation and the date of effect are not subject to the time-requirements specified above.

The Government of the Republic, when it considers that a law passed by the Regional Council exceeds the jurisdiction of the Region or is in contrast with the national interests or with those of other Regions, returns it to Regional Council within the period established for the State official to sign it.

Should the Regional Council pass it again by an absolute majority of its members, the Government of the Republic may, within fifteen days of communication of such a decision, submit the question of its legitimacy to the Constitutional Court and that of its merit, in the case of conflicting interests, to the Houses of Parliament. In case of doubt, the Constitutional Court shall decide which body has jursidiction over the matter.

Article 128

The Provinces and Municipalities are autonomous bodies in accordance with the principles laid down by the general laws of the Republic which determine their functions.

Article 129

The Provinces and the Municipalities are also territorial units of State and Regional decentralization.

For further decentralization the territory within the boundaries of the Province may be subdivided into districts with exclusively administrative functions.

Article 130

A Regional organ, constituted in accordance with the procedures established by the laws of the Republic, exercises in a decentralized form, control over the legitimacy of decisions taken by the Provinces, Municipalities and other local authorities.

In cases specified by law, control on the merit may be exercised in the form of a request, in which justifications are given, for the re-examination of decisions taken previously. This request must be submitted to the deliberating bodies.

Article 131[4]

The following Regions are instituted:

Piemonte;
Valle d'Aosta;
Lombardia;
Trentino-Alto Adige;
Veneto;
Friuli-Venezia Giulia;
Liguria;
Emilia-Romagna;
Toscana;
Umbria;
Le Marche;
Lazio;
Abruzzi;
Molise;
Campania;
Puglia;
Basilicata;
Calabria;
Sicilia;
Sardegna.

Article 132

Constitutional law allows, after having heard the Regional Councils, the merging of existing Regions or the creation of new Regions with a minimum of one million inhabitants upon request by as many Councils of Municipalities as represent at least one-third of the interested population and upon approval of

[4] As amended by article 1 of the constitutional law No.3 of December 27, 1963.

the proposal by a referendum voted by the majority of the interested population.

Consequent to a referendum the laws of the Republic, after the Regional Councils have been heard, may allow Provinces and Municipalities, having so requested, to be separated from one Region and joined to another.

Article 133

Changes of provincial boundaries and the instutution of new Provinces within the area of a Region are established by the laws of the Republic upon request of the Municipalities and with the advice of the Region.

The Region, having heard the interested population, may establish new Municipalities and modify their boundaries and names by its own enactment within its own territory.

TITLE VI
CONSTITUTIONAL GUARANTEES

Section I *The Constitutional Court*

Article 134

The Constitutional Court decides on:

Controversies concerning the constitutional legitimacy of laws and of acts having the force of laws emanating from the State and the Regions;

Conflicts arising among the constitutional powers of the State over their particular jurisdictions;

Controversies between the State and the Regions, and between Regions;

Impeachments of the President of the Republic and Ministers, according to the provisions of the Constitution.

Article 135[5]

The Constitutional Court is composed of fifteen judges, one-third of whom are appointed by the President of the Republic, one-third by Parliament in a joint sitting of the two Houses and one-third by the members of the ordinary and administrative supreme courts.

The judges of the Constitutional Court are chosen from among the judges of the High and Administrative Courts, including those in retirement, full professors of law and lawyers who have been in practice for a minimum period of twenty years.

The judges of the Constitutional Court are appointed for a period of nine years, as from the day upon which each of them shall be sworn in. They may not be appointed to this office again.

Upon termination of their period of office the judges of the Constitutional Court shall withdraw and cease all activities.

[5] As amended by article 1 of the constitutional law No. 2 of November 22, 1967.

In conformity with the provisions laid down by law, the Constitutional Court elects a President from among its members. The President remains in office for a period of three years and may be re-elected except when his term as a judge expires.

Appointment as a judge of the Constitutional Court is incompatible with membership in Parliament, Regional Council, the profession of lawyer or with the other offices indicated by law.

Proceedings against the President of the Republic and against Ministers shall be attended by the ordinary judges of the Constitutional Court and by sixteen persons drawn by lot from a list of citizens who have the necessary requirements for election to the Senate. Parliament drafts this list every nine years with an election and with the same procedure as that used for the appointment of ordinary judges.

Article 136

When the Court declares a provision of law or an act having the force of law to be unconstitutional, the provision ceases to have effect from the day following the publication of the decision.

The decision of the Court is published and communicated to Parliament and to the interested Regional Councils in order that, when they deem it necessary, a decision may be made according to constitutional procedures.

Article 137

A constitutional law establishes the conditions and forms for the decisions on constitutional legitimacy and the time limits and ways to request said decisions and furthermore establishes the guarantees for the judges of the Court.

All other provisions, necessary for the constitution and functioning of the Court, are established by law.

The decisions of the Constitutional Court may not be appealed.

Section II *Amendments to the Constitution. Constitutional Laws*

Article 138

Amendments to the Constitution and other constitutional laws must be passed twice by each House at an interval of not less than three months. An absolute majority of each House is required in the second voting.

These laws are submitted to referendum when, within three months of their publication, a demand shall be made by one-fifth of the members of either House or by five hundred thousand electors or by five Regional Councils.

A law submitted to referendum shall not be promulgated unless approved by a majority of valid votes.

No referendum is possible if the law has been approved in both Houses at the second voting by a majority of two-thirds of the members of each House.

Article 139

The Republican form of Government is not subject to constitutional amendment.

Bibliography

1. Introductory reading on Italian politics and history

ADAMS, J. C., and BARILE, P., *The Government of Republican Italy* (Boston, 1972).

ALLUM, P. A., *Italy: Republic without Government?* (London, 1973).

BOCCA, G., *Storia della repubblica italiana* (Milan, 1981).

CAROCCI, G., *Storia d'Italia dall'unità ad oggi* (Milan, 1975).

CLARK, M., *Modern Italy, 1971–1982* (London, 1984).

CLOUGH, S. B., *The Economic History of Modern Italy* (New York, 1964).

CORNER, P., *Fascism in Ferrara, 1915–25* (Oxford, 1975).

DE GRAND, A., *The Italian Left in the Twentieth Century: A History of the Socialist and Communist Parties* (Bloomington, Ind., 1989).

ELLWOOD, D., *Italy, 1943–1945* (Leicester, 1985).

FARNETI, P., *Il sistema politico italiano* (Bologna, 1976).

GAETÀ, F., *Il nazionalismo italiano* (Naples, 1965).

GINSBORG, P., *A History of Contemporary Italy: Society and Politics, 1943–1988* (London, 1990).

HARPER, J. L., *America and the Reconstruction of Italy, 1945–48* (Cambridge, 1986).

HINE, D. J., 'The Consolidation of Democracy in Postwar Italy', in G. Pridham, *Securing Democracy: Political Parties and Democratic Consolidation in Southern Europe* (London, 1990), 62–83.

JEMOLO, A. C., *Church and State in Italy 1850–1950* (Oxford, 1960).

KENT, P., *The Pope and the Duce* (London, 1981).

KOGAN, N., *A Political History of Italy* (New York, 1983).

LANGE, P., and TARROW, S., *Italy in Transition: Conflict and Consensus* (London, 1980).

LAPALOMBRA, J., *Democracy: Italian Style* (New Haven, Conn., 1987).

LEONARDI, R., and others (eds.), *Italian Politics: A Review* (annual yearbook produced since 1986) (London, 1986–   ).

LYTTLETON, A., *The Seizure of Power*, (London, 1973).

MACK SMITH, D., *Mussolini's Roman Empire* (London, 1976).

—— *Italy: A Modern History* (Ann Arbor, Mich., 1969).

PASQUINO, G., (ed.), *Il sistema politico italiano* (Rome, 1985).

PROCACCI, G., *History of the Italian People* (London, 1968).

SALAMONE, A. W., (ed.), *Italy from Risorgimento to Fascism* (Newton Abbot, 1971).

SASSOON, D., *Contemporary Italy* (London, 1986).

SETON-WATSON, C., *Italy from Liberalism to Fascism* (London, 1967).

SPOTTS, F., and WIESER, T., *Italy: A Difficult Democracy* (Cambridge, 1986).

TAMBURRANO, G., *Storia e cronaca del centro-sinistra* (Milan, 1971).

TARROW, S., 'Italian Politics and Political Change: "Eppure si muove". But where to?', *West European Politics*, 11/3 (1988), 311–24.

TONIOLO, G., (ed.), *Lo sviluppo economico italiano, 1861–1940* (Bari, 1973).

URBANI, G., *Dentro la politica: Come funzionano il governo e le istituzioni* (Milan, 1992).

VANNICELLI, P., *Italy, NATO, and the EEC* (Cambridge, Mass., 1974).

WOOLF, S., (ed.), *The Rebirth of Italy 1943–50* (London, 1972).

ZARISKI, R., *Italy: The Politics of Uneven Development* (Hinsdale, Ill., 1972).

2. The economic and social foundations of politics

ALLEN, K. J., and STEVENSON, A. A., *An Introduction to the Italian Economy* (London, 1974).

ARLACCHI, P., *Mafia Business: The Mafia Ethic and the Spirit of Capitalism* (New York, 1989).

ASCOLI, U., (ed.), *Welfare state all'italiana* (Rome, 1984).

—— and CATANZARO, R., (eds.), *La società italiana degli anni ottanta* (Bari, 1987).

BAGNASCO, A., *Tre Italie: La problematica territoriale nello sviluppo italiano* (Bologna, 1977).

—— and TRIGILIA, C., *Società e politica nelle aree di piccola impresa: Il caso di Bassano* (Venice, 1984).

—— —— *Società e politica nelle aree di piccola impresa: Il caso di Valdesa* (Milan, 1985).

BALDISSERA, A., *La rivolta dei quarantamila: Dai quadri FIAT ai COBAS* (Milan, 1988).

BANFIELD, E., *The Moral Basis of a Backward Society* (Glencoe, Ill., 1958).

BARBERIS, C., *La società italiana: Redditi, occupazione, imprese* (Milan, 1985).

BARTOCCI, E., (ed.), *Sindacato, classe, società* (Padua, 1975).

BIANCHI, P., 'The IRI in Italy: Strategic Role and Political Constraints', *West European Politics*, 10/2 (1986), 269–90.

BORDOGNA, L., 'The COBAS Fragmentation of Trade-Union Representation and Conflict', in R. Leonardi and P. Corbetta (eds.), *Italian Politics: A Review*, iii (London, 1989), 50–65.

BRUNETTA, R., *Spesa pubblica e conflitto* (Bologna, 1987).

CARBONE, C., (ed.), *Classe e movimento in Italia 1970–1985* (Rome, 1986).

CASSESE, S., BIANCHI, P., and DELLA SALA, V., 'Privatization in Italy: Aims and Constraints', in J. Vickers and V. Wright (eds.), *The Politics of Privatization in Western Europe* (London, 1989), 87–100.

CAVAZUTTI, F., *Debito pubblico e ricchezza privata* (Bologna, 1986).

CENSIS, *XXIV rapporto sulla situazione sociale del paese, 1990* (Rome, 1990).

COCCHI, G., (ed.), *Stranieri in Italia* (Bologna, 1990).

CONTINI, B., *Lo sviluppo di un economia parallela: La segmentazione del mercato del lavoro in Italia e la crescita del settore irregolare* (Milan, 1979).

DONOLO, C., *Classi sociali e politica nel mezzogiorno* (Turin, 1978).

DUGGAN, C., *Fascism and the Mafia* (New Haven, Conn., 1989).

FERRARI, S., 'The New Concordat between Church and State', in R. Leonardi and R. Y. Nanetti (eds.), *Italian Politics: A Review*, i (London, 1986), 134–45.

FERRAROTTI, F., (ed.), *Mercato del lavoro, marginalità sociale, e struttura di classe* (Milan, 1978).

FLANAGAN, R. J., SOSKICE, D. W., and ULMAN, L., *Unionism, Economic Stabilization, and Incomes Policies* (Washington, DC, 1983).

GALLI, G., *L'Italia sotterranea* (Rome, 1984).

GAMBETTA, D., 'Fragments of an Economic Theory of the Mafia', *European Journal of Sociology*, 29/2 (1989), 127–45.

GERELLI, E., and BOGNETTI, G., (eds.), *La crisi delle partecipazioni statali: Motivi e prospettivi* (Milan, 1981).

GIAVAZZI, F., and PAGANO, M., 'The Advantage of Tying One's Hands', *European Economic Review*, 32 (1988), 1055–82.

GOLDEN, M., *Labor Divided: Austerity and Working-Class Politics in Contemporary Italy* (Ithaca, NY, 1988).

GRAZIANI, A., *L'economia italiana: 1945–70* (Bologna, 1972).

GRISONI, D., and PORTELLI, H., *Le lotte operaie in Italia dal 1960 al 1976* (Milan, 1977).

HOLLAND, S., (ed.), *The State as Entrepreneur* (London, 1972).

Istituto centrale di statistica, *Sintesi di vita sociale* (Rome, 1990).

—— Associazione italiana di sociologia, *Immagini della società italiana* (Rome, 1988).

LANGE, P., 'Crisis and Consent, Change and Compromise: Dilemmas of Italian Communism in the 1970s', in P. Lange and S. Tarrow, *Italy in Transition: Conflict and Consensus* (London, 1980), 110–32.

—— 'The End of an Era: The Wage Indexation Referendum of 1985', in R. Leonardi and R. Y. Nanetti (eds.), *Italian Politics: A Review*, i (London, 1986), 29–46.

—— and REGINI, M., *State, Market, and Social Regulation: New Perspectives on Italy* (Cambridge, 1989).

—— ROSS, G., and VANNICELLI, M., *Unions, Change, and Crisis: French and Italian Union Strategy and the Political Economy, 1945–80* (London, 1982).

MAESTRI, E., 'Partiti e sistema pensionistico in Italia: Un analisi dell'azione parlamentare della DC e del PCI, 1953–75', *Rivista italiana di scienza politica*, 14/2 (1984), 125–59.

MELOGRANI, P., and SCARAFFIA, L., (eds.), *La famiglia italiana dall'ottocento a oggi* (Bari, 1988).

Ministero del tesoro, *Rapporto sulla spesa pubblica in Italia* (Rome, 1986).

NARDOZZI, G., 'Autonomia della banca centrale e istituzioni di governo', in D. Masciandaro and S. Ristuccia (eds.), *L'autonomia delle banche centrali* (Milan, 1988), 228–32.

ONIDA, V., and VIESTI, G., (eds.), *The Italian Multinationals* (London, 1988).

PACI, M., *La struttura sociale italiana* (Bologna, 1982).

—— (ed.), *Stato, mercato, e occupazione* (Bologna, 1985).

PASQUINO, G., 'Rappresentanza degli interessi, attività di lobby e processi decisionali: Il caso italiano di istituzioni permeabili', *Stato e mercato* (Dec. 1987), 403–29.

PEDONE, A., *Evasori e tartassati: I nodi della politica tributaria italiana* (Bologna, 1979).

PODBIELSKI, G., *Italy: Development and Crisis in the Postwar Economy* (Oxford, 1974).

POSNER, M., and WOOLF, S. J., *Italian Public Enterprise* (London, 1967).

REGALIA, I., REGINI, M., and REYNERI, E., 'Labour Conflicts and Industrial Relations in Italy', in C. Crouch and A. Pizzorno (eds.), *The Resurgence of Class Conflict in Western Europe since 1968*, i (national studies) (New York, 1978).

REYNERI, E., 'L'immigrazione extra-comunitaria in Italia: Prospettive, caratteristiche, politiche', in *Polis*, 5/1 (1991), 145–55.

SABETTI, F., 'The Mafia and the Anti-Mafia: Moments in the Struggle for Justice and Self-Governance in Sicily', in R. Nanetti and R. Catanzaro, *Italian Politics: A Review*, iv (London, 1990), 174–95.

SALVATI, M., *Alle origine dell'inflazione italiana* (Bologna, 1979).

SARACENO, P., *Risultati e nuovi obbietivi dell'intervento straordinario* (Rome, 1970).

SPAVENTA, L., 'The Growth of Public Debt in Italy: Past Experience, Perspectives, and Policy Problems', *Banca nazionale del lavoro Quarterly Review*, 37 (1984), 119–49.

SYLOS LABINI, P., *Le classi sociali negli anni '80* (Rome, 1986).

TREU, T., (ed.), *L'uso politico dello Statuto dei lavoratori* (Bologna, 1975).

TRIGILIA, C., *Grande partiti e piccole imprese* (Bologna, 1986).

TRUPIA, P., *La democrazia degli interessi: Lobby e decisione collettiva* (Milan, 1989).

VALLI, V., *Politica economica: I modelli, gli strumenti, l'economia italiana* (Rome, 1988).

WEITZ, P. R., 'Labour and Politics in a Divided Movement: The Italian Case', *Industrial and Labor Relations Review*, 28/2 (1975), 226–42.

3. Political parties and the party system

ACCORNERO, A., MANNHEIMER, R., and SEBASTIANI, C. (eds.), *L'identità comunista* (Rome, 1983).

ALBERONI, F., (ed.), *L'attività di partito* (Bologna, 1967).

ALLUM, P., *Politics and Society in Postwar Naples* (Cambridge, 1973).

AMYOT, G., *The Italian Communist Party: The Crisis of the Popular Front Strategy* (London, 1981).

ANDERLINI, F., 'La DC: Iscritti e modello di partitio', *Polis*, 3/2 (1989), 277–304.

ARFE, G., *Storia del socialismo italiano, 1892–1926* (Turin, 1965).

BALDASSARE, A., 'Un partito nuovo di massa?', *Democrazia e diritto* (Jan–Feb. 1983), 41–64.

BARBAGLI, M., and CORBETTA, P., 'La svolta del PCI', *Il mulino* (Jan–Feb. 1981), 95–130.

—— —— and SECHI, S., *Dentro il PCI*, (Bologna, 1979).

BELLIGNI, S., (ed.), *La giraffa e il liocorno: Il PCI dagli anni '70 al nuovo decennio* (Milan, 1983).

BERLINGUER, E., 'Riflessioni sull'Italia dopo i fatti del Cile', in E. Berlinguer, *La questione comunista* (Rome, 1975), 609–39.

BERLINGUER, L., 'Partito di massa e forme snodate di organizzazione', *Democrazia e diritto* (Jan–Feb. 1983), 19–40.

BLACKMER, D. L. M., and TARROW, S., (eds.), *Communism in Italy and France* (Princeton, NJ, 1975).

CACIAGLI, M., 'The 18th DC Congress: From De Mita to Forlani and the Victory of "Neodoroteism"', in F. Sabetti and R. Catanzaro (eds.), *Italian Politics: A Review*, v (London, 1991), 8–22.

CAZZOLA, F., (ed.), *Anatomia del potere DC: Enti pubblici e 'centralità' democristiana* (Bari, 1979).

—— 'Struttura e potere del Partito socialista italiano', in G. Pasquino (ed.), *Il sistema politico italiano* (Rome, 1985), 169–207.

CHUBB, J., 'The Christian Democrat Party: Reviving or Surviving?', in R. Leonardi and R. Nanetti (eds.), *Italian Politics: A Review*, i (London, 1986), 69–86.

CORONA, C., *Il costo della democrazia: I partiti politici italiani costi e finanziamenti* (Rome, 1984).

DAALDER, I., 'The Italian Party System in Transition: The End of Polarised Pluralism', *West European Politics*, 6/3 (1983), 216–36.

DI SCALA, S. M., *Renewing Italian Socialism: Nenni to Craxi* (New York, 1988).

DONOVAN, M., 'Party Strategy and Centre Domination in Italy', *West European Politics*, 12/4 (1989), 114–28.

FARNETI, P., *The Italian Party System (1945–1980)* (London, 1985).

GALLI, G., *Il bipartismo imperfetto* (Milan, 1984).

HELLMAN, S., *Italian Communism in Transition: The Rise and Fall of the Historic Compromise in Turin, 1975–80* (New York, 1988).

—— 'The PCI's Alliance Strategy and the Case of the Middle Classes', in D. L. M. Blackmer and S. Tarrow (eds.), *Communism in Italy and France* (Princeton, NJ, 1975), 373–419.

—— 'The Italian Communist Party between Berlinguer and the Seventeenth Congress', in R. Leonardi and R. Nanetti (eds.), *Italian Politics: A Review*, i (London, 1986), 47–68.

—— 'The Longest Campaign: Communist Party Strategy and the Election of 1976', in H. R. Penniman (ed.), *Italy at the Polls: The Parliamentary Elections of 1976* (Washington, DC, 1977), 155–80.

HINE, D. J., 'Surviving but not Reviving: The Italian Socialist Party under Craxi', *West European Politics*, 2/3 (1979), 133–48.

—— 'Italy: Parties and Party Government under Pressure', in Alan Ware (ed.), *Political Parties* (Oxford, 1987), 81–94.

HINE, D. J. 'Social Democracy in Italy', in W. E. Paterson and A. H. Thomas (eds.), *Social Democratic Parties in Western Europe* (London, 1977), 67–85.

—— 'Factionalism in West European Parties: A Framework for Analysis', *West European Politics*, 5/1 (1982), 36–53.

—— 'The Italian Socialist Party', in T. Gallagher and A. M. Williams (eds.), *Southern European Socialism: Parties, Elections, and the Challenge of Government* (Manchester, 1989), 108–30.

IGNAZI, P., *Dal PCI al PDS* (Bologna, 1992).

—— *Il polo escluso: Profilo del Movimento sociale italiano* (Bologna, 1989).

ILARDI, M., and ACCORNERO, A., (eds.), *Il Partito comunista italiano: Struttura e storia dell'organizzazione* (Milan, 1982).

IRVING, R. E. M., *The Christian Democrat Parties of Western Europe* (London, 1979).

LAPALOMBARA, J., 'Two Steps Forward, One Step Back: The PCI's Struggle for Legitimacy', in H. R. Penniman (ed.), *Italy at the Polls, 1979: A Study of the Parliamentary Elections* (Washington, DC, 1977), 104–40.

LEONARDI, R., and WERTMAN, D., *Italian Christian Democracy: The Politics of Dominance* (London, 1989).

MANNHEIMER, R., *La Lega lombarda* (Milan, 1991).

MERKL, W., *Prima e dopo Craxi: Le trasformazioni del PSI* (Padua, 1987).

MORLINO, L., 'The Changing Relationship between Parties and Society in Italy', *West European Politics*, 7/4 (1984), 46–66

ORFEI, R., *L'occupazione del potere* (Milan, 1976).

PANEBIANCO, A., *Modelli di partito* (Bologna, 1989).

PAPPALARDO, A., 'La politica consociativa nella democrazia italiana', *Rivista italiana di scienza politica*, 10/1 (1980), 73–123.

PARISI, A., (ed.), *Democristiani* (Bologna, 1979).

Partito socialista italiano, *Il Partito socialista italiano: Struttura e organizzazione* (Venice, 1975).

PASQUINO, G., *Degenerazione dei partiti e riforme istituzionali* (Rome, 1982).

—— *Party Government in Italy: Achievements and Prospects*, The Johns Hopkins University Bologna Center Research Institute, Occasional Paper no. 48 (Jan. 1985).

—— 'Mid-Stream and under Stress: The Italian Communist Party', in M. Waller and M. Fennema (eds.), *Communist Parties in Western Europe: Decline or Adaptation?* (Oxford, 1988), 26–46.

—— 'Modernity and Reforms: The PSI between Political Entrepreneurs and Gamblers', *West European Politics*, 9/1 (1986), 120–41.

—— 'Mass media, partito di massa, e trasformazioni della politica', *Il mulino* (July–Aug. 1983), 559–79.

—— (ed.), *La lenta marcia nelle istituzioni: I passi del PCI* (Bologna, 1988).

—— CORBETTA, P., PARISI, A., and ROSSI, M., 'La partecipazione politica in Italia', *Polis*, 1/1 (1987), 3–99.

PIZZORNO, A., 'Uno schema teorico per un analisi dei partiti politici italiani', in Paolo Farneti (ed.), *Il sistema politico italiano* (Bologna, 1973), 241–60.

PRANDI, A., and GALLI, G., *Patterns of Political Participation in Italy* (New Haven, Conn., 1970).

PRIDHAM, G., *Political Parties and Coalitional Behaviour in Italy* (London, 1988).

ROSSI, M., 'Un partito di "anime morte"', in A. Parisi (ed.), *Democristiani* (Bologna, 1979), 13–60.

—— 'Sezioni di partito e partecipazione politica', *Polis*, 1/1 (1987), 67–100.

SARTORI, G., *Political Parties: A Framework for Analysis* (Cambridge, 1976).

SASSOON, D., 'The PCI and the 1987 Elections', in R. Leonardi and P. Corbetta (eds.), *Italian Politics: A Review*, iii (London, 1989), 129–45.

SENSINI, A., *L'inverno della repubblica* (Milan, 1983).

TADDEI, F., *Il socialismo italiano del dopoguerra: Correnti ideologiche e scelte politiche, 1943–47* (Milan, 1984).

TAMBURRANO, G., *L'iceberg democristiano* (Milan, 1974).

TARROW, S., *Peasant Communism in Southern Italy* (New Haven, Conn., 1967).

URBAN, J. B., *Moscow and the Italian Communist Party* (London, 1986).

VALENTINI, C., *Il nome e la cosa: Viaggio nel PCI che cambia* (Milan, 1990).

4. Elections and electoral behaviour

ALLUM, P., and DIAMANTI, I., 'Ambiente sociale e comportamento elettorale nella provincia di Vicenza negli anni del primo dopoguerra', *Quaderni dell'Osservatorio elettorale*, 15 (July 1985), 65–140.

—— and MANNHEIMER, R., 'Italy', in I. Crewe and D. Denver (eds.), *Electoral Change in Western Democracies: Patterns and Sources of Electoral Volatility* (London, 1985), 287–318.

ANDERLINI, F., 'Una modellizzazione per zone socio-politiche dell'Italia repubblicana', *Polis*, 1/3 (1987), 443–79.

BARBAGLI, M., CORBETTA, P., PARISI, A., and SCHADEE, H. M. A., *Fluidità elettorale e classi sociali in Italia* (Bologna, 1979).

BARNES, S. H., *Representation in Italy: Institutionalised Tradition and Electoral Choice* (Chicago, 1977).

BIORCIO, R., and NATALE, P., 'Lo studio dei flussi elettorali: Questioni di principio e diagnostica delle distorsioni', *Polis*, 5/1 (1991), 121–38.

CACIAGLI, M., 'Erosione e mutamento dell'elettorato democristiano', in M. Caciagli and A. Spreafico (eds.), *Vent'anni di elezioni in Italia, 1968–87* (Padua, 1990), 3–30.

CAPECCHI, V., CIONI POLACCHINI, V., GALLI, G., and SIVINI, G., *Il comportamento elettorale in Italia* (Bologna, 1968).

CARTOCCI, R., 'Otto risposte a un problema: La divisione dell'Italia in zone politicamente omogenee', *Polis* 1/3 (1987), 481–514.

—— *Elettori in Italia: Riflessioni sulle vicende elettorali degli anni ottanta* (Bologna, 1990).

—— CORBETTA, P., PARISI, A., and SCHADEE, H. M. A., *Elezioni in Italia: Strutture e tipologia delle consultazioni politiche* (Bologna, 1988).

D'AMICO, R., 'La fisionomia dei partiti nel voto di preferenza', in M. Caciagli and A. Spreafico (eds.), *Vent'anni di elezioni in Italia, 1968–87* (Padua, 1990), 259–94.

D'AMICO, R., 'Voto de preferenza, movimento dell'elettorato, e modelli di partito: L'andamento delle preferenze nelle elezioni politiche italiane del quindicennio 1968–1983', *Quaderni dell'Osservatorio elettorale*, 18 (Jan. 1987), 91–147.

DANIELS, P., 'Italy', in J. Lodge (ed.), *The European Parliamentary Elections of 1989* (London, 1989), 159–78.

HINE, D. J., 'The Italian General Election of 1987', *Electoral Studies*, 6/3 (1987), 267–70.

MANNHEIMER, R., and SANI, G., *Il mercato elettorale: Identikit dell'elettore italiano* (Bologna, 1987).

NUVOLI, P., and SPREAFICO, A., 'Il partito del non voto', in M. Caciagli and A. Spreafico (eds.), *Vent'anni di elezioni in Italia, 1968–87* (Padua, 1990), 223–58.

PARISI, A., 'Un partito di cattolici? L'appartenenza religiosa e rapporti col mondo cattolico', in A. Parisi (ed.), *Democristiani* (Bologna, 1979), 85–152.

—— and PASQUINO, G., 'Changes in Italian Electoral Behaviour: The Relationships between Parties and Voters', *West European Politics*, 2/3 (1979), 6–30.

SANI, G., 'The Political Culture of Italy: Continuity and Change', in G. Almond and S. Verba (eds.), *The Civic Culture Revisited* (Boston, 1980), 273–323.

—— and SARTORI, G., 'Mass Constraints on Political Realignments: Perceptions of Anti-System Parties in Italy', in H. Daalder and P. Mair, *Western European Party Systems: Continuity and Change* (London, 1983), 307–40.

SCARAMOZZZINO, P., *Un'analisi statistica del voto di preferenza in Italia* (Milan, 1979).

—— 'Il voto di preferenza nelle elezioni politiche ed europee del 1979 e nelle elezioni politiche del 1983', *Il politico*, 4 (1983), 641–75.

SPARASCI, F., 'Alcuni aspetti delle votazioni a scrutinio segreto nei lavori dell'Assemblea costituente', in Camera dei deputati, *Il Parlamento della repubblica: Organi, procedure, apparati* (Rome, 1987), 341–64.

5. The constitutional and legal framework

AMATO, G., and BARBERA, A., *Manuale di diritto pubblico* (Bologna, 1986).

ARMAROLI, P., *L'introvabile governabilità: Le strategie istituzionali dei partiti dalla costituzione alla commissione Bozzi* (Padua, 1986).

BARENDT, E., 'The Influence of the German and Italian Constitutional Courts on Their National Broadcasting Systems', *Public Law* (1991), 93–115.

Camera dei deputati/Senato della repubblica, *Relazione della Commissione parlamentare per le riforme istituzionali*, IX legislatura, doc. XVI-*bis*, no. 3 (Rome, 1985).

CAPELLETTI, M., MERRYMAN, J. H., and PERILLO, J. M., *The Italian Legal System: An Introduction* (Stanford, Calif., 1967).

CERTOMA, G. L., *The Italian Legal System* (London, 1985).

COLOMBO, G., 'The New Code of Criminal Procedure', in F. Sabetti and R. Catanzaro (eds.), *Italian Politics: A Review*, v (London, 1991), 55–68.

CRISCUOLO, A., 'Il nuovo codice di procedura: Quale futura per la giustizia penale', *Questi istituzioni*, 17/79–80 (1989), 41–9.

DEMURO, G., 'La delegificazione', *Il foro italiano* (June 1989), 5: 355–9.

DI FEDERICO, G., 'The Crisis of the Justice System and the Referendum on the Judiciary', in R. Leonardi and P. Corbetta (eds.), *Italian Politics: A Review*, iii. (London, 1989), 25–49.

FURLONG, P., 'The Constitutional Court in Italian Politics', *West European Politics*, 11/3 (1988), 7–23.

GUARNIERI, C., 'Magistratura e politica: Il caso italiano', *Rivista italiana di scienza politica*, 21/1 (1991), 3–32.

HINE, D. J., 'Thirty Years of the Italian Constitution: Governability and Constitutional Reform', *Parliamentary Affairs*, 34/1 (1981), 63–80.

—— 'Italy: Condemned by Its Constitution?', in Vernon Bogdanor (ed.), *Constitutions in Democratic Politics* (Aldershot, 1988), 206–28.

LOMBARDO, A., *La grande riforma: Governo, istituzioni, partiti* (Milan, 1984).

PANUNZIO, S. P., 'Riforme costituzionali e referendum', *Quaderni costituzionali*, 10/3 (1990), 419–61.

PARLATO, V., (ed.), *Spazio e ruolo del riformismo* (Bologna, 1974).

PASQUINO, G., 'The Debate on Institutional Reform', in R. Leonardi and R. Y. Nanetti (eds.), *Italian Politics: A Review*, i (London, 1986), 117–33.

SARTORI, G., 'Le riforme istituzionali tra buone e cattive', *Rivista italiana di scienza politica*, 21/3 (1991), 375–407.

SPAGNA MUSSO, E., (ed.), *Costituzione e struttura di governo: La riforma dei ministeri*, (Padua, 1984), vols. i and ii.

STASIO, D., 'La giustizia alla prova della verità: Come funziona la nuova procedura penale?' *Questi istituzioni*, 17/79–80 (1989), 13–23.

ULERI, P. V., 'The 1987 referendum', in R. Leonardi and P. Corbetta (eds.), *Italian Politics: A Review*, iii (London, 1989), 155–77.

6. Legislature and political executive

BONANNI, M., (ed.), *Governi, ministri, presidenti* (Comunità, 1978).

—— 'Il governo nel sistema politico italiano (1948–1982)', *Rivista trimestrale di scienza della amministrazione*, 1 (1983), 3–46.

Camera dei deputati, Servizio studi, *Documentazione per le commissioni parlamentari: L'attuazione della 1. no. 400, 23 agosto 1989: Disciplina dell'attività del governo e ordinamento della presidenza del Consiglio dei ministri*, no. 326, x legislatura (1989).

—— Servizio studi, *Documentazione per le commissioni parlamentari: Voto palese e voto segreto*, 81, 2nd edn., x legislatura (Nov. 1988).

—— Ufficio stampa e pubblicazioni, *La Camera dei deputati dalla I alla VIII legislatura: Note e statistiche* (Rome, 1985).

CAPOTOSTI, P., 'Consiglio di gabinetto e governi di coalizione', *Quaderni costituzionali*, 3/3 (1983), 585–610.

CARLASSARE, L., 'Il ruolo del Parlamento e la nuovo disciplina del potere regolamentare', *Quaderni costituzionale*, 10/1 (1990), 7–52.

CASSESE, S., *Esiste un governo in Italia?* (Rome, 1980).

CASU, A., 'Voto segreto e voto palese nei regolamenti dal 1948 ai nostri giorni', *Rivista trimestrale di diritto pubblico*, 2 (1986), 553–93.

CAZZOLA, F., 'La solidarità nazionale dalla parte del parlamento', *Laboratorio politico*, 2 2–3 (1982), 5–43.

—— 'Consenso e opposizione nel Parlamento italiano: Il ruolo del PCI dalla I alla IV legislatura', *Rivista italiana di scienza politica*, 2 (1972).

CHELI, E., 'Il co-ordinamento delle attività di governo nell'attuale sistema italiano', *Studi parlamentari e di politica costituzionali*, 4 (1969), 4–33.

—— 'La centralità parlamentare: Sviluppo e decadenza di un modello', *Quaderni costituzionali*, 1/2 (1981), 343–51.

—— 'Ruolo dell'esecutivo e sviluppi recenti del potere regolmentare', *Quaderni costituzionale*, 10/1 (1990), 53–76.

CIRIELLO, P., *Ordinamento di governo e comitati interministeriali* (Naples, 1981).

COTTA, M., *Classe politica e parlamento in Italia 1946–76* (Bologna, 1979).

DE IONNA, P., 'Dalla legge n. 468 del 1978 alla legge n. 362 del 1988: Note sul primo decennio di applicazione della "legge finanziaro"', *Quaderni costituzionali*, 9/2 (1989), 205–27.

DELLA SALA, V., 'Government by Decree: The Craxi Government and the Use of Decree Legislation in the Italian Parliament', in R. Leonardi, R. Y. Nanetti, and P. Corbetta (eds.), *Italian Politics: A Review*, ii (London, 1988), 8–24.

—— 'The Italian Budgetary Process: Political and Institutional Constraints', *West European Politics*, 11/3 (1988), 110–25.

—— 'Parliament and the Italian Legislative Process' (D. Phil. thesis, University of Oxford, 1990).

DE VERGOTTINI, G., 'Riforma della struttura di governo ed introduzione del gabinetto ristretto', *Studi parlamentari e di politica costituzionale*, 5 (1982), 29–53.

DI PALMA, G., *Surviving without Governing: the Italian Parties in Parliament*, Berkeley, Calif., 1977).

—— 'Parlamento-arena o parlamento di trasformazione', *Rivista italiana di scienza politica*, 17/2 (1987), 179–203.

—— and COTTA, M., 'Cadres, Peones, and Entrepreneurs: Professional Identities in a Divided Parliament', E. Sulieman (ed.), *Parliaments and Parliamentarians* (New York, 1986), 41–78.

DI PASSIO, R., 'La struttura della presidenza del Consiglio dei ministri', *Rivista trimestrale di scienza della amministrazione*, 4 (1976), 606–51.

—— 'Gli organi della presidenza del Consiglio dei ministri', *Rivista trimestrale di scienza della amministrazione*, 1 (1978), 71–112.

D'ONOFRIO, F., 'Committees in the Italian Parliament', in J. D. Lees and M. Shaw (eds.), *Committees in Legislatures: A Comparative Analysis* (Durham, NC, 1979), 61–101.

FOCACCIA, G., 'Consiglio di gabinetto e organizzazione del governo', *Diritto e società*, 4 (1986), 721–57.

FURLONG, P., 'Parliament in Italian Politics', *West European Politics*, 13/3 (1990), 52–67.

FUSARO, C., 'La legge sulla presidenza del Consiglio dei ministri: Primi adempimenti a otto mesi dall'entrata in vigore', *Quaderni costituzionali*, 9/2 (1989), 374–86.

GUADAGNINI, M., 'Il personale politico parlamentare dagli anni '70 agli anni '80: Problemi di ricerca e di analisi, ed alcuni dati empirici', in Centro studi di scienza politica Paolo Farneti, *Il sistema politico italiano tra crisi e innovazione* (Milan, 1984).

GUAGLIA, G., 'Aspetti e tendenze della prassi costiuzionale in tema di ministri senza portafoglio', *Rivista trimestrale di diritto pubblico*, 34/2 (1984), 422–75.

—— 'Quale ruolo per i ministri senza portafoglio?', *Quaderni costituzionali*, 9/2 (1989), 386–90.

HINE, D. J., 'The Craxi Premiership', in R. Leonardi and R. Y. Nanetti (eds.), *Italian Politics: A Review*, i (London, 1986), 106–16.

—— and FINOCCHI, R., 'The Italian Prime Minister', *West European Politics*, 14/2 (1991), 79–96.

LABRIOLA, A., *Il governo della repubblica: Organi e poteri* (Rimini, 1989).

MANZELLA, A., 'I regolamenti parlamentari del 1971: quale riforma?', *Città e regione*, 6/4 (1980), 36–42.

—— *Il Parlamento* (Bologna, 1980).

MERLINI, S., 'Presidente del Consiglio e collegialità del governo', *Quaderni costituzionali*, 2/2 (1982), 413–37.

PASQUINO, G., 'Ricambiamento parlamentare e rendimento politico', *Politica del diritto*, 5 (1976), 543–65.

PASSIGLI, S., 'Crisi o centralità del parlamento?', *Città e regione*, 6/4 (1980), 5–11.

PITRUZZELLA, G., *La presidenza del Consiglio dei ministri e l'organizzazione del governo* (Padua, 1986).

—— 'L'organizzazione amministrativa della presidenza del Consiglio', *Il foro italiano* (June 1989), 5: 371–83.

PREDIERI, A., et al., *Il Parlamento nel sistema politico italiano* (Milan, 1975).

Presidenza del Consiglio dei ministri, *Disciplina dell'attività di governo e ordinamento della presidenza del Consiglio dei ministri*, Collana di testi e documenti, Dipartimento per l'informazione e l'editoria, no. 1 (Rome, 1989).

PRIDHAM, G., 'Parliamentarians and Their Constituencies in Italy's Party Democracy', in V. Bogdanor (eds.), *Representatives of the People* (London, 1985), 151–65.

RISTUCCI, S., *L'istituzione governo* (Comunità, 1975).

ROLLA, G., 'Il Consiglio dei ministri fra modello costituzionale e prassi', *Quaderni costitutzionali* 2/2 (1982), 393–412.

ROMANELLI GRIMALDI, C., *I ministri senza portafoglio nell'ordinamento giuridico italiano* (Padua, 1984).

ROTELLI, E., 'La prima legislatura repubblicana ed il ruolo del parlamento', *Quaderni costituzionali*, 1/1 (1981), 98–100.

RUGGIERI, E., *Il Consiglio dei ministri nella costituzione* (Milan, 1981).
SARTORI, G., *Il Parlamento italiano* (Naples, 1963).
SPAGNA MUSSO, E., (ed.), *Costituzione e strutture del governo: Il problema della presidenza del Consiglio* (Padua, 1979).
VENDITTI, R., *Il manuale Cencelli* (Rome, 1981).
VENTURA, L., *Il governo a multipolarità diseguale* (Milan, 1988).

7. Public administration

ADDIS, E., 'Banca d'Italia e politica monetaria: La riallocazione del potere fra stato, mercato, e banca centrale, *Stato e mercato* (Apr. 1987).
ARDIGÒ, A., and BARBANO, F., (eds.), *Medici e socio-sanitari: Professione in transizione* (Milan, 1981).
BILOTTA, B., 'La burocrazia italiana tra tre culture: Un'ipotesi sullo sviluppo della "meridionalizzazione" della pubblica amministrazione', *Rivista trimestrale di scienza della amministrazione*, 3 (1983), 85–101.
CALANDRA, P., *Storia dell'amministrazione pubblica in Italia* (Bologna, 1978).
CASSESE, S., *Il sistema amministrativo italiano* (Bologna, 1983).
—— 'L'amministrazione pubblica in Italia', *Rivista trimestrale di scienza della amministrazione*, 2 (1985).
—— and PEREZ, R., *Istituzioni di diritto pubblico* (Rome, 1989).
CAZZOLA, F., *Della corruzione* (Bologna, 1988).
CECORA, G., (ed.), *Il pubblico impiego: Struttura e retribuzioni* (Bologna, 1991).
CIRIEC, *Gli enti pubblici italiani: Anagrafe legislative e giurisprudenziali dal 1861 al 1970* (Milan, 1972).
Commission of the European Communities, *Seventh Annual Report to the European Parliament on the Commission Monitoring of the Application of Community Law, 1989*, Com. (90)288, Final (Brussels, 22 May 1990).
D'ALBERTI, M. , *La dirigenza pubblica* (Bologna, 1990).
DANIELS, P., HINE, D. J., and NERI GUALDESI, M., *Italy, the European Community, and the 1990 Presidency: Policy Trends and Policy Performance*, Centre for Mediterranean Studies, University of Bristol, Occasional Paper no. 3 (June 1991).
FERRARESI, F., *Burocrazia e politica in Italia* (Bologna, 1980).
FERRERA, M., 'Italy', in P. Flora (ed.), *Growth to Limits: The European Welfare State since World War Two* (Berlin, 1987), 385–480.
—— 'The Politics of Health Reformism: Origins and Performance of the Italian Health Service in Comparative Perspective', in G. Freddi and J. Bjorkman (eds.), *Controlling Medical Professionals* (London, 1989), 116–29.
—— and ZINCONE, G., (eds.), *La salute che noi pensiamo: Domande sanitaria e politiche pubbliche in Italia* (Bologna, 1986).
FINOCCHIARO, A., and CONTESSA, A. M., (eds.), *La Banca d'Italia e i problemi del governo della moneta* (Rome, 1986).
GHETTI, G., *La consulenza amministrativa*, i: *Problemi generali* (Padua, 1974).
GIANNINI, M. S., *Istituzioni di diritto amministrativo* (Milan, 1982).
GROTANELLI DE' SANTI, G., and FRANCIONI, F., (eds.), *National and Supranational Powers in the Shaping of Community Policies* (Milan, 1984).

HINE, D. J., 'Italy', in F. F. Ridley (ed.), *Government and Administration in Western Europe* (Oxford, 1979), 156–203.

'Il farmaco nel servizio pubblico: Esperienze regionali', *Salute e territorio*, 52–3 (1987).

Istituto centrale di statistica, *Statistiche sulla amministrazione pubblica* (Roma, 1989).

MASSAI, A., 'Il coordinamento interno delle politiche comunitarie', *Quaderni costituzionali* 2/2 (1982), 481–90.

PAPISCA, A., 'La Présidence du Conseil des ministres des Communautés européennes: Rapport national sur l'Italie', in C. O'Nuallain (ed.), *The Presidency of the European Council of Ministers* (London, 1985), 167–90.

PENNELLA, G., (ed.), *La produttività nella pubblica amministrazione*, vol. iii of *La produttività in Italia* (Milan, 1987).

POCUR, F., *et al.*, 'Italie' in H. Siedentopf and J. Ziller (eds.), *Making European Policies Work: The Implementation of Community Policies in the Member States*, ii (national reports) (London, 1988), 449–518.

RONZITTI, N., 'European Policy Formulation in the Italian Administrative System', *International Spectator*, 22 (1987), 207–15.

—— 'The Internal Market, Italian Law, and the Public Administration', *International Spectator*, 25 (1990), 38–44.

RUSCIANI, M., *Il pubblico impiego in Italia* (Bologna, 1978).

8. Regional and local government and politics

BALBONI, E., and PASTORI, G., 'Il governo regionale e locale', in G. Amato and A. Barbera (eds.), *Manuale di diritto pubblico* (Bologna, 1986), 575–626.

BARBANO, F., (eds.), *Le frontiere delle città: Casi di marginalità e servizi sociali* (Milan, 1982).

BARTOLE, S., *et al.*, 'Le regioni, le province, i comuni', in G. Branca (ed.), *Commentario della costituzione*, i (Bologna, 1985).

BARUSSO, E., *Il nuovo ordinamento delle autonomie locali: Commento alla legge 8-6-90 n. 142* (Naples, 1990).

BETTIN, G., and MAGNIER, A., *Chi governa la città? Una ricerca sugli asessori comunali* (Padua, 1991).

CASSESE, S., 'La regionalizzazione economica in Italia: Un sistema alla ricerca di un equilibrio', in *Studi in memoria di Vittorio Bachelet*, iii: *Amministrazione e economia* (Milan, 1987), 165–77.

Commission of the European Communities, *Fourth Periodic Report on the Development of the Regions*, Com. (90) Final (Brussels, 9 Jan. 1990).

CORSO, G., 'L'intervento per il mezzogiorno', in Progetto CER-CENSIS, *Publico e privato: Secondo rapporto CER-CENSIS sull'economia italiana*, i: *Mutazioni, confini, intrecci, modelli* (Milan, 1987), 469–86.

DEGANELLO, R., 'La dirigenza nelle amministrazioni regionali e locali', in M. d'Alberti (ed.), *La dirigenza pubblica* (Bologna, 1990), 91–118.

DELLA PORTA, D., 'Risorse e attori nella corruzione politica: Appunti su tre casi di governo locale in Italia', *Polis*, 4/3 (1990), 499–532.

DENTE, B., *Governare la frammentazione: Stato regioni ed enti locali in Italia* (Bologna, 1985).

DESIDERI, C., and TORCHIA, L., *I raccordi fra stato e regioni* (Milan, 1986).

FONDAZIONE OLIVETTI, *Le regioni: Politica o amministrazione?* (Milan, 1973).

FRIED, R., *The Italian Prefects* (New Haven, Conn., 1963).

GIARDA, D. P., 'Vicende e problemi della finanza regionale', *Quaderni regionali* 9/1 (1990), 23–32.

—— *Finanza locale: Idee per una riforma* (Milan, 1982).

LEONARDI, R., *La regione Basilicata* (Bologna, 1987).

—— NANETTI, R. Y., and PUTNAM, R., 'Italy: Territorial Politics in the Postwar Years: The Case of Regional Reform', *West European Politics*, 10/4 (1987), 88–107.

MALTINI, G., and PETRETTO, A., (eds.), *Finanziamento ed efficenza della spesa pubblica locale* (Turin, 1987).

MANNOZZI, S., and VISCO COMANDINI, V., *Le funzioni del governo locale in Italia*, ii: *Verifica dell'effettività* (Milan, 1990).

MERLONI, F., (ed.), *La nuova provincia nella riforma del governo locale*, Unione delle province italiane, Quaderni delle autonomie, no. 1 (Rome, 1988).

PUTNAM, R., LEONARDI, R., and NANETTI, R., *La pianta e le radici* (Bologna, 1984).

ROLLA, G., 'La determinazione delle materie di competenza regionale nella giurisprudenza costituzionale', *Le regioni* (1982), 100–30.

TARROW, S., *Between Center and Periphery: Grassroots Politicians in Italy and France* (New Haven, Conn., 1977).

VANDELLI, L., *I controlli sull'amministrazione regionale e locale* (Bologna, 1984).

Index